BACTERIAL DISEASES

ENCYCLOPAEDIA OF ANIMAL DISEASES-III

BACTERIAL DISEASES

By

Ashok Kumar

Dept. of Zoology
Bundelkhand University
Campus Department
Jhansi

DISCOVERY PUBLISHING HOUSE PVT. LTD.
NEW DELHI-110 002

Published by:
Tilak Wasan

DISCOVERY PUBLISHING HOUSE PVT. LTD.
4383/4B, Ansari Road, Darya Ganj
New Delhi-110 002 (India)
Phone : +91-11-23279245; 23253475; 43596065
E-mail : discoverybooksindia@gmail.com
discoverypublishinghouse@gmail.com
namitwasan9@gmail.com
web : www.discoverypublishinggroup.com

Edition: **2020**

ISBN: 978-81-8356-206-5 (Set)
ISBN: 978-81-8356-284-3

Bacterial Diseases

Printed at:
Infinity Imaging Systems
Delhi

PREFACE

The **Bacterial Diseases** has been carefully compiled and edited to meet the long felt needs of increasingly large number of those who have to deal with the different aspects of human diseases in colleges, universities and research institutes. It provides a stimulating and important new view of interaction between animals and pathogens causing diseases. The objective is to introduce to students the essential principles for understanding various aspects of diseases. Most of diseases constitute the largest part of human pathology and are the primary cause of death. Hence, special importance is given to the study of such diseases.

The book is intended to acquaint students of various fields involved directly or indirectly with the major principles of human diseases. The book may be helpful as well to practitioners and those engaged in medical research.

In the preparation of this book large number of books and research papers have been consulted. So no authenticity is claimed.

The author wishes to express his deepest appreciation to the many people who have contributed in one way or the other to the preparation of this title.

The author expresses his gratitude to Mr. Wasan and staff of M/s Discovery Publishing House for their whole hearted co-operation in the publication of this book.

The author tried hard to be accurate and upto date in statement and realises the impossibility of completely avoiding errors therefore, the author will greatly appreciate having his attention called to any questionable statement.

Author

CONTENTS

INTRODUCTION

In nature, almost all kinds of bacteria or fungi, including the disease-producing species, live naturally in more or less intimate association with other kinds. Therefore, the primary culture from almost any source will be a *mixed culture* containing organisms of several different kinds. But in the laboratory the various species may be separated from one another and cultivated by themselves. A culture which contains just one species is called *a pure culture*. An organism must be obtained and studied in pure cultures before the properties peculiar to itself may be learned.

The process of obtaining a pure culture by separating one kind of bacterium or fungus from a mixture with other kinds is spoken of as *isolation* of the organism.

PRINCIPLE OF ISOLATION METHODS

The earliest workers to study bacteria in the laboratory used only liquid culture media. The task of securing pure cultures using liquids only was naturally very difficult, and only men of the highest mental attainment and possessed of the patience of genius, like Pasteur and Lister, could make much headway in the study of micro-organisms. We have already explained how *Robert Koch*, in 1881, by the use of solid culture media and the plate method, simplified the entire procedure of securing pure cultures. The methods for isolating bacteria used today are essentially the same as those of Koeb. These methods depend upon (1) *dilution of the original material in solid media cultures in order to secure separated, pure colonies, and* (2) *transfer of a pure colony to a fresh sterile medium,* without contamination from the neighbouring growth. The process of picking out a single colony for a smear or transfer is called *fishing.*

DILUTION METHODS WITH AGAR MEDIA

Just as in planting a vegetable garden it is necessary to scatter the seed over the ground so that the plants which later develop *will* not be too close together, so the bacteria which are to be planted upon culture media must be thinned out so that separate, typical, pure colonies will appear. Any method of diluting the original material will serve as long as extraneous bacteria are not introduced.

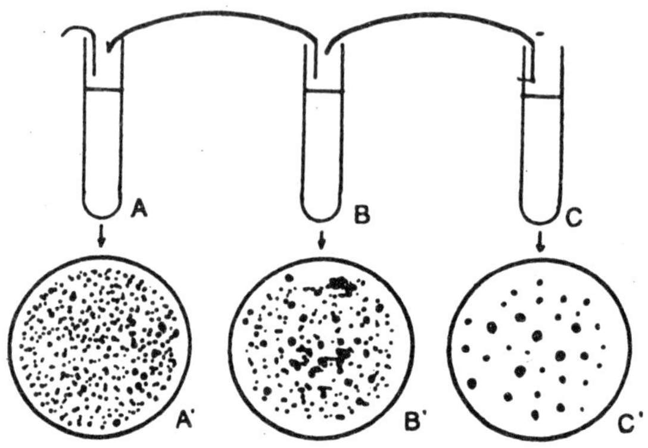

Fig. 1.1. Pour plate culture, illustrating the effect of dilution of the inoculated material. A, B, C, tubes of melted agar, inoculated in series as indicated by the arrows. A', B', C, pour plate cultures made from A. B, and C, respectively, showing the growth resulting after incubation. Compare with streak plate cultures as a means of securing isolated colonies of bacteria.

THE POUR-PLATE TECHNIQUE

The forerunner of the present pour-plate method was developed in the laboratory of the famous bacteriologist *Robert Koch.* Today this technique consists of cooling melted agar-containing medium (1.5% agar) to approximately 42° to 45° C, inoculating the medium with a specimen and immediately pouring it into a sterile Petri plate, allowing the freshly poured medium to solidify, and incubating the preparation at the desired temperature. In several instances, in which the magnitude of the bacterial population in the specimen to be studied is not known beforehand, suitable dilutions must be created in order to ensure isolated colonies. By means of the pourplate method, bacteria are distributed throughout the agar and are trapped in position. Although the solidified medium restricts bacterial movement from one area to another, it is soft enough to permit growth, which occurs both on the surface and in the depths of the inoculated medium. In addition to the qualitative application of this procedure to isolate and detect bacterial species contained within a mixed culture, it is also useful in quantitative measurements of bacterial growth.

Unfortunately, however, there are several disadvantages to this technique. Colonies of several species may present a similar appearance in the agar environment, thus making differentiation difficult. Certain species of bacteria may not grow under the cultural conditions of the method and difficulty may be encountered in removing colonies for further study.

THE STREAK-PLATE TECHNIQUE

This procedure' is also a dilution method. It was originally developed by two bacteriologists, Loefler and *Gaffky*, in the laboratory of *Robert Koch*. The modern method for the preparation of a streak-plate involves the spreading of a single loopful of material containing microorganisms over the surface of a solidified agar medium. The "clock-plate technique" is one of the more generally used forms of this procedure. Here the inoculum is first spread over a small portion of the medium's surface ; then the inoculating loop is flamed to destroy

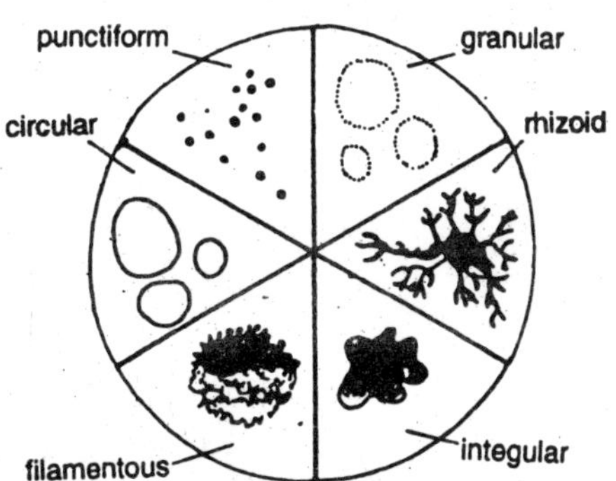

Fig. 1.2. Selected characteristics of bacterial colonies. A-Diagrammatic representation of colonial forms of growth.

any residual bacteria, and the plate containing the medium is rotated approximately one quarter of a turn. The flamed loop is next used to make a second set of streaks, thus diluting (spreading) the bacterial population in the original set of streaks. The original surface streaks are crossed only once. Further dilutions of the specimen are carried out by repeating this sequence; flaming the loop, rotating the medium, and making additional streaks. If this technique is properly performed, well-isolated colonies should grow after incubation at an appropriate temperature. Supposedly, one colony develops from a single cell, thereby producing a pure culture. It is customary to "pick" (transfer) a small portion of a desired colony to a tube of medium, such as broth or agar slant. and utilize the culture as a source of organisms for additional studies.

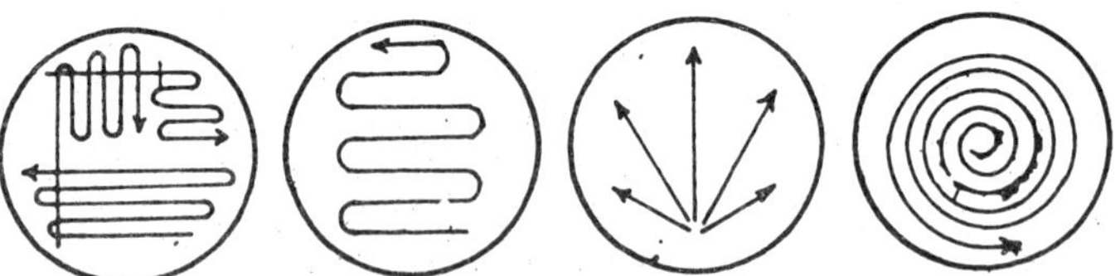

Fig. 1.3. Representative streaking patterns used in the isolation of bacteria.

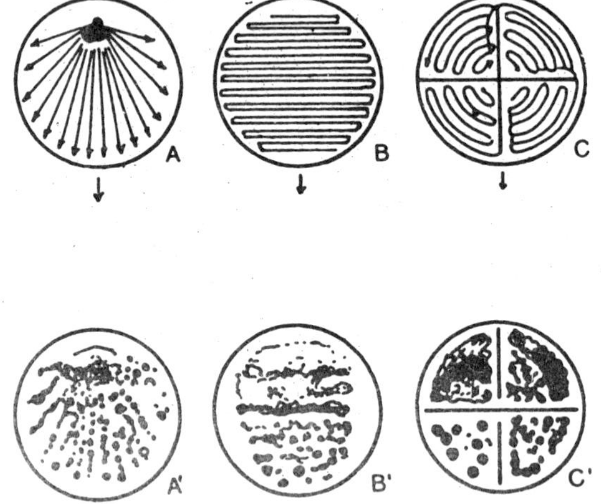

Fig. 1.4. Streak plate culture. A.B.C. methods of inoculating streak plates. In method C the needle is sterilized after streaking a quarter of the plate. then recharged with the organisms by passing it across the section just previously streaked. .4 B: C: the growth resulting after incubation, when inoculated as in A. B. and (.7. respectively. Compare with pour plate cultures as a means of searing single colonies of bacteria..

Another technique, the "spread-plate" procedure, is used in certain types of investigations. Here a bacterial specimen is placed on an agar medium and spread over its surface with the aid of a sterile bent glass rod. The agar plate can be placed on a rotating wheel device to aid the spreading out of the bacterial specimen. Because of the high concentration of water in agar preparations, condensation forms in most Petri plates. To avoid such *water of condensation* on media surfaces, which may cause bacterial colonies to run together, plates should be incubated in an inverted position.

FISHING

The process of picking up bacteria from a single colony with a sterile needle, without touching neighbouring colonies, is often a delicate task requiring much care and skill. This is particularly true when pathogenic organisms are being isolated because their colonies are usually small.

A straight needle is always used for fishing. Often it is an advantage to have the end of the needle bent at a right angle and filed to a fine point. Colonies to be fished from plate cultures may be marked by drawing a ring about them with a wax pencil on the bottom of the dish. The colonies may be given numbers, and smears or cultures trade from them may be correspondingly numbered. In fishing, as in any other procedure, the culture must be protected from contamination, and the complete removal of the cover of a Petri dish is avoided whenever possible. Fishing from 'plate cultures is much easier if performed with the aid of a low power dissecting microscope.

STUDY AND IDENTIFICATION OF PURE CULTURES

Once a pure culture is obtained, a long study is usually required before the organism can be fully identified and named. It is necessary to determine

(1) its morphological properties and staining reactions, (2) its cultural characteristics, (3) its physiological requirements and chemical activities, and (4) its pathogenicity (disease-producing power). Also tests would be made (5) to see whether the organism will agglutinate, or otherwise react specifically, with an immune serum known to contain antibodies for the species to which the organism appears to belong. This will identify the unknown organism positively in most cases.

Morphological Study : Staining reactions

Microscopic studies will reveal the form (coccus, bacillus, or spirillum), and the characteristic arrangement and grouping of the cells, their size, and the presence or absence of spores, capsules, granules, or other peculiarities of structure. Examination of hanging drop preparations will show whether the organisms are motile or not. If so, the flagella may be stained. The reaction to the Gram stain is of great help in determining the class to which the unknown bacterium belongs. In case the organism is acid-fast, this will be revealed by the acid-fast staining method. These studies supply a great deal of information about an organism and may give a strong hint as to its identity, but *a species of bacteria can never be identified with certainty on the basis of morphology and staining alone.* There are only three basic shapes which bacteria may take, and only a few other morphological features which help to differentiate organisms from one another, yet there are hundreds of different species. Organisms which stain alike and look alike under the microscope may be totally different in other and more important characteristics. Thus, nearly every type of disease germ is duplicated, so far as morphology and staining are concerned, by other species which are harmless.

Cultural characteristics

Further information about an organism is obtained by observing the way it grows in various kinds of culture media. Certain species have a very characteristic manner of growth in broth or milk, in agar, or other media. Illustrates some of the forms of growth commonly seen.

The agar *colonies* are sometimes so distinctive that they give a valuable clue to the identity of the organism. Plate cultures are most conveniently used for the study of colony characteristics. The colonies may be observed with a hand lens, or they may be studied under a dissection microscope or under the low power objective of the ordinary microscope. In the description of colonies, the following points are usually considered *:form, size, colour, optical characteristics, surface, elevation, edge, internal structure,* and *consistency* when touched with a needle. Thus, a colony of staphylococcus might be described as follows: a circular, orange-coloured, opaque mass, about 2mm, in diameter, with a smooth, glistening surface and regular edge, slightly convex, showing a homogeneous, granular, internal structure, and having a soft consistency.

Physiological requirements and chemical activities

The most significant properties of an organism are learned by a study of its physiology and its biochemical reactions. The following points are among those usually investigated

(1) *Food requirements*

Does the organism grow upon the simpler agar and broth media, or does it require media enriched with blood or other body fluids ?

(2) *Temperature relations*

Does it grow best at body temperature ? If not, what is its optimum growth temperature ? Minimum and maximum growth temperature ?

(3) *Relation to oxygen*

Does it grow best under aerobic or anaerobic conditions, or under partially reduced O_2 tension ?

(4) Pigment production

Does it develop a coloured growth on agar slants or other cultures?

(5) *Proteolytic action*

Does it liquefy gelatin ? Cause digestion of coagulated blood-serum, meat, and similar substances ? Does it form indol ? (Indol is a product of the decomposition of tryptophane, one of the amino-acids composing proteins.)

(6) *Fermentation of carbohydrates*

Does the organism produce acid, or acid and gas, in culture media containing dextrose, lactose, maltose, sacchrose, or other carbohydrates?

When these facts are known it often becomes possible to recognize the species, or at least the group of closely related species, to which the unknown organism belongs.

PATHOGENICITY

One other important property remains to be tested, however Will the organism produce disease in laboratory animals ? The animals most commonly used in laboratories are guinea pigs, rabbits, white mice, and white rats. For certain special work monkeys, dogs, cats, or other animals may be needed. Pathogenicity tests are usually made by inoculating the organisms under investigation into these animals *subcutaneously* (*just under the skin*), *intraperitoneally* (into the peritoneal cavity), or *intravenously* (into a vein). Other possible routes of injection are *intradermal* (into the skin just under the epidermis), *intramuscular* (into the muscles, as of the thigh), and *intracerebral* (*directly* into the brain through the skull).

Such animal inoculations are often of great value in identifying a particular organism. Also they help in securing pure cultures of disease germs. If a material contains acid-fast bacilli, for example, and there is doubt as to whether they are tuberculosis bacilli or not, the matter can be settled by inoculating a guinea pig. If the material injected contains tubercle bacilli, the guinea pigs will develop tuberculosis in a few weeks. It is difficult to cultivate the tubercle germs upon culture media directly from sputum or other matter containing them, but if this material be inoculated into a guinea pig, the germs can easily be obtained in pure culture from the lesions in the animal.

IDENTIFICATION BY AGGULTINATION REACTIONS AND OTHER SEROLOGICAL TESTS

One final method of identifying a species of bacteria is by use of serological tests. If, for example. we have a Grain negative bacillus which has the characteristics of the typhoid gear. a final test of its identity may be made by mixing a suspension of the organisms with a blood-serum known to contain antibodies for that species. If agglutination occurs under properly controlled conditions, the organism must be a typhoid bacillus.

Counting Bacteria by Cultural methods

In the examination of water, sewage, milk and other materials, it is often necessary to make a count of the number of bacteria. The method is simple, but the cultures must be made very carefully in order to assure consistent results. The *standard methods* for counting the bacteria in water and milk, published by the American Public Health Association, are used almost universally. It is necessary (1) to secure a representative sample of the material to be examined in a sterile container. Then (2) the sample is diluted in a definite quantitive manner and (3) the diluted material is inoculated into agar media. Then (4) the colonies which develop are counted, and, assuming that each colony represents a single living organism in the original sample, (5) the number of bacteria per cubic centimeter of the sample is calculated.

Technique

The method of counting of bacteria in water may be taken as an example. The technique is as follows:

(1) Shake the water sample thoroughly, and transfer, with a sterile pipette, lc.c. of the sample to a bottle containing 99 c.c of *sterile* water. (This is called *a water blank*). The sample is thus diluted 1:100. If 1 c.c of this thoroughly mixed dilution is added to another 99 c.c . water blank, this will give a dilution of 1:1000. As many dilution as are necessary (depending upon the number of living organisms in the original sample) are made in this way.

(2) Place 1 c.c. of each dilution in the bottom of a separate sterile Petri dish. Mark the dishes accordingly. Then pour melted agar, cooled

to about 45°C, into each dish, and mix it thoroughly with the water by gently tilting and rotating the dish. It is best to make these plates in duplicate or triplicate.

(3) Allow the agar to harden. Then invert the dishes and incubate them for twenty-four to forty-eight hours.

(4) Discard those plates which contain more than 300 colonies, because a count based upon them could not be accurate. Count the colonies in each of the other plates. Each colony is assumed to represent a single organism in the original water sample. Multiply this individual plate count in each case by the dilution of the sample in that plate, so as to get the number in 1 c.c. of the original sample. Take the average of the individual plate counts as the final figure.

CONDITION OF INCUBATION

Aerobic incubation

Microbial growth, as noted previously, can be dependent upon suitable levels of oxygen and carbon dioxide. While aerobic organisms may be able to grow under anaerobic conditions, the obligate aerobes, such as *Acetobacteri* spp., must be in intimate contact with air, or approximately 20 per cent oxygen. Many organisms have less stringent oxygen requirements and will grow well in the depths of liquid or solid media. Therefore, cultivation of aerobic or facultative anaerobic bacteria is relatively simple under usual laboratory conditions.

Once an appropriate solid or liquid medium has been inoculated and protected from contamination, all that remains to be controlled is the,. temperature and occasionally the level of humidity. Standard laboratory incubators usually are sufficient to maintain such environmental factors.

With any incubator, it is advisable to employ a maximum minimum thermometer to determine the temperature range provided by the thermostatic control. One type of maximum minimum recording thermometer consists of a bimetallic coil (in the form of a strip), a dial equipped with a needle indicator to register the temperature, and two hands. The hands are moved by the temperature indicator ; one remains set at the highest and one at the lowest temperature value. Periodic recordings of the daily extremes give advance notice of the possibility that the controls may be wearing out, and can provide warning of the instrument's malfunctioning in time to repair it before any serious damage occurs, such as cooking the cultures.

Capneic Incubation

Air enriched with carbon dioxide is required by some bacteria,

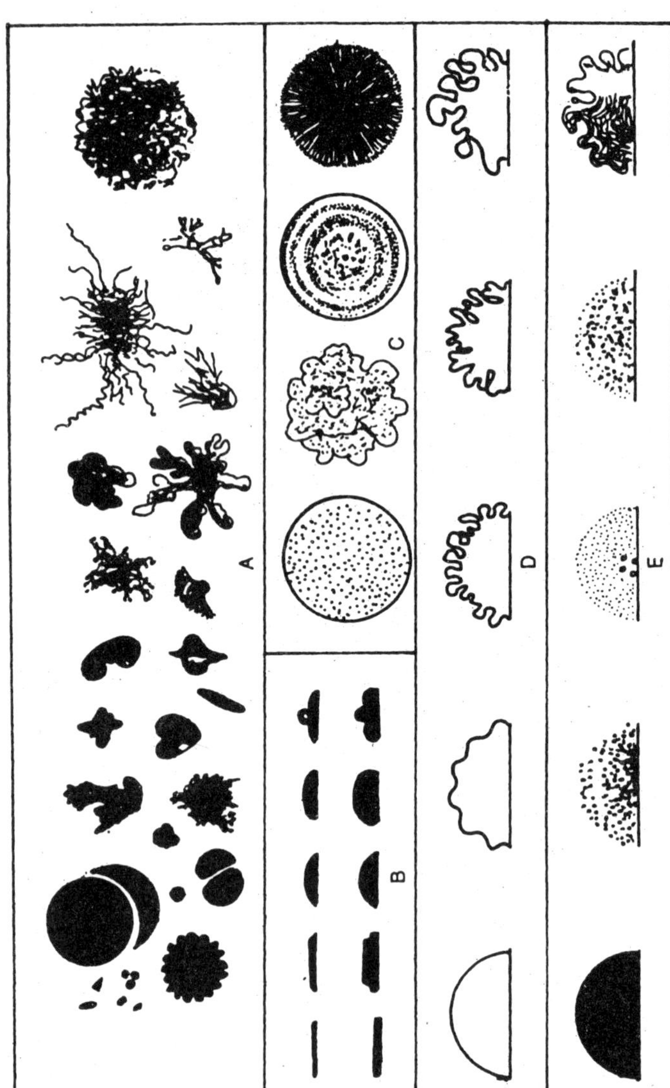

Fig. 1.5. Colonies of bacteria in Agar culture. A, various forms of colonies; B, cross sections; C, surface appearances; D, character of edges; E. internal structure

including *Neisseriagonorrhoeae*, *N. meningitides*, and ***Brucella spp.***, for their primary isolation from clinical specimens. As mentioned earlier, many other *microorganisms*, such *as Mycobacterium tuberculosis*, appear to grow better if allowed to incubate under these capneic conditions. This form of enriched atmosphere can be supplied in a variety of ways. The candle jar technique is routinely used for *N. gonorrhoeae* cultivation. With this technique, Petri plates and/or tubes with inoculated media are placed in a jar with a candle. The lighted candle will continue to burn after the lid has been placed on the jar, until the CO_2 concentration increases to the point which stops combustion, usually around 3 to 5 per cent CO·· This should not be considered to represent complete combustion of oxygen as aerobic organisms will grow and strict anaerobes will not grow in such a candle jar.

Fig. 1.6. The Candle Jar.

For a laboratory which is primarily concerned with the maintenance of *N. gonorrhoeae* on slanted media, the test tube capneic system is worthy of consideration.

In this system a capsule of sodium bicarbonate is added to a small tube of dilute sulfuric acid and the large tube is immediately stoppered. The reaction here is the same as that used in fire extinguishers: acidification of bicarbonate to release CO_2.

Anaerobic Incubation

Certain anaerobic microorganisms are known to be responsible for a variety of diseases. while others are functional in several industrial fermentation processes. Some of these anaerobes appear to be *-aerotolerant* they can withstand oxygen to a limited degree. Others of them can survive only in an environment without oxygen and*are obligate anaerobes.* One explanation for their sensitivity to an oxygen environment is related to the role of the oxygen in the formation of hydrogen peroxide (H_2O_2) during microbial metabolic processes. This product alone can be quite destructive, as shown by the fact that it is commonly used as a disinfectant. Some bacteria produce an enzyme. catalase, which breaks down the peroxide to oxygen (O_2) and water (H_2O). Strict anaerobic bacteria do not appear to have catalase. and are therefore poisoned by the peroxide.

An additional explanation for the lack of growth by anaerobes in the presence of oxygen concerns the oxidation- reduction potential (Elm) of the media, which may be the more $_s$ignificant mechanism responsible for the anaerobes' oxygen intolerance. The oxidation-reduction potential is an electrical phenomenon that indicates the electron-accepting e yielding potentialities of substances. When the Eli of a medium is lowered by the addition of a reducing or oxygen-absorbing compound, such as cysteine or thioglycollic acid, many anaerobes will grow.

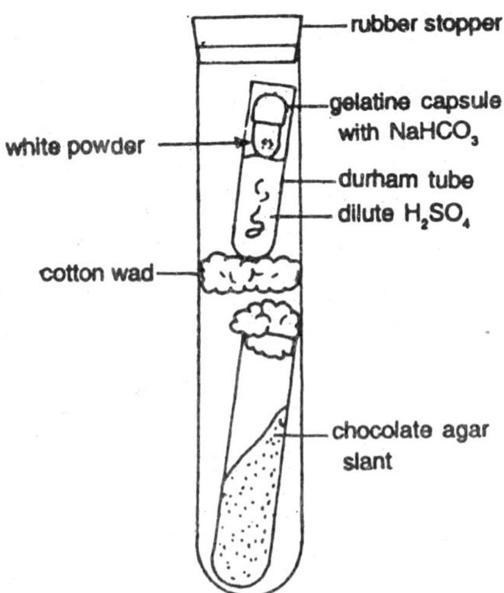

Fig. 1.7. The test tube capneie system- A capsule of sodium bicarbonate is added to a small tube is dilute sulphuric acid and the large tube is immediately stoppereit The reaction is the same as that used in fire $_{ex}$tinguishers-acidification of bicarbonate to release CO_2 The example shown is a chocolate agar slant culture inoculated with Neisseria $_g$onorrhoeae'

Anaerobic Transfer

The lack of growth of many clinical isolates may not be due to the Eh of the properly prepared anaerobic medium, but in reality to transient exposure to air during the piOcedure for specimen collection, transportation to the laboratory, or after groom, during the transfer of organisms to subculture media. In order to prevent inactivation of anaerobes when transferring them, the operation should be performed mouse of a pipette stream of nitrogen for cultures on solid media, or by the use of a pipette with liquid media. For example in the transfer of cultures from thioglycollate broth to a fresh tube of medium, a pipette should be introduced into the bottom of the tube with the finger on the mouth-piece. By carefully lifting the finger. inoculumn from the most anaerobic area is allowed into the pipette. Next, with the finger on the moullipiece, the pipette is removed and inserted into the bottom of a fresh tube of thioglycolate. The finger than is quickly removed, which causes the release of the inoculum into the most anaerobic portion of the medium. Following this step, the pipette is removed and the newly inoculated preparation is incubated at the desired temperature.

Methods of anaerobic incubation

Incubation under anaerobic conditions can be accomplished with vacuum devices. Incubators for this use are usually fitted with gaskets and Ports for evacuation and flushing with inert gases. One method commonly used involves flushing a specially equipped incubator with 95 per cent N_2 and 5 per cent CO_2 to remove any oxygen and to introduce CO_2 into the system. The latter gas may enhance growth. Hydrogen also may be used for flushing, but it forms an explosive mixture with oxygen. If for some reason anaerobic hydrogen bacteria are to be grown hydrogen should be bubbled through water first; an explosion will not occur with wet hydrogen.

Before the advent of the anaerobic incubator, *Brewer* invented two systems for culturing anaerobic bacteria. In one system thioglycollate agar is inoculated and poured into a Petri dish. The cover for this Brewer plate forms a seal with the surface of the agar and with the edge of a slight concave opening, to allow a limited surface for organisms on which to grow. The trapped oxygen is rapidly reduced by the thioglycollate, thus producing anaerobic conditions.

An alternative to the Brewer plate is the Spray dish. This device consists of a deep, double-well dish and cover. The intent is to permit separation of an alkaline solution, such as potassium hydroxide (KOH), and pyrogalic acid. These chemicals when combined absorb oxygen and produce anaerobic conditions. When this system is used, an inoculated Petri plate is inverted over the bottom dish and sealed into place. The dish is then tipped to permit the mixing of the chemicals, thus resulting in anaerobiosis.

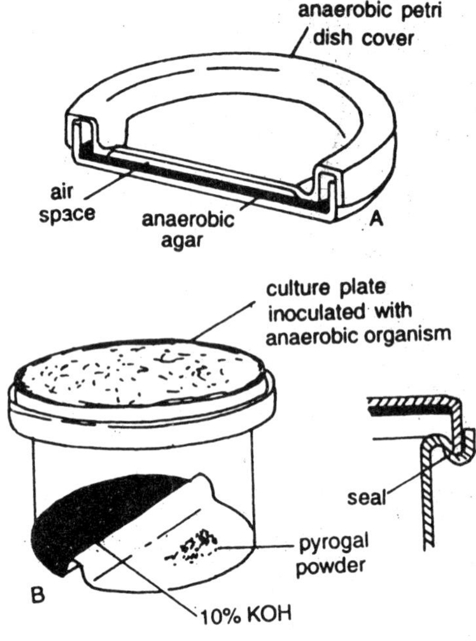

Fig. 1.8. A cut-away drawing of a Brewer Petri dish. B-spray dish for anaerobic incubation.

The Brewer jar was developed in an attempt to have a larger incubation system for anaerobic organisms. In this system, the inoculated plates and/or tubes are placed in the jar, the cover issealed into place, the air in the container is immediately evacuated, and the system is flushed with hydrogen. Subsequently, a catalyst, such as platinum, is heated in the lid by an electric current, with the result that the hydrogen combines with residual oxygen to form water. A slight vacuum is created in the chamber due to the combustion reaction.

A recently developed alternative to the Brewer Jar is the Bio Quest disposable Gas Pak. This enveloped unit is a self contained hydrogen generating and catalyst system. much simpler to use than the Brewer Jar. The plates and or tubes are placed in ajar with a

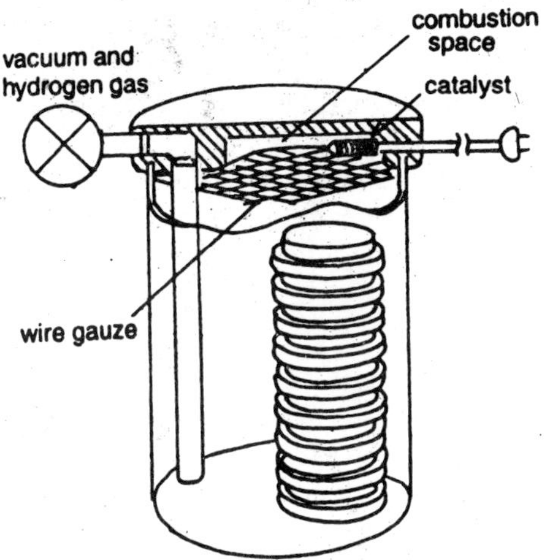

Fig. 1.9. The Breiter anaerohic jar.

Gas Pak envelope. The envelope is opened, water is added to the reagents, and the jar is sealed immediately. The generation of hydrogen in the presence of air and the catalyst causes reduction of the oxygen to water, which condenses on the side of the jar. This system eliminates the need for hydrogen and nitrogen tanks and vacuum pumps, which greatly enhances the ability of a small clinical laboratory to carry out anaerobic cultivation.

ANAEROBIC INDICATORS AND CHECKING THE EFFICIENCY OF ANAEROBIC SYSTEMS

Anaerobic incubation systems should be checked whenever possible to provide assurance that adequate conditions have been obtained and maintained during incubation. One system used for this purpose incorporates Bacto-OR Indicator Agar (Difco Laboratories). This medium uses methylene blue as an indicator of oxidation-reduction potential. It is usually dispensed into small screw-capped vials and autoclaved (sterilized under pressurized steam). This reduces the methylene blue to a colourless state, leucomethylene blue. The procedure for testing involves placing an opened vial of medium in the incubator and initiating the anaerobiosis environment. After a suitable incubation period the vial is removed and examined. If anaerobic conditions were maintained during the test period, the methylene blue should still be in the reduced state, i.e., leuco. However, if anaerobiosis was not achieved, the medium will be oxidized and appear blue. (Note that, in the first case, the brief exposure to air may cause a slight oxidation of the leuco- methylene blue at the surface of the medium).

Another system for checking the efficiency of an anaerobic incubator involves subculturing an obligate anaerobic bacterium in the same incubator as other specimens. If the indicator organism grows, satisfactory conditions were met. Organisms that may be used for this purpose include certain *Clostridium* and *Bacteroides* spp. However, the use of chemical indicators is recommended due to their simplicity and reliability.

Biological or "Sterlity Test" Cabinets

A definite need exists to provide protection from airborne contamination. Such units have value in laboratories that handle "biohazardous" substances, the preparation bacteriological media, sterility testing, and the inoculation of a variety of media.

Cabinets of this type are equipped with a double polycarbonate viewscreen which provides a functional visual working angle and contributes to the protection of individuals within the confines of the working area. A recirculating vertical airflow unit creates a "front air barrier" at the opening of the work area. This "barrier" protects both the laboratory personnel and materials from contamination by preventing airborne particulates from leaving or entering the cabinets. Air entering and leaving the working area passes through HEPA (High Efficiency Particulate Air) filters which remove particles of 0.3 μm (μ) and greater. Although contamination of personnel and materials is prevented in a unit such as the one described, workers must still observe aspetic precautions and techniques.

Culture and Susceptibility

Many microbiologists believe that the culture and susceptibility is the most important clinical test performed, because the results will provide the physician with significant information about the pathogen and how to control it. *A culture and susceptibility test* is the growth of a known pathogen in pure culture and its exposure to numerous antibiotics of different concentrations to determine which drug will kill or inhibit growth of the microbe. The smallest amount of the drug that prevents the microbe's growth is called the *minimal inhibitory concentration* (*MIC*). The drug with the lowest MIC is usually the one selected by the physician for use in treatment. The culture and susceptibility test, and determination of the MIC have become greatly important due to the increasing number of antimicrobial agents available to physicians, and because of an increase in the number and types of pathogens that have become resistant (unaffected) to these drugs. Two methods commonly carried out to determine the susceptibility of a microbe to an antimicrobial agent are the tube dilution method and the agar diffusion (disk susceptibility) method.

The *tube dilution method tests* the susceptibility of a bacterium to antibiotics and is performed by inoculating the bacterium into a serial dilution of the antibiotic. Each tube contains an appropriate culture medium and a specific concentration of the anitbiotic. If the bacterium is inhibited by the drug, there will be no growth in the tube and the medium will remain clear. If microbe is resistant to the effects of the drug, it will grow and produce a cloudly tube. Several antibiotics are compared using this method in order to determine which inhibits the bacterium in the lowest concentration. If more than one drug successfully controls growth, all the inhibiting drug's names are sent to the physician for consideration. This testing procedure may be used to determine the susceptibility of microbes from blood cultures, the susceptibility of patients who have undergone a relapse during therapy, and the susceptibility of patients who have not responded to the use of an antimicrobial drug. This method is time-consuming and becomes fairly expensive when testing a number of antibiotics. Therefore, most labs are prepared to run a tube dilution series, but prefer the agar diffusion (disk susceptibility) method.

The *disk susceptibility* (sensitivity) method is probably the most widely used and quickest susceptibility test used in hospital labs. In this method, the medium (usually Mueller-Hinton) is inoculated by swabbing the bacteria over the entire surface so that they will grow into a "lawn." Small disks of paper impregnated with various antibiotics of different concentrations are placed on the surface of the plate. The plate is incubated overnight and checked the following day for growth inhibition. During the incubation period, the antibiotic molecules diffuse from the disks over the surface of the bacteria-coated agar. If the concentration of an antibiotic is strong enough to inhibit the bacteria's growth, there will be a zone of inhibition around the disk impregnated with that drug. If the bacteria are resistant to the drug, there will be little or no zone of cleaning and the bacteria grow close to the disk. The diameter of the inhibition zone designates the relative effectiveness of the drug or the bacteria's susceptibility to the antibiotic. The zone is measured from the edge of the antibiotic disk to the edge of the cleared area that shows no visible growth. The size is then compared to a table that has been developed from disk susceptibility tests run on known *EE coli* and *Staphylococcus aureus* culture. This is known as the Kirby Bauer technique. The table lists the antibiotic agents, concentrations used in the disks, and the inhibition zone diameters measured from the standard E. *coli* and *S. aureus*. The inhibition zones are divided into three ranges; resistant, intermediate, and susceptible. Disk susceptibles that show clearing only to the resistant level have not been inhibited by the drug. Drugs that have cleared to the intermediate range may be used to control the pathogen, but may be required in high dosages. If this is the case, another drug may better be used. Dmgs that have resulted in large zones of clearing on the agar surface and fall in the susceptible range are those that may be expected to inhibit the pathogen in the patient. They may be recommended for use in controlling an infection caused by the bacterium being tested. The disk susceptibility method is quick and accurate, but there are several sources of error in the test. These possible errors make it essential that a qualified technician perform and interpret the results.

1. Inoculum density not carefully standardized larger zones of inhibition may result with a light inoculum, smaller zones with a more dense inoculum.

2. Using a mixed culture : the standardized test is based on the use of pure cultures, a mixed culture can yield completely erroneous susceptibility results.

3. Excessive moisture on the surface of the medium may yield very confluent growth and reduce the diameter of the inhibition zone even though the density of inoculum is correct.

4. A very dry surface may result in poor growth, yielding a larger inhibition zone.

5. Mishandling of susceptibility disks by permitting moisture uptake and prolonged exposure to room temperature results in deterioration of most antibiotics.

All of the information gained from culturing microbes is sent to the physician. The physician then interprets this information and decides on an appropriate course of treatment in light of the patient's condition (both mental and physical), the available health care facilities, chemotherapeutic drugs, and the time needed for treatment. In order to ensure successful treatment of the patient and containment of the infection, the lab must perform another essential service known as *sterility testing*.

Hospitals use a great many sterile materials in the care and treatment of patients. Bandages, dressings, hypodermic needles and syringes, glassware, scissors, catheters, and surgical instruments must all be checked for contamination by bacteria, fungi, and yeasts before they are used. Usually a sample from a batch of sterilized instrument is taken to the lab for testing. If the sample is found to be free of all living things, the entire batch is considered sterile and safe for use. The item to be sampled is opened using proper aseptic technique and sampled either with a sterile moist swab or with RODAC plate. (RODAC is an acronym for Replicate Organism Detecting and Counting). Swabs are typically used to sample hard surfaces such as utensils, glassware, or instruments while the RODAC plates are used to sample linens, gauze, and flat surfaces. The RODAC plate is a small petri dish filled with so much culture media that it can be pressed directly onto the surface of the material being tested. The plate is incubated for forth-eight hours after which the colonies may be counted and identified. Another technique is used to check the efficient operation of the autoclave and other hospital sterilization equipment. Special paper strips containing endospores of the bacteria *Bacillus* stearothermophilus and Bacillus subtilis are placed in the autoclave with the material to be sterilized...,

COLLECTION OF SPECIMENS FOR BACTERIOLOGICAL EXAMINATION

The laboratory examinations of pus, urine, feces, sputum, or other material collected from the living patient, is relied upon to furnish the final diagnosis, and often to determine or control the treatment, of many of the most common diseases. A bacteriological study of material secured from the dead body at autopsy often serves to explain the cause of death.

The value of the laboratory examination of any material is in large part determined by the care and intelligence with which the specimen is collected. If the proper technique is not employed at the time of collection, or if the specimen is not properly cared for after collection, an examination of it may be impossible or useless. It is frequently desirable to reach a diagnosis in as brief a time as possible in order to permit the proper treatment to be given, and delay or error in diagnosis, by reason of an improperly collected specimen, may be a very serious matter.

General rules

(1) Secure an uncontaminated specimen

Avoid contamination of the specimen with organisms from other sources. Use *a sterile container*, and protect the specimen from contamination with dust bacteria as you would any culture tube. When cultures or smears are made directly from an infected part of the body, *sterile swabs* or *needles* must be used, and the greatest care must be taken to avoid picking up organisms from adjoining tissues or other sources. This is not in every case an easy matter, but an effort must always be made to secure as nearly pure a specimen as possible.

(2) Label specimen fully and accurately

Every specimen, smear, or culture must be fully, clearly, and accurately labelled. The label should indicate unmistakably the patient from whom the material was obtained, the date, the nature and source of the specimen, and the kind of examination desired. Special pains should be taken to see that the name attached to a specimen is the proper one, for serious results may follow failure to associate a patient with his own specimen. If a printed form is to accompany the specimen to the laboratory, this must be filled out completely, accurately, and in a legible manner. The bacteriologist is able to save time, to perform a more intelligent examination, and to preserve more accurate records if the fullest possible information is given him as to the clinical state of the patient, the exact nature of the specimen. the time or the manner in which it was secured. and the kind of studies he is expected to carry out.

(3) Do not add a disinfectant unless this is especially ordered

As a rule disinfectants are not to be added to a specimen intended for bacteriological examination, because the bacteriologist may wish to cultivate the microbes in the specimen or to observe them in a living state. The only exception to this rule is in the case of sputum or feces from a case of suspected tuberculosis. Ordinarily, this material is used solely for making smears. But here also it is best to omit the disinfectant, so that the bacteriologist may make cultures from the specimen if he desires.

(4) Handle with care to avoid infection

Since no disinfectant is added, specimens may contain very many living germs in a highly dangerous state. The outside of the specimen bottle or other container should not be soiled, so that it may be handled without contaminating the fingers.

(5) See that specimens reach the laboratory promptly

Place cultures in a 37.5 °C *incubator, and other specimens in a refrigerator, immediately after collection.* It is often very important that the examination be made as soon as possible after collection. The best results are obtained when the bacteriologist brings his swabs and culture media to the bedside, or takes his specimen from the patient directly to the laboratory. Failing this, the most reliable results are secured when the material is studied within one or two hours after collection. A specimen of pus, feces, or sputum is practically useless for cultures when more than four hours old.

(6) No time muse be lost in getting cultures to the incubator

The incubator temperature of 37.5°C. (body temperature) will favour the development of the pathogenic types of organisms which are being looked for. But if the culture is permitted to stay long at room temperature, some nonpathogenic types may grow so rapidly that they overwhelm the disease germs.

Specimens of urine, feces, sputum, pus, spinal fluid, and similar material must often be kept for a short time before they can be examined. ***During this interval between collection and examination, they must be kept continuously in a refrigerator.*** Usually a single kind of pathogenic organism is to be looked for in a specimen- the typhoid bacilli in feces, for example, or pneumococci in sputum. If the specimen is allowed to stand in a warm place, the numerous other kinds of bacteria always present in the.tnaterial night multiply to such an extent that the germs would be very difficult to find.

Collection of Particular Specimens

Pus From wounds and other lesions is usually secured with a sterile cotton swab. Abscesses are sometimes lanced and a sample of the pus collected on sterile gauze or in a sterile test tube. A cotton-plugged sterile capillary pipette may often be used to advantage ; its tip may be sealed in the flame before sending it to the laboratory.

Sputum for bacteriological examination should be collected carefully, with attention to a number of details. The mouth should be clean; the patient should rinse it with a mouth wash just prior to collection of the specimen. The specimen must contain true sputum, raised from the deeper air passages by *a cough,* and not merely saliva. The best time to collect the specimen is in the early morning, because patients frequently find it easier to raise sputum at the first expectoration in the morning than at any other time. The sputum must be received in a sterile Petri dish or a clean cup and transferred to a sterile widemouthed container. Sputum is examined in cases of pulmonary tuberculosis, pneumonia, influenza, whooping cough, bronchiectasis and lung abscess, and in other forms or acute infection of the deeper parts of the respiratory tract.

Feces are collected in a clean, preferably sterile pan. Portions may be placed in sterile wide-mouthed bottles or large test tubes, making the transfer with sterile sticks or large swabs. Fecal material may be secured from very young infants by inserting a sterilized glass tube into the rectum. The feces are always examined in cases of typhoid and paratyphoid fever, dysentery, cholera, and other diseases of the intestinal tract. Cultures are often made from the feces of healthy persons in order to discover carriers of typhoid bacilli and other germs. Feces are examined microscopically for hookworms and other intestinal parasites.

Urine is collected for bacteriological examination in cases of suspected infection of the urinary tract. It also may be examined in typhoid fever and other intestinal diseases, in tuberculosis of the urinogenital organs, and occasionally in pneumonia or septicemia, and other diseases. The external genitals and the lower part of the urethra always contain many bacteria, and these must be avoided in order to -secure an uncontaminated specimen of urine. A satisfactory sample may be obtained from males if the glans and meatus are first thoroughly cleansed with soap and water. The first urine voided. should be discarded, and only the last portion collected in a sterile, wide-mouthed bottle. From a female, a urine sample satisfactory for bacteriological examination can be secured only by use of a catheter-a small rubber tube inserted into the bladder or ureter. The part must first be washed with soap and water. The catheter must be sterile, and the first portion of urine should be rejected.

Peritoneal or *pleural fluid* is collected by inserting a sterile needle through the wall of the abdomen or chest and withdrawing the fluid in a sterile syringe or allowing it to run into sterile test tubes. The skin at the site of the puncture must be disinfected, of course, and every aseptic precaution must be taken as in any operation.

In heart and kidney disorders, and in some other organic disease conditions, there may be an accumulation of very large amounts of sterile fluid in the peritoneal cavity. This condition is cared ascites and the liquid is called *ascitic fluid.* Similarly, an excess of fluid may accumulate in the pleural or pericardial cavities. *Sterile fluids* of this sort, originating from some cause other than an infection, are called *transudates. Ascitic fluid*, aseptically collected, is used in the bacteriological laboratory as an enrichment for culture media.

Spinal fluid is obtained for examination by a process known as *lumbar puncture.* A large sterile hollow needle or trochar is passed into the spinal canal through a sterilized and anesthetized spot on the skin of the back, slightly to one side of the midline, between the third and fourth lumbar vertebrae. The strictest asepsis is observed throughout this operation and at its completion the puncture wound is protected with a sterile dressing. In pathological conditions the spinal fluid is usually much increased in amount and under much greater pressure than normal, so that it flows readily from the needle. It may be allowed to run directly into sterile centrifuge tubes. When fluid from the same patient is collected in several tubes, these must be numbered to show in what order the specimens were obtained. Often blood appears in the first drops of fluid collected, while later, unmixed spinal fluid is secured.

The spinal fluid is normally a clear liquid, containing only a few leukocytes, and *sterile. Therefore*, if bacteria, or an unusual number of pus cells, are found in it, this is evidence of a diseased condition. The fluid may still appear clear and yet be very abnormal. In syphilis and infantile paralysis (poliomyelitis), it is usually clear; and in tuberculous meningitis, it is either clear or slightly cloudy. In cases of acute meningitis, however, due to *Sterptococcus*, *Pneumococcus*, *Meningcoccus* or other bacteria, the fluid is usually very cloudy and contains many pus cells.

Spinal fluid from cases of syphilis is not used for cultures or smears. but only for a Wassermann or other diagnostic test. The sample should be sterile.

BLOOD

Many important facts are learned from examination of the patient's blood. The blood may be collected for study of the blood cells, or for tests on the blood-serum, or for smears or cultures to detect micro-organisms that may be in it. There are two common methods of securing blood for examination. These are: (1) the skin puncture method, by which a few drops of blood are secured from a puncture wound of the finger or ear, and (2) the venous puncture method, by which a considerable amount is obtained through it hollow needle inserted into a vein.

TECHNIQUE OF SKIN PUNCTURE METHOD

The lower lobe of the ear or tip of the finger is prepared for puncture by cleaning throughly with and alcohol sponge. An increased flow of blood to the fingers may be secured by shaking or swinging the hand vigorously, and the ear may be rubbed gently. After the alcohol has dried, the skin is then punctured, *not cut*, with a quick determined movement. A special blood lancet may be used for the puncture, but a sharpened, stiff needle or pin, or half of an ordinary writting pen, will serve. The puncture needle must be sterile. The blood should well out of the puncture wound spontaneously. It is best to avoid squeezing the ear or finger in order to secure enough blood. When the bleeding process is completed, the puncture wound is wiped with an alcohol sponge or touched with tincture of iodine.

Use of skin puncture method

This way of obtaining drops of blood serves for smears to be examined for malaria parasites and other organisms.

Also this method is used to secure blood for a determination of the number of red blood cells ("red count"), or white blood cells (" white count"), and for making smears from which to determine the relative proportion of the various types of white blood cells ("differential count"). The amount of hemoglobin the coagulation time, and other properties of the blood may be tested also.

The cell counts are made by drawing up a small amount of blood from the drop on the finger or ear into special blood counting pipettes, which accurately measure and dilute the blood. Drops of this diluted blood are examined in special chambers under the microscope and an actual count is made of the number of red or white blood cells in a known number of blood. From this, an estimate is made of the total number of the cells in a cubic millimeter of the patient's blood. The differential count is made by counting the first 200 white blood cells seen in a stained smear of the blood and classifying them into the various types- the polymorphonuclear leukocytes, lymphocytes, and so forth. The percentage of each type present is then determined. This differential count and the white count are very important in case of germ disease, because they serve as an index of the severity of the disease and of the resistance of the patients has.

Technique of venous puncture method

In adults the veins at the bend of the elbow are used. A bandage of cloth or a tourniquet of soft rubber tubing is applied to the upper arm and the patient is made to clench the fist. This makes the veins at the elbow and lower arm stand out prominently. The skin about the veins is cleansed with soap and water (if necessary), then washed with 70 per cent alcohol. Tincture of iodine may be used. A sterile hypodermic needle is then inserted into the vein and the blood is caught in a sterile tube. When the bleeding is complete, the tourniquet is immediately removed and an alcohol sponge is pressed firmly against the puncture wound until the bleeding stops.

When it is necessary to secure blood from an infant, for the Wassermann or other tests, the skin of the finger or heel may be punctured, or the blood may be secured from the large vein that lies just below the anterior fontanel (the soft spot on top of the head). This area is shaved and cleansed, then a sterile needle is thrust into this vein and the blood withdrawn into a syringe.

Use of venous puncture method

This method is used whenever considerable amounts of blood are required for chemical or bacteriological tests upon the *blood serum.* Blood for the *Wassermann test* (for syphilis) is always secured in this way. The blood is allowed to *clot* in the sterile collection tube, and the clear serum which separates off from the clot is used for the test. The specimen should be sterile, and must be kept in a refrigerator until the test is made.

CULTURES AND SMEARS FROM THE LIVING PATIENT

Blood cultures

The blood of healthy persons is sterile

But in various diseases living bacteria may be present in it and cultures of the blood serve as one of the most important methods of diagnosis. Usually 10 c.c or 15 c.c. are with drawn with a syringe from the arm vein as described above. *The blood is at once expelled into a flask of sterile broth.* Bile broth is used when typhoid bacilli are likely to be present in the blood, and brain broth when the presence of streptococci, pneumocoeci, meningococci, or other organisms is suspected. Some of the blood may be added to melted agar the agar poured into Petri dishes. If the blood must be carried some distance to the laboratory before it can be inoculated into media, it can be caught in a flask containing a sterile, 10 percent solution of sodium citrate. Enough of this solution should be used to give a final concentration of about 0.1 per cent of sodium citrate after mixture with the blood. This will be sufficient to prevent clotting.

Cultures from the nose and throat

Material for nose cultures is secured by passing a small, sterile, cotton swab straight back through the nostril. The swab must not be large, or loose upon the stick, otherwise it may catch in the nose.

Cultures from the throat are made by touching a sterile swab to the *diseased part only*. There must be plenty of light in the throat so that it is possible to see exactly what is being done. When the presence of diphtheria bacilli in the nose or throat is suspected, the medium used must be Loeffler's serum medium. For all other purposes, blood agar is the most suitable medium.

Cultures from the nasopharynx

The nasopharynx is the upper part of the throat back of the soft palate. Cultures from this region are made by use of a special swab. The cotton is wrapped about the end of a wire having a nearly right angle bend, which is enclosed in a glass tube similarly bent. The tube is introduced into the mouth and the curved end passed back of the soft palate. The swab is then pushed out and rubbed across the nasopharynx, then withdrawn into the tube before it is removed from the mouth.

Other cultures

Cultures from the *eyes* may be made by rubbing a small sterile cotton swab wet with sterile salt solution very gently over the surface of the conjunctiva.

Cultures from the *cervix* or *uterus* can be made only when the parts are exposed by the use of a sterile speculum. The very greatest care is required not to contaminate such cultures with organisms from the vagina.

Direct smears

There is frequently more to be learned form a smear made directly from an exudate or lesion than from cultures of the same material. Smears alone are relied upon for the diagnosis in cases of acute gonorrhea. Vincent's angina, and in some other diseases. Often the examination of smears from the pus of abscesses, wounds, inflamed eyes or ears, and other lesions, gives important clues as to the cause of the infection. Smears must be *thin*, and of good size. The slide must be clean and not greasy. When smear is to be made with a swab, *roll* the swab over the slide and avoid unnecessary pressure, so that the pus cells will not be broken up.

2

ANAEROBIC BACILLIAND WOUND INFECTIONS

CLOSTRIDIUM

The clostridia are large, gram-positive, endospore-forming rods that are unable to use molecular oxygen as a final electron acceptor. They are also unable to synthesize the prosthetic heme component necessary for a cytochrome system and the enzyme catalase, or superoxide dismutase. and must, therefore, be grown under anaerobic conditions. This can be done by placing cultures in a container and replacing the air with N_2 or H_2, or by using a liquid medium containing 0.1% agar and a reducing agent such as sodium thioglycollate or dithiothreotol.

The natural habitats of the clostridia are soil and the intestinal tracts of humans and animals. Some are saccharolytic and will ferment carbohydrates to form produts such as butyrie acid, butanol, isopropanol, and acetone, whereas others are proteolytic and will metabolize proteins, often yielding rather foul-smelling amines as end products.

In general, the clostridia are not invasive organisms, and those that produce disease do so as a result of the formation and liberation of destructive enzymes and toxic exotoxins.

The pathogenic *clostridia* are characterized by their ability to produce powerful exotoxins. They fall naturally into three groups: the gas-gangrene organisms, which infect only when the tissues have been traumatized and devitalized; *Cl. tetani*, which produces an insignificant local infection but general intoxication when introduced into the tissues under certain specific conditions; and the *botulinunt* species, which do not invade the body but synthesize exotoxins in certain food products which poison after ingestion.

The gas-gangrene infections will be discussed in this chapter, and tetanus and botulism food poisoning in subsequent chapters.

Many anaerobic, spore-bearing bacilli are normal inhabitants of the intestinal canal of man and animals. Soils fertilized with natural manures contain many more of these organisms than virgin or desert soils. Since it has been shown that *Cl. perfringens* can grow and multiply in the soil, it would not be surprising if all *clostridia* possess this capacity.

Wound infections are characterized by a mixed flora, and primary cultures rarely yield a single species. Stained smears of secretions usually show the presence of gram-positive cocci, and often of gram-negative bacilli of the coliform types, in addition to the large gram-positive rods which are characteristic of the *clostridia*. In the studies of gas gangrene, made during World War I single species of *clostridia* were found in about 40 per cent of the cases while two or more species were present in 60 per cent. The average number found per case in World War II varied from 2.56 to 2.84. One highly pathogenic species may be accompanied by another highly pathogenic one, such as C1. *perfringens* and *Cl. tetani*, or by one or more species which have little if any primary pathogenicity. It is essential, therefore, that plating methods be employed and colonies of varying morphology be isolated for detailed study.

Stock cultures of *clostridia* usually grow readily on ordinary laboratory media when incubated under anaerobic conditions, but richer media and meticulous care are required for primary isolation. Chopped meat and milk media have been used for many years for obtaining primary mixed cultures. Most, but not all, species form spores readily in these media. Those which form spores are easily purified by heating to 80°C for one hour to kill the vegetative forms and associated aerobic bacteria.The resistant spores are then streaked on suitable media and incubated under anaerobic conditions. Brewer's thioglyc-ollate broth is probably the best medium for obtaining initial mixed cultures.

TABLE 2.1. INCIDENCE OF CLOSTRIDIAL FLORA OF GAS GANGRENE

	Percent of Cases		
organism	*MacLennan (146 cases)*	*Stock (25 cases)*	*Smith and George (119 cases)*
Cl. perfringens	56	80	39
Cl. novyi	37	48	32
Cl. septicum	19	4	
Cl. histolyticum	6		
Cl. tetani	13	8	4
Cl. bifermentans	4	20	54
Cl. sporogenes	37	72	54
Cl. tertium	30	8	3
Cl. multifermentans		5	
Cl. butyricum	13	4	3
Cl. capitovale	5		3
Cl. fallax	1	4	3
Cl. cochlearium	9	4	2
Cl. putrificum	19		2
Cl. regulare			2
Cl. sphenoides	3		2
Cl. paraputrificum			1
Cl. hastiforme	3		
Cl. tetanomorphum	2		

The identification of the more pathogenic and more frequently encountered species of *clostridia* are shown in Table. This table was constructed from data in the books of *L. de S Smith* and *Holderman*, *Prevot*, and *Dowell* and *Hawkins*.

Clostridium Perfringens and Gas Gangrene

Cl. perfringens is the organism most frequently found in gas gangrene. It was present in about 72 to 80 percent of the cases of gas gangrene studied during Word War I and World War II. It has been associated consistently with civilian cases of gas gangrene and generally is considered the most important etiologic factor in this disease. It must be remembered, however, that the bacillus frequently is present in wounds which never develop gangrene. *Cl. perfringens* was discovered independently in three countries. It was discovered in the United States in 1892 by *Welch* and *Nuttall*, who named it *Bacillus aerogenes capsulatus*. In 1893 Fraenkel isolated a similar organism in Germany from several cases of gaseous phlegmons. He called it *B. phlegmonis emphysematosae*. The organism was described again by *Veillon* and *Zuber* in France and called by them *B. perfringens*. *B. welchii*, *B.aerogenes capsulatus*, *Fraenkel bacillus*, and *B. perfringens* all refer to the same organism.

MORPHOLOGY AND STAINING

Cl. perfringens is a short, plump, spore-bearing, gram-positive bacillus, occurring singly or in pairs Chains are not formed as a rule. It is nonmotile and has a capsule.

Cultural Characters

It grows best under strictly anaerobic conditions, but its requirements for anaerobiosis are less rigid than those of *C. tetani*. It grows well in media containing tissue. such as cookedmeat medium, after all the air has been expelled by simple boiling. With milk, boiling is not always sufficient to obtain good growth, and it is best to put milk tubes in anaerobic jars. The majority of strains do not form spores readily.

There seems to be an inverse relationship between the ability to form spores and to form toxins. The more toxins, the fewer spores and vice versa. The has been reported for *C. perfringens*, and for *C. novyi*. *A* detailed study of the cell wall and spore formation has been made with the electron microscopy by *Hoeniger* and her associates. *C. perfringens* ferments the muscle sugar, producing gas in the tissues and for this reason, commonly is called the "gas" bacillus. The crepitation thus produced is characteristic of gas gangrene and, indicates the extent of the infection.

Antigenic Structure

The capsular material is a polysaccharide and is heat-stable. Although all strains produce the same exotoxins, precipitin reactions with extracts of capsular substance and agglutinations.with intact bacilli show that the strains are heterologous.

Toxin

The types of *C. welchll* differ in the combinations of various toxic and enzymic factors that they produce. Several of these factors have haemolytic, lethal or necrotizing properties and others have enzymic activity against biological substrates.

Table shows that the various types of *C. welchii* can be differentiated on the basis of their production of the four major lethal toxins. Type-A strains produce alpha toxin; type- B strains typically produce alpha, beta and epsilon toxins; type-C strains produce alpha and beta toxins; Type-D strains produce alpha and epsilon toxins; and type-E strains produce alpha and iota toxins.

Neutralization tests may be performed by intracutaneous or intravenous administration of mixtures of toxin and antitoxin to guineapigs or mice respectively. Epsilon and iotatoxins do not occur in fully active form in cultures and these prototoxins require to be activated by trypsinization of samples of the culture filtrates prior to neutralization tests.

Alpha Toxin

Alpha toxin is produced by all types of *C. welehii* but notably by type-A strains. This is the most important of the lethal toxins of the organism and is generally considered to be the main cause of the profound toxaemia associated with gas gangrene in man. The alpha toxin is lethal for laboratory animals and it is necrotizing on intradermal inoculation. It is relatively heat stable. being only 50 per cent inactivated after five minutes at 100°C. The toxin is an enzyme-phospholipase (lecithinase C). In the presence of free. Ca_2^+ or Mg_2^+ ions it can split lipoprotein complexes in serum or eggyolk preparations with resulting opalescence. The reaction can be inhibited by specific antitoxin.

The phospholipase also attacks constituents of the membranes of red blood cells of various animals, and the alpha toxin is thereby haemolytic for the red cells of most species except the horse and the goat. The clear zones of haemolysis typically seen around colonies of classical type-A strains of *C. welchii* grown on horse .blood agar are produced by the theta toxin and not by the alpha toxin. With the re l cells of the sheep in particular the alpha toxin provides an example of a 'hot-cold' lysin. The alpha toxin similarly damages the membranes of other types of tissue cells and is thus a general cytotoxin.

Nagler's Reaction

Several clostridia and other bacterial species are able to produce opalescence in both human serum and egg-yolk media, due to the production of phospholipases that cause visible precipitates in these media. The reaction was first demonstrated with the alpha toxin of *C. welchii* and is specifically neutralized by *C. welchii* alpha antitoxin (but the serologically related phospholipase of *C. bifermentans* is also inhibited). This reaction has been utilized for the rapid detection of *C. welchii* in direct plate culture, and allows a serologically controlled identification of the o: ganisms to be made within 20 hours of inoculating the plate from the wound exudate. Further developments of this type of medium have included the incorporation of neomycin sulphate to inhibit aerobic sporeforming and coliform bacteria.

Beta toxin. Types B and C produce this toxin, which is lethal and necrotizing.

Epsilon toxin is produced by type-B and D strains as a prototoxin which is thereafter activated by proteolytic enzymes. It is lethal and necrotizing. Filtrates may be trypsinized before assay.

Iota toxin. Only type-E strains produce this toxin, which is also lethal and necrotizing and, like epsilon toxin, is formed as a prototoxin which is then activated by proteolytic enzymes.

Theta toxin is an oxygen-labile haemolysin that is antigenically related to streptolysin O: it is a lethal toxin and a general cytolytic toxin. It is produced by most strains of *C. welchii*, types A-E, but is not produced by typical food poisoning strains or by strains associated with enteritis necroticans in man. It lyses the red cells of the horse, ox, sheep and rabbit, but is virtually inactive against mouse erythrocytes.Many animal sera inhibit theta toxin and, although this may be due to contained antibodies, it is known that tissue lipids and cholesterol inactivate it.

Gamma toxin is a minor lethal toxin.

Delta toxin is lethal. It is also haemolytic for the red cells of even-toed ungulates (sheep, goats, pigs, cattle).

Eta toxin is said to be an insignificant lethal toxin.

Kappa toxin is a collagenase which attacks native collagen as well as hide powder and gelatin.

Lambda toxin is a proteinase and gelatinase. It will decompose hide power, but it does not attack native collagen.

Mu toxin is a hyaluronidase.

Nu toxin is a deoxyribonuclease.

C. welchii thus produces a wide range of potentially toxic or aggressin-like substances. In addition, cultures of this organism have been shown to possess other enzymic properties. Enzymes are produced, particularly by some type-B strains, that destroy blood-group substances. The organism also renders red blood cells inagglutinable by the myxoviruses by destroying virus receptors at the red cell surface. This is due to a receptor destroying enzyme (neuraminiddase) similar to that of *brio cholerae*. *C. welchii* renders red blood-cells panagglutinable by exposing their Tant:gensso that they lose theirspeetfieity and reset with any of the ADO antisera. A diffusible haemagglutinin elaborated by *C. welchii* causes agglutination of the red blood cells of man and most animals. It is produced by some strains after prolonged artificial subculture, but it is not produced'by freshly isolated strains. Virulent strains of *C. welchii* are said to produce an aggressin that has been named 'bursting factor' but this agent has not yet been adequately characterized. The organism also produces a deeonjugase enzyme that releases free bile acid from bile salt.

Epidemiology and Pathogenesis of Gas Gangrene

Gas gangrene results from the contamination of wounds with *Clostridlum* spores. Since all of these organisms are anaerobic, they are able to germinate and grow in deep wounds that become necrotic as a result of a diminished blood supply. After germination, the organisms secrete their exotoxins and enzymes into the surrounding environment, causing more tissue destruction and resulting in a rapid and fulminating spread of the organism in the necrotic environment. In addition, carbohydrates may be fermented, resulting in the production of large quantities of gas in the tissues. The pressures resulting from the gas information may cause still more restriction of the blood supply to adjoining tissue and, hence, still more necrosis. In the absence of surgical and antitoxic treatment, severe toxemia and death frequently ensue.

The toxins and enzymes produced by the various species of the gas gangrene group are similar, but not identical, from one species to another. Actually, most of them have not been purified or characterized, and are lumped under the general name "lethal toxins". The products produced by *C. perfringens* have received the most study, at least 12 different toxins and enzymes have been described and labelled with Greek letters. Not all serologic strains of *C. perfringens* produce all, 12 products or even similar quantities of certain toxins and enzymes.

The most extensively studied toxin is the a toxin, a lecithinase that hydrolyzes the phospholipid lecithin to a diglyceride and a phosphorylcholine. Since lecithin is a component of cell membranes, its hydrolysis can result in cell destruction throughout the body.

Another toxin produced by this group is the*a toxin*, a lethal hemolytic product characterized by its effect on the heart- more precisely. its cardiotoxic properties. Other toxic enzymes produced by the gas gangrene group include a collagenase that hydrolyzes the body's collagen, a hyaluronidase, a fibrinolysin that breaks down blood clots, a DNase, and a neuraminidase that can remove the neuraminic acid from a large number of glycoproteins. With such a vastarray of toxic substances, it is no wonder that gas gangrene was one of the major causes of death in the American Civil War-and, undoubtedly, in many other wars.

TABLE 2.2. TOXINS AND TOXIGENIC TYPE OF CLOSTRIDIUM PERIFRIGENS

		Bacterial Types				
	Toxins	*A*	*B*	*C*	*D*	*E*
α	(lecithinase)	+++	+++	+++	+++	+++
β	(lethal, necrotizing)		+++	+++		
γ	(lethal)		++	++		
δ	(lethal, hemolytic)		+	++		
ε	(lethal, necrotizing)		+++	-	+++	
η	(lethal)	+	p	p	p	
θ	(lethal, hemolytic)	+	++	+++	+++	+++
τ	(lethal, necrotizing)					+++
K	(collagenese)	+	+	+++	++	+++
λ	(proteinase)		+	-	++	+++
μ	(hyaluronidase)	++	+	+	++	
ν	(deoxyribonuclease)	++	+	++	++	++

+++ = most strains; ++ = some strains; + = a few strains; — = not produced.

In addition to battlefield casualities, automobile and farm equipment accidents nifty also cause traumatic wounds resulting in gas gangrene. Also, because *C. perfringens* can be part of the normal flora of the female genital tract, induced abortions may result in uterine gas gangrene.

Clostridia may also cause a diffuse spreading cellulitis accompanied by an overwhelming toxemia. Such infections. probably originate from the large intestine, either from a bowel perforation or from a contaminated injection site. Gas may be produced, but the cellulitis differs from the classic gas gangrene in that muscle necrosis is not involved.

Pathological-changes

Gas gangrene is a condition of massive necrosis of the affected tissue with gas formation. This is produced by the toxin of anaerobic bacteria of the clostridium group. The condition should, therefore, be differentiated from moist gangrene, in which gas production is a putrefactive process occurring in the tissue, already dead of dying. In this case, the infection is a primary factor. The earliest pathological change is a rapidly spreading oedema of the subcutaneous connective tissue and muscle with accumulation of gas. Collagen fibres are swollen, fragmented and cellular elements of the connective tissue are broken down.The blood vessels are damaged with destruction of their endothelial cells and this helps the . necrotic process to proceed further. Gas bubbles spread along the long axis of the muscle sheath. The spread of infection is helped by production.of exudationof haemorrhagic fluid and gas, which cuts off the nutrition of the muscle. The muscle loses its striation and passes through various stages of degeneration with - loss of nuclei until a coagulation necrosis sets in. The pathological changes seen in the nucleus are loss of contractility and the normal healthy colour of the muscle becomes brick red and later yellow in colour with crepitation due to gas bubbles. It becomes soft, friable and defluent and ultimately the muscle becomes black in colour due to the action of sulphurated hydrogen on iron liberated from broken down muscle haemoglobin. The gas is chiefly hydrogen and odourless at first (saccharolytic organisms) but soon it becomes foetid due to the production of sulphurated hydrogen. ammonia: and volatile gases by the action of the proteolytic group of organisms.

Histopathology

The invading organism is seen growing in the muscle sheath. Muscle fibres lose their striations and are separated from the sheath by accumulation of fluid and gas. Later the muscle sarcolemma disappears. and the whole fibre becomes hyalinised, necrotic, deeply stained with eosin, with disappearance of nuclei. The muscle fibres are completely disintegrated.

Food poisoning in man

Hobbs and his associates reported that, heat resistant *C. welchii* type A, may produce symptoms of intoxication causing food poisoning. The organism is nonhaemolytic on horse blood and feebly toxigenic. The spores resist boiling for several hours. They occur in human faeces. But human carrier rate for typical food poisoning is about 2.2 per cent in general population but it is 20 to 30 per cent in hospit personnels. The food poisoning usually appears 8-12 hours after ingestion of food'and diarrhoea is extremely common but vomiting is rare; whereas vomiting is very common in staphylococcal food poisoning. Abdominal pain is present but pyrexia is absent; prostration is common.

For diagnosis, the stools should be inoculated in Robertson's meat broth and heated at 1000C for one hour. The tubes are then incubated over-night at 37°C to allow the spores to germinate. Subcultures are made on blood agar plates and incubated at 37°C for a period of further 24 hours under anaerobic condition. *Nonhaemolytic colonies* characteristic of heat resistant *C. welchii* should grow in the plate. Although, the strains may produce lecithinase and doubtful haemolysis, they lack in the production of theta toxin, which causes complete beta haemolysis, typical of classical *C. welchii.*

Clostridium Perfringens and Food Poisoning

In addition to being the major etiologic agent in wound infections, *C. perfringens* is also an important cause of food poisoning. Most outbreaks are caused by C *perfringens* type A strains that produce a heat-labile enterotoxin only when the vegetative cells sporulate in the small intestine, releasing the newly synthesized enterotoxin. Symptoms of acute abdominal pain and diarrhea begin 8 to 24 hours after ingestion of the contaminated food and usually subside within 24 hours. The mechanism of action of the enterotoxin is unknown, but the effect is similar to that produced by the enterotoxigenic *E. coli.*

Rare but severe cases of food poisoning, characterized by hemorrhagic enteritis and a high mortality rate, are caused by *C. perfringens* type C. Such cases have been reported primarily from Germany and new Guinea. Those in New Guinea (known as pig-bel) have been associated with the eating of pork that had been insufficient cooked and improperly handled and cooled. Type C organisms produce a sporulation enterotoxin indistinguishable from that produced by type *AC. perfringens*, but they also produce laige amounts of a toxin and the lethal, necrotizing R toxin. It appears that the severe hemorrhagic enteritis is primarily a result of the action of the P toxin.

Because of the severity and high incidence of this disease a program of active immunization with *C. perfringens B* toxoid was initiated in 1980. Current data indicate that the use of this vaccine has resulted in a dramatic decrease in the incidence of pig-bel in the New Guinea highlands.

Clostridium Difficile

Pseudomembranous colitis is a severe, necrotizing process that occurs in the large intestine following antibiotic therapy. This syndrome has been associated with a number of antimicrobial agents, but the antibiotics clindamycin and ampicillin have been most often incriminated. The mechanism of this severe diarrhea was elucidated in 1978 when it was observed that the use of these antibiotics resulted in an overgrowth of an organism in the intestine identified as *Clostridium difficile.* This organism appears to be part of the normal intestinal flora of certain persons, but only when antibiotic-sensitive organisms are eliminated from the intestine is it able to grow to sufficient numbers to produce disease.

Clostridium difficile produces disease by the elaboration of two distinct exotoxins, which have been designated as A and B. Toxin A is an enterotoxin that is primarily responsible for the diarrhoea associated with this disease. Toxin B is a cytotoxin that demonstrates a lethal effect on cultured tissue cells. It is believed that toxin B causes the cell necrosis associated with pseudomembranous colitis, and preliminary data suggest that toxin A may stimulate guanylate cyclase, resulting in increased concentrations of cyclic guanosine monophosphate (cCMP).

Clostridium Botulinum

Clostridium botulinun is the causative agent of a highly fatal food pöisoning that usually follows the ingestion of a performed toxin produced by the organisms while growing in the food. A total of 118 cases of botulism occurred in the United States in 1984. This included 92 cases of infant botulism, 20 cases of food-borne botulism, and 6 cases designated as "classification undetermined."

Prevention and Control of Gas Gangrene

Surgical cleansing of wounds to eliminate extraneous material or necrotic tissue is undoubtedly the most important control mechanism foi gas gangrene. Additionally, antitoxin against the bacterial filtrates can be used-when complete surgical debridement is not possible. Antibiotics, such as penicillin or the tetracyclines, would be effective in tissues still receiving a blood supply but are of little value in necrotic areas. Hyperbaric oxygen chambers, in which an infected area is placed in a chamber containing pure oxygen under pressure, have been used with some success to stop the growth of these obligate anaerobes.

3

PNEUMOCOCCUS

By "Pneumonia" is meant an inflammation of the walls of the alveoli, or air sacs, which make up the lung tissues, as a result of which the alveoli become filled with exudate. This disease may be *primary i.e.*, a well person may suddenly develop an acute pneumonia. In this case, the infection almost invariably involves one *entire lobe*, or two or more entire lobes of the lung. This is called *acute lobar pneumonia*. Another form of pneumonia is *secondary*, ie., it occurs as a complication to some other disease condition. In this case the infection usually results from an extension of an acute bronchitis into the alveoli, and the lung is involved only in scattered patches. about the inflamed bronchioles. This is called bronchopneumonia.

Secondary Pneumonia

We have already pointed out that measles, whooping cough, and influenza are especially liable to be complicated by a secondary infection of the lungs in the form of a bronchopneumonia, and have mentioned that this complication is responsible for nearly all the deaths of patients with these diseases. This type of lung infection may also complicate a great many other diseases, and in fact a terminal bronchopneu monia is the immediate cage of death in the great majority of cases of chronic tuberculosis, cancer, and various other. pathological conditions. Though not always fatal, a secondary pneumonia is a very dangerous infection, because the Patient is usually greatly weakened by pre-existing disease.

No single kind of germ is responsible for all cases of secondary pneumonia and there is a mixture of bacteria in the inflamed lung, but in groups of cases occurring in the same place a particular species often predominates. Thus, Streptococcus homolyhcus is frequently the most abundant germ, while in other groups of cps *pneumonci*, Staphylococci, or Hemophilus influenzae may be predominate- These germs an doubtless present in the throat before the disease begins in many cases. and invade the lung only when the resistance of the patient becomes sufficiently low.

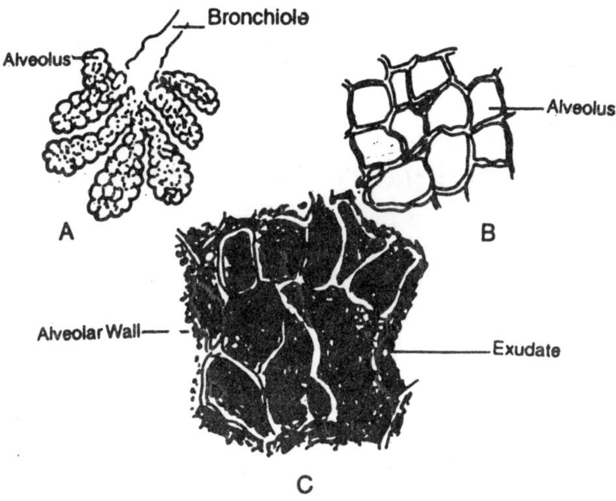

Fig. 3.1.A, diagrammatic representation of a terminal bronchiole and the group of tiny air sacs, or alveoli. attached. The lungs'are made up of innumerable units of this nature. B, section of the normal lung. showing the thin-walled of alveoli filled with air. C. section of the hung in lobar pneumonia.' showing how the alveoli become solidly filled with a purulent exudate

Occasionally the bronchopneumonia is caused by the germ which is, responsible also for the primary infection as, for example, the typhoid bacillus in cases of tyhphoid-fever.

History and Classification

While working on rabies, Pasteur in France and Sternberg in New York isolated and cultured a capsulated diplococcus. Pasteur found it in the saliva of a child but he did not ascribe the diplococcus as the causative organism of pneumonia. He also described it as the causative organism for septicaemia in rabbits. Albert Fraenkel and Weichselbaum independently established beyond doubt the importance ofthis organism as the aetiological agent in a large majority of cases of lobar pneumonia. Schottmueler described, and organism under the name of*Streptocaccusmucosus*, which is now known as pneumococcus type III. Neufield and Handel showed that pneumococci could be divided into specific serological groups. Cole, and Dochez and Gillespie differentiated the organism into definite types, namely; I, II, Ill, and Group IV, the last one being a heterogeneous group. Cooper and her associates differentiated group IV, serologically into 30 odd types; at present, seventy-seven different types of pneumococci have been identified by antisera.

Habitat

D. pneumoniae can be isolated from upper respiratory tract of 25 per cent of healthy human subjects and of these, about 50 per cent belong to group IV.

MORPHOLOGY AND STAINING

The pneumococci are rather large, lancent-shped cocci which usually occur in pairs and are surrounded by definite capsules. In smears the cocci also may be found singly, in short chains, and occasionally in long chains; and in the latter condition the capsule appears to enclose the entire chain with or without indentations opposite the points of division.

Type III pneumococci are characteristically spherical in shape both in exudates from the body and in culture.

The pneumococcus it nonsporogenous and nonmotile and possesses no flagella. The organism stains readily with the usual aniline dyes and is gram-positive when fresh, actively growing cultures are examined, but numerous gram-negative forms may be found in old cultures. Capsules are produced by virulent strains.

Pneumococci are bile-soluble. Rapid autolysis in bile or 10 percent deoxycholate within 5 to 10 minutes is the most reliable test for the differentiation of pneumococci from other coccal forms. If glucose is present in the both in which the pneumococci are grown, the increased acidity causes a precipitation and gelling after addition of the deoxycholate solution unless the culture has been readjusted to pH 7.4.

A more rapid test for solubility has been described by Hawn and Beebe. With the aid of a hand lens, a loopful of 2 percent sodium deoxycholate (pH 7.0) is deposited on an isolated colony present in the original primary culture. After reincubation for 30 minutes at 37°C the colony disappears.

Pneumococci require choline for growth, and the choline becomes a constituent of teichoic acid in the cell wall. If ethanolamine is substituted for choline, the pneumococci will grow, but they are then no longer sensitive to lysis, nor can they be genetically transformed. Apparently, the incorporation of ethanolamine in place of choline causes steric differences that result in major changes in cell properties.

Nutritionally, the pneumococci need an enriched medium for growth and, like other streptococci, lack both cytochromes and catalase. All pneumococci produce alpha-hemolysis when growing on a blood agar medium and, therefore, closely resemble the viridans streptococci in colonial appearance and morphology.

Antigenic Structure

The pneumococci can be subdivided into more than 80 types on the basis of antigenic differences in their polysaccharide capsule. (The ability to transform one type of *S. pheumoniae* to a new type using purified DNA was discussed. They also contain a C carbohydrate analogous to that used by Lancefield to group the streptococci and a type-specific M protein. Unlike the group A streptococci, however, pneumococcal M protein is not antiphagocytic, nor are antibodies to the M protein protective.

Pneumococcal Infectious

The pneumococci are alpha-hemolytic and excrete a cytolytic toxin called *pueumolysin*, which binds to cholesterol in host cell membranes. The role of pneumolysin in the pathogenesis of pneumococcal infections is obscure, but preliminary reports indicate that it may function by inhibiting the antimicrobial properties of neutrophils and the opsonic activity of serum. It appears, however, that the pneumococcus can survive and produce disease in the host primarily because of its capsule. Once a strain loses its capsule, it can be readily phagocytosed and destroyed. Thus, immunity is the result of humoral antibody directed against the capsule and is, therefore, type specific.

Interestingly, *S. pheumoniae* is carried as part of the normal flora of the respiratory tract in many health individuals. We do not understand why carriers do not suffer from pneumonia, but it appears that the normal lung is quite resistant to infection and that pneumococcal pneumonia occurs most frequently in conjunction with viral infections of the upper respiratory tract. The disease also occurs in persons whose respiratory drainage is impaired, that is, bedridden patients, heavy smokers, and persons who have inhaled toxic irritants.

Pneumococcal Pneumonia

The estimated incidence of pneumococcal pneumonia varies considerably with an individual's age, conditions of crowding, and occupation. In the United States, the incidence is thought to be 300,000 to 400.000 cases per year, with an overall mortality of 15,000 to 60,000. Military personnel living in a closed group have an incidence 10 to 20 times higher per 1.000 population; the rates ofpneumococcal pneumonia in African gold miners is about 100-fold greater than that for the genbral population.

The disease is characterized by an acute lung inflammation, which. in adults, is usually lobar; that is. involving the tissues in one or more lobes of the lungs, whereas in children or the elderly, it frequently causes a more restricted bronchopneumonia. It is usually sudden in onset and is characterizedby chills, fever, and pleural pain (in the area surrounding the lung). The alveoli fill with exudate and, in about 25% of cases, bactremia is found early in the course of the disease.

Pneumococci may also invade other tissues, particularly the sinuses, the middle ear, and the meninges. Other possible secondary complications include septicemia, endocarditis (inflammation of the heart and valves), pericarditis (inflammation of the pericardium, the membrane surrounding the heart), and empyema (an infection of the pleural cavity).

Recovery is characteristically abrupt and coincides with the appearance of circulating anticapsular antibodies.

Meningitis

The pneumococcus is the second most common cause of bacterial meningitis in adults. Meningitis may arise as a complication of pneumonia or sinusitis, in which the bacteria reach the meninges by way of the bloodstream, or it may result from a skull fracture or other injury, permitting organisms from the nasopharynx to enter the meninges.

Otitis Media

At least 75% of all children have middle ear infections by age 6 years, and the pneumococcus is the etiologic agent for about half these infections; such infections are rare in adults. Children experiencing an initial middle ear infection during the first year of life are likely to have recurrent otitis media during early childhood, resulting in reduced hearing acuity. Surprisingly, not all pneumococcal types cause this infection; only types 6, 14; 19, and 23 can be isolated from more than half the cases of pneumococcal otitis media.

CULTURAL CHARACTERISTICS

The pneumococci lack cytochromes. They can utilize oxygen through a flavoprotein enzyme system, but cannot degrade the hydrogen peroxide which is produced. Catalase to destroy the hydrogen peroxide can be supplied by the addition of defibrinated blood to the basic media which usually contain meat extracts or tryptic digests of soy beans. Glucose is usually the limiting growth factor in most media. The addition of glucose to provide a final concentration of 1 percent increases the total growth but results in the production of inhibiting amounts of lactic acid which can be neutralized by.sodium hydroxide, sodiwn bicarbonate, or calcium carbonate. The pH of the media should be adjusted to 7.6.

Austrian and Collins found that 8 percent of primary isolates from human secretions would not grow On the surface of solid medium unless 20 Percent of CO_2 was provided. However, these same strains would grow in a mouse, in liquid medium, or under aerobic or anaerobic conditions on solid media if CO_2 was supplied.

On meat infusion blood-agar plates the pneumococci develop, after 24 to 48 hours incubation, small, round, somewaht flattened, transparent colonies. In suitable nutrient broth growth is rapid, and within 24 hours' incubation, pneumococci produce in the depth of the medium small, round, compact colonies swrounded by a zone of greenish discoloration which is identical in appearance with that formed by colonies of α-hemolytic streptococci.

Inulin is fermented by most but not all strains of pneumococci; a positive test is therefore confirmation, but a negative test does not exclude the possiblity that the organism is a pneumococcus. Pneumococci, in contrast to other cocci, are inhibited by quinidine. Colonies suspected of being pneumococci are streaked over the surface of blood-agar plate, and paper disks are applied after streaking. If the organism in question is a pneumococcus, there will be a clear zone free of organisms about each disk.

The intraperitoneal inoculation of a white mouse is not only the most rapid and most reliable method of obtaining pure cultures of pneumococci from contaminated maaterials, but it is also an accurate means of determining the pathogenicity of the strain. Type XIV, however, is aviruient for the mouse, and type III. A 66 is almost aviruient for the rabbit.

Direct typing can be done on broth culture after 12 to 18 hours' incubation or from sputum or peritoneal exudate of mice which have been inoculated with sputum. This is known as the Quellung method. In the presence of the specific anti-serum the capsule becomes easily visible. It was assumed, as the name Quellung suggests, that the capsule became swollen. Later it was believed that the effect was to make the capsule more visible but not to increase the size. However, the recent study of Baker and Loosli with the electron microscope shows that both are true, the capsule does swell and also becomes more refractile.

Pacamococci do resemble streptococci in many ways and are included as a species of streptococcus by English microbiologists. The evidence of the close relationship depends upon the following cha.acteristics. Both pneumococci and streptococci have a specific M protein which is near the surfate of the cell wall. The specific M protein does not correspond to the specific capsular polysaccharide but can be transduced from one M type pneumococcus to another but not to streptococci. Both have a group-specific carbohydrate which is highly antigenic. Streptomycin resistance can be transferred front to streptococci and vice versa. However, the pneumococoi differences are greater than the resemblances. The specific capsular polysaccharide is essential for the virulence of the pneumococci while the specific M protein plays the same role with streptococci. The M protein cannot be transferred from pneumococci to streptococci. The pneumococci are much more virulent for mice than streptococci, and classical lobar pneumonia in man is produced by pneumococci but not by streptococci.

THE CASE OF DEATH IN PNEUMOCOCCAL BACTERIA

The amount and quality of the known toxin produced by the pneumococci is not sufficient to explain the sudden collapse and death of patients and of experimentally infected animals. Robson and Cluff have found that experimental, lethal pneumococcal infections in rabbits produce progressive failing cardiac output and progressive rising peripheral resistance. Hydro cortisone acts in man and in infected animals to increase the cardiac output and lower the peripheral resistance. These investigators found that the administration of hydrocortisone and penicillin saved a higher percentage of the animals than when penicillin was used alone. They also found that there was a critical dose of pneumococci which always killed the animals regardless of the treatment used. When a sufficient initial dose was given to produce a pneumococcal bacteremia of 10^6 pneumococci per milliliter of blood within four hours after infection, the animals always died even though treatment with penicillin markedly reduced or eliminated the pneumococci. The same phenomenon has been observed by others with the plague bacillus, anthrax, and coliform bacteria. These three types of bacilli produce known toxins and it was assumed that death would always occur when a fatal dose of toxin had been grown even when the living organisms were all eliminated by antibiotics. But with the pneumococci we know of no such toxin.

Recent studies on pneumococcal neuraminidase suggest that this enzyme may act as a toxin. It is produced by all pneumococci freshly isolated from man. It is actively secreted by growing, dividing cells, not autolysing' cells. It seems to be a group not type-specific antigen for pneumococci since it is neutralized by both homotypic and heterotypic antibody. The mechanism of action may be the enzymatic cleavage of sialic acid from the sialic acid-glycoprotein conjugate of the cell membranes, modifying or inhibiting active cation transport.

The enzyme seems to be of relatively low molecular weight and is not antigenic for rabbits when injected alone, but is antigenic, when injected as a part of the whole pneumococcal cell.

The creactive protein is not a metabolite of the pneumococcus or a specific antibody to the somatic group carbo hydrate but is an abnormal protein that appears in the serum of patients with pneumonia and other diseases and has the peculiar property of precipitating the C carbohydrate of pneumococci.

Pathogenesis

It is important to distinguish two main categories of disease syndromes associated with the pneumococcus. One category includes lobar pneumonia and some suppurative infections, e.g. meningitis and peritonitis, which are mostly caused by a limited number of pneumococcus serotypes 1, 2, 5, 7, 12, 14possessing infectious and invasive qualities that facilitate primary attack on healthy tissues. The other category includes secondary infections of upper and lower respiratory tracts, e.g. sinusitis, bronchitis, broncho pneumonia, by opportunistic or potentially pathogenic pneumococci -types 4, 6,10, 18, 19, 22, 23, etc.-already resident in the oro-or nasopharynx and ready to attack tissues of lowered resistance. Two pneumococcus types, 3 and 8, are probably intermediate in invasiveness but, because they are rich in capsular substance, they may produce very severe infections, particularly in elderly debilitated persons.

In lobar pneumonia, the highly virulent pneumococcus, once it has penetrated the bronchial mucosa, spreads diffusely through the hitherto healthy lung via the peribronchial tissues and lymphatics. In bronchitis and bronchopneumonia, on the other hand, the pneumococci, which are generally less virulent, spread along the mucosal surface to the bronchial tree, which is probably already damaged by a predisposing viral infection or other condition, and invade the lung tissues only to a short distance from the mucosa. The causal role of pneumococci, like that of *Haemophilus influenzae,* in chronic bronchitis and its acute exacerbations is probably facilitated by the excessive secretion of bronchial mucus in that syndrome which may be due primarily to tobacca smoking, atmospheric pollution, allergy or other as yet unknown causes.

Pneumococci are frequently inhaled into the upper and lower respiratory tracts but the usual outcome of such intreductions is elimination of the organisms by phagocytosis and other normal defence mechanisms. In some persons the introduction leads to the establishment of symptotnless carriage in the nasopharynr. It is possible that the introduction of a virulent type of pneumococcus sometimes causes nasophatyngitis, but whether pneumococci can act as primary pathogens in producing an exogenous clinical infection of the throat is uncertain. The available evidence suggests that pneumonia is seldom if ever caused by the direct inhalation of pneumococc from the environment into the lungs i.e. by direct exogenous infection. Probably the infecting pneumococcus first becomes established in the nasopharynx and then some days or weeks later, if the carrier is subjected to a predisposing condition, it may spread to and infect the lung, the middle ear, a paranasal sinus or the meninges. The conditions most commonly predisposing to pneumonia are probably virus infections, including the common cold, but chilling, excessive intake of alcohol and deep anaesthesia, conditions that predispose to aspiration of secretions from the throat into the lower respiratory tract, may also be effective.

Capsule as Virulence Factor

The main virulence factor of the pneumococcus is its capsular polysaccharide which, because of its highly acidic and, hydrophilic properties, renders the pneumococci, when suspended in fluid, very difficult for phagocytes to trap and ingest Non-capsulate mutant (R) forms of pneumooocci lack this resistance to phagocytosis and are entirely non-virulent for experimental animals like the mouse and rabbit, and presumably also for man. Capsulate pneumococci, although resistant to phagocytosis when suspended in fluid, are nevertheless moderately susceptible to phagocytosis when lying on a surface e.g. a bronchial or alveolar wall, or a deposit of fibrin, against which the phagocytes may trap them. Infection of the respiratory tract is therefore facilitated by conditions, such as primary virus infections, that cause an excessive secretion of mucus, since this mucus protects the pneumccocci from 'surface' phagocytosis and allows their free growth. There is evidence suggesting that lobar pneumonia may be produced in the hitherto healthy lower respiratory tract of a throat carrier of pneumococcus when, in the course of a viral infection of the upper respiratory tract, nasopharyngeal secretion containing pneumococci is aspirated into the lower tract.

Toxins

Pneumococcus is generally cited as an example of a pathogen combining high invasiveness with minimal toxigenicity. The failure to demonstrate its production of a significantly potent toxin has left in doubt the mechanism by which it causes death in cases of pneumonia and septicaemia. A weak oxygen- labile haemolysin (pneumolysin) and a weak oxygen-labile leucocidin with some general cytotoxic activity have been demonstrated in bacteria-free filtrates or centrifuged supernates of cultures, but their role is unknown.

Immunity

Since the antiphagocytic capsule is the principal virulence factor of the pneumococcus, the principal protective antibody is antibody specific for the capsular polysaccharide. This antibody exerts a strong opsonic effect so that the capsulate pneumococcus is easily phagocytosed. Production of anticapsular antibody in the course of infection is probably the main factor bringing about recovery, for example by 'crisis', that often takes place about the 7th or 8th day in untreated cases of lobar pneumonia. Since the anticapsular antibody is type-specific, the acquired immunity is specific for each of the 80 different types of pneumococcus, and a person recovered from pneumonia due to one type of pneumococcus may at any time suffer a second attack of pneumonia due to infection with a pneumococcus of a different type. In the period before sulphonamides and penicillin became available for the treatment of pneumococcal pneumonia, horse or rabbit antiserum was administered to patients with a beneficial and often life saving effect; it was necessary for this purpose that the type of the pneumococcus infecting the patient should be determined and that antiserum specific for this type should be given. Similarly if vaceines are to be used effectively for active immunization against pneumococcal infection, they must contain a mixture of the capsular polysaccharides from all the more common types of pneumococcus likely to cause infection in the community.

Many persons who are not known to have suffered pnetmococcal infection nevertheless possess antibodies to various types of the organisms. They may have developed these antibodies either as a result of having carried the corresponding pneumococci for a long period (e.g. many months) in the nasopharyx or by ingestion of cross-reacting antigenic polysaccharides in vegetable foodstuffs. If prolonged throat carriage does lead to the production of protective antibodies, then the danger of endogenous infection being induced in a carrier through exposure to a precipitary factor, such as an upper respiratory tract virus infection, must be limited to the early weeks after the start of carriage.

Laboratory Diagnosis

Pneumonia. which on the basis of clinical and radiological 'findings is divisible into lobar. segmental, and lobular and broncho-pneumonia is a disease syndrome of varied microbial aetiology For these pneumonias and for other severe chest infections, e.g. bronchiolitis and croup in children, chronic bronchitis, primary atypical and interstitial pneumonias in adults. precise-(aetiological diagnosis is often essential for effective antimicrobial therapy and good medical care. Sputum that has been coughed up (not salivary secretion) or, when sputum is not available, a laryngeal swab should be transmitted to the laboratory as early and as quickly assessible with all relevant information including any history of anti-microbial therapy before admission. In addition, blood for culture and for the first of two serum specimens for virus antibodies and cold agglutinins should also be obtained on admission. Sputum is Homogenized by shaking with water and glass beads in a mechanical shaker and inoculated on plates of blood agar and heated blood agar. It may also be injected intraperitoneally into a mouse when a search is to be made for scanty pneumococci. The inoculated plates are incubated for 18 hours at 37°C in an atmosphere of 5 to 10 par cent CO_2 and suspected colonies to bacterial pathogens-pneumococci, *H. influenzae*, staphylococci and 0-haemolytic streptococci are picked for further identification. The second serum specimen is taken after 2 to 3 week: and the paired sera are tested for antibodies against influenza and parainfluenza viruses, the adenovirus group, psittacosis Q fever, and cold agglutinins or antibodies to mycoplasme infection.

In a series of 156 adult patients with pneumonia or severe bronchitis, admitted to an Edinburgh hospital, pneumococci were isolated from sputum and/or blood in 44 per cent; in 13 per cent of these cases there were associated *H. influenzae* which were also isolated as the main pathogen in another 10 percent of cases. *Staphylococcus aureus* was the significant pathogen in 8 per cent. In 38.5 per cent of all patients, no bacterial pathogens were isolated; since a quarter of these cases were classified as lobar pneumonia in which the pneumococcus is much the commonest pathogen and since 39 per cent, of all patients had antimicrobial drugs before admission, it was assumed that many of the pathogen-negative cases were in fact pnewnococcal infections. Serological evidence of recent virus infection was found in 1 8 per cent of all cases.

It has been argued that routine blood culture and pneumococcus serotyping are worthwhile procedures in adult cases of pneumonia because of their prognostic significance. Austrian reported a case-fatality of 18 percent in a large series of bacteriaemic pneumococcal pneumonias; in type 3 pneumococcus infections it was 48 per cent. In an Edinburgh series of 137 cases of pneumococcal pneumonia. 50 (36 per cent) were type 3 infections and 5 of these died (4 with positive blood culture) : the overall case fatality was 7.3 per cent.

For the isolation of bacterial pathogens in lower respiratory tract infections of young children, a serum-coated laryngeal swab, plated on blood agar and certain selective media, gave satisfactory results in a London series of 191 hospitalized patients (mostly under 5 years of age) in whom Pneumococci were the most common pathogens followed by *Staphylococcus aureus, H. influenzae*, O-haemolytic streptococci and coliform bacilli in that order of frequency. If there is likely to be delay in the swab reaching the laboratory, it should first be inoculated into a modified Pike medium and plated out after overnight incubation.

Chemotherapy

The pneumococcus is snesitive to a wide range of anitimicrobial drugs includings the penicillins., tetracyclines and sulphonamides in the treatment of pneumonia in adults or children at home or in hospital, identification of the infecting pathogen may not be sought or is known only after chemotherapy has been started. In such circumstances, broad spectrum bactericidal drugs like ampicillin or the combination of trimethoprim and sulphamethoxazole (cotrimoxazole), both of which can be given orally is likely to be effective. In severe infectious, parenteral injections of combined penicillin and streptomycin may be preferred. If and when the infecting pathogen has been identified and its drug sensitivity ascertained, a switch may have to be made to the appropriate antimicrobial drug. Tetracycline-resistant pneumococci are now not uncommon and recently, penicillin resistant pneumococci, developing sometimes in the course of treatment or chemoprophylaxis, have been encountered.

Epidemiology

The number of deaths from pneumonia in England and Wales has been increasing in recent years and with bronchitis and influenza these respiratory infections rank fourth to cardiovascular diseases, cancers and cerebrovascular diseases in the mortality table. The increase in deaths and in mortality rates from pneumonia probably reflects the greater longevity of the population and the weakening of resistance to infection in old age; seven-tenths of all pneumonia deaths occur in persons over 65 years of age. Young children are the other highly susceptible age group and account for one-tenth of all deaths from pneumonia. Although the death rate from pneumonia at all ages is almost equal in male and females it is much higher for men than for women in the age group 55 to 64 years (71 versus 40 per 100000) and this disparity is even greater for the death rates from bronchitis in the same age-group (217 versus 39). In the Morbidity Statistics for General Practice respiratory infections constituted one quarter of practitioner consultations, the age groups most affected being 0 to 5 years and 65 years or over. The highest.consultation rates were in urban communities and the lowest in rural areas; and they were, of course, highest in the winter months. There was a steeply rising gradient from social class 1 *tea* V of consultation rates for pneumonia and bronchitis among males aged 15 to 64 years and for bronchitis in children aged 0 to 5 years.

Source and Mode of Infection

Pneumococci of one or other type are found growing, apparently like comrnensals, in the nasopharynx of about 30 per cent of healthy persons examined on a single occasion, and in lesser numbers in the oral and nasal secretions of many of these throat carriers. The pneumococcus is relatively resistant to drying and other common environmental conditions and it therefore may readily be spread from the throat of one person to that of another by any of the routes generally applicable to respiratory-tract infections, e.g. by the distribution of dust derived from dried respiratory-tract secretion, which may become airborne and be inhaled, by contact with fingers and other articles soiled with secretion and possibly, by secretion droplet-spray and droplet-nuclei.

It is important to emphasize that meet of the severe chest infections at the extremes of life are endogenous infections by opportunistic resident bacteria such as pneumococci, H. influensae and staphylococci and that they develop when respiratory mucosal resistance is lowered by antecedent virus infections or from social and environmental causes. On the other hand, most, cases of lobar pneumonia in older children and healthy adults .are primarily exogenous infections derived from cases or carriers of the limited number of the more infectious and invasive pneumococcus types. Outbreaks of ldhar pneumonia are rare but have occurred in army training camps and in heavy industries such as steel works. Because most of the younger patients with lobar pneumonia respond well to chemotherapy, they are nowaap Olden treated of home whereas older persons with severe respiratory in>1kd are try admitted to hospital. When detailed investigations ittt g pasnmococcus typing are made in these hospitalized cases, pftmococcus type 3 is found to be the most frequent pathogen and with type : 8 accounts for over 50 per cent of the pneumoeoCCal pneumonias; 30 to 40 years ago Pneumococcus types I and 2 were the causal agents in I Pneumonias of 50 to 70 per cent of the hospitalized patients, large proportion of whom were 20 to 40 year-old adults.

Clinical Types of Infections in Man

Pneumococcal pneumonia, particularly the lobar type, the most characteristic of pneumococcal infections. In addition to pneumonia, pneumococci can produce sinus infection otitis media, osteomyelitis, arthritis, peritonitis, corneal ulceration, and meningtis. The common complications of pneumococcal pneumonia are septicemia, empylma, endocarditis, pericarditis, meningitis, and arthritis. Secondary pneumococcal (pneumonias follow viral infections, such as measles and influenza, less frequently than streptococcal ones but more frequently than staphylococcal infections.

Recurrent Pneumonia

True recurrences, after months or years, are observed more frequently in pneumonia than in any other acute infectious disease. Recurrences are particularly common in patients with, congenital or acquired agammaglobulinemia.

Blood cultures in pneumonia

During the course of pneumonia, *pneumococcus septicemia* is common. Frankel in 1902 stated that he believed in most, if not all, cases of pneumonia the organisms are present in th blood stream at some stage of the disease.

Mortality

The death rate in pneumonia depends upon the race, sex age, and general condition of the patient, the type of infecting pneumococcus, the degree of involvement of the lung, thg presence or absence of septicemia, the occurrence of complications, the promptness of specific therapy, and many other factors. General experience has indicated that the average case mortality varies from 20 to 30 per cent in untreated patients. The highest death rates occur in infections with types II and Ill, ranging from about 35 to 50 percent. When patients with pneumococcal pneumonia are not diagnosed and treated with antibiotics. the mortality remains as high as, before. With prompt antibiotic therapy the death rate has been reduced to 5 percent, and the failure is primarily in, elderly people and in those with debilitating diseases. The poorest results in primary pneumococcal infections are found in patients with pneumococcal meningitis. especially in those with pneumococcal otitis media and meningitis.

Transmission

Considering that 25 to 50 per cent of the population carryvirulent pneumococci in their nasopharyhges, one alternately wonders why pneumococcal attack rates are not infinitely higher and why anyone over gets clinical pneumonia. Pneumococci disappear from the nasopharynx of the convalescent case in two or three weeks unless he has a focus in a nasal sinus. Straken, Hill, and Lovell have shown that even the asymptomatic carriers constantly are losing old types and acquiring new types of pneumococci. Smillie and Jewett and Finland have traced the asymptomatic epidemic spread of.a. specific type of pneumococcus through a family group and observed the sporadic development of clinical cases of pneumonia.

Treatment

A prompt diagnosis is essential in obtaining the best results with either antibiotic or sulphonamide therapy. Fortunately, it is not necessary to type the pneumococcus before starting. treatment, since all types are equally susceptible to these, therapeutic agents.

Pneumococci are very susceptible to penicillin and to the broad-spectrum antibiotics. In ordinary pneumococcal pneumonia, even with septicemia, doses of 500,000 to 1,000,000 units of penicillin daily effect a prompt cure. In contrast, truly heroic doses are required in pneumococcal meningitis to effect a transfer of the antibiotic through the blood-brain barier of the meninges. We quote the doses suggested by Spink fot treating the disease. Penicillin should be given intravenously in a dose of 1,000,000 units.per hour until definite improvement occurs. This should be followed by intramuscular penicillin every six hours in doses of 4,000,000 to 5,000,000 units and continued for two to three weeks. Sulphadiazine is 'given orally as long as penicillin is administered. Intrathecal administration of penicillin is not recommended.

The greatest hazard in the treatment of pneumonia in the present era is not the elimination of the pneumococcus but the development of a secondary and often fatal infection with staphylococci and other organisms.

Active Immunization

During World War II MacLeod, Hodges, and Heidelberger injected one half of the soldiers in an Army Air Force technical school with a single dose containing 0.0 3 to 0.06 mg of polysaccharides from types I, II. V, and VII pneumococci. These types, together with types IV and XII. were the predominant types present in that camp during. the previous winter. For control purposes, types IV and XII were not included in the mixture. There was a reduction in pneumonia from all types after vaccination but most sharply in those types included in the polysaccharide vaccine. Evidence of immunity appeared in two weeks, reached a maximum in six weeks, and lasted for at least six months.

The mortality from pneumococcal pneumonia increases in individuals over age 50. Shortly after the successful trials of pneumococcal polysaccharide vaccine in soldiers, Kaufman vaccinated 500 individuals 50 years old or older with polysaccharide from types I, II, and III. Another 500 individuals of the same age were not vaccinated. During the next year there were only 3 cases of pneumonia and 1 of bacteremia among the vaccinated, but 30 cases of pneumonia with 12 instances of bacteremia among the controls. The great success of penicillin therapy caused a loss of interest in prophylactic vaccination. However, with the changing frequency of the specific types and the development of penicillin sensitivity in the population there may be a place for specific vaccination in certain high-risk groups.

ENTEROBACTERIACEAE

GENERAL CHARACTERS

The family Enterobacteriaceae consists of numerous interrelated bacteria, which are Gram-negative rods, motile with peritrichate flagella, or nonmotile. They do not form spores. All of them rapidly ferment glucose with or without formation of gas and reduce nitrates into nitrites. Some of them are pathogens, most of them are commensals or opportunists and a few of them are saprophytic and found in solid and water.

These organisms have intergeneric relationships amongst typical strains of their genera. The tribe salmonellae is divided into 2 genera; salmonella and shigella. The original ancestors of the family Enterobacteriaceae must have a full complement of enzymes; from these, descendants arose with different biochemical reactions and evolution of different antigenic types. These changes are due to dissociations and transformations. It is frequently seen that, a recently isolated motile strain often loses its motility or lose some of its biochemical characters. These strains should be classified with the species to which majority of its biochemical reactions correspond. The phenomenon of *transduction* induced by lysogeruc bacteriophage has been observed in salmonella.

S. typhosa and some other members of the salmonella group possess Vi surface antigen resposible for greater pathogenicity and the same antigen is shard by *S. paratyphi C* and by the relatively avirulent Ballerup strains of Bethesda-Ballerup groups and also by certain avinilent strains of *E. coli*.

Selecting Specimens for Planting

For most enteric bacteria an ordinary stool is satisfactory for planting on special media, but this is not true of the *Shigella*. These organisms occur concentrated in bits of epithelium or in blood-stained mucus and pus on the surface of the stool. Furthermore, they die rather quickly if not cultured on appropriate media. Specimens may be obtained directly from the intestine through a proctoscope, by rectal swabs, or from a freshly passed and still warm stool. Selective material of this type can be added to preservative solutions.

TABLE 4.1. THE PRINCIPAL DIVISIONS AND GROUPS OF ENTEROBACTERIACEAE

Tribe I.	*Eschericheae*
Genus 1.	*Escherichia*
Genus 2.	*Shigella*
Tribe II.	*Salmonelleae*
Genus 1.	*Salmonella*
Genus 2.	*Arizona*
Genus 3.	*Citrobacter*
Tribe III.	*Klebsielleae*
Genus 1.	*Klebsiella*
Genus 2.	*Enterobacter*
Genus 3.	*Serratia*
Tribe IV.	*Proteeae*
Genus 1.	*Proteus*
Genus 2.	*Providencia*
Tribe V.	*Edwardsielleae*
Genus 1.	*Edwardsiella*
Tribe VI.	*Edwinieae*
Genus 1.	*Edwinia*

Preserving Specimens

Three methods are available for preserving specimens for shipping or holding, but none of these is as effective as direct plating. Coleman recommends the use of buffered glycerolsaline solutions, which should contain sufficient phenol red to give the solutions a distinctly red colour. An acid reaction often kills the dysentery bacilli. *Banxgang* and *Eliot* devised a buffered saline solution which contains sodium citrate and sodium desoxycholate. Approximately 1 g of feces should be added to 8 to 10 ml of either of these solutions and thoroughly emulsified. As a last resort, small particles of feces may be dried on blotting paper or filter paper and stored at room temperature in the dark.

Enrichment media

Enrichment media are designed to suppress the normal flora of the stool and favor the multiplication of pathogens and are most useful when the latter are present in very small numbers, as often occurs late in the disease and among carriers. Two types of enrichment media are in common use. The tetrathionate broth of Moeller, as modified by *Kauffmann* by the addition of brilliant green and bile, is probably best for the isolation of the *Salmonella*, particularly when subsequent plating is on brilliant green-phenol red agar. The addition of 8 to 16 mg of sodium sulphadiazine per 100 ml of this medium inhibits overgrowth by *Pseudomonas* and the multiplication of the *Proteus* organisms. The latter may be suppressed in commercial tetrathionate broth by the addition of 0.125 mg of sodium sulphathiazole. Typhoid bacilli and *Shigella* are usually inhibited by tetrathionate broth particularly if used with brilliant green. The second type of enrichment medium is the selenite broth of Leifson, which is recommended for the isolation of typhoid bacilli and *Shigella.* The addition of cystine to selenite broth improves its efficiency when growing *Salmonella* from powdered eggs.

Approximately 1 g of fresh feces, or 2 to 3 ml of faces in preservative media are added to 8 to 10 ml of the enrichment media and incubated for 16 to 18 hours before streaking plates. When possible, both types of enrichment media should be employed.

Differential, Inhibiting, and Selective Media

In many laboratories bismuth sulphite agar and S. S. agar are used for typhoid patients and suspected carriers; S.S. agar and eosin-methylene blue for *Shigella:* desoxycholate agar and brilliant green agar for *Salmonella;* and eosin-methylene blue and blood agar for the pathogenic serotypes of E. *coli.* The strongly inhibitory media should be used when plating feces from the enrichment media.

Isolation of colonies

The streaked plates are examined after 18 to 24 hours'incubation at 37°C for the presence of potential pathogens. Little difficulty is encountered if the original material contains a reasonable number of pathogens, but not infrequently there are only one to five potential pathogens in the entire plate and these colonies are not always typical.

TABLE 4.2. BIOCHEMICAL SERIES 1

Test or Substrate	*Escherichia*	*Klebsiella*	*Enterobacter*	*Citrobacter*
Indola	+	–,+	–	–
Methyl red	+	–	–	+
Voges-Proskauer	–	+	+	–
Ctrate	–	+	+	+
Ornithine	+, –	–	+	–, +
Motility	+	–	+	+

Symbols : + = Positive reaction: – = negative reaction: +, – = may be either+ or –

TABLE 4.3. BIOCHEMICAL SERIES 2

Test or Substrate	*Salmonella*	*Serratia*	*Hafnia*	*Klebsiella*	*Enterobacter*
Arabinose	+	–	+	+	+
Raffinose	–	–	–	+	+
Rhamnose	+	–	+	+	+
Sorbitol	+	+	–	+	+
Indole	–	–	–	–, +	–
Voges-Proskauer	–	+	+, –	+	+
Ornithine	+	+	+	–	+
Motility	+	+	+	–	+

Symbols : + = positive reaction; – = negative reaction; +, – = may be either + or –

TABLE 4.4. BIOCHEMICAL SERIES 3*

Test or Substrate	*Shigella*	*Escherichia coli*
Acetate	–	+ (rare –)
Mucate	–	+ (rare –)
Xylose	–	+ (rare –)
Salicin	–	+, –
Motillity	–	+, –
Citrate	–	– (very rare +)

Symbols : – = negative reaction; +, – = may be either + or – ; usually two or more of the first four reactions are positive with E.coli.

The colourless colonies are potential pathogens, but a number of nonpathogenic species also fail to ferment lactose and also produce colourless colonies. The most commonly encountered are *Proteus*. *C. freundii*, *Pseudomonas*, and the *Alcaligenes*, and the slow lactose fermenters formerly called paracolon bacilli.

For thus reason several colonies should be picked and carried through the diagnostic scheme and followed up by additional tests shown in Tables.

The colony should be picked with a slightly curved needle, after which the needle should be plunged into the center of the solid agar in the bottom of the tube and rubbed lightly over the slanting agar as it is withdrawn.

Another result of the excessive use of penicillin and broadspectrum antibiotics has been the increase in the gram-negative bacillary infection of the urinary tract. The distribution found among 597 positive urinary cultures from the Massachusetts General Hospital of Boston are shown in Table.

A corresponding change has occurred in patients with chronic bronchial and broncho-pulmonary bacterial infections after prolonged antibiotic therapy. One or more species of cocci may be accompanied by one to three different species of gram-negative bacilli and all may show partial or even complete resistance to well-known antibiotics.

TABLE 4.5 BIOCHEMICAL SERIES 4

	H_2S+		H_2S-	
Test or Substrate	*Proteus vulgaris*	*Proteus mirabilis*	*Proteus morganii*	*Proteu rettgeri*
Indole	+	–		
Ornithine	–	+	+	–
Citrate			–	+
Mannitol			–	+

Symbols: + = positive reaction; – = negative reaction.

Blood agar and the usual enteric type media should be streaked for the isolation of the individual species. An additional plating medium has been recommended by Mandel and his associates. Most of the gram-positive organisms are inhibited. All acid-producing colonies are yellow and are surrounded by a yellow zone. *Mimeae* and *Herellae* colonies are more mucoid than they are on nutrient agar or blood agar. These colonies are a pale lavender which is the colour of the medium. *Pseudomonas* colonies are gray green in colour. *Proteus* colonies are not inhibited and are colourless or will have a brown colony surrounded by a light brown zone if 5 g of phenylalanine and 0.5 g of ferric ammonium citrate are added to the medium.

TABLE 4.6. FREQUENCY OF ISOLATION OF ENTEROBACTERIACEAC

Organism	*Lac+*	*Lac–*	*Total*
Shigella			0
Escherichia coli	282*	25	307
Salmonella			0
Arizona group			0
Citrobacter	11	3	14
Klebsiella	157	0	157
Enterobacter	17	7	24
Hafnia			0
Serratia	0	6	6
Proteus vulgaris	0	1	1
P. mirabilis	0	119	119
P. morganii	0	21	21
P.rettgeri	0	40	40
Providencia	0	14	14

Figures refer to number of specimens from which respective organisms were isolated in significant quantities (>30 colonies).

Individual colonies of gram-negative bacilli from the blood agar plates, enteric plates, or Mandel plates can be transferred to Sellers tubes. The results are shown in Table.

The frequency of the *tribeMimeae* has been reviewed by Gilardi and the use of serologic and immunofluoreseent methods for the identification of the gram-negative bacilli by *Maiztegui*, *Biegeleisen*, *Cherry*, and *Kass*.

Biochemical Properties used for Classification

Early taxonomic schemes relied heavily obn the organisms ability to ferment lactose, and numerous differential and selective media have been devised to allow one to recognize a lactose-fermenting colony on a solid medium. The effectiveness of such differential media is based on the fact that organisms fermenting the lactose form acid, whereas nonlactose fermenters use the peptones present and do not form acids in these media. The incorporation of an acid-base indicator into the agar medium thus causes a colour change around a lactose-fermenting colony. This has been a valuable technique for selecting the major nonlactose-fermenting pathogens that cause salmonellosis or shigellosis. we shall see. however. that under special conditions, many lactose fer menters also cause a variety of infectious diseases.

TABLE 4.7. CLASSIFICATION OF THE ENTEROBACTERIACEAE

Ewing and Martin		*9th EdBergey's Manual*
Tribe	***Genera***	***Genera***
Escherichieae	Escherichia	Escherichia
	Shigella	Shigella
Edwardsielleae	Edwardsiella	Edwardsiella
Salmonelleae	Salmonella	Salmonella
	Arizona	Citrobacter
	Citrobacter	Klebsiella
Klebsielleae	Klebsiella	Enterobacter
	Enterobacter	Hafnia
	Serratis	Serratia
Proteeae	Proteus	Proteus
		Providencia
		Morganella
Erwineae	Providencia	Yersinia
	Erwina	Erwinia
	Pectobacterium	

In addition, many enterics ferment lactose only slowly, requiring several days before sufficient acid is formed to change the indicator. Such organisms were at one time all placed into a large category called the *paracolon bacteria*. However, it is now known that these bacteria are a heterogenovs group, they all synthesize beta-galactosidase, the enzyme that splits lactose into glucose and galactose but lack the specific permease necessary for the transport of lactose into the cell. One can easily determine whether an organism is a slow lactose or nonlactose fermenter by mixing a loopful of bacteria with ortho-nitrophenyl-beta-galactoside (ONPG) dissolved in a detergent. The linkage of the galactose in ONPG is the same as its linkage in lactose; in as much as the ONPG can enter the cell in the absence of a permease, an organism possessing beta-galactosidase will hydrolyse ONPG to yield galactose and the very bright yellow compound, ortho-nitro-phenol. Thus, a slow lactose fermenter is an ONPG-positive organism that does not possess a specific lactose permease but does possess beta-galactosidase.

In addition, a number of selective media have been devised that contain bile salts, dyes such as brilliant green and methylene blue, and chemicals such as selenite and bismuth. The incorporation of such compounds into the growth of medium has allowed for the selective growth of the enterics while inhibiting the growth of gram-positive organisms.

Some other biochemical properties used to classify members of the Enterobacteriaceae include the ability to (1) form H_2S; (2) decarboxylate the amino acids lysine, ornithine, or phenylalanine; (3) hydrolyse urea into CO_2 and NH_3; (4) form indole from tryptophan; (5) grow with citrate as a sole source of carbon; (6) liquify gelatin; and (7) ferment a large variety of sugars.

Laboratory Identification of the Enterics

As you can imagine, the complete identification of one of the enterics requires the use of dozens of different types of media. The modem clinical laboratory, which may have many isolates at one time, has devised a number of ingenious procedures to accomplish an identification in the shortest possible time. One procedure uses a plastic strip with about two dozen microwells containing different kinds of dehydrated media. A single isolated colony is suspended in 5 ml of saline, and this is used both to rehydrate and to inoculate the microwells.After 18 to 24 hours, positive reactions are read and an identification is made by referring to a standard chart.

An automated system is also available, which uses a plastic card that contains 30 microwells of various kinds of dehydrated media. The wells are simultaneously rehydrated and inoculated with a suspension of the unknown organism. The card is then placed in a special incubator, where, after about 8 hours, it is automatically read and results are transmitted from the reader incubator to a programmed computer, which prints the identification of the unknown organism.

Serologic Properties Used for Classification

No other group of organisms has been so extensively classified on the basis of cell-surface antigens as the Enterobacteriaceae. These antigens can be divided into three types, designated 0, K, and H antigens.

O Antigens

As described in Chapter all gram-negative bacteria possess a lipopolysaccharide (LPS) as a component of their outer membrane. This toxic LPS, or as it is also called, endotoxin, is composed of three regions : lipid A, core, and a repeating sequence of carbohydrates called the O antigen. Based on different sugars, alpha-or beta-glycosidic linkages, and the presence or absence of substituted acetyl groups, *Escherichia coli* can be shown to possess more than 164 different O antigens, and 64 have been described in the genus *Salmonella*.

Sometimes, after continuous laboratory growth, strains *will*, though mutation, lose the ability to synthesize or attach this oligosaccharide. O antigen to the core region of the LPS. This loss results in a change from a smooth colony to a rough colony type, and it is referred to as an S to R transformation. Interestingly, the R mutants have lost the ability to produce disease.

K Antigens

K antigens exist as capsule or envelope polysaccharides and cover the O antigens when present, inhibiting agglutination by specific O antiserum. Most K antigens can be removed by boiling the organisms in water.

H Antigens

Only those organisms that are motile will possess H antigens, because these determinants are in the proteins that make up the flagella. However, to complicate matters, members of the genus *Salmonella* will alternate back and forth to form different H antigens. The more specific antigens are called phase 1 antigens and are designated by lower case letters (a, b, c, and so on), whereas the less-specific phase 2 H antigens are given numbers. The mechanism of this phase variation provides an interesting way in which a cell can regulate the expression of its genes. In short, *Salmonella* possesses two genes, HI encoding for phase 1 flagellar antigens, and H2 encoding for phase 2 flagellar antigens. The transcription of H2 results in the coordinate expression of gene *rhl.* which codes for a repressor that prevents the expression of HI. Approximately every 10^3 to 10· generations, a 900 base-pair region, containing the promoter for the H2 gene, under-goes a sitespecific inversion, stopping the transcription of both H2 and *rhl.* In the absence of the *rhl.* gene product, the HI gene is then transcribed until the 900 base-pair region in the H2 promoter is again inverted, resulting in the expression of H2 and *rhl.*

After obtaining the serologic data, one can write an antigenic formula such as *E. coli* 0111: K58: H6, meaning this *E. coli* possesses 0 antigen 111, K antigen 58, and H antigen 6, the formula *Salmonella togo* 4, 12: 1, w : 1,6 indicates this serotype of *Salmonella* possesses 0 antigens 4 and 12, phase 1H antigens 1 and w, and phase 2 H antigens 1 and 6.

Coliforms

The meaning of the term *coliform* is somewhat arbitrary, but it usually refers to those members of the Enterobacteriaceae that are normal inhabitants of the intestinal tract. With certain exceptions, these do not cause gastrointestinal-type diseases, and, using this definition, the coliforms can be separated into two major groups: (1) *Escherichia.* and (2) *Klebsiella, Enterobacter, Serratia,* and *Hafina.*

Escherichia coli is an obligate intestinal parasite that cannot live free in nature, and its presence in water supplies is, therefore, evidence of recent *fecal* contamination.

Strain of *Escherichia coil* and related coliform bacteria predominate among the aerobic commensal flora present in the gut of men and animals and are also widely distributed in the environment. All persons have a rich flora of *Esch. coil* in the lower ileum and in the colon. It is acquired in the first few days after birth, when the child ingests bacilli derived from its mother or attendant. *E. coil is* incriminated as a pathogen outside the gut and particularly in the urinary tract and in wounds where the infection may be endogenous from the patient's own intestine or acquired from an exogenous source. Some antigenically identifiable strains with special enterotoxic characteristics also cause gasto-enteritis, particularly in infants.

Some species of coliform bacteria such as *Klebsiella aerogenes* and *Citrobacter freundii* commonly grow in the soil, vegetation, natural waters and other environments outside the body. *E. coli*, on the other hand, appears to grow only as a parasite of man and animals, mainly in the intestine. Being excreted in very large numbers in faeces, it comes to contaminate the environment, including the soil, very widely and the bacilli may survive without growth for several days to a few weeks outside the body. When *E. coli* is found in a water supply, it is considered to indicate that the supply has recently been subjected to contamination with human or animal faeces.

MORPHOLOGY AND STAINNING

E.coli is a short, plump rod, 0.4 to 0.7g in width and 1 to 4tt in length. Coccoid forms and short chains of organisms are found often in exudatesand young cultures. Motility varies greatly in different cultures, some strains showing active motility, others moving sluggishly, and some showing no motility whatever. Spores are not formed but capsules occur in a small percentage of the strains. The organisms are grain negative and stain uniformly with the usual aniline dyes. No characteristic internal structures occur.

Cultural Characteristics

The colon bacilli are aerobic but facultatively anaerobic. They grow readily in 24 hours on all the usual laboratory media at temperatures ranging from 20° to 40°C. Their synthesizing powers are so well developed that the bacilli *will* grow in a medium consisting of inorganic salts, an ammonium salt. and glucose.

On agar plates surface colonies appear within 12 to 24 hours, reaching a size of 2 to 3 mm in 48 hours. There is considerable variation in the appearance of individual colonies.The typical colony is low, convex, smooth, and colourless but rather opaque, with an entire edge.

Glucose, lactose, maltose, and other sugars are fermented with the production of acid and gas. About 50 percent of the strains ferment sucrose and have been named *E. toll communior*, while the other 50 percent, which fail to ferment this sugar, are called *E. coil communis*. The failure to ferment sucrose has no biologic significance.

Cultures of the colon bacilli are characterized by a fetid odor not unlike that of diluted feces. The acid formed by carbohydrate fermentation is chiefly lactic acid with smaller amounts of formic and acetic acids. Both carbon dioxide and hydrogen are produced in approximately equal amounts.

Biochemical Reaction

E. coli ferments a wide range of sugars, forms indole, gives positive MR test but the VP test is negative; it does not utilize citrate. The acids produced are chiefly lactic acid smaller amounts of formic and acetic acids. Both CO_2 and H_2 are produced in equal amounts. IMViC (Indole, MR, VP, and citrate utilisation) reactions = ++ - - in typical faecal *E. coli*.

Viability

Thermal death point of *E. coli* 60 °*C* for 10 minutes. It can resist sunlight for weeks and months and also drying for a longer period. In water, it retains its viability for a prolonged period. *Brilliant green* selectivity inhibits the growth of*Esch. toll*, *K aerogenes* and *shigella* but it is less effective for salmonella. Sod. *desoxycholate* in presence of sod. citrate inhibits *E. coli*, and *K aerogenes* with little effect on *salmonell* and *shigella. Potassium tellurite selenium salts, tetrathionate* have differential inhibiting actions on colon bacilli and members of the enteric group. This knowledge of inhibition is applied in differentiating and selective media to suppress the growth of *E. coli* and Gram-positive organisms favouring the selective growth or *salmonella* and *shigella.*

Variations

E. coli may show growth of M. S and R types of colonies. M. phase is less frequent than S and less pathogenic than some S forms. Most strains after isolation are motile and remains in the S phase. Small G,type colony is also known. *Esch. coli mutabile* grows profusely in lactose broth but ferment this sugar after 7 days or later. In Endo's medium, they show rapidly growing colourless colonies till they show red papillae on the mother colony. Further subcultures show red lactose fermenting colonies; whereas, subcultures from colourless. parts of colonies maintain the colourless character. The colourless colonies produce lactose-fermenting variants at a constant ratio of 1 in 10.

Toxin Production

Toxin is of the nature of endotoxin which is liberated after disintegration of the bacillus. Strains producing pathogenic lesions often produce a powerful haemolysin for human red cells. This can be elicited by adding a suspension of human red blood corpuscles to the filtrate after the growth of the organism in liquid media.

Antigenic Structure

E. coli are serologically heterogeneous and *Kauffman et. al.* established a diagnostic antigenic scheme. They distinguished 3 types of antigen, namely, (i) monophasic flagellar or H (thermolabile), (ii) somatic thermostable antigen, resembling those of salmonallae and (iii) thermolabile K-capsular or envelope (somatic) antigen. Except these antigens, there is also heat labile fmbrial antigen. K antigen is farther subdivided into L, A, B, according to their heat stability. L or Labile antigen is reduced at 60°C in one hour and destroyed at 100°C; B is destroyed at 100°C in 1 hour but A remains intact. K antigen occurs as envelope or capsule and interferes with specific agglutination by O antiserum, unless destroyed by heating at 100°C or 121°C. The capsular antigen is like Viantigen of salmonella and prevents O agglutination of living cells by homologous O antisera. *Esch. cola* is divided into 135 O groups, besides this 40 H, 77 capsular or envelope K antigens are recognised. K antigens are farther subdivided into 30 L, 21 B and 26 A antigens according to their thermostability.

The Pathogenicity of *E. coli* depends upon the presence of O and K somatic antigens. Strains containing K antigens are more toxic and more resistant to normal defensive mechamism of the host. In fact, O antigens of some 10 serotypes of *Shigella* are identical with certain serotypes of *E. coli*. 0112a and 112c, which cause epidemic diarrhoea in infants have same 0 antigen with K (B) antigen of Sh. *dysentery* serotype 2.

Bacteriophage

These are limited to their ability to infect strains of *E. coli* devoid of capsule or envelope antigens but some types specific for capsular antigen have been reported.

Colicines

Some strains of *E. coli*. Produce antibodies "colicines", the nature of which is still undetermined. They are diffusible and capable of killing certain other coliform species. A number of types of colicine have been distinguished on the basis of strains against which they are active. Production of colicines is likely to be associated with the somatic antigen and they may play a part in permitting certain coliform strains to establish themselves in the intestine.

Pathogenicity (in laboratory animals)

Guineapigs, rabbits and mice are killed by endotoxin of *E. coli*. When injected subcutaneously, abscesses are produced by strains producing necrotoxin. Intra-tracheal injections of living or dead cultures in rabbits produce pneumonitis. O111 B4 causes epidemic diarrhoea in monkeys.

Pathogenicity in man. Vehlne showed that, pathogenic strains of *E. coli*. belong to limited O groups and majority are O inagglutinable due to the presence of L antigens. As a contrast, commensals isolated from faeces belong to many O group and minority are O inagglutinable. They are characterised by inagglutinability with anti-O sera, marked toxicity, presence of haemolysin and necrotising toxins. Special serotypes have been worked out for infantile diarrhoea.

LESIONS IN MAN

Occurrence

E. coli are commensals of the intestine, usually appear within 2 to 3 days after birth and remain in the large intestine all through life. They are most frequently present in pyogenic infections of the urinary tract, namely; pyelitis, cystitis either in pure culture or often mixed with pyogenic cocci. These are. also responsible for producing cholecystitis, cholangitis, appendicular abscesses, peritonitis and wound infections. In the intestine, it usually lives a symbiotic life in man and animals and maintains an equilibrium under ordinary conditions of life. Special strains of *E. coli* often cause gastroenteritis in infants. These organisms contain 'B' surface antigens.

Factors Determining Infection

The exact factor is not definitely known but infection may take place under the following conditions, e.g... (1) The in- fecting strains possess pathogenic qualities. (2) Virulence of the ordinary commensal strains is increased. (3) Resistance of the mucosa is lowered by physical or chemical agents, or by infection of bacteria like salmonelly or food poisoning.

Mode of infection

There are three possible modes of infection other than the. intestine. (1) *Direct Extension.* It is due to the immediate, transference of the organism and this may be from the colon to pericolic tissue, gall-bladder or pelvic cellular tissue. (2) *Lymphatics.* The infection may spread along the lymphatics, to the neighbouring viscera. (3) *Haemaiogenous.* In many cases, bacteraemia is present in this type of infection.

Colitis

Many of the patients suffering from vague intestinal intoxication or chronic colitis are probably cases of subclinical infection caused by *E. coli*, but at present the criteria for judging such an infection are lacking. Agglutination reaction, which is rarely positive in this infection is of little value for the diagnosis of such a condition.

Appendicitis and other lesions

Appendicitis, diverticulitis, pericolic suppuration, local peritonities as a complication of intestinal infection are often caused by *E. coli.* In these cases, there may be secondary organisms like Clostridia, *Pr. vulgaris*, *Ps. aeruginosa* and *Str faecalis*.

Infection of Portal Vein

Infection through the portal vein usually occurs from suppurative appendicitis or septic haemorrhoides and these two important conditions are responsible for infective pylephlebitis and portal pyaemia. The infected thrombus from the tributaries of protal vein may often produce multiple abscesses of the liver.

Gall-bladder

E. coli is the causative agent in 28 per cent of cases of cholecystitis both acute and chronic. The infection occur commonly through the haematogenous route. In this, the organism is excreted through bile but the gall-bladder might be infected through the lymphatic route. The organism may also enter through and ascend along the common bile duct from the duodenum. The condition may harmonise with gall-bladder infection during typhoid fever. Urinary infection is usually associated with cholecystitis, which often reacts favourably upon the concomitant treatment for urinary infection. Subclinical infection with *E. coli* is one of the important factors, associated with the evolution of cholelithiasis.

Incomplete obstruction of the bile duct caused by biliary calculus, helps the organisms to produce a condition of suppurative cholangitis.

Blood circulation

E. coli may enter into the circulating blood, producing a condition of temporary bacteraemia and brief intermittent excretion of bacilli is not unusual in the urine through the kidney filters to produce a condition of sebacilluria. When the infection is overwhe-lming, a condition of septicaemia producing diarrhoea, frequency of micturition. pain and strangury are often present or frank haematuria may result in certain cases. In fact, a large number of obscure haematuria cases can be accounted for *E. coli* infection. The onset is often associated with chill and rigor followed by sweating. There is remittent type of temperature like that of enteric fever, but with slight leucocytosis. In children, the onset is rather dramatic, associated with rigor, lassitude and often stupor. The organism can be isolated by blood culture.

Urinary Tract Infection

Infection of the urinary tract caused by *Esch. coli* occurs through (a) direct extension, (b) hacmatogenous route, (c) lymphatics in ascending infection.

(a) Direct extension

It is possible through urethra extending to urinary bladder in female children specially in napkin age and this explains the greater incidence in them. Cystitis that follows the use of catheter is an example of direct infection. There is also a possibility of direct infection from the colon, which may reach the kidney either directly or through the lymphatic vessels. Such a conception would also explain pyelitis in women, who are liable to colon sepsis and affection to the kidney, which is in close relation to the hepatic flexure.

(b) Haematogenous route

It is important to note that, mere presence of the organism in urine does not mean infection. The excretion of bacilli through kidney filter may occur without any pathological lesion. But excretion of bacilli with pus cells indicates some infected focus in the urinary tract. When the infection is haematogenous, the determining factor is some local lesion like stone, caudal calyx. congenital malformation, pyonephrosis or obstruction of an.. kind. In pregnancy, pressure upon the right ureter by the enlarging uterus may result in urinary sepsis and predispose to pyelitis.

(c) Lymphatics

Ascending infection occurs by the lymphatic spread from the urinary bladder and produce as condition of pyelitis and pyelonephritis. The mucosa and the submucous tissue of the bladder are richly supplied with an extensive net work of lymphatics, which pass up the wall of the ureter, congregate in the pelvis and the capsule of the kidney, and pass to the perinephric lymphatics, which drain into the lumbar group of lymph nodes. These lymph nodes drain in their turn into the thoracic duct and ultimately into the right side of the heart. This is what happens in catheter fever. Lymphatic spread may also occur through intertubular lymphatics from the pelvis of the ureter to the cortex of the kidney.

Pyelitis

It affects females more than males, specially as a complication of pregnancy. According to the mode of onset it may be acute or chronic. The infection is usually caused by *Esch. coli* and often of haematogenous origin. In this, the renal pelvis is chiefly affected without any affection of parenchyma in the initial stage. In haematogenous infection, the determining factor is some local lesion, stone, obstruction or malformation, which renders the pelvis unduly susceptible. In pregnancy, the pressure upon the right ureter may result in urinary stasis followed by pyelitis. The infection may also extend from the bladder, either through the dilated lumen in pregnancy or through the periureteral lymphatics.

Pyelonephritis

Here the infection affects the pelvis and the renal parenchyma as well. The disease may be unilateral or bilateral depending on the site of obstruction. At first the inflammation is limited to mucous membrane of the pelvis and calyces, which are intensely congested and oedematous and later numerous small abscesses form at the cortical substance of the kidney. In chronic pyelonephritis, there is scarring of the kidney with adhesions of the capsule. In the region of scarring, there is interstitial fibrosis with loss of kidney parenchyma (tubules and glomeruli). The kidney parenchyma shows cellular infiltration. The tubules are filled with hyaline casts. In this infection, *E. coli* is often present along with other organisms like staphylococci, streptococci and proteus group of organisms. The infection may be haematogenous; but more frequently it is derived from the lower urinary tract by ascending infection, when it reaches the kidney through the periureteral lymphatics.

Perinephric Abscess

The infection may spread to perinephric tissues and cause perinephric abscesses.

Urinary Bladder

It is often the site of inflammation caused by *E. coli* as a primary condition or secondary to infection of pelvis of the kidney. Obstruction to the urinary passage caused by enlarged prostate, structure of the urethra, calculus, tumour, or tuberculosis often predispose to ascending pyelonephritis.

In females, infection with *E. coli* is very frequent, the reason being

(a) shortness of the urethra, (b) pressure effect during pregnancy, (c) loaded sigmoid colon or constipation, which might press upon the ureter. Obstruction causes difficulty in free flow of urine with loss of resistance of the urethral mucous membrane. The uterus and the Fallopian tubes are sometimes the sites of infection in puerperal sepsis, but in those cases, the infection is often a mixed one along with streptococci.

Courses of Genito-urinary Infection

This varies but usually symptoms last for about 3 weeks or for several weeks. Relapses are common in spite of adequate treatment with chemotherapy. Recurrent cases are not uncommon. In some cases, the condition becomes chronic due to various causes of obstruction. Tuberculosis of the kidney may keep up the condition.

Complications

Prostatitis, epididymitis and less often ureteritis, pyelonephritis, hydronephrosis or pyonephrosis may occur. Renal complications in a young individual may lead to renal failure in later life.

Wound Infection

Esch. coli often produces deep-seated abscesses in the region of the buttock and thigh. This often shows secondary infections with other organisms.

Bone Infection

It may infect bone, producing a condition of osteomyelitis or arthritis.

Septic Endocarditis

It is rarely produced by *E. coli*.

Laboratory Diagnosis

This is done by finding of the organism in urine or discharge, which are examined under the microscope by preparing a smear or by culture of the centrifuged deposit of urine. Serological methods are of little help in the diagnosis of infection caused by *E. coli.*

Examination of Urine

Chemical

The urine is highly acid in reaction and often contains albumin. *Microscopically*, pus-cells and Gram-negative bacteria are present in large numbers and RBCs may be present in the centrifuged deposit.

Collection of urine for culture. A catheter specimen of urine should always be collected aseptically in a sterile flask and carefully plugged. *In males* a mid-stream urine may serve the purpose. In such a case, the sample is collected after carefully cleaning the glans penis and the external urethral meatus with an antiseptic swab. The patient is asked to micturate. The first portion of the urine is discarded; whereas, the mid-stream sample of urine is collected for culture in a sterile wide mouth flask. In the case of a *female patient*, collection of a catheter. specimen is essential.

Culture

The urine is usually cultivated in MacConkey's and blood agar plates directly from the centrifuged deposit of a sample of urine by streak method and also after enrichment for 24 hours. Any growth of the organism, namely; *Esch. coli* (lactose fermenting, pink colonies), enterococcus, proteus and other organisms should be investigated for identification. *E. coli* should be investigated for pathogenicity and tested by haemolytic properties on blood agar; but it should be finally tested by adding the broth culture to 5 per cent suspension of human RBC in normal saline for the production of haemolysin.

Treatment

The replacement of the depleted water and electrolytes usually effects a cure in the summer diarrhea syndrome. Chloramphenicol, the tetracyclines, and neomycin have been used with success in the epidemic diarrhea of infants. The sporadic infections of the internal organs are treated with the same series of antibiotics but are *difficult* to cure since resistant strains develop with great rapidity.

Infections of the urinary tract resulting in cystitis, pyelitis. and pyelonephritis are so common that the question of a defect in the immune mechanism has been suggested.

Kass and others have emphasized the importance of detecting significant bacteriuria before the patient becomes symptomatic. It is generally accepted that bacterial concentrations greater than 100.000 per ml in clean, voided urine suggest a urinary tract infection.

Prevention

The epidemic diarrhea of infants can be prevented by rigid isolation technique in the nursery.

Bacteriuria is a frequent complication subsequent to the use of indwelling catheters. The use of a three-way catheter system to allow for rinsing the bladder reduces the infection rate. If nitrofurazone or a mixture of neomycin-polymyxin are used for the irrigation the infection rate is materially reduced. Meyers and his associates found neomycin-polymyxin somewhat superior to nitrofurazone.

The Microbacterium

MYCOBACTERIUM LEPRAE (HANSEN)

Leprosy is an ancient disease. It was known in India as an old disease when mentioned in the Vedas of 1400 B. C. Not all the skin lesions called "leprosy" in the old Testament of the Bible were leprosy, but almost certainly some of them were.

The lepra cell, which is a modified monocyte, was recognized by Danielssen in 1840, and his son-in-law, Hansen, discovered the bacilli in the lepra cell in1874; Neisser confirmed the observation of Hansen.

Myco. leprae of man and *Myco. lepraemurium* of rats are the causes of human and rat leprosy. These two antigenically independent species have both achieved a status of complete parasitism and cannot be grown on artificial media.

In some parts of the tropics leprosy occurs in an active or progressive form in 1 percent of the population. Trautman estimates that there are 20 million patients with leprosy in the world at the present time. The U.S. *Public Health Service* knows that there were approximately 2,000 cases of leprosy in the Unites States in 1967. This disease is endemic in some parts of Louisiana, Texas, Florida, and California and all parts of Hawaii and Puerto Rico.

A total of 166 cases of leprosy has been followed at the leprosy clinic in San Francisco for a period of seven years among 198 family contacts of patients with lepromatous leprosy 16 developed clinical leprosy. This represents an attack rate of 80.8 per 1,000 contacts examined. Badger studied the spread of leprosy in white and Negro families in Louisiana.

MORPHOLOGY AND STAINING

When stained by the Ziehl-Neelsen method, the leprosy bacilli are found predominantly in modified mononuclear or epithelioid structures called lepra cells. Large numbers of bacilli are packed in the cells in an arrangement which suggests packets of cigars. The individual rods van in length from I to 7*t* and in width from 0.2 to 1.4g. The rods usually are straight or slightly curved and when stained may appear solid red or show granules and bids which are slightly larger than the average diameter of the cell. *Myco leprae* is acid-fast, grain- positive,.and nonsporogenous.

Walters and Rees noted a drop in the solid staining rods from 54 percent, to 3 percent in lepromatous patients who had received chemothetapy for six months. Their observation on patients was confirmed by Shepard and McRae in Shepard's experimental model where *Myco. leprae* from patients were introduced into the foot pad of mice.

Prabhakaran and Kirchheimer found that *Myco. leprae* separated from lepromatous skin nodules oxidizes 3, 4-dihydro xyphenylalanine (dopa) to colourless products.

A study of thin sections of *Myco. leprae* in lepromatous nodules shows that this organism's structure resembles that of *Myco. tuberculosis* with a three-layered cell wall and a complex intracytoplasmic membrane system which connects with the plasma membrane. Surrounding the individual bacilli was another structure of low density which could have been a product of the cell or a product of the host.

Cultivation

All well-controlled attempts to cultivate *Myco. leprae* have met with failure, including the attempt to grow the organism in cultures of various types of human cells.

Antigenic Structure

Patients with leprosy may give Positive skin tests with lepromin prepared from leprous nodules but react equally well to PPD or to tuberculin made from the acid-fast saprophyte, *Myco. phlei*. In complement-fixation tests using as the antigen cultured strains of *leprosy bacilli, Myco. tuberculosis* and *Myco. phlei*, the same percentage of positive reactions was obtained with all antigens. One interesting relationship was observed. the more active cases gave the highest percentage of positive complement fixation, while the less active cases had the highest percentage of positive skin tests.

Rees and his associates have separated leprosy bacilli from the tissues of lepromatous nodules by differential contrifugations and then immunized rabbits with the bacilli. Subsequently the antiserum was used in the agar-gel diffusion method and most of the antibody was directed toward the specific antigens of the bacilli, with only a little cross-reaction with the human tissue. The latter could be removed by absorption. In two patients lepromatous antigens were demonstrated in the serum. The serum of the other patients with lepromatous leprosy gave a very faint line with bacillary antigens but very heavy lines when antigens from human tubercle bacilli were used. This confirmed the presence of cross-reaction antibodies which gave the complement-fixing reaction to human and *Hlei* antigens.

Levine found that patients with lepromatous leprosy frequently had hemagglutinin titers to soluble tuberculin antigen which were much higher than found in patients with active tuberculosis, although their skin tests were negative to both lepromin and to PPD made from the human tubercle bacillus.

Active cases of leprosy have a high percentage of positive Wassermann and Kahn reactions, but Neurath and others who studied these reactions showed that they belonged to the biologically false positive group.

BACTERIAL METABOLITES

Dharmendra has analysed leprae bacilli obtained from nodules of patients with lepromatous leprosy by the chemical methods deveolped by Anderson for the study of human tubercle bacilli from cultures, and found proteins, polysaccharides, phosphatide, and wax. The protein was antigenic and gave a 24- to 48- hour tuberculin-like reaction in patients with tuberculoid leprosy.

Classification

According to the International Congress of Leprosy Madrid, 1953, case of Leprosy are classified as follows

Lepromatous Type (L)

This is the open or the malignant type, specially stable, strongly positive, bacteriologically presenting infiltrating skin lesion and the subject is negative to lepromin. The peripheral nerve trunks become manifestly involved with the progress of the disease, habitually in a symmetrical fashion on advanced stages. There may be erythematous macule, diffuse infiltration or nodular lesions. *Histopathologically*, the lesions are characterised by the presence of histiocytes, in which the protoplasm has undergone fatty changes with the formation of vacuoles (foamy cells of Virchow or lepra cells) and contain bunches of acidfast bacilli. The dermal nerves stand out prominently with out marked cellular infiltration and Ziehl-Neelsen stain shows innumerable acidfast bacilli.

Tuberculoid Type (T)

This is usually benign. relatively stable. often bacteriologically negative: lesions are flat or elevated at the margin or more extensive; positive to lepromin. Nerve trunk involvement as a sequela may develop in certain proportiii of cases producing serious and disabling deformity, which is often asymmetric and unilateral. According to the thickness of the lesion they are macular tuberculoid (Tm) with very little thickening maculo-anaesthetic or pretuberculoid); minor tuberculoid (T) with slight thickening; or major tuberculoid (TT) with considerable thickening. The lesions are, usually anaesthetic. *Histopathologically*, there is cellular infiltration with variable amount of epithelioid cells and giant cells. The infiltration is perivascular, perineural, perifollicular, and periglandular.

Nerves are infiltrated (endoneural), bacilli are few and more frequently encountered inside nerves.

Indeterminate group (I)

This is a relatively unstable form, rarely bacteriologically positive, presenting flat. hypopigmented macular lesions and the reaction to lepromin may be negative or positive. Neuritic manifestations are more or less extensive in long standing cases. This group consists essentially of simple macular cases and may evolve either, towards lepromatous or towards tuberculoid type or may remain unchanged. *Histopathologically*, round cell infiltration is characteristic in these cases.

Borderline (Dimorphous) Group (B)

The lesions in this group share some characters of both to tuberculoid and lepromatous types. It is an unstable form. Lesions are bacteriologically positive but nasal mucosa is often bacteriologially negative; lepromin reaction is generally negative. The skin lesions are often plaque, band, nodular with distribution like that of lepromatous type except that there is a conspicuous asymmetry. Ear lobules may give the appearance of lepromatous infliteration.

The lesions are often soft and succulent and the periphery slopes away from the centre and unlike the tuberculoid type, do not present clearcut margins. They often look like lepromonas. The lesions are smooth with a shiny appearance and aviolaceons hue on a brownish or sepia background.

Epidemiology and Pathogenesis of Leprosy

Very little is known about the epidemiology of leprosy. but it is an infectious disease whose transfer may depend in large part on the susceptibily of certain persons. Children appear to be more susceptible than adults. and on a worldwide basis, leprosy is twice as common in males as in females. In general, it seems that infection requires only relatively brief contacts for "susceptible" persons. but most persons probably cannot be infected by any means.

It is generally believed that human constitute the only source of *M. leprae* and that it may be acquired by susceptible person by way of skin-to-skin contact. In case of lepromatous leprosy, however, the nasal discharge may contain over 10^8 organisms per ml, and it is believed that such discharges provide the major means of spread for this disease.

Clinically, the disease may occur in either of two major forms lepromatous leprosy or tuberculoid leprosy. There is, however, no distinct separation between these two manifestations of leprosy and a five-group system of classification is used that includes tuberculoid (TT), borderline tuberculoid (BT), borderline (BB), border up lepromatous (BL), lipromatous (LL).

Lepromatous Leprosy

This is a progressive, malignant form of the disease, which, if untreated, routinely ends in death. The organisms are found in essentially every organ of the body, although the major pathologic changes occur in the skin, nerves, Skin lesions may be hypopigmented or nodular, and Lesions of mucous membrane may involve the nose, causing severe nasal deformities owing to the destruction of the cartilaginous septum. Nerve involvement invariably occurs, and tends to be bilateral and symmetric. In advanced cases, the eye is usually infected, and eventual blindness is common.

Lepromatous leprosy occurs in persons with defective cellular immune systems. Thus, lepromatous patients reject skin allografts very slowly, and their lymphocytes are unable to release macrophage migration inhibition factor when exposed to lepromin. The reason for the inability to mount a cell-miediated immune response is unknown, but it does very form only a slight disability in borderline tuberculoid cases to complete energy for the full lepromatous disease. Moreover, the non specific depresion of the cell-mediated response is not nearly as severe as the specific impairment of the cell-mediated response to *M. leprae.* Some preliminary evidence has suggested that this unresponsiveness may result, at least in part from the stimulation of an immunosuppressor regulatory mechanism.

TABLE 5.1. SUMMARIZES THE CHARACTERISTICS OF BOTH FORMS OF LEPROSY AND COMPARISON OF PROMINENT FEATURES DISTINGU-ISHING LEPROMATOUS LEPROSY FROM TUBERCULOID LEPROSY.

Characteristics	*Lepronwtous*	*Tuberculoid*
Clinical Features		
Sites of infection	Skin (and nerves)	Nerves(and skin)
Visceral lesions	Many subclinical	(lymph nodes?)
Mucosal lesions	Often and early	Nose only
Eye lesions	Often, late	Rarely
Pale macules	Sometimes	Frequently
Annular plaques	Sometimes	Frequently
Fever	-Jn reactions	Not seen
Eyebrow *loss*	Common	Not seen
Symmetry of lesions	Common	Often lAcking
Nerve elargement	*Slow*, symmetric	Rapid, asymmetric
Nerve damage	*Slow*	Rapid
Anesthesia	Glove and stocking	*In* mascules or plaques; circumscribed
Bacterioscopy		
Acid-fast bacilli	Always abundant	Rare except in reactions
Immunology		
Cellularaimmunity		
Humoral immunity	Very *low*	High
Lepromin reaction	High	Low
False positive serology for syphillis	Negative 40%-60%	Positive None
Course		
Untreated	Progression	Spontaneous recovery often

Tuberculoid Leprosy

Tuberculoid leprosy is frequently a self-limiting, disease that may even regress spontaneously. Skin lesions occur, and nerve involvement producing areas of anesthesia is the most conspicuous feature of this form of leprosy. Unlike the lepromatous form of leprosy, organisms are extremely rare and may note seen in skin scrapings or biopsies. The major characteristic accounting for this form of the disease is a normal cellular immune response mounted against the leprosy bacillus. Thus, nerve damage (which occurs much more rapidly than in the lepromatous form) actually results from inflammation that occurs during a cellular immune response to the bacilli in the nerves.

Laboratory Diagnosis of Leprosy

Although there are an estimated 15 million cases of leprosy in the world, including about 1000 in tbi United States, the rarity of the disease plus its ability to mimic other diseases makes diagnosis very difficult.

The occurrence of anesthesia and the presence of acid-fast rods that cannot be cultured are, actually the major criteria available for diagnosis. Lepromin, purified from infected tissues, is analogous to tuberculin, but it is of no aid in the diagnosis of leprosy for two reasons : (1) lepromatous patients have an impaired cellular immune response and hence will not react; and (2) most persons will give, a positive reaction to lepromin.

A trisaccharide containing glucose and rhamnose, found in large quantities in a species specific plycolipid, has been synthesized and conjugate to bovine scrum albumin. This conjugate holds promise for an early serodiagnosis of leprosy.

LEPOMIN TEST

This test was introduced by Mitsuda with the hope that it would be as specific in leprosy as the tuberculin test is in tuberculosis. Lepromin is made by grinding lepromatous nodules into a paste which is then diluted with physiologic saline to 20 ml for each gram of tissue. The supernate, after filtration, is sterilized by autoclaying at 120°C for 15 minutes and preserved by the addition of 0.5 percent of phenol. Good preparations contain many more leprac bacilli than tissue fragments. The test dose is 0. 1 ml of lepromin injected intracutaneously as in the tuberculin test. Two types of reactions occur : the early reactions resemble the tuberculin reactions and appear in 24 to 48 hours, and the late reactions begin between the seventh and tenth days as a small papule which gradually increases in size by the twenty-fifth to thirtieth day. In the more severe reactions the center of the nodule becomes necrotic and sloughs out. The late lepromin reactions are caused by the intact leprosy bacilli in the lepromin, and if they are removed by filtration or broken up by supersonic vibration or by chemical treatment, the tuberculin-like reaction is intensified and the late lepromin reactions reduced or eliminated.

The negative lepromin reaction in the acute lepromatous stage of the disease can be explained by assuming that the patient is in the preallergic stage analogous to the preallergic stage in tuberculosis, in which the bacilli multiply in mononuclear cells before the tuberculin reaction becomes positive.

Positive lepromin tests can be elicited in patients with tuberculosis in areas of the world where tlere is no leprosy, and positive lepromin tests can be induced in normal, healthy children by vaccination with BCG. which is an attenuated bovine tubercle bacillus.

Guinto, Mabalay, and Doull elicited a delayed lepromin- like test by injecting the whole dead bacilli of human, avian, or Battery types of Mycobacterium.

Clinical types of Disease in man

Leprologists recognize four different types of leprosy. These are lepromatous, tuberculoid, dimorphous, and indeterminate. In the dimorphous or intermediate form, some of the lesions resemble the lepromatous and some the tuberculoid forms. The term, indeterminate

TABLE 5.2. THE CORRELATION OF PATHOLOGY, IMMUNOLOGY, AND BACTERIOLOGY OF LEPROSY

Pathology	*Immunology (Lepromin Test)*	*Bacteriology (Pos. Smears Or Sections)*
Lepromatous	0	+
Diffuse		
Infiltrated		
Nodular		
Tuberculoid	+	-
Major		
Minor		
Dimorphous	±	±
Indeterminate	±	±

form of leprosy is used for a very early form which can either heal spontaneously, as it does frequently, or evolve through the dimorphous form to either lepromatous or tuberculoid forms.

The Prognosis is poor in the lepromatous type of leprosy, Where the lepromin test is negative and bacilli are found in great abundance in the lesion. The outlook is best in the tuberculoid type, where the lepromin test is positive and bacilli are few or absent.

Diagnosis

The diagnosis may be suspected from the symptoms and the type and distribution of the lesions plus a history of living in an endemic area, but the diagnosis is made by the demonstration of acid-fast bacilli in smears of skin, in nasal scarpings, impossible to detect in tissue from the typical tuberculoid leprosy. However, the admonstration of corticoid hormones, which increase the lesions. also promotes the growth of *Alvco. leprae* in the local lesions and thus makes the diagonsis easier. One such case was reported from New Jersey in 1965 and we saw one here at Duke University of this type in 1966.

Transmission

The clinical evidence for the transmission of leprosy is quite conclusive. There are many examples of Europeans developing leprosy after a single contact with South Sea Island prostitutes. It must be emphasized, however, that man actually is very resistant to the development of leprosy even when exposed over a period of years.

The incubation period is difficult to determine. It seems to vary from a minimum of a few months to a maximum of 30 years, with an average fo 2 to 7 years. Black refers to a 15 year-old girl in whom he demonstrated leprosy bacilli in smears from an apparently normal ear lobe 2 years before the patient developed cutaneous and neural leprosy of forearms and legs. In India 25 of 254 contacts had leprosy bacilli in their skin, and 4 of these subsequently developed clinical leprosy.

CONTROL MEASURES

Lepromin: BCG Vaccination

Lepromin, as ordinarily used, is a boiled unstandardized extract of leprous tissue which, when injected intracutaneously, produces an area of nodular infiltaration reaching its maximum in 3 to 5 weeks (Mitsuda reaction) in cases of tuberculoid leprosy and in a proportion of apparently healthy people. The reaction is usually negative in cases of lepromatous leprosy. Recently, efforts have been made to 'clean' and standardize lepromin by treatment in a tissue blender, washing, centrifugation, etc. in order reduce the tissue content and homogenize the bacterial suspension. As a result, an antigen containing 160 million *Tepra bacilli* per ml has been recommended as a standard lepromin of which a 1 in 4 dilution containing 40 million bacilli would on intradermal inoculation be adequate to produce a nodule of 3 mm or more after 4 weeks as the criterion of positivity. A positive Mitsuda reaction indicates resistance to leprosy and the negative reaction in lepromatous cases may be related to a deficiency of cell mediated immunity.

There is considerable overlap with positive tuberculin tests for this and other reasons. controlled trials of BCG vaccines as a prophylactic against leprosy have been carried out in three regions Uganda, Burma and New Guinea. The most promising results wre obtained in Uganda against tuberculoid leprosy in childern aged 0 to 15 years with a protection rate of 82 per cent among the vaccinated children over a period of 6 years. BCG vaccination gave some protection. particularly in the age range 10 to 29 years in an aboriginal population in New Guinea with a high prevalence of tuberculoid leprosy and very little tuberculosis whereas a controlled trial among children in Burma where lepromatous leprosy is common gave negative results. Obviously, further evidence is needed before BCG vaccination can be reconmmended for routine prophylaxis agianst leprosy.

Chemotherapy and Chemoprophylaxis

Oral adminstration of sulphones, in particular dapsone (4,4'-diamino-diphenylsulphone, or DDS) has become the most practical chemo-therapy for mass campaigns against leprosy. The recommended dosage, after tolerance to the drug has been established, has ranged from 6.0 to 10 mg per kg. body weight per week over a period of 3 to 5 years or more, depending on the nature and extent of the infection. Smaller doses are recommended by some leprologists as being less likely to provoke severe lepra reactions or other secondary effects. The long-acting or respository sulphone, acedapsone (DADDS), or the riminophenazine, clofazimine (formerly known as B 663 or lamprene), or other more bactericidal drugs are presently on trial.

Controlled trials in the long-term chemoprophylaxis of leprosy with dapsone among child contacts of infective cases have given encouraging results in India and the Philippines.

Health education is an important element in any leprosy control programme, with the main objective of creating in the minds of the community, the patient and their families. a resoned attitude towards leprosy, which neither exaggerates the danger nor minimizes it.

Prevention

There is now some reason for being optimistic about the prevention of leprosy and perhaps the eventual elimination of the disease from the world. Man is the only host and the *Myco. leprae* organisms cannot multiply in the soil or spontaneously in animals.

The elimination of the disease in endemic areas would logically begin with the early detection and rigid isolation of all acute lepromatous and nonspecific or indeterminate types of cases. The diagnosed cases should be isolated in 1) leper colonies or 2) the leprosy villages. This should be followed by 1) prophylacitc chemotherapy for individuals in close contact with the patient and 2) active immunization with BCG of remaining children in the village,

Rat leprosy

This disease, caused by *Myco. lepraemurium*, was discovered among rats in odessa by Stefanskv in 1903. Since then it has been found in many parts of the world. Rat leprosy occurs spontaneously among house rats and is characterized by subcuaneous indurations, swelling of lymph nodes, emaciation, and sometimes ulceration and loss of hair. The disease is chronic, and rats often live for six months to one year after becoming infected. The characteristic lesion is a thickened area under the skin of the abdomen or flank which resembles adipose tissue except that it is less shiny and more nodular and gray than fat. The resemblance to fat is so close, however; that it is often overlooked by those unfamiliar with the condition. Acid-fast bacillie resembling *Myco. leprae* are found in large numbers in the mononuclear cells of the subcutaneous tissues and in the lymph nodes and nodules in the liver and lungs.

Rats can be infected by direct inoculation of infected tissues, but the disease probably is transmitted naturally from rat to rat by fleas.

Although the disease is not exactly like leprosy, the resemblance is sufficiently great to suggest that rats are a potential source of human leprosy. The distribution of the disease in various parts of the world, however, does not correspond with the distribution of human leprosy, and the rat cannot be infected with tissues from cases from of human leprosy.

The natural host for both *Myco. leprae* and *Myco. lepraemurium* is the monocyte and Chang and his associates were logical in choosing to develop cultures of monocytes from mice which could be maintained for months in tissue cultures. *Myco. lepraemurium* grew in these cells and could be transferred from culture to culture. The average generation time was seven days.

Rees and his co-workers found that solid staining forms of*Myco. lepraemurium* would grow in cultured macrophages while the beaded and grandular ones would not. These investigators assumed that the solid staining forms of Myco. leprae were alive.

However, the studies of Chang and Andersen on the cultivation of *Myco. lepraemurium* demonstrated that there were two causes for beaded or absent staining. One was the death of the organism while the other was a change which immediately precedes rapid growth and division.

Garbutt and her associates and Rees and his co-workers have cultured that rat-leprosy bacilli in cultures of rat fibroblasts. They have collected the specific antigens elaborated by the bacilli in culture and studied them with the gel-diffusion method., using antisera produced by rats infected with the organisms and antisera induced in rabbits by injecting bacilli freed from experimental lesions in rats. There seemed to be one or more specific antigens characteristic of *Myco. lepraenturiunt* with very little cross-reaction with *Myco. tuberculosis* of man.

MYCOBACTERIUM

The most obvious characteristic of the Mycobacterium is the large amount of lipid present in their cell walls-approxirfiately 40% of the total cell dry weight-causing them to grow as extremely rough, hydrophobic colonies. Mycobacteria are also difficult to stain, but, once stained, they resist decolouration-even when washed with 95% ethanol containing 3% Hydrochloric acid. Organisms with the ability to retain a stain in spite of washing with acid alcohol are referred to as acid fast. Only the members of the genus *Mycobacterium* and a few species of *Nocardia* possess this property, and this characteristic-helps in detecting mycobacteria in body fluids such as sputum or gastric washings.

There are many nonpathogenic mycobacteria, as well as -many pathogens whose range of host animals is narrowly restricted. Human mycobacterial infections are primarily of two types; (1) tuberculosis, usually a respiratory infection but occasionally acquired by ingestion of the organisms, and (2) leprosy, primarily a disease of the skin. Both diseases are chronic infections and may last for many years, causing destructive lesions as a result of a cellular immune response to the organisms and their products.

History

The modern knowledge of tuberculosis started from the work of Laennec, a French clinician, who himself was a consumptive and succumbed to the disease. He gave an accurate description of tuberculous lesion and in 1819, he described follicular (miliary) and infiltrative (exudative) forms Of tuberculosis. Villemin, a French, military surgeon, experimentally demonstrated that the disease could be transmitted to animals by inoculation of tuberculous materials. Robert Koch discovered tubercle bacillus and successfully cultivated the organism from tuberculous material. He also inoculated the material to experimental animals successfully. The acidfast nature of the organism was discovered by Ehrlich in the same year and the present method of acidfast staining, was developed by Ziehl and subsequently modified by Neelsen, and hence the name Ziehl-Neelsen stain. Robert Koch maintained that, there was only one mammalian *Myco. tuberculosis*. The credit of distinguishing human and bovintypes lies in the work of Theobald Smith.

Habitat

Myco. tuberculosis (Matmnalian) is a strictly parasitic organism. They are usually found in the sputum and faeces of cases of pulmonary and intestinal tuberculosis and in other organs of the body including lymph nodes, bones, kidney, meninges, etc. It is also present in dust contaminated with infected sputum.

MORPHOLOGY AND STAINING

Tubrcle bacilli are slender, straight, or slightly curved rods with rounded ends. They vary in width from 0.2 to 0.5 μ and in length from 1 to 4μ. True branching is seen occasionally in old cultures and sometimes in smears from caseous lymph nodes. Branching forms may be produced at will under certain specific cultural conditions.

The bacilli are acid-fast, nonmotile, and non-sporogenous', and have no capsules. Electron micrographs of thin sections show that the rather thick wall is composed of three layers enclosing a plasma membrane which is also three layers in thickness.

Tubercle bacilli from either cultures or secretions usually are stained by the Ziehl-Neelsen method. The carbolfuchsin is allowed to act for 12 to 24 hours, or the process can be speeded up by steaming the preparation for 5 to 10 minutes. The excess stain is washed off with water, and the side is decolourized by washing for a few seconds with 95 per cent alcohol containing 5 per cent HCl. After counterstaining for 1 minute with methylene blue, the bacilli are seen as brilliant red rods against a deep, sky-blue background. The bacilli can be stained without heating if the detergent tergitol is added to the carbolfuchsin.

The physical structure of the all resembles that of gram-negative organisms although the main structural materials are lipids. Murohashi and his associates have found that it is the physical structure which gives the organisms its acid fastness and gram-positiveness and not the mycolic acid and other lipids.

Thacore and Willett have produced spheroplasts from tuberce bacilli by cultivation in the presence of lysozyme and a high concentration of sucrose.

Much's Granules

Some specimens of pus from tuberculous abscesses, serous exudates, lymph nodes or sputum contain no acid fast- organisms but produce tuberculosis when inoculated into susceptible animals. In 1908 Much demonstrated gram-positive granules in short chains or irregular clamps in these materials. Later studies by Kahn and Brieger have demonstrated that these non-acid-fast forms are indeed alive.

Cultural Characteristics

Tubercle bacilli will not grow on the usual type of media but do grow slowly in inspissated serum, coagulated egg, or potato medium after two to three weeks incubation at 37°C. Youmans found that the generation time of tubercle bacilli on the Proskauer-Beck basal synthetic medium was 20.5 to 24 hours but could be shortened to 13.2 to 15.7 hours by adding beef serum or proantithrombin to the basal medium. The addition of 5 per cent glycerin inhibits the growth of the vole bacillus, has little or no effect on the bovine bacillus, but accelerates appreciably the growth of the human and avian strains. Tubercle bacilli will grow over a pH range of 6.0 to 7.6. The optimal pH for the maintenance of virulence is pH 6.8. The optimal temperature for the isolation of avian strains is 40°C, human and bovine strains 37°C, and bacilli from cold blooded animals 25°C. After a number of generations in the laboratory, however, temperature requirements of the organisms are less exacting.

Tubercle bacilli are obligate aerobes and will not grow in the absence of oxygen. Even a moderate reduction in the oxygen tension results in an appreciable decrease in the metabolism of the bacilli.

Human and bovine strains grow slowly on inspissated serum or coagulated egg medium, producing, after 10 to 20 days, small, dry, scaly colonies with corrugated surfaces. The bovine strains grow more slowly and less luxuriantly than bacilli of human origin. On glycerin both, prepared by adding 5 per cent glycerin to beef or veal infusion peptone broth, growth of the human and bovine strains is confined to the surface of the medium. A thin, gray, almost transparent, veil-like film grows over the surface of the broth. This film gradually thickens into a white or slightly yellowish, wrinkled membrane which covers the entire surface of the culture fluid.

Dubos and Davis found that a derivative of a long-chain fatty acid known commercially as Tween 80 alters the surface conditions of the organism in both media so that tubercle bacilli multiply much more rapidly, giving a smooth. homogeneous type of growth throughout the culture medium. On hydrolysis free oleic acid, which is toxic for the organisms is liberated but this effect may be neutralized by adding small amounts of bovine albumin to the medium. Since homogeneous suspensions of organisms grown on other types of media are prepared with great difficulty, the advantages of Dubos' medium are obvious.

After primary isolation, tubercle bacilli grow readily on synthetic media containing glycerol, asparagme, citrate, and inorganic salts. While growing on synthetic media, the tuberce bacillus synthesized all the known B-complex vitamins. The addition of vitamins of synthetic media does not increase appreciably either the rate or quantity of growth.

A relatively rich medium is required for primary isolation. Contaminated sputum, or other materials, should be treated with a solution containing sodium hydroxide (2 per cent) and sodium citrate (0.05 M) to which is added 0.5 g of N-acetyl-L'cystein for each 100 ml of solution.

The specimen and the decontaminating solution are mixed in equal volumes in a 50 ml centrifuge tube, shaken for 5 to 30 seconds, and allowed to stand at room temperature for 15 minutesimenThen s Phosphate buffer is added to make a 50 ml volume and the specimen is centrifuged for 30 minutes after which the supernate is discarded abnd 1 ml ofbovine albumin is added to the sediment. The specimen is diluted 10 times with sterile physiologic saline and planted on Lowenstein Jensen medium and Middlebrook's 7H10 agar. Incubation under increased CO_2 increases the yield of positive cultures. This method of decontamination and culture increases the number of positive cultures of *Myco. tuberculosis* and also the positive cultures of atypical mycobacteria and *Nocardia*.

Resistance

Tubercle bacilli may remain viable in culture media for 2 to 8 months. Organisms from cultures are killed in 2 hours when exposed to direct sunlight, but bacilli contained in sputum require an exposure of 20 to 30 hours. When protected from direct sunlight, they live in putrefying sputum for weeks and in dried sputum for as long as 6 to 8 months. Droplets of dried sputum adhering to dust particles in the air may be infectius for 8 to 10 days. Tubercle bacilli are resistant to the usual chemical disinfections. A 5 percent solution of phenol requires 24 hours to distinfect sputum.

Fortunately, tubercle bacilli possess no greater resistance to moist heat than other bacteria. Pasteurization temperatures are, therefore, efficacious in eliminating them from milk and milk products.

Streptomycin was the first specific antibiotic which could kill tubercle bucilli. But resistant strains developed in a few months unless a second specific antibiotic was given simultaneously. Para-aminosalicylic acid (PAS) given simultaneously with streptomycin or isonicotinic acid hydrazide (INH) delays the appearance of resistant strains for one year or more.

At the present time six additional anti-tuberculosis drugs are available. The last one, ethambutol, was approved by the council on Drugs of the AMA in 1969. A seventh drug, rifampin, is proving effective.

Variability

Tubercle bacilli were dissociated by Petroff in the Trudeau Laboratory in 1927. The standard nomenclature employed since 1936 uses S to designate a smooth colony and R to designate a rough one. With few exceptions the virulent organisms produce R colonies, but there also are R colonies which are aviruent.

Antigenic Structure

By agglutination, agglutinin, absorption, and complement-fixation, the acid-fast bacteria may be separated into mammlian, avian, cold-blooded, and'saprophytic types. The avian bacilli have specific antigens by which they can be seperated into subtypes and also have an antigen in common with both human and bovine organisms.

Parlett and Youmans have investigated the antigens of mycobacteria by the Ouchterlony diffusion precipitation technique.

Middlebrook has extracted from tubercle bacilli one or more antigens which are capable of sensitizing either sheep or human erythrocytes in such a manner that they agglutinate with the sera of patients having tuberculosis and the sera of individuals with tuberculosis infection in the absence of clinical disease. These antigens are present in old tuberculin. If the erythrocytes are treated with tannic acid by the method of Boyden they absorb more and different types of antigens.

Takahashi's studies suggest that the sera of patients may contain anti-polysaccharide, antiprotein, and anti-phosphatide antibodies. The first are detected by the original Middlebrook test, the second by the tanned red cells of Boyden, and the third by the phosphatide kaolin-agglutination test of Takahashi.

Latex particles coated with tubercular protein have been used in an agglutination test for antibodies in the patient's serum by a number of investigators. The results were reviewed by Duboczv and White in 1969.

Ching-Tsai-Kuo demonstrated antibodies in spinal fluid of the patients with tuberculosis meningitis of 97.1 percent of patients. To achieve this he used a modified hemagglutinin test and concentrated the protein from 5 to 10 ml of spinal fluid.

Most patients with active tuberculosis do have antibodies by all these tests. Some severely ill patients are negative and some healthy individuals with positive tuberculin test have antituberculous antibodies. There is no reliable serologic test for clinically active tuberculosis.

All attethpts to transfer immunity from one animal to another of the same species have failed, and there are many reasons for believing that immunity is not mediated by the classical types of Immoral antibodies. In contrast to these negative findings, Lurie demonstrated that monocytes from immunized rabbits retained their ability to destroy tubercle bacilli when transferred to the anterior chamber of the eyes of normal rabbits.

The detailed work of Fong, Chin, and Elberg revealed that PMN's did not transfer resistance; lymphocytes transfer hypersensitivity but not resistance; while histocytes transfer immunity which was still detectable after a second transfer to a normal animal.

Hypersensitivity to tuberculoprotein lean be transferred from animal to animal and from tuberculin-sensitive individuals to previously tuberculin-negative ones by the injection of white blood cells. This phenomenon was discovered by Chase and confirmed by a number of other investigators. Cortisone can suppress completely the tuberculin skin lest without interfering with the passive transfer of hypersensitivity to a normal animal. The specific alteration required for passive transfer develops with surprising speed, since Tomcsanyi and his associates found that white cells from the peritoneum of guinea pigs, 24 hours after infection, could effect the transfer. The sensitivity transferred by white cells of ordinary stock guinea pigs persists for only a few weeks, in contrast to that in man. Lawrence also found that disrupted human cells could transfer the tuberculin sensitivity and named the unknown substance the transfer factor.

George and Vaughan observed in 1962 that peritoneal exudate cells from guinea pigs with positive tuberclin reaction were inhibited from migrating out of capillary tubes onto glass. David and have associates have improved the method and showed that the inhibiting factor was not antibodies in the serum, or complement, but sensitivity of the cell itself to tuberculin.

Factors Influencing Virulence

It has not been possible to identify a particular structure, antigen. or toxin which could explain the virulence of tubercle bacilli. Middlebrook, Dubos. and Pierce in 1947 noted that virulent strains of human and bovine bacilli grew in strands or cords while avirulent dissociates of the same strains showed no particular arrangement of the organisms.

Bacteriophage

Freshly isolated strains of human tubercle bacilli can be separated into Types A, B, C and an intermediate between A and B. Type A is found most frequently in Japan, Hong Kong and Rhodesia; Type A and B occur with equal frequency in Britain; Type A and intermediate Type A-B in Madras; and Type C predominantly in the United States. By bacteriophage typing, Stead and Bates demonstrated that a soldier who acquired an infection with Type A in the Far East transmitted bis type to two civilians after returning to this country.

Bacterial Metabolites

The acid-fast bacilli produce neither exotoxins nor endotoxins. The "cord factor" described by Bloch and Noll has some toxicity for mice when given in very large doses. This factor is found primarily in the wax C fraction and appears to inhibit various dehydrogenase systems in the animal.

The violent toxic symptoms induced in spontaneously infected humans and in experimentally infected animals by the injection of minute amounts of tuberculin are manifestations of allergy to tuberculoprotein and not endotoxin reactions.

Catalase is produced by both virulent and saprophytic strains of mycobacteria, but the ability to synthesize Catalase seems to be one of the factors necessary for virulence, since there is a reasonably good correlation between the loss of ability to synthesize catalase and the loss of virulence in strain which have become resistant to INH.

TUBERCULIN

Between 1891 and 1901 Koch prepared a series of tuberculin and subsequently more than 50 kinds of tuberculin were investigated of which only 2 have survived the test of time. These are Koch's original preparation known as old Tuberculin (OT) and Seibert's purified protein derivative (PPD).

The purified protein derivative of tuberculin contains a mixture of tuberculoproteins having molecular weights of 2.000 to 9.000. in contrast to the native antigens tuberculo protein studied by Seibert, which had a molecular weight of 32,000.

PPD is a dry powder which is "dry diluted" with lactose and made into tablets in the proper proportions so solutions can be made which will contain 0.000 2, 0.000 1, or.005 mg in the injection dose of 0. 1 ml. Some errors may occur in making the "dry" dilutions of 0.00002 and 0.0001 mg; hence it is more accurate and more economical to use a tablet of 0.005 mg diluted in buffered saline to make the 0.0001 and 0.00002 mg strengths.

False positive tuberculin reactions will not develop in individuals who are skin tested over a period of months or years with 0.0001 or 0.005 mg of PPD, provided that the individual has never been infected with either a tubercle bacillus or one of the other classified or unclassified mycobacteria. However, individuals who give small reactions or even zero reactions to the 0.0001 mg dose but who are positive to the 0.005 mg dose often get a booster effect from the 0.0001 mg dose; this reaction is not evident in 2 to 4 days but appears after 1 week, reaches its maximum at 1 month, and persists for 6 to 12 months.

However, Mohr and his associates have demonstrated that positive skin tests to 5 TU doses of tuberculin can be possitively transferred if fresh blood, from donors with positive skin tests, is given in routine transfusions.

Tuberculin Test

This is an allergic reaction in which old tuberculin was originally employed but nowadays purified protein derivative obtainable in tablet form is used. The tablet keeps well in dry form but deteriorates within a few days after being dissolved in the diluent solution.

Methods

The method that were employed in the past are cutaneous method of Pirquet, subcutaneous method of Koch, ophthalmic reaction of Calmette. Nowadays, quantitative intracutanceous test of Mantoux is used. Patch test of Vollmer, percutaneous test of Monro are also used by some. Recently, the Mantoux test has been replaced by purified protein derivative (PPD) in epidemiological·

Intraeutaneous Method of Mantoux (Quantitative)

This is done with a dilution of old Tuberculin 1 : 10,000 (0.01 mg))· Sterilise the skin on the flexor surface of the forearm and with the help of a tuberculin syringe with No. 19 needle, inject 0.1 ml of 1 : 10,000 O.T. (0.01 mg) to make a wheal of about 8 mm in diameter. A control is similarly done on the same forearm. Take the reading after 48 hours or later. In this test, the reaction may be local, focal or general.

Local reaction

Erythema and induration indicate a positive reaction. (1) A definite induration with a diameter of 10 nun and erytheina indicate positive reaction one plus. (ii) Erythema and induration 10 to 20mm-two plus. (iii) Erythema and induration more than 20 mm-three plus. (iv) Erythema and induration with necrosis-four plus (Plate VII).

The reaction is negative, when the induration is less than 6 mm. or there is no induration at all. Non-specific reaction usually fades away within 48 hours. In case the test with. 1 : 10,000 dilution is negative, a similar test is performed with 0.1 mi of 1 : 2000 or 1 : 100 dilution (1 mg).

Focal reaction is characterised by exacerbation of the lesion and *general reaction* is associated with malaise, fever and other constitutional symptoms.

Test with (PPD)

The tablet is dissolved in supplied along with the Phosphate buffer solution, supplied along with the tablets, so that when 0.1 m is injected intradermally, it contains 0.00002 mg equivalent to 1 . 110,000 of old tuberculin. Take the reading after 48 hours. If test is negative, the higher dose (0.005 in 0.1 MJ) is injectd Readings are taken as in the case of Mantoux test.

Interpretation

(I) A negative reaction indicates that patient has not been infected with tubercle bacilli and has not acquired allergy. (II) Positive reaction

indicates a past, latent or an active infection either bovine or human. For all practical purposes, a positive reaction with 1 : 10,000 indicates active lesion. *A* dilution of 1 : 100 when negative, excludes active tuberculosis.

Delayed reaction

This appears weeks and months after the Mantoux test. This only indicates that since the test was performed, infection has occurred and induced allergy.

Serological Method *(specific)*

Immune bodies can be demonstrated *by complement-fixation test* with W K K antigen due to the presence of antibodies in the serum. It becomes positive in chronic cases only and this is why, it has not gained popularity as a practical method of diagnosis. *Haemagglutination test.* In this, sheep red cells are sensitised with extract of tubercle bacillus of old tuberculin. The cells are then mixed with varying dilutions of patient's serum from which heterophile antibody is removed by adsorptions. In presence of specific antibody, the cells are agglutinated and the degree of reaction is indicated by the highest dilution of serum producing haemagglutination.

Cyto-Diagnosis

Tuberculous exudate shows a preponderance of the mono-nuclear cells. The inflammatory exudates from tl a pleura Peritoneum, synovial membrane and the C S F often shows preponderance of lymphocytes.

Histophathology

Microscopic examination of a tuberculous granuloma shows a typical picutre, i.e., a central with giant cells, epithelioid cells adn lyumphocytes around which tere are fibroblasts.

Both OT 'Jhd PPD are standardised reactivity as shown in table. *weighted mean* often show laevo deviation.

Arneth index or *Cooke's weighted mean* often show laevo divaiation. Erythrocyte sedimentation rate is increased, as in any other infection. It has a limited value in the diagnosis of Tuberculosis. It is rather a useful test in detecting the programs of a case and the sedimentation rate diminishes as the patient improves.

Special Bacteriological Examinations

Pulmonary Tuberculosis

Uniform films are prepared from the muco-purulent portion of the sputum and examined by Zichl-Neelsen and Fluorescence microscopy methods. if the acidfast organisms are not found in direct smear, concentration method should be tried. This dissolves the mucus and it becomes easy to inoculate into a guineapig or culture tube.

Gastric layage

The gastric lavage in an empty stomach may be a useful method for detecting tubercle bacillus but care should be taken to wash the stomach with fluids, which do not contain saprophytic acidfast bacilli.

Faeces

Children and others Who swallow a but faeces may contain bacilli in the faeces as in the gastric tovag saprophytic acidfast bacilli. In such cases, therefore, an animal inoculation after concentration is almost an essential Procedure to be adopted.

Laryngeal swab

For this, a swab at the end of a long wire, of the nature of West's swab may be used. The Swab is passed down the larynx to the vocal cords. The material thus obtained may be cultured. The contaminating bacteria are killed by i,mrunersing the swab in 6 per cent sulphuric acid and then in N. NaOH for 1/2 minute before the cultures are made.

Pathogenesis of Tuberculosis

Humans become infected with *M. tuberculosis* most frequently by inhaling droplet nuclei that contain tubercle bacilli. Droplet nuclei are expelled by infected individuals and. because of their very small size (1 μm—10 μm in diameter). they-remain airborne for long periods of time. Infection may also result from ingestion or, rarely, through the skin.

Tuberculosis appears to be a highly infectious disease, as manifested by the minor epidemics initiated by infected schoolteachers, students, bus drivers, or others who come into contact with large numbers of people. Humans tend, however, to vary considerably in their response to infection by tubercle bacilli, and active disease can, in general, be thought of as resulting either from a primary infection or from a subsequent reactivation of a quiescent infection.

Primary Infection

Following inhalation, tubercle bacilli initiate small lesions in the lower respiratory tract and drain from these lesions to the regional lymph nodes. This primary complex, as these lesions are called, frequently heals to form tiny "tubercles" which are too small to be seen by x-rays but may continue to harbor the viable tubercle bacilli indefinitely. In other cases, multiplication of the bacilli continues, and the lesion expands, destroying the normal tissue and leaving the necrotic tissue in a semisolid, cheesy state. This process, call caseation necrosis, may eventually heal and become infiltrated with fibrous tissue and calcium deposits; or the lesion may continue to expand, leaving cavities in the lung after the clearance of necrotictissue. The lesion might also involve a pulmonary vein, allowing the organisms to spread by way of the bloodstream.

During the early part of the infection, the organisms, encounter little, if any, host resistance, and the lesions, called exudative lesions, are characterized by the presence of polymorphonuelear leukocytes, fluid, and inflammation. At this time, most tubercle bacilli are found growing intracellularly in macrophages. Later, as the host develops a cellular immunity or allergy to the tubercle bacilli, the lesions are called productive lesions, or tubercles, and the organisms, which are few in, number, are now mostly extracellular, surrounded by necrotic tissue and large mononuclear macrophages known as epithelioid cells. Some of the epithelioid cells fuse to form large, multinucleate giant cells. The necrotic tissue and epithelioid cells are, in turn, surrounded by lymphocytes and fibrous tissue. Which wall off the tubercle from the normal tissues of the lung.

Reactivation Infection

Whether or not the primary infection heals early or late, the walled-off tubercle is believed to contain viable organisms. which probably persist for the remaining life of the host. It is estimated that two thirds of all new active cases of tubetculosis represent a reactivalion of a healed primary infection. This postulation is difficult to prove, but it is strongly supported by the observation that over 80% of all new cases reported occur in persons over 29 years of age. Also, it has been shown that the majority of new cases of active tuberculosis among Navy recruits occur in persons who exhibited positive skin reactions to tuberculin at the time of their enlistment.

Nonpulmorlary Infectious

Tubercle bacilli may spread hematogenously from lesions in the lung, resulting in infection of every organ of the body. Invasion of the central nervous system, resulting in tuberculosis meningitis, is probably the most lethal form of tuberculosis. The organisms may also produce tubercles in the kidney, causing a genital tuberculosis. Bone and joint involvement, particularly in the spine and the weight-bearing joints, also may occur. Other possible complications include peritoneal tuber- culosis, tuberculous pericarditis, and a diffuse pattern of tubercles throughout the body known as miliary tuberculosis. Infection of the cervical lymph nodes, with or without infection at other sites, is not an unusual manifestation of this& disease. This syndrome has been known for thousands of years as scrofula.

CONTROL MEASURES

Tuberculosis is an infectious disease; it is also a social disease with its highest incidence among poor, malnourished and crowded communities. Control measures must therefore be directed at (a) reducing the load of infectious cases by case- finding and effective chemotherapy; (b) protecting the susceptible members by vaccination or, sometimes, by chemopro phylaxis and (c) improving personal, social and environmentals conditions.

Case-finding and Chemotherapy

Reduction of the load of infection by lease-getting, or case-finding followed by effective chemotherapy has played a major part in the dramatic reduction of mortality and Morbidity from tuberculosis in sophisticate communities,'. Open cases of Pulmonary tuberculosis become nearly non-infectious within a few weeks after the start of effective chemotherapy and remain so during maintenance of such therapy. Chest clinics to which-suspected cases are referred by general practitioners have given the best returns in case-finding, with a current rate of 4 per 1000 referrals in England and Wales. The organization of chest clinics, long since established in Britain. needs to be developed, perhaps in special units in health centres or Polyclinics, in countries where a large proportion of the cases of Pulmonary tuberculosis already have extensive disease before they are seen medically. In such countries, microscopic examination of sputum smears is the best and cheapest method of screening for infectious cases. Case-finding by mass miniature radiography is expensive and impracticable in most developing countries and should not be used until the load of infection has been reduced to reasonably low levels when it can help in detecting disease in older people and in spacial groups such as teachers, nurses and medical students, workers in certain industries, and staff in medical laboratories.

When an infectious case has been recognized, treatment with two or three of the first-line drugs must be initiated and maintained for at least one year and for two years in advanced cases in order to minimize the risk of relapse. Controlled trials of the treatment of infected cases in hospital or at home leave shown that domiciliary treatment can be as effective as Hospital treatment but sonic countries prefer to begin treatment with a spell of 2 to 3 months in hospital. The dangers of the development of drug-resistant strains of tubercle bacilli and of clinical relapses associated with ineffective chemotherapy have been illustrated by reports from many countries. In Britain, fortunately, surveys have shown that only 4 per cent of strains from untreated cases are resistant to one or more of the first-line drugs and 3 per cent are resistant to one drug only.

BCG Vaccination

Killed vacceines of the tubercle bacillus give little or not protection against tuberculosis. In 1921, two French workers, Calmette and Guerin, introduced a living vaccine prepared from a bovine strain that had been cultured for 239 subcultures on a bile-potato medium during the course of many years. This Bacille Calmette-Guerin (BCG) vaccine was at first given orally, but following Scandinavian practice is now given mostly by intradermal injection. Its value in the prophylaxis of tiuberculosis has been much disputed, but in recent years controlled trials in different countries and with different communities and, age-groups have demonstrated conclusively that BCG vaccination may give protection of the order of 80 per cent against clinical infection. Thus, in large-scale trials among school- leavers (14 to 1 5 years of age) in industrial areas in England. the incidence of clinical disease was reduced by approximately 80 per cent in the vaccinated groups during a follow-up period& of 15 years. In a study among North American Indians (0 to 20 years old) a similar degree of protection persisted for some ten years after vaccination.

These findings are in striking contrast to the poor results, reported by Palmer and his colleagues from two controlled trials (a) in Puerto Rico where the protection rate was 31 per cent and (b) in Georgia and Alabama where it was only 14 per cent. Various factors have been blamed for these discrepant findings, such as malnutrition, variations in the protective potencies of the BCG vacceines, the strength of tuberculin used a to distinguish susceptible from resistant individuals, and, in particular, the high level of non-specific hypersensitivity found, in warm-climate countries. A critical assessment of these factors has recently been made by Hart, who, while admitting some protective effect from nonspecific hyper- sensitivity, suggests that the low immunizing potency of the vaccines used in some of the American trials may have been, the main contributor to the poor protection. Large-scale trials are at present being carried out in India in an attempt to solve these controversial problems.

Mycobacterium murium, the vole bacillus, causes tuberculosis in voles but is non-pathogenic to man. It has been used is a prophylactic vaccine and gives protection of the same order as that of BCG. However, it may give rise to local lupus-like reations and its use has been discontinued.

Chemiprophylaxis

Isoniazid, usually in a dose of 5mg/kg body weight daily for one year, has been used for the chemoprophylaxis of tuberculosis in the U.S.A. where BCG vaccination has not been generally advocated. Best results have been obtained in young children with primary tuberculosis diagnosed by a positive tuberculin reaction (secondary chemoprophylaxis); these children have a relatively high risk of developing extrapulmonary complications; and with close child contacts of active cases of pulmonary tuberculosis who are at special risk of infection within the first year after recognition of the index case. However, the need to maintain treatment for a year among children who are not obviously sick must militate against the large-scale use of chemoprophylaxis in poor class communities where the need will be greatest.

Hygienic Measures

Tuberculosis has its highest incidence in poor-class urban communities where overcrowding, poor housing and matnutrition are the main contributors. But even in such communities, the prevalence of infection, as indicated by the tuberculin test, is much higher in families where an adult (father, other grandparent) is an infectious case than in families without. Thus the public must be taught that early recognition of pulmonary tuberculosis (persistent cough and spit. sometimes frank haemoptysis. fever and sweating) is advantageous both to the patient and to his family. Particular attention should be given to elderly, apparently bronchitic individuals. Avoidance of open coughing or spitting in the home, at the factory or in public transport has now become good social practice; good standards of household hygiene, lighting and ventilation *will* help to reduce the risks of family intection. Malnutrition is recognized as an important factor in reducing resistance to clinical disease. Persistent health education can help to direct attention to these hygienic and health measures but since social environmental betterment takes time, most emphasis must be given to the more specific measures of casefinding, effective chemotherapy and prophylactic vaccination for the control of tuberculosis.

STREPTOCOCCI

Those invasive cocci that are frequently involved in purulent (pus forming) lesions are usually referred to as the *pyogenic cocci*. Many secrete toxic substances, undoubtedly responsible for the pathology of the lesions they produce, but the major property permitting them to cause disease is their ability to resist phagocytosis in the absence of specific antibodies. Thus, we shall see that one's principal defense against the pyogenic cocci is the production of humoral antibodies (opsonins) that stimulate their phagocytosis and destruction. We shall also see that some infections caused by the pyogenic cocci can be acute and, without antibiotic therapy, an antibody response may not be sufficiently rapid to overcome the infection.

Streptococci

Streptococci are important pathogens both because of the many severe infections they produce and because of the Complications (sequelae) that may occur after recovery from the acute infection.

The bacteria classified in the genus *Streptococcus* share certain morphologic and biochemical characteristics, of which the most noticeable is their appearance. They are spherical cells that divide in only one direction but, rather than separating into individual cocci, the daughter cells tend to remain together, forming pairs or chains of cocci. The length of chain likely to be observed when stained specimens are examined depends to some extent upon the species of streptococcus (e.g., *Streptococcus pneumoniae* has a tendency to remain in pairs), whether the organisms were grown on solid or liquid medium, and how roughly they were handled in the process of making. a smear. The streptococci are all grain positive and non-motile.

History and Classification

The tern Streptococcus was first introduced by Bilroth and the term *Str. pyogenes* was used by Rosenbach. Who isolated it from suppurative lesions in nian. Fehteisen. isolated a strain of streptococcus from erysipelas and called the causative agent *Str. evsipelatis*. Schottmueller classified streptococci on the basis of heamolysis, when the organism was grown on blood agar plates. *Str. haentolvticus* produced definite clear zone of haemolysis and is arranged in long chains, whereas, *Str. viridans* produced greenish zone of heamolysis with formation of short chains. Classification on the basis of biochemical reaction was introduced by Gordon, and Andrews and Horder. The results of biochemical reactions obtained by different workers were not constant. Holman utilised haemolytic properties of these organisms and tried to correlate them with biochemical reactions. Fermentation, however, helped only in the subgrouping of the organisms. Although, Mandelbaum emphasised the importance of the study of colony characters on blood-agar, it was left for Smith and Brown to devise a new technique of pour-blood-agar plate and classified streptococci into a, (3 and y types on the basis of heamolysis.

Haemolysis

(*a*) *Alpha-haemolysis*. It is characterised by greenish di-s colouration of red cells round the colony on blood agar plate within 24 hours with obscure margin. The discolouration is due to peroxide formation and the resultant production of inethaemoglobin. The colour change is best studied in chocolate agar due to oxidation product of haematin. This corresponds to *Str. viridans* of Schottmueller.

(*b*) *Beta-haemolysis*. The colonies are characterised by clear zone of complete haemolysis 2.5 mm. in diameter in 24 hours. with sharp clear cut demarcation of the margin. This is seen in *Str. pyogenes* (*Str. haemolyticus* of *Schottmueller*). Alpha- haemolysis does not give a clear cut heamolytic zone.

(*c*) *Gamma-haemolysis*. In this, no change is noticed on the red blood cells round the colonies on blood agar media. They correspond to *Str. faecalis* or commensals at the throat.

Serological Types

The modern classification of streptococci is based on their

antigenic characters. At present 1 5 groups of aerobic streptococci namely; A, B, C, D, E, F, G, H, K, L, M, N, O, P, Q, have been included on the basis of 15 different C substances, which are group specific polysaccharides, haptens, and give precipitation reactions. Human pathogenic strains of *Str. pyogenes* (*Str. haemolvticus*) belong to group A: but a few other strains belong to group C and G. Group D includes non-Haemolytic faecal streptococci and also certain haemolytic strains of low pathogenicity. The remaining groups are mostly pathogenic to animals and occasionally produce lesions in man. Members of group N are, essentially non-haemolytic. Streptococci of Lancefield's group A were further divided into by Griffith types according to surface protein antigens; M, T, and R. Lancefield typed matt colonies of streptococci of group. A on the basis of M protein, which is type specific as demonstrated by agglutination and precipitation.

Biochemical Reactions

These were used in the past to differentiate haemolytic streptococci but have since been replaced by serological procedure. The reaction is now used to differentiate organisms of D group.

MORPHOLOGY AND STAINING

The individual streptococcus is a spherical microorganism measuring from 0.5g to 1 it in diameter. In the characteristic,chains, however, adjacent cocci are elongated in the axis of the chain. The pathogenic streptococci, when grown upon favourable fluid and certain solid media, often produce long chains made up of eight or more individuals.

Streptococci from human infections are gram-positive, although certain varieties isolated from human feces and animal tissues are gram-negative. The cocci are gram-positive in young cultures but variable or even gram-negative in cultures several days old. They are nonsporogenous and, except for a -few saprophytic srtains, nonmotile. Virulent strains produce a capsule which contains both hyaluronic acid and M-type specific protein.

Metabolism

Nutritionally, the streptococci are very demanding in their growth requirements, having lost the ability to synthesize many essential nutrients. For example, some streptococci require as many as 15 different amino acids, all the known B vitamins, and some purines or pyrimidines for growth. Obviously, such a complex synthetic medium would be used only in a research laboratory. For routine culturing of streptococci, a complex, undefined medium containing peptones, meat infusion, salts, glucose, and agar for solidification is used. To this is added 5% sterile defibrinated blood before the medium is poured into petri dishes. The resulting plates are usually referred to as blood agar plates, valuable both for growing and for identifying the streptococci.

Most streptococci are aerotolerant anaerobes. although there are obligatory anaerobic streptococci that are normal inhabitants of the female genital tract. The term *aerotolerant anaerobe* is used because the streptococci obtain all their energy requirement's from the fermentation of sugars to lactic acid, whether they are growing aerobically or anaerobically. They have no aerobic metabolism because they are unable to synthesize heme, a necessary prosthetic group of the cytochromes.

Thus, they have no mechanism for an aerobic metabolism requiring the transport of electrons through a cytochrome system to molecular oxygen. Their growth in the presence of air is also limited because of the spontaneous aerobic oxidation of reduced pyridine nucleotides (NADH or NADPH). In the absence of cytochromes, this results in a two-electron transfer to oxygen to form H_20_2. Aerobic bacteria can protect themselves from the killing effect of H_2O_2 because they synthesize the enzyme catalase, which quickly converts H_2O_2 to H_2O and O_2. However, the streptococci are unable to synthesize the heme prosthetic group for this enzyme and, as a result, may form lethal amounts of H_2O_2 during aerobic growth. In laboratory practice, the streptococci are grown on blood agar plates, and red blood cells provide a good source of catalase for the destruction of any H_2O_2 formed during aerobic metabolism.

Hemolysins

As streptococci grow, they secrete a large number of toxins and enzymes. We do not know the exact role of many of these products in the development of disease, but some of them are used for the identification of the streptococci and, in some cases, for the diagnosis of a recent streptococcal infection. Among these secreted products may be one or more hemolysins that cause the lysis of red blood cells in the medium. Although there is, no evidence that the hemolysis of red blood cells plays Any part in the disease syndrome, the streptococci are divided into three groups based on the presence or absence of hemolysis and on the type of red cell destruction caused by the hemolysin.

When grown on a blood agar plate, the alpha-hemolytic streptococci produce an incomplete hemolysis of the red blood cells, resulting in a greenish-brown discolouration surrounding the colony. The partially opaque area contains unlysed red blood cells and a green, unidentified, reduced product of hemoglobin. (The streptococci producing alpha-hemolysis are also called *viridans streptococci.*)

The beta-hemolytic streptococci cause a hemolysis of red blood cells surrounding the colony, resulting in a completely clear zone in which no colour remains. This beta-hemolysis is due to the secretion of one or both of two different hemolysins by the streptococci-designated streptolysin S and streptolysin O. Streptolysin S was so named because early work with this hemolysin showed that it could be extracted from the streptococci with serum. However, because it is stable in the presence of atmospheric oxygen (streptolysin O is not), the S could represent "stable" as well as "serum extractable." Streptolysin O is reversibly inactivated in the presence of oxygen, and the beta-hemolysis one sees on the surface of a blood agar plate is primarily the result of streptolysin S rather than streptolysin O. If, however, the streptococci are grown anaerobically, both hemolysins produce beta-hemolysis.

The third major group of streptococci produces no hemolysins and, hence, has no'effect on blood cells in an agar medium. Members of this group of streptococci are sometimes called the *gamma-hemolytic streptococci*, although the term is really a misnomer because they are not at all hemolytic.

CLASSIFICATION

Until the 1930s, the classification of the streptococci was confusing. Many streptococci were considered specific for the disease entity from which they were isolated and were given names based on that type of infection. Examples were such, names as *Streptococcus erysipelatis* for an organism isolated from the skin infection erysipelas, and *Streptococcus scarlatinae* for one isolated from scarlet fever. A biochemical classification system proposed by J.M. Sherman in 1937 proved valuable in the overall classification of this genus, but, since essentially all acute infections were caused by organisms in Sherman's pyogenic group, this classification was of little value to the medical epidemiologist. The present classification of the streptococci still uses the criteria proposed by Sherman but, in addition, uses antigenic properties to subdivide most of the streptococci into groups and types. This latter classification system was originally proposed by Rebecca

Lancefield in 1933. and, as a result of her system, it became obvious that a single streptococcal species could be responsible for a variety of disease entities.

Lancefield found that if streptococci are placed in dilute acid (pH2) and heated at 100°C for 10 minutes, a soluble carbohydrate antigen is extracted from their cell walls. This carbohydrate, which she called C *carbohydrate*, can also be extracted with formamide by heating the cells at 150°C for 15 minutes.

All streptococci except the viridans group possess, a C carbohydrate, and, when the C carbohydrate from many different streptococcal isolates was categorized using antibodies obtained by immunizing rabbits with the streptococci it was found that there were 13 different antigenic C carbohydrates. Based on these antigenic differences in their C carbohydrate, Lancefield divided the stroptococci into groups designated by letters. Thus, the organisms in group A all possess the same antigenic C carbohydrate, and the organisms in group B all possess another C carbohydrate. The C carbohydrate from group A has been shown to consist of a long polymer of rhainnose to which are attached residues of N-acetylglucosamine. Further more, it soon became apparent that each group had a more or less specific habitat, that is, group A were primarily human pathogens, group B primarily cattle and human pathogens and so on. Although common, these habitats are nor rigid.

TABLE : 7.1. MAJOR CRITERIA USED IN SHERMAN'S BIOCHEMICAL CLASSIFICATION OF THE STREPTOCOCCI

Group	*Characteristics*
Pyogenic (all Lancefield groups except D and N)	Mostly beta-hemolytic, will not grow at 45°C or in the presence of 6.5% NaCI
Viridans (not classifiable in Lancefield's classification	Alpha-hemolytic; will grow at 45°C but not in the presence of 6.5% NACI.
Lactic (LanceReld's Group N)	Nonhemolytic; will not grow at 45°C or in the presence of 6.5 % NaCI; will grow at 10°C in the presence of 0.1% methylene blue in milk
Enterococcus (Lance-field's Group D)	Usually not hemolytic; will grow at 45°C in the presence of 6.5 NaCL will grow at pH 9.6

In addition to the carbohydrate used to classify the streptococci into groups, other antigens are present in each group. Some of these antigens are not involved in the virulence of the streptococci, nor are they of value in a specific classification; thus, they will not be discussed her. However, each lancefield group does contain a type-specific substance that allows a further subdivision of the group into specific types. The type specific antigen in some groups is a carbohydrate (different from the C carbohydrate), whereas in group A, which contains the major human pathogens, it is a cell wall protein called the *Mprotein.*

Cultural Characteristics

Only a limited number of strains will grow in a chemically defined medium. Streptococci grow best at a pH of 7.4 to. 7.6. With most species growth is optimal at 37°C and sharply reduced at 40°C.

The pyogenic streptococci grow readily on all the richer artificial media. For primary isolation the media should contain whole blood, blood serum. or transudates. such as ascitic or pleural fluids. The addition of glucose in 0.5 percent concentration increases the rate of growth of the organism but causes a change in the ability of the organism to lyse red blood cells.

TABLE : 7.2. LANCEFELD'S GROUP CLASSIFICATION AND NORMAL HABITAT OF STREPTOCOCCI.

Group	*Normal Habitat*
A	Humans
B	Cattle and humans
C	Wide variety of animals and humans
D	Intestinal tract of humans and animals (enterococci)
E	Swine
F	Humans
G	Humans and dogs
H	Humans
K	Humans
L	Dogs
M	Dogs
N	Dairy products (Never hemolytic on blood agar)
O	Humans

On blood-agar plates at 37°C small, grayish, and delicate opalescent colonies are visible usually within 18 to 24 hours. They are round with smooth or very slightly corrugated edges, and on the surface of the medium they resemble small droplets of fluid. Depending upon the phase of dissociation, the colonies may vary from the slimy or mucoid type to the finely granular or even dry form. In poured blood-agar plates hemolysis of the red cells in the medium surrounding, the colony is characteristic of certain streptococci. The hemolytic effect is usually less intense in streaked blood-agar plates.

Brown based his classification on the hemolytic properties as produced on blood-agar as follows : (a) the a type, which produced a greenish discolouration and partial hemolysis of the red cells surrounding the colony, although an outer clear zone may develop on preservation of the cultures in the ice- box; (b) the 3 type, which produced a clear zone of hemolysis about the colony with no intact corpuscles and no further extension of the area on refrigeration; and (c) the y type, which exerted no effect upon the red blood cells in the medium. To obtain clearly differentiated types of hemolysis.horse's or rabbit's blood should be used, and the medium should be glucose-free.

Resistance

Some varieties of streptococci die after 10 minutes' exposure to temperatures of 55°C, and practically all species are killed in 30 to 60 minutes at 62°C. The pasteurization temperature of 62°C (143.6°F) for 30 minutes destroys all pathogenic streptococci in milk.

Practically all varieties of pathogenic streptococci are susceptible to the bacteriostatic effects of the sulphonamides, except *S. faecalis* and other members of the enterococcus group. Resistance to the effects of the drug, however, is acquired readily when inadequate doses are administered, and these resistant strains may induce epidemics. Penicillin is very effective in relatively small doses against the beta-hemolytic streptococci belonging to Lancefield's group A but is somewhat less efficacious against organisms belonging to groups B, C, E. F, and G. Many individual strains require very large doses and the enterccocci are resistant. Anaerobic hemolytic streptococci may be 250 times as resistant to penicillin as the aerobic streptococci. Fortunately, in the animal resistance to penicillin is acquired slowly, if at all, so that prolonged and repeated treatment with penicillin is practical.

Streptococci in general are susceptible to tetracycline. Streptomycin is very variable in activity : some strains are inhibited by as IMP, as 1 μg and others require as much as 120 gg per ml of culture fluid.

Antigenic Structure

The antigenic structure of streptococci is extremely complex in contrast to the simplicity of the pneumococci. They were divided into groups by Rebecca Lancefield in 1933 on the basis of specific carbohydrates which could be extracted from the cell walls. The groups extended from A to O).

Groups A and D are the most common cause of disease in man. However, in recent years the other groups have been found either in blood cultures or from local lesions.

The group A strains are divided into specific immunologic types by the M, T, and R proteins. The group D and N streptococci are characterized by the presence of glycerol teichoic acids.

At least 50 serotypes of group A streptococci can be identified by the seriologic specificity of the M protein.

Group B is a common cause of mastitis in cows and has recently been identified as the causes of a fatal sepsis in a newborn child. Group B is the exception to the rule in streptococcal groups since it has a complex polysaccharide capsule rather than a hyaluronic acid capsule or no capsule at all.

The *Streptococcus lactic* type from milk and cream, group N, are not hemolytic but do have a group-specific carbohydrate. Heidelberger and Elliott have reported that the group N carbohydrate is an intracellular teichoic acid which shows precipitation in antipneumococcal horse serum types VI, XIV, XVI, and XXVII. Groups B and G share L-rhamnose and cross-react with antipneumococcus serum type XXIII.

M Protein

The specific types of streptococci in group A are now classified by means of the M protein, which is a surface protein. This method of classification was worked out by Lancefield and her associate. Each type has a single specific type of M protein, with the single exception of type 14. where some strains have one M protein and some a different protein but never both at once.

In group A streptococci the M protein corresponds to the capsular polysaccharide of the pneumococcus, since that is not only specific for the type but is essential for the virulence of the organism. Here immunity to the M protein is equivalent to immunity to that strain of streptococcus, and clinical recurrences are rare with the same type of streptococcus.

In many strains hyaluronic acid forms a capsule enclosing the surface M antigen. The ability to resist phagocytes seems to depend upon the combined effect of the M protein and the hyaluronic acid capsule. The presence or absence of the hyaluronic acid does not seem to influence the intraperitoneal infection of mice, but when mice are challenged by the aerosol method, both M protein and hyaluronic acid are necessary for infection. Not all the factors necessary for virulence have been delineated.

TABLE :19.3. ANTIGENIC CLASSIFICATION OF STREPTOCOCCI

Group	*Species*	*Habitat*
A	S.pyogenes	man
B	S.agalactiac	mastitis in cows
C	S.equi	horses
	S.zooepidemicus	animals
	S.equisimilis	man and animals
	S.dysagalactiae	man and animals
D	S.faecalis	milk, man and animals
	S.durans	milk, man and animals
	S.zymogenes	man
	S. liquefaciens	man and animals
E	1 type	milk and swine
F	4 type	man
G	S anginosus	man and dog
H	S.sanguis	man
K	1 type	man
L		man, dog and pig
M		dog and man
N	S. lactis	milk
	S.cremoris	cream
O		man
Viridans group		man
Mieroaerophilie streptococci	(Meleney 1931, 1935)	man
Anaerobic streptococci	13 *species*	man

Fox and Wittner reported that small amounts of purified M protein absorbed to aluminum hydroxide or injected with an oil adjuvant produced high titers of protective antibody in rabbits and man.

The *T* and *R Antigens*. Griffith determined the specific types of streptococci in group A by the agglutination method. The protein on the surface of the streptococci which stimulates the formation of agglutinins is called the T protein. Some T antigens are restricted to a single type of streptococci. but others arc shared by several different types.

The T proteins are readily destroyed by heat and acid pH and are absent from the usual M-containing extracts. In contrast the T proteins are resistant to proteolytic digestion so they can be separated readily from the M protein by proteolytic enzyme action.

A third class of surface-protein antigens has been called R antigens. The type 28 R antigen resists tryptic digestion but is destroyed by pepsin and very slowly by heat and acid pH. This R protein has been recovered from M types 2, 28, and 48. A second R protein occurs in M type 3.

The antigenic complexity of the group A streptococei is emphasized by the tests of Halbert and Auerbach, who studied sera from patients with clinical and subclinical streptococcal infections and found 12 antibodies by electrophoresis and at least 15 by agar gel diffusion.

The Alpha type streptococci

The alpha-hemolytic streptococci of the viridans type have no common carbohydrate but for convenience have been included in Table as have the microaerophilic and anaerobic streptococci. Horsfall found six serologic types of *S. salivarius* with capsular polysaccharides.

Bacteriophages

Bacteriophages which lyse types 1, 6, 12, 25, and human C hemolytic streptococci have been studied by Krause and McCarty. Other phages have been isolated from group D organisms.

Bacterial Metabolites

The injection of washed, heat-killed, intact streptococci into experimental animals produces surprisingly little reaction suggesting that the somatic antigens have little toxicity and that the endotoxins are not very potent. As they grow on suitable media, however, they liberate a variety of specific toxic and nontoxic substances.

TABLE 7.4. BACTERIAL METABOLITES

Extracellular metabolites	*Antibodies*
Erythrogenic toxin	Antitoxin
Streptolysin-O	Antistreptolysin-O
Streptolysin-S	None
Alpha hemolysin	
Diphosphopyridine	Antibody nucleotidase
Streptokinase	Antistreptokinase
Deoxyribonuclease A	
Deoxyribonuclease B	
Deoxyribonuclease C	
Deoxyribonuclease D	
Ribonuclease	
Hyaluronic acid	None
Hyaluronidase	Antihyaluronidase
Proteinase	Antiproteinase
Amylase	?
Esterase	?

Erythrogenic Toxin

This is the toxin which produces the characteristic signs and symptoms of scarlet fever in man. Most strains of group A streptococci and a few of groups C and G can produce an exotoxin of this type. Zabriske in 1964 showed that certain temperate bacteriophages could induce the cell to produce this toxin.

Streptolysin-O

This toxin is readily inactivated by oxygen but has the potency reactivated by reducing agents, such as sulfhydry compounds. It is assumed to be a protein because it is readily destroyed by proteolytic enzymes. Weismann found that the lysosomes of mammalian cells were disrupted with the release of lysosomal enzymes. Infections with group A streptococci results in the production of antistreptolysin (ASO). ASO antibodies in excess of 125 units indicates either recent or previous infection with streptococci.

Streptolysin-S

This toxin is oxygen-stable and can hemolyze the red cells about the colonies growing aerobically on the surface of blood-agar plates. Streptolysin-S was isolated in 1967 by Bemheimer and found to haveaa molecular weight of about 20,000. Its polypeptide moiety only has a molecular weight of 2,800, which is probably too small to induce antibodies.

Weismann and his associates have shown that both streptolysin-S and-O disrupt the lysosomes of mammalian cells and release lysosomal enzymes.

Alpha Hemolysis

The green zone observed around the colonies of alphahemolytic streptococci was formerly attributed to the direct action of hydrogen peroxide, but later work suggests the presence of an oxidation-reduction system in which one component is intracellular. Other organisms such as pneumococci. micrococci. and *E. coli*, also produce green discolouration of blood media by the same mechanism.

Nicotinamide Adenine Dinucleotidase (NADase)

Bernheimer and his associates reported good correlation between the ability of the streptococcal strain to produce NADase and leukotoxicity.

Streptokinase

Tillett and Garner found that filtrates of streptococcal cultures would promote the lysis of human fibrin clots.

Dillon and Wannamaker have reported that group A strains can produce two types of streptokinase with different electrophoretic motility.

Deoxyribonuclease

In 1948 McCarty and Tillett and their associates recognized an enzyme in streptococcal culture filtrate which would depolymerize deoxyribonucjease. Most group A and some C and G strains produced this enzyme. Wannamaker separated four different enzymes by zone electrophoresis and named them A, B, C, and D. Each enzyme stimulates its own specific antibody but all act on the same deoxyribonuclease.

Hyaluronidase

Some streptococci can synthesize a hyaluronic-acid capsule and also a hyaluronidase which can destroy the capsule. McCarty has suggested that the two functions are to some extent mutually exclusive but a single strain may produce capsules while growing under one set of conditions and hyaluronidase while under other conditions. Most group A strains of type 4 and type 22 produce large amounts of hyaluronidase in the culture fluid but do not form capsules. Most other group A strains produce very little hyaluronidase under cultural conditions but may make more in the body since most patients recovering from streptococcal infectious have increased titers of antibodies which inhibit hyaluronidase preparations obtained from types 4 and 22.

Streptococcal Proteinase

Most of our information about this enzyme was contnouied by Elliott and his associates. The poteinase and its inactive precursor have been obtained in crystalline form by Elliott. The precusor is autocatalytically converted to active proteinase under suitable conditions which require a pH between 5.5 and 6.5 and probably activation by sulf iydryl compounds. The cultural conditions which favour the production of this enzyme automatically result in the destruction of the M protein streptokinase, and hyaluronidase.

Amylase

Most of our knowledge of this enzyme has been published by Crowley. Some group A strains synthesize extracellular amylase when grown in the usual poptone media but the yield is much greater if a substrate is present in the medium, such as human plasma, starch, glycogen, and maltose.

Esterase

This enzyme was discovered by Stock in 1961 in group.4 *streptococci.*

It acts on the substrate, P-naphthyi acetate. Antibodies are found in rabbits and in man but the antisera do not inhibit the action of the enzyme.

L-Forms of Streptococci

L-form colonies appear spontaneously but can be induced at will by treating the culture with penicillin or bacitracin but not with novobiocin. L forms occur spontaneously in mice which have not been treated with antibiotics and appear in man in the absence of antibiotics.

Allergy

Lawrence found that 45 percent of 472 adult patients, without evidence of streptococcal infections, gave positive skin tests of the delayed type to intact streptococcal cells or certain isolated fractions of the cells. Sensitivity of the delayed type was transferred to a group of originally negative reactors by the injection of viable leukocytes from streptococcus-positive human donors. These obs&.rvations provide a solid basis for suspecting that allergy to streptococci or their products may play an important role in rheumatic fever and certain types of nephritis.

The specific allergy to M protein investigated by Fox and his associates is even more impressive than the reactions to the whole cell or a mixture of cell-wall components. These investigators found that only 8 percent of infants but 80 percent of adults showed the delayed type of sensitivity to the M protein.

Clinical Infections Due to Strept. Pyogenes

The most common and most typical infection caused by *Strept. pyogenes* is an acute sore throat called tonsillitis if the tonsils are maximally involved or pharyngitis if there is little or no tonsillar tissue in the fauces. There is acute inflammation often with oedema and exudate on the faucial tissues including the soft palate, accompanied by fever and usually an associated cervical adenitis. If the infecting streptococcus is capable of producing a considerable amount of an erythrogenic toxin and the host has not developed antibodies to this toxin, the sore throat may be accompanied by a generalized punctate erythema or rash and this syndrome is called *scarlet fever.* Local extension of the streptococcal infection from the throat may result in such complications as peritonsillar abscess (quinsy), sinusitis, otitis media, mastoiditis or meningitis.

Puerperal sepsis or child- fever is traditionally associated with infection with *Strept. pyogenes* although there are other causal agents. Besides local inflammation of uterine tissues, infection may spread to the adnexa (pelvic cellulitis or peritonitis) or may become generalized (septicaemia). Wounds. burns and chronic skin lesions (eczema. psoriasis) may become infected with *Strept. pyogenes;* these superficial infections may extend in the local tissues (cellulitis) or be carried by lymphatics to regional lymph glands (lymphadenitis) or get into the blood stream.

Strept. pyogenes may cause two types of skin infection- erysipelas and impetigo. The former infection is a spreading inflammation of the dermis seen most commonly on the face and neck and may be associated with antecedent-streptococcal infection of nose, throat or ear. Repeated attacks may occur, which maybe related to an allergy to the streptococcal toxins. Impetigo contagiosa, characterized by multiple vesiculo-pustular or ulcerated skin lesions usually on exposed parts of the body (legs, arms, face) and affecting mostly school and pre-school children, is nowadays uncommon in temperate climates but is prevalent in many warm-climate countries where it is a more likely precursor of acute glomerulonephritis than is streptococcal sore throat. Impetigo may also be caused by *Staphylococcus aureus :* the primary skin lesion may be bullous rather than vesicular (bullous impetigo or pemphigus neonatorum).

Scarlet Fever

Scarlet fever, a specific infectious disease, most often consists of a combination of streptococcal sore throat and a generalized erythema; occasionally the rash will accompany a streptococcal or staphylococcal wound infection (surgical scarlet fever). The rash is due to an erythrogenic toxin produced by the infecting organism in the primary lesion; only strains of *Strept. pyogenes* that have been infected with temperate bacteriophage, i.e., are lysogenic, can produce the erythrogenic toxin (cf. toxigenic diphtheria bacilli). The toxin, suitably diluted, may be used to test susceptibility or immuuity to scarlet fever by intradermal injection; a localized erythema appearing within 8 to 12 hours indicates susceptibility (positive Dick test). Conversely, serum from a convalescent case of scarlet fever or artificially prepared streptococcal antitoxin will, when injected intradermally, cause local blanching of a scarlatinal rash (Schultz-Charlton reaction) due to neutralization of the toxin.

In localized outbreaks of scarlet fever, as in a school, there are usually cases of sore throat without rash and many healthy throat carriers; serological examination of the streptococci will show that these children are infected with the same streptococcal type as those with scarlet fever. They have developed streptococcal antitoxin which protects them against the rash (but not against the primary streptococcal infection), presumably because of previous infections by strains that produce small amounts of toxin. Laboratory studies have shown that there are many different serotypes of *Strept. pyogenes* but only one main ervthrogenic toxin. An individual may therefore suffer from frequent attacks of streptococcal sore throat but only one attack of scarlet fever. Specific antibodies to the M protein, the virulence antigen of the infecting streptococcus, develop slowly after sore throat or other streptococcal illness and persist for a long time so that repeat attacks by the same streptococcus serotype are unlikely; but this specific antibody does not protect against infection with other serotypes.

Besides the acute inflammatory and septic lesions caused *by Strept. pyogenes*, there are two other syndromes, acute rheumatic fever and acute glomerulonephritis (q.v.) that may folfbw an antecedent streptococcal infection. These two diseases are usually regarded as allergic tissue manifestation affecting predominantly heart and joint tissues (rheumatic fever) or kidney tissue (glomerulonephritis).

Pathogenesis

The most common route of entry of *Strept. pyogenes* is by theupper respiratory tract where the primary infection is established, usually in the throat. As is customary with this and other pathogens, only a proportion of infected individuals develop a clinical syndrome such as tonsillitis, pharyngitis or scarlet fever. The others may have mild a typical inkctions or become symptomless carriers. The nose is much less .frequently infected and the streptococci usually disappear much earlier from the pose than from the throat. After an acute attack of sore throat the convalescent patient may carry the infecting streptococci in the fauces for some weeks; a few of these convalescent carriers may continue to carry the streptococci in throat or nose for much longer (persistent or chronic carriers), more especially if there is diseased tonsillar tissue or nasal deformity. A nose carrier sheds far greater numbers of streptococci (e.g., 100 fold) into the environment than dose a throat carrier and consequently nasal carriers, often with an associated sinusitis, are more likely sources for the spread of infection than are throat carriers although numerically nose carriers are much less, common. The saliva of both cases and carriers may become contaminated, sometimes heavily, with haemolytic strep and may be responsible for spreading infection.

Strept. pyogenes is well-endowed with secretory enzymes or 'toxins', including two forms of *haemolytin*, streptolysin-O which is oxygenlabile and streptolysin-S which is not (these are toxic to a variety of tissues); *streptokinase* which lyses fibrin; *hyaluronidase* which increases tissue permeability by hydrolysing the tissue cement, hyaluronic acid; *DNAase* and *leueocidin* which destroy leucocytes. One or more ofthese substances may help the streptococcus in its attack or defence against the host tissues but the invasiveness or virulence of- *Strept. pyogens* is related particularly to a surface antigen, the M-protein, which is present during the acute phase of infection but may be scanty or absent in the later convalescent phase when variant forms of the coccus are present. Two other surface proteins. T and R, do not play any part in virulence but are useful in identification of the infecting serotype. The M-protein is responsible for the virulence of *Strept. pyogenes* because it is the main anti-phagocytic factor of the *cofcus*. Hyaluronic acid capsules are produced by the cocci when spreading fit the blood and tissues and in the early hours of artificial culture, but they have only a weak antiphagocytic effect. Antibodies to M-protein are the antibodies mainly responsible for immunity to *Strept. pyogenes*. They act as opsonins, counteracting the anti-phagocytic action of the M-protein and they are effective only against the homologous serotype of streptococcus.

A characteristic feature of streptococcal infections, whether the portal of entry be the throat or the skin or the genital tract, is the spread permeation of the inflammation through the tissues in contrast to the much more localized inflammatory lesion which is characteristic of staphylococcal infections. A classical example of the spreading lesion is erysipelas and it is tempting to suppose that this permeation of the infection through the skin is related to the production of hyaluronidase; but *Straphylococcus aureus* also produces hyaluronidase and rarely causes spreading infections in the skin.

Laboratory Diagnosis

Since sore throat, with or without inflammatory exudate, may be caused by different agents and consequently requires different treatments, the physician should, whenever possible, obtain a laboratory report on material taken from the throat and, if need be, from the blood. The differential diagnosis may rest between streptococcal or viral infection, diphtheria, Vincent's angina, thrush, infective mononucleosis (glandular fever) and such blood dyserasias as agranulocytosis and leukaemia when the throat becomes 'dirty' because of the absence of the normal scavengers. the phagocytes.

In taking a throat swab, the doctor or nurse must have a good view of the fauces, which means a good light and in most young children. a tongue depressor, the child's hands and head may have to be held by an attendant. T f there is likely to be a delay of more than a few hours between taking the throat swab and its arrival at the laboratory. the swab should be placed in a transport or holding niediurn. e.g. Pike semi-solid agar or a scrum-coated swab pray be used. When search is being made for carriers. e.g. in an institutional outbreak of sore throat and/or scarlet fever, deep nasal as well as throat swabs must be taken. In many cases, and Particularly in children over 3 years of age, a specimen of saliva expectorated into a wide-mouthed container is easier to obtain and gives a higher proportion of positive results than a throat swab in both covalescent and chronic carriers. It may be desirable in the differential diagnosis to collect a sample of blood for leucocyte count (total and differential), erythrocyte sedimentation rate, and antistreptolysin or other streptoc-occal antibody tests.

Chemotherapy

Strept. pyogenes is highly sensitive to a wide range of antibacterial drugs-penicillin, erythromycin, tetracyclines, sulphonamides, etc.-but strains resistant to sulphonamides and tetracyclines are fairly common-A penicillin preparation is the drug of choice; penicillin-resistant strains of *Strept. pyogenes* are unknown, so that antibiotic-sensitivity tests are unnecessary if *Strept. pyogenes* is identified as the infecting organism. In an acute infection, early dosage should be given parenterally, e.g., a combination of benzy and proaine penicillin, or a long-acting Penicillin, e.g., benzathine penicillin (Penidural), which obviates the need for continuing oral penicillin therapy for 7 to 10 days. This prolongation of treatment for some days afterthe clinical infection has subsided is required if the infecting streptococcus is to be eliminated from the throat and the risk of septic and allergic complications (rheumatic fever, glomerulonephritis) reduced to a minimum. Bacteriostatic drugs like sulphonamides or tetracyclines should not be used for this purpose.

Although 50 to 70 per cent of cases of acute sor throat are caused by pathogenes other than *Strept. pyogens, e.g.*, rhino, adeno-myxo and entero-viruses which are not sensitive to anti-bacterial drugs, it seems wise to initiate antibiotic therafy in all cases and decide on the continuation or not of drug therapy after the laboratory report on the throat swab is received.

Epidemology

The severity of streptococcal infections has become steadily. and markedly reduced in many countries in the past, century The strongest evidence in support of this statement comes front the mortality rates for scarlet,fever which has long been a notifiable disease. Death rates in Britain from this once dreaded disease have fallen from approximately 1000 per million population in the decade 1860-69 to virtually zero at the present time. The remarkable reduction in the severity of scarlet fever was accompanied by declines in the incidence, and mortality, of other severe streptococcal infections such as septicaemia, puerperal sepsis and malignant endocarditis and, was apparent before the chemotherapeutic era. This general amelioration was probably related to a steady improvement in nutrition and in social and environmental conditions compared with the abject poverty and gross overcrowding during and after the industrial revolution when the rapid transfer of *Strept. pyogenes* in a highly susceptible population probably led to an exaltation in the virulence of the pathogen However, despite the great reduction in severity, it is doubtful if there has been a corresponding reduction in the incidence of the commonest streptococcal syndrome, sore throat. It is true that notifications of scarlet fever have declined markedly in recent years but the doctor is not likely to notify what is nowadays a mild infectious disease which can be effectively treated at home without upsetting the family with notification and household disinfection.

Sources and Modes of Spread

Streptococcal throat infections have their highest incidence in school children in the age range 5 to 8 years and are rare (or rarely detected) in children under 2 years. The attack rates among school children in temperate climates are probably around 10 to 20 per cent per annum and may be higher among troops in training or in other closed or semi-closed communities. Streptococcal throat infections, and in particular scarlet fever, are much less commonly recognized in tropical countries, but such complications as otitis media and rheumatic heart disease are common enough. Glomerulonephritis is prevalent in some tropical and semi-tropical countries but the antecedent infection is more likely to be streptococcal impetigo than sore throat.

If a throat carrier of *Strept. pyogenes* speaks, coughs or sneezes towards an exposed blood-agar plate within a radius of 1 to 2 feet front his mouth, very few of the expelled droplets will carry haemolytic streptococci. A nose carrier, on the other hand, sheds large numbers of streptococci which abundantly contaminate his clothing and his environment and cart be readily recovered from floor dust, bedding, books and the like in his immediate vicinity, where they may remain alive for days, weeks or months if shielded from daylight. This environmental contamination suggested that dust and fomites were more likely vehicles for the spread of streptococcal infections than droplet spray, and this view was supported by the studies of Wright, Cruickshank and Gunn on the controlof secondary streptococcal complications among hospitalized cases of measles by dust-suppressive measures. However, later studies by American workers showed that men in barracks were remarkably resistant to primary throat infection from dust or bedding heavily contaminated with streptococci. Instead, there was a direct relationship between the incidence of infection and the proximity of the contact (a radius of about 8 feet) to the infected patient so that early transfer of *moist* secretions from an acute case or heavy nasal carrier by direct contact or by contaminated fomites may be the main mode of spread of primary streptococcal infection in healthy subjects. Dried secretions in contaminated dust and the like may nevertheless commonly infect highly susceptible tissues such as burns, or the respiratory musca after a primary virus infection, e.g.,measles, influenza or common cold.

Besides the acute case of sore throat and the nasal or saliva carrier, other dangerous sources of infection are patients with streptococcal otitis media, vulvo-vaginitis or infected skin lesions. Although the nose carrier is the most likely focus for the initiation of streptococcal infections the throat and/or saliva carrier is the more common and more persistent reservoir of *Strept. pyogenes;* some 5 to 10 per cent of children will be throat carriers at any one time and this proportion increases sharply at times and in places of greater prevalence of clinical infection. The throat carrier rate may be 2 to 3 times higher in children with tonsils than in .those without, and acute streptococcal infections tend to be more common in the former group; but this is not an argument in favour of indiscriminate tonsillectomy.

Control of Streptococcal Infections

The early treatment of patients with streptococcal sore throat or other streptococcal infections with a bactericidal drug, such as penicillin or erythromycin, will quickly reduce the numbers of streptococci in the lesion to nil or to small numbers. At the same time as treatment is begun, a swab from the lesion should be sent to the laboratory for bacteriological examination, since more than half of sore throats are non-bacterial in origin. In streptococcal sore throat complete elimination of the infecting organisms can be obtained only if treatment is continued for 7 to 10 days with an oral penicillin or erythromycin, or by giving a single large injection of a longacting penicillin. e.g., benzathine penicillin. However, this last,drug is more likely to produce sensitizing reactions than are other penicillins given orally. Unfortunately, a large proportion of children with sore throats will not be seen by a doctor during the acute episode : such patients will disseminate the infecting organism in the community and be themselves liable to develop secondary septic or non-septic complications.

In outbreaks it is important to search as early as possible for the dangerous spreader, most commonly a nasal carrier, but it may be a child with suppurating otitis media or an infected skin lesion. Such individuals should be isolated and treated with antimicrobial drugs. Heavy nasal carriers are best treated with systemic rather than local therapy, as there is often an associated sinusitis. Treatment of these dangerous carriers is particularly important in children's wards, where young sick patients may develop serious secondary infections. In some hospitals admission swabs are taken to detect a dangerous carrier so that he may be temporarily isolated. Because gross environmental contamination quickly occurs in closed spaces, such as hospital wards, dormitories, and barracks, where there may be dangerous 'shedders' of haemolytic streptococci, bedding and floors should be washed and disinfected regularly and particularly after an outbreak of infection. In children's wards the communal use of toys, books, pencils, and the like should be prohibited. Dust control measures in hospitals or barracks, such as oiling of floors and blankets, present technical difficulties and are probably not of much value unless there are patients with highly susceptible tissues, e.g., burns or virus respiratory infections.

NON-SUPPURATIVE COMPLICATIONS OF STREPTOCOCCIAL INFECTION

1. Rheumatic Fever

There is nowadays general agreement that an attack of acute rheumatic fever is related to an antecedent streptococcal throat infection occurring 1 to 5 weeks earlier. Support for this association is based on epidemiological, bacteriological, serological and therapeutic evidence.

Outbreaks of streptococcal sore throat in schools have been followed a few weeks later by a crop of cases of rheumatic fever; in army training camps in North America, 3 to 4 per cent of patients with proven streptococcal tonsillitis or scarlet fever have developed rheumatic fever: and in institutions for convalescent cases of rheumatic fever, outbreaks of streptococcal infection have been followed by a high incidence of rheumatic fever relapses. Sometimes the association is much less obvious. Among school children suffering from streptococcal sore throats, rheumatic fever is nowadays a rare sequela occurring in, perhaps, 1 in 500 to 1 in 1000 of such cases. However, rheumatic heart disease may be. discovered in children with no clear history of antecedent sore throat or rheumatic fever: this finding occurs particularly in tropical countries were the rheumatic syndrome has its greatest loci-deuce in young children (3 to 7 years old) in comparison with the later peak (8 to 12 years) in Britain, and even later in U.S.A.

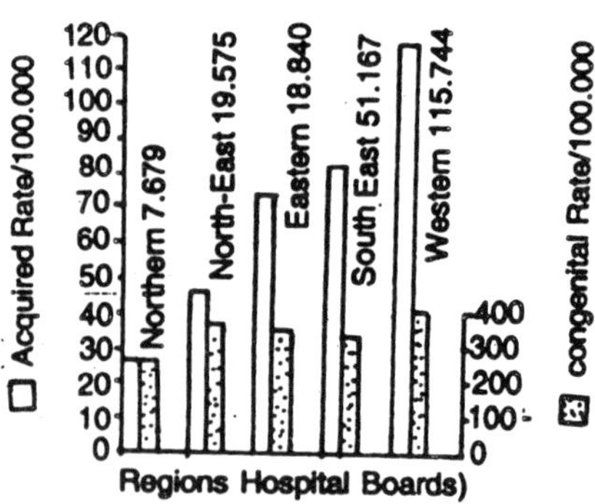

Fig. 7.1. Organic heart disease in Scotland, from the school medical inspection in 1964. Rate per 100.000 per region.

Laboratory evidence for antecedent streptococcal infection is based on bacteriological and serological data. *Strept. pyogenes* has been isolated from the throats of 50 to 80 per cent of cases of rheumatic fever occurring a few weeks after an untreated primary sore throat; and the social class and age distribution of the rheumatic syndrome correlates well with the distribution of streptococcal carrier rates. The demonstration of raised or rising levels of streptococcal antibodies, e.g., antistreptolysin 0 and/or antistreptokinase, antihyaluronidase antiDNAase in 95 percent of cases of rheumatic fever is perhaps the strongest evidence of the association with an earlier streptococcal infection. These antibodies are usually at higher levels and persist for longer periods in rheumatic disease than happens in uncomplicated streptococcal infections.

The supporting chemotherapeutic evidence comes mainly from the prophylactic value of prolonged therapy with penicillin or sulphonamides in patients who have already suffered from one or more attacks of rheumatic fever. Recurrent attacks are not uncommon (20 to 50 per cent) after a fresh streptococcal infection and these can be largely prevented by the long-term administration of an antistreptococcal drug. preferably one of the penicillins. Similarly. if the patient is under medical care. treatment of' the primary streptococcal throat infection with pencilin for 7 to 10 days will eliminate the pathogen and minimize the risk of a subsequent attack of rheumatic fever.

In summary there is conclusive evidence of the association between rheumatic fever and an antecedent streptococcal throat infection but not with primary streptococcal infections of other tissues. The streptococci are not present in the lesions in the heart and joints, No particular streptococcus serotypes are incriminated as happens with glomerulonephritis and it is for this reason that repeat throat infections with different serotypes occur and cause. relapses of rheumatic fever; the evidence indicates that some antigenic component of *Strept. pyogenes*, cellular or extracellular, is involved, perhaps in association with cardiac tissue (muscle or valve) in establishing an allergi

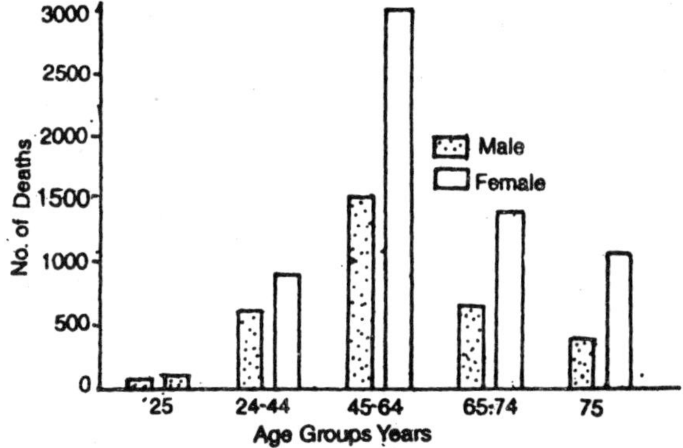

Fig. 7.2. Deaths in males and females from rheumatic heart disease.

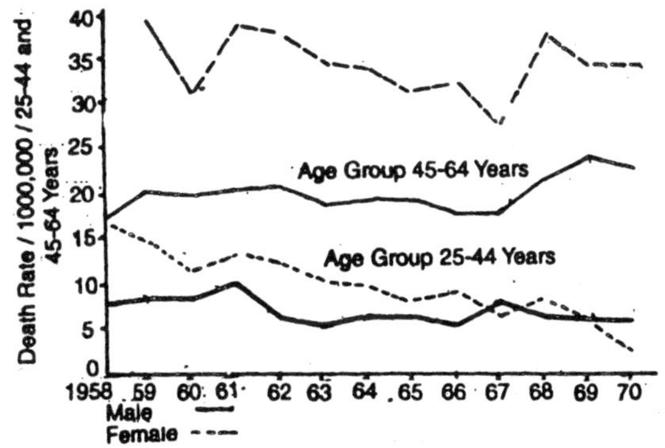

Fig. 7.3. Death rates in male and female from rhumatic heart disease.

chypersensitivity which produces the syndrome of rheumatic fever. There can be little doubt that selected individuals are prone to develop the rheumatic syndrome and the patient with this rheumatic genotype, once he has suffered an initial attack of rheumatic fever, is particularly liable to recurrent attacks after farther streptococcal sore throats. However, the significance of the hereditary predisposition in families is very difficult to disentangle from predisposing environmental factors.

Of these factors, the most important is overcrowding in families and in communities which facilitates the spread of streptococcal infection. For example, the rates of rheumatic heart disease among school children in Scotland is lowest in the Northern and North-Eastern regions (28 to 46 per 100 000), intermediate in the Eastern and South-Eastern regions (75 to 95 per 100 000) and highest in the Western region (116 per 100000) which corresponds with the degree of urbanization and overcrowding in these five regions. On the other hand, congenital heart disease, with much higher rates, shows little variation in the four more populous regions. This factor of crowding is the main reason for the high prevalence of rheumatic heart disease in the cities of many developing countries. Another interesting but unexplained phenomenon is the increasing disparity in the deaths from rheumatic heart disease between men and women with advancing age. Although the primary rheumatic infection has similar morbidity and mortality rates in the two sexes, total deaths from rheumatic heart disease in Scotland have been in the ratio of 2 : 3 for males and females in the age-range 25 to 44 years, about 1 : 2 in the age-range 45 to 64 years and nearly 1 : 3 in those aged 65 years or older. The sex difference in the death rates has been maintained in the 45 to 64 years age group in recent years, but has gradually disappeared in the younger, 25 to 44 years age group.

2. Acute Glomerulonephritis

Acceptance of the association between acute glomerulonephritis and an antecedent streptococcal infection is based on similar evidence to that for rheumatic fever. The pathogenesis of this form of nephritis is possibly similar to that of the rheumatic syndrome; that is, an acquired tissue hypersensitivity or autoimmune disease with the kidney as the involved organ developing I to 4 weeks after a primary streptococcal infection. *Strept. pyogenes* is not found in the kidneys or urine. There are several distinctive features about this streptococcus mediated disease; (a) it follows infection with a limited number of streptococcal 'nephritogenic' serotypes; (b) the primary infection may affect the skin and not the throat; in warm climate countries particularly. streptococcal impetigo or secondarily infected scabies is more likely to be the antecedent infection than a sore throat : and (c) second attacks are very rare. In throat infections, the infecting streptococcus is most commonly Griffith type 12, less often types 4 and 25; in impetigo, type 49 is most commonly incriminated, but types 2, 52, 55, 57 have also been involved; the M antigen may be masked by an associated T antigen of another type, e.g., T type 14 antigen may mask the M '49 antigen.

In temperature climates, the incidence of acute glomerulonephritis tends to be episodic dependent, presumably, on the occurrence of primary throat infectious with nephritogenic streptococci. School children and young adults are most often affected; mild or atypical cases with transient albuminuria and haematuria are found during outbreaks in institutions or epidemic waves in a community. However, recognized nephritogenic types, e.g., type 12, may cause epidemic or sporadic throat infections without an associated nephritis. In tropical countries, the age of attack is earlier than in temperate climates with the peak around 3 to 4 years of age. Experimentally, Matheson and Reed were able to produce acute nephritis in rabbits and monkeys after intravenous injection of a culture filtrate of nephritogenic streptococcus type 12 or of a purified polypeptide fraction. Other workers have been less successful. Early penicillin therapy of the primary streptococcal infection seems to reduce the risk of subsequent kidney disease.

OTHER BETA-HAEMOLYTIC STREPTOCOCCI

Beta-haemolytic streptococci of groups other than group A are only occasionally incriminated as human pathogens; such strains belong almost invariably to groups C, G, B and D of the 18 Lancefield groups, labelled A to T.

Group C streptococci are predominantly animal parasites; 4 biochemical types are recognized and that designated srept. equisimils is the one most commonly associated with human disease, e.g., it has been found in cases of puerperal infection, and has also been isolated from cases of cellulitis, tonsillitis. wounds and scarlet fever.

The majority of group G strains have been found as commensals in the human oropharynx; its pathogenic role is restricted to occasional cases of puerperal infection and possibly pharyngitis, it has been responsible for epidemics..of canine tonsillitis.

Colonies of Group β on blood agar do not produce such marked β-haemolysis as do group A strains. Some strains give α-haemolysis or are non-haemolytic. It 'is encountered as a commensal in the human vagina and throat but is only rarely pathogenic.t the human subject: it may cause pharyngitis and has been recorded in a few cases of puerperal infection and ulcerative endocarditis. As *Strept. agalactiae*, it is the most common cause of bovine mastitis.

Streptococcus Viridans Bacterial Endocarditis

Streptococcus viridans, so-called because of the green pigmentation that surrounds colonies of the organism grown on blood agar and more distinctively on heated (chocolate) blood agar, is a normal commensal of the oropharynx. Morphologically it resembles *Strept. pyogenes* and has a tendency to occur in short chains when grown in a fluid medium. It is non-capsulate. On ordinary blood agar, colonies are small and convex and are surrounded by a zone of partial haemolysis alpha-haemolysis) and green discolouration; there may be a thin outer rim of complete lysis, especially after overnight refrigeration. Because of the green pigmentation colonies of *Strept. viridans* resemble pneumococcal colonies but *Strept. viridans* is distinguishable from the pneumococcus by being non-capsulate, non-bile-soluble, resistant to optochin and nonvirulent for the mouse. Biochemical reactions and antigenic characters are little used in identification or classification although several distinct serotypes have been recognized in strains isolated from the oropharynx and from cases of bacterial endocarditis. *Strept. viridans* is not a single defined species but is the name given to streptococci belonging to several species that produce alpha-haemolysis, *e.g.*,*Strept. mitis*, *Strept. sanguis* and *Strept. salivarius*.

Pathogenicity

Strept. viridans is a constant and numerous commensal of the mouth. being present in most persons throughout life in numbers in the order of 10^9 Per ml saliva. It has little intrinsic pathogenicity, but may act as an opportunistic pathogen and attack tissues with lowered resistance. It is one of the varieties of non-haemolytic streptococci which play a major role in the causation of dental caries (q.v.) and is a pathogen in periodontal infections. It is. however., its causative role in subacute bacterial endocarditis that has given *Strept. viridaus* an important place in medicine. This infection, which before the advent of penicillin was almost invariably fatal after a febrile course of 6 to 10 weeks, affects heart valves that have been. damaged by antecedent rheumatic infection, syphilis and, in more recent years. arteriosclerosis or malignant disease, or are congenitally malformed: other congenital abnormalities such as ventricular septal defects and aortic stenosis also predispose to infection. When rheumatic fever was more common than it is nowadays, subacute bacterial endocarditis occurred most frequently among young adults; in recent years a much higher proportion of the cases occur in the age range 40 to 70 years and tend to run a more rapid course. In the earlier period, *Strept. viridans* was the causal organism in approximately 90 per cent of cases and there was a close association between periodontal sepsis and/or tooth extraction and the onset of bacterial endocarditis due to the bacteriaemia that generally is ploduced for 5 to 15 min after dental extractions. With the shift to the older age groups, the range of incriminated bacteria has widened and includes non-haemolytic and micro-aerophilic streptococci,

Strept.faecalis, Staphylococcus albus, Haemophilus influenzae, bacteroides, and *Coxielia burnetei*, with presumably other primary foci than the oropharynx such as the respiratory and urinary tracts. In a proportion of cases (10 to 20 per cent), repeated blood cultures have failed to isolate any bacterium. Since *Staph. albums* from the skin is the commonest contaminant of blood cultures the finding of *Staph. albums in* a blood culture-requires confirmation by further blood culture and its significance proved by the demonstration of specific antibody to the isolated staphylococcus.

Treatment

With the greater range of incriminated bacteria, the rational and optimal antimicrobial therapy of patients with bacterial endocarditis requires close collaboration between the bacteriologist and the physician. Although *Strept. viridans* is generally more resistant to penicillin than is *Strept. pyogenes*, a penicillin preparation is still the first drug of choice but with more resistant bacteria such as *Strept. faecalis* a combination of penicillin and streptomycin may be required or other drugs may be used according to the drug-sensitivities of the infecting organism. Treatment with adequate dosage must be continued for 4 to 6 weeks; even so, the case-fatality for patients under 40 years of age with *Strept. viridans* infections will vary from 20 to 30 per cent) and in the older age groups with underlying cardiac or other disease, the case mortality will be much higher (60 to 80 per cent). Any patient with recognized valvular disease of the heart or congenital cardiac abnormality who requires dental treatment should be given penicillin (10000 units benzyl penicillin, plus 300000 procaine penicillin) *one half to one hour and no earlier* before treatment and this prophylaxis against bacteriaemia should be continued for 24 to 48 hours. The pathoggnesis and treatment of bacterial endocarditis was fully discussed in a recent R.C.P. Symposium.

Subacture Bacterial Endocarditis

Although acute endocarditis may be caused by *Staphylococcus aureus*, *Streptococcus pyogenes*, *Diplococcus pneumoniae*, *Neisseria gonorrhoeae*, *Brucella*, and occasionally other organisms, most instances of endocarditis are of the subacute variety and are caused by the *viridans* or *enterococcus* group (group D) types of streptococci. In a few instances *Haemo philus parainfluenzae*, microaerophilic and anaerobic streptococci, *Erysipelothrix erysipeloides*, *Candida krusei* and *Histoplasma capsulatum* have been isolated from the blood or from the heart valves at necropsy. The presence of a congenital heart lesion or an active or -healed rheumatic valvular lesion predisposes to the development of endocarditis.

Treatment

There was'a recovery rate of less than 1 per cent in cases of subacute bacterial endocarditis before the introduction of penicillin. Most strains of the viridans group of streptococci are moderately susceptible to penicillin.

Penicillin-susceptible strains usually respond readily to 1,000,000 units daily given for six to eight weeks. Resistant strains may require 10,000'000 to 20,000,000 units and supplementary treatment with streptomycin and the newer antibiotics. Resistance does develop to the newer antibiotics more rapidly than to penicillin but less rapidly than to streptomycin. By early diagnosis and adequate treatment a recovery rate of over 90 per cent can be expected.

Prevention

Patients with congenital heart lesions or old rheumatic carditis should be given prophylactic penicillin therapy before the extraction of teeth or undergoing operations upon the upper respiratory tract.

Streptococcus Faecalis Enterococcus

This streptococcus which almost constantly inhabits the intestine of man and animals as a commensal is oval in shape and occurs in pairs (like spectacles) or short chains. Ordinarily, its colonies do not cause any change in blood agar but a variant causes a clear zone of haemolysis without producing soluble haemolysin and the species is classified antigenically as Lancefield group *D. Strept.* faecalis grows on MaoConkey's and other bile-salt lactose media (forming very small. pink colonies) and also in the presence of a high salt content (6.5 per cent). Characteristic features are its resistance to heat at 60°C for half an hour. fermentation of aesculin and of mannitol with gas formation.

At most, it is an opportunistic pathogen when it gains access to the urinary tract, either alone or more often in association with coliform organisms. It is also one of the less common streptococci in cases of subacute bacterial endocarditis. It has a high degree of resistance to many antimicrobial drugs.

STREPTOCOCCI AND DENTAL DISEASE

Certain alpha-haemolytic and non-haemolytic streptococci, e.g., *Strept. mutans*, *Strept. sanguis*, *Strept. mitis* and *Strept. faecalis*, are commonly found in large numbers in dental plague, carious teeth and root abscesses and probably play an important part in initiating caries and periodontal disease.

Dental Caries

When fed on a sucrose-rich diet, rats and hamsters with a normal oral flora develop caries. Germ-free animals fed on the same diet remain free from caries but readily develop it when they are later infected with a pure culture of *Strept. muans* or *Strept. sanguis* and sometimes do so when infected with *Lactobacillus casei* or *L. acidopliilus*.

In man, streptococci form about half the bacterial population of 'plaque', a soft whitish meterial that accumulates on the surfaces of the teeth if they are not regularly cleaned. *Strept. mutans* and *Strept. sanguis* are the principal bacteria in the plaque that forms on smooth surfaces and are the cause of smooth-surface caries. They convert dietary sucrose into dextran, an insoluble, inert, gelatinous polysaccharide which enables them to adhere to the dental surface. These streptococci, as well as the less numerous but more highly aciduric lactobacilli present in the plaque, ferment part of the sucrose and other dietary carbohydrates to form lactic acid. The acid is held locally by the diffusion-inhibiting dextran and protected from neutralization by the saliva. It dissolves the hydroxyapatite (calcium phosphate/hydroxide) of the tooth enamel and dentine, allowing lactobacilli to invade the tubules of the dentine and continue the process. *Fissural caries*, which begins in crevices protected from mechanical scouring, is caused by a variety of streptococci and lactobacilli, including, non-dextran-producers. without need for the production of a very gelatinous plaque.

Periodontal Disease

Plaque that forms in the angle around the crown of the tooth just above the margin of the gum. contains *principally Sirept. mitis* and. *Strept. faecalis*. When teeth are not brushed. this marginal plaque grows down into the gingival crevice: where it induces a change of flora to one dominated by anaerobic Gram-negative cocci (veillonellae), bacilli, vibrios and spirochaetes and this change leads to the development of gingivitis and pyorrhoea.

Anaerobic Streptococci

Streptococci that can grow only as obligate anaerobes have undoubted pathogenicity for man. Peptostreptococcus putridus, is the best documented species.

They are Gram-positive cocci resembling facultatively anaerobic streptococci but frequently much smaller (0.5 tm or. less) and exhibiting pleomorphism in artificial culture. After anaerobic incubation for 48 hours, colonies on blood agar are smooth, low-convex, approximately 1 to 2 mm in diameter; no alteration occurs in the medium. Cultures in meat broth are proteolytic and usually give off an exceptionally foul odour.

Attempts have been made to classify the anaerobic streptococci on their biochemical reactions; provided that a sulphur compound is present (e.g. 0.1 per cent sodium thioglycollate) in the medium, *Pepto putridus* strains ferment glucose, maltose and fructose with abundant gas production.

Pathogenicity

The main normal habitats of the anaerobic streptococci are the vagina and the intestine. *Pepto. putridus* is incriminated in low-grade puerperal sepsis, probably as an endogenous infection precipitated by trauma and the presence of necrotic material; characteristically it produces as septic thrombophlebitis in the pelvic veins with metastatic abscesses in the lungs. It has also been isolated from brain abscess, infected wounds, e.g., post-operative synergistic bacterial gangrene, and anaerobic streptococcal myositis. Strains are sensitive to penicillin which should be used in large doses therapeutically for 1 to 2 weeks.

Laboratory Diagnosis

Strictly anaerobic methods are required if isolation is to be successful. Inoculation of blood agar plates and incubation for 48 hours in a McIntosh and Fildes' jar produces colonies as described above. For details of the classification and pathogenicity of anaerobic species other than *Pepto. putridus* the report by Thomas and Hare should be consulted.

Scarlet Fever

Sydenham in 1675 gave the first detailed and accurate description of the infection we now call scarlet fever. The discovery of the erythrogenic toxin by Dick and Dick and Dochcz and Sherman explained most of the puzzling features of the disease. The Dick test is performed by injecting intradermally into the skin of the forearm 1 STD of toxin contained in 0.1 ml of volume. A positive Dick test indicates. that the individual is susceptible to the disease. On the other hand, a positive Schultz-Charlton reaction, performed by the injection of antitoxin into a reddened area of skin, indicates, the presence of scarlet fever.

The erythrogenic toxin explains many of the various clinical features of the disease. Scarlet fever rarely occurs infants under 6 months of age or in adults over 50 years of age. If a group of children is exposed to a patient with scarlet fever, some will not be infected, some will develop scarlet fever, and, others may develop no more than an acute pharyngitis and yet, transmit scarlet fever to other susceptible children.

Zabriskic has reviewed the evidence which supports the belief that only streptococci which are carrying a lysogenic phage can produce erythrogenic toxin. The two most serious complications of scarlet fever, acute hemorrhagic glomerular nephritis and acute rheumatic fever, will be discussed later in this chapter.

Treatment

Both sulphonamides and penicillin are very effective. Penicillin eliminates the toxicity and fever of scarlet fever, reduces the number of complications, and shortens the carrier period.

Prevention

The control of scarlet fever has been attempted by quarantine, pasteurization of milk, active immunization, passive. Immunization, and sulphonamide prophylaxis. Oral penicillin is better than sulphonamide as a prophylactic agent and will not induce the appearance of penicillin-resistint strains.

Rheumatic Fever

Cheadle in 1889 suggested that polyarthritis, Sydenham's chorea, and heart disease were all a part of the same clinical syndrome. One of the chief manifestations of rheumatic fever is damage to the heart and the resulting syndrome is known as rheumatic heart disease.

Rheumatic fever is rare in children under three years of age and after middle life. Taranta's studies of twin siblings suggests that genetic susceptibility is not likely.

Hemolytic streptococci are known to be associated constantly with the onset and with recurrences of the disease, but not necessarily with the active phase of the infection. The clinical evidence is almost conclusive that rheumatic fever, follows an infection by streptococci, but many different types of group A streptococci are involved and no one metabolitc can be incriminated, such as the erythrogenic toxin in scarlet fever.

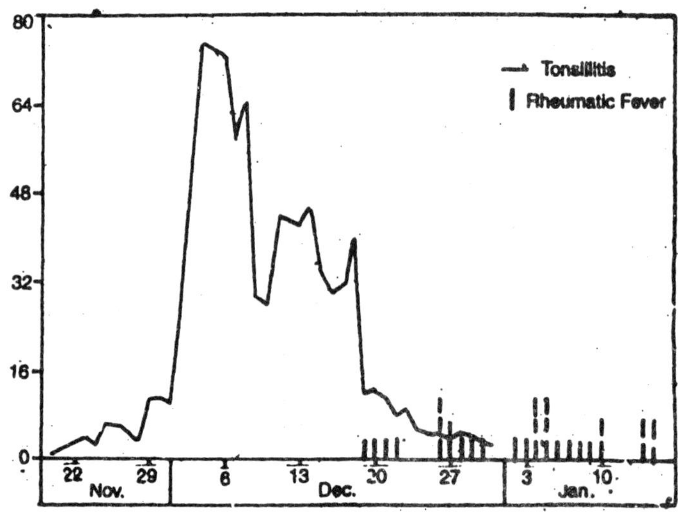

Fig. 7.4. Epidemiology of rheumatic fever.

Kaplan and Meyesenan in 1962 reported that there were antigenic cross-reactions between certain group A streptococcal antigens and human heart tissue. This suggested the possibility that the streptococci might, under certain specific conditions, induce the formation of autoantibodies to patients own heart antigens. Zabriskie and Freimer located the cross-reacting antigen in the cell membranes of all group A streptococci.

The damage to the heart valves and to the joints and subcutaneous tissues is as characteristic of rheumatic fever as damage to the heart muscle.

In1967, Halpern and Goldstein demonstrated that group, A streptococci, but not streptococci of other groups, crossreact with the structural glycoproteins of heart valves of man and-oxen. Presumably the same glycoproteins are present in the joints.

Treatment

Prolonged rest in bed, for weeks or months, is essential for, the heating of the myocardial lesions. Salicylates reduce fever and improve the general symptoms.

Prevention

The prevention of streptococcal infections prevents rheumatic fever. Prompt and vigorous treatment of streptococcal infections with sulphonamides and penicillin reduces but does not entirely eliminate the disease.The administration of cortisone in small doses during the acute phase of infection does not prevent the development of rheumatic fever. Penicillin does not Ilnfluence the course of *rheumatic* fever but when given as a prophylactic prevents streptococcal infections, and thereby subsequent recurrences of the disease. Group A streptococcii rapidly develop resistance to sulphonamides and tetracycline but not to penicillin and erythromycin. Carriers, of beta-hemolytic streptococci of group A can be protected from an'attack of rheumatic fever for a period of six weeks by a doseof 1,200,000 units of penicillin.

The occurrence of rheumatic fever among the recruits of the Navy's training centers at Great hakes was reduced by 93 percent by giving 1.2 million units of beuzathine penicillin G (Bicdlin) parenterally once on induction and again in the fourth week of training.

The study of Feinstein and his associates demonstrated that a single injection of penicillin G benzathine was superior to oral sutphadiaiine or any of the oral penicillin regimens in preventing rheumatic fever.

Acute Hemorrhagic Glomerulonephritis

Acute nephritis occur as a complication of scarlet fever in 0.03 to 18 percent of patients. It occurs also as a complication of acute rheumatic fever, but in a completely irregular and unpredictable percentage. It appears most frequently after rather mild pharyngeal infections, which are not followed by either scarlpt fever or acute rheumatic fever. The irregular manner in which the disease follows streptococcal infections led Reed and Rann elkamp and Weaver to the conclusion that a particular type of group A-hemolytic streptococcus was the etiologic agent. The investigations of Rammelkai# and his associates and others have conifirmed' this theory. ost cases, of acute hemorrhagic glomervlonephritis.follow infection with type 12; but some follow types 1, 4,18, 25, or 49. Wannamaker and Pierce reported an outbreak of acute nephritis associated with type 49 streptococcus.

Some patients die in the acute phase of the disease,. but those that recover have type-specific antibodies in their serum which are present for a period of years. Recurrences are rarely seen even though the patient may carry the specific type of streptococcus in his nasopharynx for 14 weeks to 10 months or longer.

The general clinical picture is not unlike the hemorrhagic nephritis occasionally occurs with serum sickness and which is presumably the result of an antigen-antibody reaction. Antibodies are readily demonstrated to the specific types of group A streptococci which cause the disease but not to other types. Derrick and his associates have demonstrated. a complement consuming antigen-antibody reaction. Only the plasma membrane of specific streptococcus absorbed the immunoglobulin fraction. The antibodies produced to the streptococcal plasma membrane react in a destructive manner with basement membrane of the glomerulus. The clinical syndrome was reproduced in rats by Vosti and his associates.

Subacute and Chronic Glomerulonephritis

This common form of nephritis rarely follows the acute hemorrhagic form discussed above. Only a few specific types can produce the acute form. Almost any of the group A streptococci may be present in the throat immediately before and during an acute recurrence of chronic nephritis. These observations suggest the possibility that subacute and chronic glomerrlonphritis is mediated by a delayed type of allergy from group A streptococci.

Lawrence has demonstrated the frequency of positive delayed skin test to streptococci and has shown that this type of allergy to streptococci can be passively transferred from man to man with white blood cells.

Zabriskie and his associates showed in 1970 that lymphocytes from patients with progressive glomenrlonephritis showed significant inhibition of cell migration in the presence of group A streptococcal particulate antigens.

If allergy to streptococci is indeed the cause of subacute and chronic glomerrlonephritis then autogenous streptococcal vaccines from the throat of the patients may be of help in therapy. The method of making and standardizing autogenous vaccines can be found in the chapter on staphylococci.

Recurrent Aphthous Stomatitis

Recurrent aphthous stomatitis is characterized by painful, recurrent, single, and multiple necrotizing ulceration of mucosal tissue.

For some years it was assumed that these lesions were caused by the herpetic virus which is known to produce similar lesions of the mucocutancous surfaces. However, the failure of 'smallpox vaccination to reduce the number or severity of the attacks resulted in this theory losing support.

This disease has been studied at the National Institute of Dental Research for several years. Neither herpes simplex virus or other viruses were isolated; however a pleomorphic alpha-hemolytic streptococcus could be demonstrated in 94 percent of histologic sections of aphthous ulcers. When guinea pigs were injected with viable, dead, or cell wall group substances, the animals became allergic to skin test with these materials. A vaccine was prepared from the alpha-hemolytic streptococcus strain 2A23 HOT, and used for skin testing 30 patients with recurrent aphthae. All 30 patients gave delayed tuberculin-like skin test to the. vaccine. Less frequent and less severe reactions were found in the controls. Oral suspensions' of tetracycline, which were held in the mouth for a minute, produced rapid improvement but the patient usually relapsed later. Steroids were effective, which supports the idea that the real immunologic defect is the presence of the tuberculin like allergy to the green streptococci. Other treatment, such as antihistamines, gamma globulin, smallpox vaccination, and vitamins, did not improve the lesions or prevent their recurrence.

We studied two patients with aphthous stomatitis before we learned of the study at the National Institute of Dental Rgsearch and more than 30 patients subsequen'tiy. We grew alpha-fidmdlytic streptococci from all patients; it was usually the predominant organism on the blood-agar plates, but most patients also had Neisseria species in smaller numbers. Some had S *epidermidis*, diphtheroids, or other organisms in small numbers in addition to the alpha streptococci. and Neisseria. Autogenous vaceines were prepared from each isolated organism by the method described in the chapter on staphylococci, and the patients then skin tested. The vaccines giving positive reactions were mixed and the patients hyposensitized. A number of weeks are required to complete the series of injections. Generally, the results have been favourable; some patients have remained free of ulcers for 2 to 3 years. Others have. relapsed and had lobe treated a second or third time. The alpha streptococci are always present, but the associated organisms may be different.

Erysipelas

In the Middle Ages both erysipelas and acute ergot poisoning were called Saint Anthony's fire. Fehleisen in 1883 isolated a hemolytic streptococcus from the lesions and reproduced the disease in man by intradermal inoculation of the organisms from cultures.

The streptococci which cause erysipelas belong to several specific types of group A. The potent erythrogenic toxins produced by these erysipelas strains can be neutralized by both erysipelas antitoxin and the scarlet fever antitoxin.

The disease is contagious from person to person but does not produce explosive epidemics analogous to scarlet fever. In contrast to scarlet fever, one attack of erysipelas may predispose the individual to additional attack.

Recurrent Erysipelas

There are two clinical types of recurrent erysipelas. The first type occurs early, often within a few weeks after the original infection. The same skin area is involved, and streptococci are present in the skin, but the symptoms are usually milder than those of the primary attack. The second type of recurrence occurs months and years later, with an explosive onset of fever and redness of the area involved in the original attack. Streptococci usually cannot be recovered from the inflamed skin. It is thought that the recurring attacks are due to the hypersensitiveness of the patient to streptococcus proteins as a result of the original infection. Skin sensitivity in the area of the original disease is greater thani that in other areas of the body.

Treatment

Sulphonamides and penicillin are effective in the primary and early recurrences. Recurrent attacks. of the late ,type do not respond so dramatically, and such patients should be treated for sensitivity to Strept-allergens and desensitized. Desensitization rarely is permanent and should be repeated from time. Careful foot hygiene should be exercised to prevet attacks of "athlete's foot" which open, the way for the streptococcal infection.

Epidemic Sore Throat

Epidemics of sore throat traceable to milk have been observed in England since 1875. The onset is usually accompanied by sudden chilliness, with muscular soreness, headache, and nausea. The cases are similar to' the milder forms d"fitfluenza Epidemics of this type have practically disappeared with universal pasteurization of milk. However, epidemics can still occur when the proper- group A streptocoacusfinds another suitable carrier. In 1968, over 1,200 U.S.

Air Force Academy Cadets developed streptococci pharyngitis. The food carrier was boiled eggs used in the preparation of tuna salad. The'specific streptococcus was a type 12 but a new M type by agglutination.

Puerperal Sepsis

Before the work of Semmelweis was accepted, women died by the tens of thousands from streptococcal puerperal infections carried, for the most part. on the hands and in the nasopharnyx of the attending physician.

The most dangerous and rapidly fatal form of puerperal fever is caused by various types of group A-and human C-hemolytic streptococci. The studies of Harris and Brown and Colebrook have shown that anaerobic streptococci which are normal inhabitants of the vagina also less frequently cause the disease. *Staphylococcus aureus*, *Bacterioldes*, and the *Clostridium* group of anaerobes, including the tetanus bacillus, and the colon bacillus, and other organisms, occasionally cause puerperal fever.

Treatment

Infections witlthe hemolytic streptococci respond readily to treatment with the sulphonamides and penicillin. The anaerobic streptococcus infections are quite resistant to these bactericidal agents, but the progress of recovery often is aided by very large doses of penicillin supplemented by erythromycin and other antibiotics.

Prevention

Every effort should be made to protect the prospective mother from contact with individuals carrying hemolytic streptococci. Scrupulously aseptic techniques in predelivery examinations and in delivery rooms are now routine, and adequate protection from droplet infections should be the objective. Prophylactic treatment with penicillin has materially reduced morbidity.

Rheumatoid Arthritis

Rheumatoid arthritis is a chronic disease with systemic manifestations involving especially the synovia linings of the joints.

At one time rheumatoid arthritis was thought to be another disease precipitated by a previous streptococcal infection. Some of the joint symptoms were similar and a considerable number of patients had agglutinins in their blood for group A streptococci. In 1948 Rose and his associates detected the presence of a peculiar antibody in the serum of most arthritic, patients. This antibody became known as the rheumatoid factor. At the present time there is more evidence that rheumatoid arthritis is one of the collwn diseases and that the rheumatoid factor in human sera is antibodies to the patients' own gamma globulin. The present status of rheumatoid arthritis was reviewed by Kunkle and Williams in 1964 and the nature of the antibody by Christian in 1963. A final summary can be found in the publication of Hirose and Osler in 1965. It appears that autologous gamma globulin becomes denatured in vivo as a result of antibody-antigen complexes and this modified globulin becomes the antigen to which the individual produces a macroglobulin complex of 7S and 19S components. The secondary or tertiary structure of the original gamma globulin is altered in the antigen-antibody complex and can be altered by heat aggregation. TheL chains are inactive but the H polypeptide chains, as well as heat-aggregated F and S fragments, react with the rheumatoid factor.

Treatment

The dramatic response of patients with acute rheumatoid arthritis following ad!ninistration of corticoid hormones is suggestive evidence that an allergic reaction is involved in this disease. The evidence is not nearly as conclusive that streptococci cause the initial sensitization.

Miicroaerophilic and Anaerobic Streptococcal Infections

Microaerophilic streptococci associated with a chronic, burrowing type of gangrene of the subcutaneous tissues have been studied by Meleney. They are associated at times with micrococci and colon bacilli but often occur alone. They are found to be anaerobic on primary isolation but adjust themselves to aerobic conditions after a few transfers.

The strictly anaerobic streptococci have been studied by a number of investigators. These organisms are apparently normal inhabitants of the vagina and frequently cause puerperal fever. Anaerobic streptococci have ban isolated from empyema. They also are a part of the fusospirochetal symbiosis which causes the most common. of pulmonary abscess and gangrene.

Melency found that the local lesions caused by microaerophilic streptococci respond slowly to treatment with zinc peroxide or zinc peroxide supplemented by sulphonamides. Both microaerophilic and anaerobic streptococci are rather resistant to penicillin but somewhat more susceptible to the newer antibiotics, particularly bacitracin and eWorampheniool. The use of two or more antibiotics simultaneously may give better results than one alone. These two groups of streptococci, deserve more study.

8

STAPHYLOCOCCUS

In 1894, *J. Denys* first studied the staphylococcal food poisoning/ food intoxication syndroms and later in 1914, *Barber* produced in himself the signs and symptoms of the disease by consuming milk that had been contaminated with a culture of *Staphylococcus aureus*. The capacity of some strains of *S. aureus* to produce food poisoning was proved conclusively in 1930 by *G.M. Dack et at.*, who showed that the symptoms could be produced by feeding culture filtrated of *S. aureus*. This type of food associated illness is refered by some authors as food intoxication rather than food poisoning, the designation gastroenteritis obviated the need to indicate whether the illness is an intoxication or an infection.

Some strains of *S. aureus* that produce coagulase usually produces staphylococcal gastroentritis. This enzyme is elaborated by growing cells and is identified by its capacity to clot blood plasma. Some coagulase-negative strains are associated with the gastroenteritis syndrome, but coagulase-positive strains are by far the most frequently involved. An extracellular substance designated as enterotoxin cases all symptoms of staphylococca gastroenteritis and these specific enterotoxins are not known to be produced by any other organisms.

An extensive literature exists on staphylococci and the food-poisoning syndrome, much of which goes beyond the scope of this chapter. For more extensive information, other references should be consulted including *Bryan*, *Bergdoll*, *Minor and Marth*, and Smith et at.

POTENTIALLY PATHOGENIC SPECIES/STRAINSQ

The taxonomy of the genus *Staphylococcus* has been the subject of intense study during the past fifteen years, resulting in the assignment of more species to the genus. Two species; *S. aureus* and *S epidermidis* were recognized is the seventh edition of *Bergevs Alanual.* The eighth edition recognized these two and one additional species—*S. saphrophiticus.* It appears that at least fifteen species will be recognized when the next edition of*Alanual* is published. Because of the application of more sensitive and extensive methods of analysis such as DNA-DNA hybridization the enlargement of the genus has come about in part. The expanded genus results in part from the classification of staphylococci by *Baird-Parker* who established six subgroups with the classical S *aureus* strains placed in subgroup I, and from the work of Kloos and others in biotyping host-adapted strains of staphylococci. In Biotype A most human strains, in biotype B poultry and porcine strains while in biotype C most bovine strains are placed.

The species and strains of current potential interest in food microbiology are summarized in Table. *S hyicus* subsp. *hyicus* and S. *intermedium* both of which are important in determining the potential enterotoxigenicity of staphylococcal isolate may produce both coagulase and thermostable nuclease. In one study, S *hyicus* subsp. *hyicus* filtrates from four strains produced emetic responses in monkeys but were negative for either of the known enterotoxins, suggesting that one or more new enterotoxins may have been involved. These authors found one strains that produced enterotoxin B (SEB) but was more closely related to S *epidermidis* and S *aureus.* Evidence to date suggests that S. *intermidius* and S. *hyicus* subsp. *hyicus* cannot be overlooked when examining foods for staphylococci of health significance. While in the past organisms resembling *S. aureus* that produce coagulase, thermostable nuclease, protein A, or the clumping factor could be reasonably presumed to be S *aureus*, additional characteristics need to be determined before the identity of this species is certain. With the other three species noted in Table, inhibition was achieved by from 0.4 to 3.2μg/ ml. While susceptibility to acriflavine appears to be diagnostic of *S. aureus* > 10 jig/ml required for its inhibition.

Habitat and Distribution

Nasal cavity in man, is the man reservior of S *aureus* are either directly or indirectly from this source the organism find their way to the skin and into wounds. While the nasal carriage rate varies, it is generally about 50% for adults and somewhat higher among children. The most common skin sources are the arms, hands, and face, where the carriage rate runs between 5 and 30%. In addition to skin and nasal cavities, *S. aureus* may be found in the eyes, throat, and in the intestinal tract. From these sources, the organism finds its way into air and dust, onto clothing, and in other places from which it may contaminate foods. Nasal carriers and individuals whose hands and anus are inflicted with boils and carbuncles. who are permitted to handle foods are the two most important sources to foods.

The chances of contracting food intoxication are excellent if milk from infected cows is consumed or used for cheese making though most domesticated animals harbor *S. aureus*, Staphylococcal mastitis is not unknown among dairy herds. There is little doubt that many strains of this organism that cause bovine mastitis are of human origin. However, some are designated as " animal strains". In one study, staphylococcal strains isolated from parts of raw pork products were essentially all of the animal strain type. To a point where none of the original animal strains could be detected in finished products, these animals strains during the manufacture of pickled pork products were gradually replaced by human strains during the production process.

TABLE 8.1. SPECIES AND STRAINS OF STAPHYLOCOCCI IMPORTANT IN FOODS

Characteristic	*S. aureus*	*S. hyicus subsp. hyicus*	*S. hyicus subsp. chromogens*	*S. intermedius*
coagulase(rabbit plasma)	+	+[1]		+
Thermostable nuclease	+	+	–[2]	+
Clumping factor	+	–	–	+[1]
Pigment	+	–	+	–
α, β, or δ hemolysins	+	–	–	+[1]
Phosphatase	+	+	+	+
Sensitivity to acriflavine[3]	>10	<5	<5	<5

[1] 11 to 89% of strains.

[2] Slight of none.

[3] MIC ig/ml.

Incidence in Foods

Unless heat processing steps are applied to effect staphylococci's destruction they may be expected to exist in any or all food products that are of animal origin; or in those that are handled directly by man, at least in low numbers. They have been found in a large number of commercial foods by many investigators.

Nutritional Requirements for Growth

Staphylococci are typical of other gram-positive bacteria in having a requirement for certain organic compounds in their nutrition. Amino acids are required as nitrogen sources, and thiamine and nicotinic acid are required among the B vitamins. They appear to require uracil when grown anaerobically. In one minimal medium for aerobic growth and enterotoxin production. Monosodium glutamate serves as the C, N, and energy sources. In addition to inorganic salts, this medium contains only three amino acids (arginine, cystine and phenylalanine) and four vitamins (pantothenate, biotin, niacin and thiamine). Arginine appears to be essential for enterotoxin B production.

Temperature Growth Range

Some strains of *S. aureus* can grow a temperature as low as 6.7°C. thought it is mesophile with time of incubation food poisoning strains decreased at 116°-120° F but grew in custard at 114°F which was found by latter authors. They grew in chicken a lacking at 112°F but failed to grow in ham salad at the same temperature. In general, growth occurs over the range of 7°—47.8° C, and enterotoxins are produced between 10° and 46°C, with the optimum between 40° and 45°C. Optimal conditions relative to other parameters are assumed by these minimum and maximum temperatures of growth and toxin productions, and the ways in which they interact to raise minimum growth or lower maximum growth temperature are noted below.

Effect of Salts and Other Chemicals

Some strains can grow in 20% while S. *aureus* grows well in 7-10% concentration and even in culture media without NaC1..The maximum concentrations that permit growth actually depend on other parameters such as temperature, pH, a_w, and Eh.

Compounds such as tellurite, mercuric chloride, neomycin, polymyxin, and sodium azide, all of those compounds are used as selective agents in culture media, with S. *aureus* having high degree of tolerance. S *aureus* can be differentiated from other staphylococcal species by its greater resistance to acriflavine. In the case of borate, *S. aureus* is sensitive while *S. epidermidis* is resistant. With novobiocin. *S. saprophyticum* is resistant whereas S. *aureus* and S. *epidermidis* are not. Members of genus micrococcus are widely distributed in nature and occur in foods generally in greater numbers than staphylococci having capacity to tolerate high levels of NaCl and certain compounds making the recovery of the latter more difficult. The effect of other chemicals on S. *aureus* is presented.

Effect of pH, a_w and Other Parameters

Regarding pH, *S. aureus* can grow over the range of 4.0-9.8 but its optimum is in the range of 6-7. As is the case with the other growth parameters, the precise minimum growth pH is dependent upon the degree to which all other parameters are at optimal levels.

Besides any other nonhalophilic bacteria the staphylococci are unique in being able to grow at lower values, with respect to $a_{w.}$ Growth has been demonstrated as low as 0.83 under otherwise ideal conditions, although 0.86 is the generally recognized minimum a The interrelationship of a_w, pH, NaCl level, and temperature of incubation is discussed below.

NaCl and pH over the pH range 4.00-9.83 with no NaCl growth and production of enterotoxin C occurred by using a protein hydrolysate medium incubated at 37° C for 8 days. With 4% NaCl, the pH range was restricted to 4.4-9.43. Toxin was produced 10% NaCl with a pH of 5.45 or higher, but more was produced at 12% NaCl.

TABLE 8.2. THE EFFECT OF pH AND NACI ON THE PRODUCTION OF ENTEROTOXIN C BY AN INOCULUM OF 10^8 CELLS/ML OF *S. AUREUS* 137 IN A PROTEIN HYDROLYSATE MEDIUM INCUBATED AT 37°C FOR 8 DAYS

pH range	4.00-9.83	4.4-9.43	4.50-8.55	5.45-7.30	4.50-8.55
NaCl content (%)	0	4	8	10[1]	12
Enterotoxinproduction	+	+	+	+	-

[1]Enterotoxin was detected also with an inculum of 3.6 × 106 at pH 6.38—7.30.

At pH 4.8 and 5% NaCl S. *aureus* growth is inhibited in both as shown, while in 10% NaCl at pH 6.9 growth and enterotoxin B production by strain S-6 occurred, as once not with 4% at pH 5.1 revealed in another study. The general effect of increasing NaCl concentration is to raise the minimum pH of growth. At pH 7.0 and 37° C enteroxtoxin B was inhibited by 6% or more NaCl.

pH, a_w and Temperature. No growth of a mixture of S. *aureus* strains occurred in brain heart infusion (BHI) broth containing NaCl and sucrose as humectants either at pH 4.3, a_w of 0.85, or at 8° C. No growth occurred with a combination of pH <5.5, 12°C, and aw of 0.90 or 0.93; and no growth occurred at pH<4.9, 12°C, and a_w of 0.96.

$NaNo_2$, Eh, pH, and Temperature of *Growth.* Under anaerobic conditions with brine content upto 9.2%, not below pH 5.30 and 30°C or below pH 5.58 at 10°C, *S. aureus* strain S-6 grew and produced enterototoxin B in cured ham. Under arobic conditions, enterotoxin production occurred sooner than under anaerobic conditions. As the concentration. of HNO_2 increased, enterotoxin production decreased.

Staphylococcal Enterotoxins—Types and Incidence

Seven different enterotoxins are recognized and designated A, B. C_1, C_2. C_3, D, and E, by use of serologic methods. Not identical to SEC_1 and SEC_2, enterotoxin C, (SEC_3) is chemically and serologically related to it. The latter two show some cross reactivity. Preliminary reports during the early 1980s that the toxic shock syndrome toxin was SEF were subsequently not confirmed.

In table the relative incidence of entertotoxins is presented generally with SED being second most frequent, SEA is recovered from food poisoning outbreaks more often than any of the others. The fewest number of outbreaks are associated with SEE. The incidence of SEA among 3,109 and SED among 1,055 strains from different sources, and by a large number of invesugators, was 23 and 14%, respectively. For SEB, SEC, and SEE, 11, 10 and 3%, respectively, were found among 3 367, and 1.072 strains.

The relative incidence of specific enterotoxins among strains recovered from various sources varies widely. Over 50% of isolates secrete alone from human specimens in the United States or in combination from human isolates, in Sri Lanka SEA producers constitued only 7.8%. Unlike other reports, the latter study found more SEB producers than any other types. Wide variations are found among S. *aureus* strains isolated from foods. While in one study *Harvey et al.* found SED to be associated more with poultry isolates than human strains, in another study these investigators found no SED producers among fifty-five poultry isolates. SED were produced by the 2 of 3 atypical S. *aureus* isolates which were negative for the anaerobic fermentation of mannitol and produced a slow, weak positive or negative coagulase reaction. The isolates were from poultry. From Nigerian ready-to-eat foods, about 39% of 248 isolates were enterotoxigenic, with 44% of these producing SED. Of 48 isolates from dairy and 134 from meat products, 45.8 and 48.5%, respectively, were enterotoxigenic and, of 80 strains from food-poisoning outbreaks, 96.2% produced SEA.

Depending on the source of isolates widely different percentages have been found, regarding the percentage of strains that are enterotoxigenic. Only 10% of 236 raw milk isolates were enterotoxigenic while 62.5% of 200 food isolates were positive. In a study of S. *aureus* from chicken livers, 40% were enterotoxigenic. In another study, 33% of 36 food isolates were enterotoxigenic.

TABLE 8.3. PERCENT INCIDENCE OF STAPHYLOCOCCAL ENTEROTOXINS ALONE AND IN COMBINATION FROM VARIOUS SOURCES.

			Enterotoxins				
Source	*No. cultures*	*% enter-otoxic*	*A*	*B*	*C*	*D*	*E*
Human specimens	582	—	54.5	28.1	8.4	41.0	—
Raw milk	236	10	1.8	0.8	1.2	68	—
Frozen foods	260		3.4	3.0	7.4	10.4	—
Food-Poisoning outbreaks	80	96.2	77.8	10.0	7.4	37.5	—
Foods	200	62.5	47.5	3.5	12.0	18.5	6.5
Poultry	139	25.2	1.4	0	0.7	23.7	0
Humans	293	39	7.8	17.7	7.2	6.8	0.7
Poultry	55	62	60.0	1.8	36	0	0

Fermentation of various carbohydrates and attempts to associate enterotoxigenicity with other biochemical properties of staphylococci such as getatinase, phosphatase, lysozyme, lecithinase, lipase, and DNAse production have been unsuccessful. Enterotoxigenic strains appear to be about the same as other coagulase-positive strains in these respects. Attempts to relate enterotoxigenesis with specific bacteriophage types have been unsuccessful also. Most enterotoxigenic strains belong to phage Group III, but all phage groups are known to contain toxigenic strains. Of fifty-four strains from clinical specimens that produced SEA. 5.5, 1.9 and 27.8% belonged respectively to phage Groups I, II, and III, with 20.4% being untypable. Among poultry isolates, 49% were found to be phage untypable. Various studies suggested that the bruised poultry tissue served as the source of staphylococci to the handlers as in bruised poultry tissue the same phage types were found on the hands and in lesions of handlers as in the bruised tissues.

Chemical and Physical Properties of Enterotoxins

Both these properties being simple proteins upon hydrolysis, yield eighteen amino acids with aspartic, glutamic, lysine, and valine being the most abundant, are summarized in table. The amino acid sequence of SEB was determined first. Its N-terminal is glutamic acid, and lysine is the C-tenninal amino acid. SEA, SEB, and SEE are composed of 239 to 296 amino acid residues, SEC, contains 236 amino acid residues and the N-terminal is serine, while the N-terminal of SEC, is glutamic acid. The disulfide bond in enterotoxin B is not essential for biological activity and conformation. Biological activity of SEA is destroyed when the abnormal tyrosyl residues are modified. The effect of acetylation, succinylation, guanidination, and carbamylation on the biological activity of SEB from strain S-6 has been studied. It was found that guanidination of 90% of the lysine residues had no effect on emetic activity or on the combining power of antigen-antibody reactions of SEB. The toxin was reduced, however, when acetylated, succinylated, and carbamylated. Amino groups which contributed the net positive charge of the enterotoxin is decreased by the investigators. The normal positive charge of the enterotoxin is thought to play an important role in both its emetic activity and in its combining with specific antibody. The enterotoxins are sensitive to pepsin at a pH of about 2 and are resistant to proteolytic enzymes such as trypsin and chymotrypsin, remain and papain, in their activate states, while the various enterotoxins differ in certain physiochemical properties, each has about the same potency. Although biological activity and serologic reactivity are generally associated, it has been shown that aerologically negative entrotoxin may be biologically active.

After heating for 16 h at 60°C and pH 7.3, the biological activity of SEB was retained because as noted above, it is observed that the enterotoxins are quite heat resistant. Heating of one preparation of SEC for 30 min at 60°C resulted in no change in serologic reaction. The heating of SEA'of 80° C for 3 min or at 100°C for 1 min caused it to lose its capacity to react serologically.

The thermal inactivation of SEA based on cat emetic response was shown by *Denny et al.* to be 11 min at 250°F (F^{48}_{250} = 1 1 min). When monkeys were employed, thermal inactiviation was F^{46}_{250} = 8mins. These enterotoxin preparations consisted of 13.5-fold concentration of casamino acid culture filtrate employing strains 196-E. Using double -gel-diffusion assay, *Read* and *Bradshaw* found the heat inactivation of 99+% pure SEB in veronal buffer to be F = 16.4min. Intravenous injection of cats was identical to the end point for enterotoxin inactivation by gel diffusion. The slope of the thermal inactivation curve for SEA in beef bouillon at pH 6.2 was found to be around 27.8°C (50°F) using three different toxin concentrations (5,20 and 60 gg/ml, 26). In table some D values for the thermal destruction of SEB. It has been found that purified toxins are less resistant to crude toxin preparations. It may be noted from Table that staphylococcal thermonuclease displays heat resistance similar to that of SEB. In one study. SEB was found to be more heat sensitive at 80°C than at 100^0 or 110°C. The thermal destruction was more propounced at 80°C than at either 60° or 100°C when heating was carried out in the presence of meat proteins. To destroy these toxins present thermal process treatments for low-acid foods are adequate in spite of the generally high degree of heat resistance.

TABLE 8.4. D VALUES FOR THE HEAT DESTRUCTION OF STAPHYLOCOCCAL ENTEROTOXIN B AND STAPHYLOCOCCAL HEATSTABLE NUCLEASE.

Conditions	*D(C)*
Veronal buffer	D_{110} = 29.7[a]
Veronal buffer	D_{110} = 23.7[b]
Veronal buffer	D_{121} = 11.4[a]
Veronal buffer	D_{121} = 9.9[b]
Veronal buffer, pH 7.4	D_{110} = 18
Beef broth, pH 7.4	D_{110} = 60
Staph. nuclease	D_{130} = 16.5

[a]Crude toxin.

[b]99+percent purified.

As may be noted from D values presented in Table from the various heating menstra that S. aureus cells are considerably more sensitive to heat. The tells are quite sensitive in Ringers solutions at pH 7.2 (D_{140} °F = 11), and much more resistant in milk at pH 6.9 (D_{140} °F = 10). In f ankfurters, heating to 71.1°C was found to be destructive to several strains of S. *aureus* and microwave heating for 2 min was destructive to over 2 million cells/g.

When the cells were grown in heart infusion broth containing soy sauce and monosodium glutamate (MSG) its effects were shown on the maximum growth temperature and heat resistance of S. *aureus* strain MF 31. Without these ingredients in the broth, maximum growth temperature was 44°C but with them the maximum was above 46. The most interesting effect of MSG was on Dr C values determined in Tris buffer at pH 7.2. With cells grown at 37° C, the mean D60°C value in buffer was 2.0 min, but when 5% MSG and 5% NaCI were added to the buffer, D60°C was 15.5 min. Employing cells grown at 46°C, the respective D 60°C values were 7.75 and 53.0 min in buffer and buffer-MSG-NaCl. Though changes of this magnitude is unusual, it is well known that heat resistance increases along with increasing growth temperature.

Production

Optimum growth conditions of pH, temperature, Eh and so on, are all discussed in Table and they in general tends to favoured enterotoxin production. It is well established that staphylococci can grow under conditions that do not favour enterotoxin production.

Even over a slightly narrow range than growth, enterotoxin production (except for SEA) occurs with respect to a_w.

TABLE 8.5. D AND Z VALUES FOR THE THERMAL DESTRUCTION OF S. *AUREUS* 196E IN VARIOUS HEATING MENSTRA AT 140°F

Products	*D(F)*	*z*
Chiken a faking	5.37	10.5
Custard	7.82	10.5
Green pea soup	6.7-6.9	8.1
Skim milk	3.1-3.4	92
0.5 percent NaCl	2.2-2.5	10.3
Beef bouillon	2.2-2.6	10.5
Skim milk alone	5.34	—
Raw skim milk + 10% sugar	4011	—
Raw skim milk + 25% sugar	6.71	—
Raw skim milk + 45% sugar	15.08	—
Raw skim milk + 6% fat	4.27	—
Raw skim milk + 10% fat	4.20	—
Tris buffer, pH 7.2	2.0	—
Tris buffer, pH 7.2, 5.8% NaCl or 5% MSG	7.0	—
Tris buffer, pH 7.2, + 5.8% NaCl + 5% MSG	15.5	—

In precooked bacon incubated aerobically at 370C, *S. aureus A* 100 grew rapidly at a_w as low as 0.84 and produced SEA. The production of the individual enterotoxins is more inherent to the toxin tlhan to the strain that produces them. SEA but not SEB has been shown to be produced by L-phase cells. In pork, SEA production occurred at a 0.86 but not at 0.83; and in beef at 0.88 but not at 0.86. Under conditions of a_w that do not favour SEB, SEA can be produced. IN general, SEB $_{pro}$duction is sensitive to a_w while SEC is sensitive to both a_w and temperature, Regarding NaCl and pH enterotoxin production has been recorded at pK 4.0 in the absence of NaCl,. The effect of NaCl on SEB synthesis by strain S-6 at pH 7.0 and 37°C is presented. Although this strain produces both SEA and SEB, neither was produced above 10% NaCl. In general SEA production is less sensitive to pH than SEB. When the medium is unbuffered or buffered in the acid range. More SEB is leaded than the buffering of a culture medium at pH 7.0, and rather than 7.0, at controlled pH of 6.5 a similar result was noted.

With respect to growth temperature, SEB production in ham at 10°C has been recorded, as well as small amounts of SEA, SEB' SEC, and SED in cooked ground beef, ham and bologna at 10°C. The optimum temperature for SEB and SEC is 40°C in a protein hydrolysate inediutn and for SEE- 40°C at pH 6.0, though the production has been observed at 46°C. The growth of S. *aureus* on cooked beef at 45.5°C for 24 h has been demonstrated, but at 46.6°C the initial inoculum decreased by 2 log cycles over the same period. For SEB in a culture medium at pH 7.0 the optimum temperature was 39.4°C. Thus, the optimum temperature for enterotoxin production is in the 40-45°C range.

Through the stationary phase and into the transitional phase increase the staphylococcal enterotoxins which have been reported to appear in cultures as early as 4-6 h. Enterotoxin production has been shown to occur during all phases of growth although earlier studies revealed that with strain S-6, 95% of SEB was released during the later part of the log phase of growth. Even in non growing cells the production of SEB have been demonstrated by the latter authors. On the other hand, strain S-6 was found not to produce detectable quantities of SEB during exponential growth, but did during the postexponential phase in association with total protein synthesis. Enterotoxins appearance was inhibited by chloramphenicol, suggesting that the presence of toxin was dependent upon *de novo* protein synthesis.

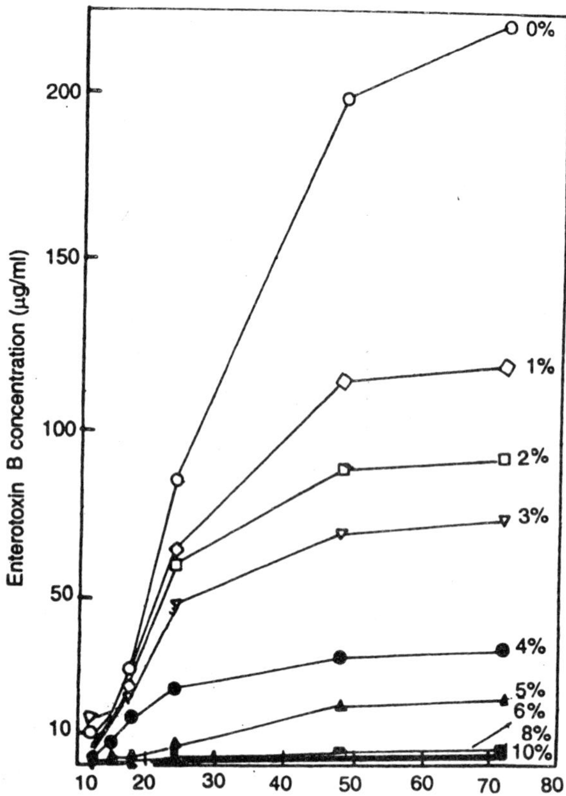

Fig. 8.1. Staphploccal enterotoxin B. prodution in different NaCl concentration in 4 % NZ-Amine NAK medium at pH 7.0 and 3 7°C.

Under ideal condition the maximum amount of enterotoxin A that can be produced in culture media is about S-6μglml, while levels of 350 and 60 gg/ml or more of SEB and SEC, respectively, can be produced. In protein hydrolysate media, up to 500 gg/ml of SEB may be produced. A study by *Chesbro et al.* suggests that SEB is heterogeneous. They found that two electrophoretically distinct toxins can be identified in cultures, one produced in early to mid-log and the other in mid-late log phase growth. The presence of both should be show by analyses of old cultures.

It has been found that excess glucose in the medium repressed the SEB production. Streptomycin, actinomycin D, acriflavine. Tween 80, and other comounds have been found to inhibit SEB synthesis in broth in unbuffered media. SEB production is inhibited by 2-

deoxyglucose and the inhibition is not restored by glucose, indicating that this toxin, at least, is not under catabolite control. While actinomycin D has been shown to inhibit SEB synthesis in strain S-6, the inhibition occurred about 1 h after cellular synthesis ceased. The latter was immediately and completely inhibited. A possible conclusion from this finding is that the mRNA responsbile for enterotoxin synthesis is more stable than that for cellular synthesis.

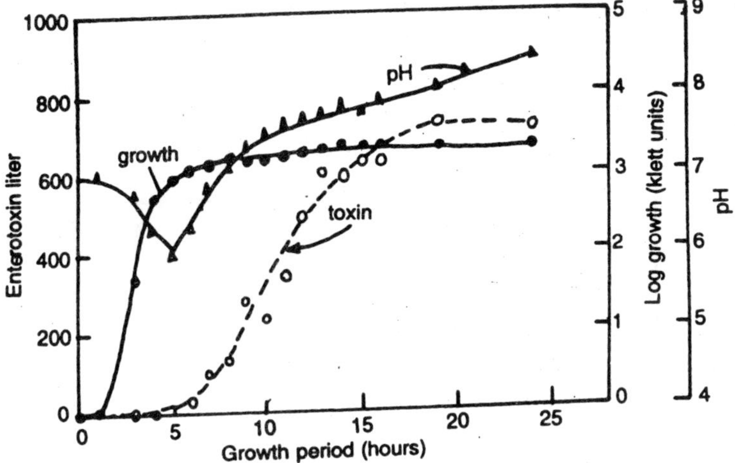

Fig. 8.2. Enterotoxin B production growth, and the pH changes in Staphylococcus aureus at 37°C.

The minimum number of cells of S. *aureus* required to produce that minimum level of enterotoxin considered necessary to cause the gastroenteritis syndrome in man (1 ng/g) appears to differ for substrates and for particular enterotoxin. Withcounts of 10^7 in milk, SEA and SED were detected, but not below this level. Employing a strain of *S.aureus* that produces SEA, SEB, and SED. SEB and SED were detected when the count reached 6 x 10^6/ml and the enterotoxin level was 1 ng/ml, while SEA at a level of 4 ng/ml was detected with a count of 3 x 10^6cfu/ml. In imitation cheese with pH of 5.56-5.90 and a,. of 0.94-0.97, enterotoxins were first detected at the following count: SEA at 4 x 10^6/g; SEC at 1 x 10^8; SED at 3 x 10^6; SEE at 5 x 10^6; and SEC and SEE at 3x 10^6/g. In precooked bacon, SEA was produced by strain A100 with cells >10^6/g. In certain vegetable products no toxin was detected with counts up to log $_{,0}$ 10.00/g, but in meat products and vanilla custard, SEA was produced with > log $_{10}$ 7.2 cells/g.

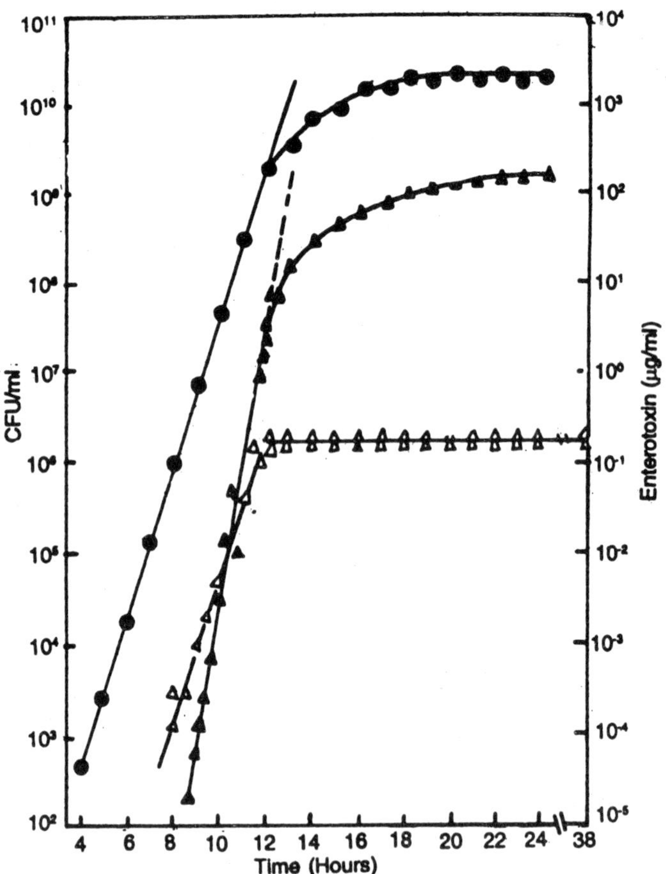

Fig. 8.3. Rates of growth and enterotoxin A and B synthesis by Staphylococcus aureus S-6. Symbols; • CFU/ml; Δ enterotoxin A; Δ enterotoxin B.

Chromosomal gene is not a stable chromosomal entity though SED has been determined to be under its control. Temperature polymorphic phages that integrate with the bacterial chromosome carries the gene for SEA in some wild-type strains of S *aureus*. This explains why SEA is produced generally under all conditions that support growth of SEA-producing strains, and perhaps why this enterotoxin causes more food-poisoning outbreaks than any other, at least in the United States. Chromosomal genes are more stable than plasmid-borne genes. In strain S-6, the SEA gene has been shown to occur on the chromosome very close to the alpha-hemolysin gene, but the strain FRI-196E it appears to be in another position. A chromosomal location has been reported at least for some strains, as in case of SEB, it appears to be plasmid borne. SEB and SEC, genes are carried on a penicillinase bearing plasmid, where they may serve either as structural genes for the synthesis of these two enterotoxins, or as essential regulatory genes that switch on cryptic structural genes in recipient cells.

Evidence has been presented for SEB that the kinetic precursor of the extracellular product is a larger membrane bound from designated pSEB with respect of enterotoxin synthesis. This latter investigators believe that the temporary sequestering on the membrane may be critical to the mechanism that facilitates the transfer of SEB through the cell wall. After its release from the membrane, the enterotoxin appears to be transiently sequestered by the cell wall before its ultimate release into the extracellular environment. A similar pattern of synthesis, sequestering, and release has been shown for SEA. While SEA, SED, and SEE and assembles in one way, SEB and SEC synthesized in another as presented by evidence regarding intracellular synthesis.

Detection in Foods

Serologic and *in vitro* methods for detecting enterotoxins are presented and *in vivo* and related methods. An appropriate refgrence in Table should be consulted. For the extraction of foods for enterotoxins.

THE GASTROENTERITIS SYNDROME

Though a range from 1 to 6 h has been reported, but within 4h, symptoms of staphylococcal food poisoning develops upon the ingestion of contaminated food. The symptoms consist of nausea, vomiting, abdominal cramps(which are usually quite severe), diarrhea, sweating, headache, prostration, and sometimes a fall in body temperature. The symptoms generally last from 24 to 48 h, and the mortality rate is very low or nil. Bed rest and maintenance of fluid balance is the usual treatment for healthy person. Upon cessation of symptoms, the victim possesses no demonstrable immunity to recurring attacks, although animals become resistant to enterotoxin after repeated oral doses. Though rare, it is conceivable that stool cultures might be negative for the organisms, since the symptoms are referable to the ingestion of pre-formed enterotoxin. Proof of staphylococcal food poisoning is established by recovering coagulase-positive, enterotoxigenic staphylococci from leftover food and from the stool cultures of victims. Attempts should be made to extract enterotoxin from suspect foods, especially when the number of recoverable viable cells is low.

A syndrome can be produced by a dosage of 20-35 μg of pure SEB as is shown by a data obtained from the use of three human volunteers so the minimum quantity of enterotoxin needed to cause illness in man is about 1 ng/g. From sixteen incidents of staphylococcal food poisoning enterotoxin levels of <0.01-0.25 tg/g offood were found.

TABLE 8.6. FOODS INCRIMINATED IN STAPHYLOCOCCAL FOOD POISONING OUTBREAKS.

Food Products	*No. of Outbreaks*	
Meat		251
Ham products	137	
Beef products	60	
Uncured pork products	27	
Others/combinations	27	
Poultry		102
Turkey products	52	
Chicken	50	
Custards and cream-filled pastries		55
Fish and shellfish		34
Salads (nonmeat)		31
Eggs and egg products		17
Milk and milk products		14
Vegetables		9
Cereal products		6
Miscellaneous products		59

In man the pathogensis of enterotoxin is not yet clear as they act upon the intestine to induce vomiting and diarrhea, the same effects can be achieved by injections. When SEA was administered IV to monkeys, an initial state of lymphopenia was induced,which lasted for 1 to 2 days and was followed by the release of new immature cells that had greater DNA synthesis activity.

Incidence and Vehicle Foods

The incidence of staphylococci in a variety of foods is presented, they may be expected to occur in a wide variety of foods not given heat treatments for their destruction.

Usually products made by hand and improperly refrigerated after being prepared, a large number has been incriminated in outbreaks with regard to vehicle foods for staphylococcal enteritis. Of selected cases of staphylococcus poisoning over the period 1961-73, meat products were involved in over 40% of the cases. Of the 251 meat products, 76 were baked ham. The precise number of cases in the United States is not known, but various investigators have placed the number in the tens of thousands/ years. The small outbreaks that occur in homes are not reported to public health officials so the problem here is one of reporting. A large percentage of the reporting that result from banquets, generally involving large numbers of persons.

Wild mushrooms in vinegar were traced, which was caused by SEA and Shl) in unusual outbreak and the food contained 10 ng SEA and 1 ng of SED/g.

Ecology to S. Aureus Growth

In general, the staphylococci do not compete well with the normal flora of most foods, and this is especially true for those that contain large numbers of lactic acid bacteria where conditions permit the growth of the latter organism. *S aureus* inability to compete in both fresh and frozen foods have been shown by a large number of investigators. At temperatures that favour staphylococal growth, the normal food saprophytic flora offers protection against staphylococcal growth through antagonism, competition for nutrients, and modification of the environment of conditions less favourable to S. *aureus*. Bacteria known to be,antagonistic to S. *aureus* growth include *Acinetobacter Aeroinonas*, *Bacillus*, *Pseudomonas*, *S. epidermidis*, the Enterobacteriaceae, the Lactobacillaceae, streptococci, and others are included in the bacteria which are known to be antagonistic *to S. aureus* growth. SEA has been shown to be resistant to a variety of environmental stresses, but growth of several lactic acid bacteria did lead to its reduction and to a suggestion that toxin reduction might have resulted from specific enzymes or other metabolites of the lactic acid bacteria. The' generally higher incidence of food poisonings of all types over the past decade may simply reflect the general improvement in food plant sanitation and the fact that improving technology enables food producers to produce more lowcount foods. Before this picture can be made clearer more studies on the ecology of staphylococcal growth are necessary.

Prevention of Staphylococcal and other Food-Poisoning Syndromes

If kept either below 40° or above 140°F until consumed,

susceptible foods which are produced with low numbers of staphylococci, will remain free of enterotoxins and other food poisoning hazards. For the years 1961-72, over 700 food brone disease outbreaks were investigated by Bryan relative to the factors that contributed to the outbreaks, and of the sixteen factors identified, the five most frequently involved were:

1. inadequate refrigeration
2. preparing foods far in advance of planned service 3. infected persons practicing poor personal hygiene
4. inadequate cooking or heat processing
5. holding food in warming devices at bacterial growth temperatures

25.5% of the contributing factors alone comprises of inadequate refrigeration. The five listed above contributed to 68 percent of outbreaks. Susceptible foods should not be held within the staphylococcal growth range for more than 3-4 h.

9

FOOD POISONING CAUSED BY SPORE- FORMING BACTERIA

Bacterial food poisoning is known to be caused by at least three grain-positive sporeforming rods : *Clostridium perfringens* (*welchii*), *C. botulinum, and Bacillus cereus*. The incidence of food poisoning caused by each of these organisms is related to certain specific foods as is food poisoning in general.

CLOSTRIDIUM PERFRINGENS FOOD POISONING

Anaerobic sporeforming rod widely distributed in nature is the causative organism of this syndrome which is a grain- positive. Based upon their ability to produce certain exotoxins, five types are recognized types A, B, C, D, and E. The food-poisoning strains belong to type A as do the classical gas gangrene strains, but unlike the latter, the food-poisoning strains are generally heat-resistant and produce only traces of alpha toxin. Some type C strains produce enterotoxin and may cause a food poisoning syndrome. By not producing beta toxin, the classical food-poisoning strains differs from type C. The latter, which have been recovered from enteritis necroticans, are compared to type A heat-sensitive and heat- resistant strains in Table.

McClung mode the first clear-cut demonstration of its etiological status in food poisoning, investigating four outbreaks in which chicken was incriminated, while since 1895 *C. perfringens* has been associated with gastroenteritis. The first detailed report of the characteristics of this food- poisoning syndrome was that of*Hobbs et. al.* in Great Britain. While the British workers were more aware of this organism as a cause of food-poisoning during the 1940s and 1950s, few incidents were recorded in the United States prior to the publication by*Angelotti et. al.* of methods of recovery and quantitation of the organism. It is now known that C. *perfringens* food poisoning is widespread in the United States and many other countries.

DISTRIBUTION OF C. PERFRINGENS

In soils, water, foods, dust. spices, and the intestinal tract of man and other animals the food-poisoning strains of C. *perfringens* exists. The incidence of the heat-resistant. nonhemolytic strains have been reported by many authors to range from 2-6% in the general population. Between 20 and 30% of healthy hospital personnel and their families have been found to carry these organisms in their feces, while the carrier rate of victims after 2 weeks may be 50% or as high as 80%. The heat-sensitive types are common to the intestinal tract of all humans. *C. perfringens* gets into meats either directly from slaughter animals or by subsequent contamination of slaughtered meat from containers, handlers, or dust. The adverse environmental conditions of drying, heating, and certain toxic compounds can be with stood, since it is a sporeformer.

TABLE 9.1 TOXINS OF CLOSTRIDIUM WELCHII TYPES A AND C.

					Toxins						
Cl. welchii	α	β	γ	δ	Σ	θ	ι	κ	λ	μ	υ
Heat-sensitive											
Type A	+++	-	-	-	-	++	-	++	-	+ or -	+
Heat-resistant											
Type A	± or tr	-	-	-	-	-	-	+ or -	-	+++ or -	-
Heat-resistant											
Type C	+	+	+	-	-	-	-	-	-	-	-

Characteristics of the Organism

If incubated under anaerobic conditions, or if provided with sufficient reducing capacity food poisoning as well as most other strains of C. *perfringens* grow well on a variety of media. Strains of C. *perfringens* isolated from horse muscle grew without increased lag phase at an Eh of-45 or lower, while more positive Eh values had the effect of increasing the lag phase. Although it is not difficult to obtain growth of these organisms on various media, sporulation occurs with difficulty and requires the use of special media such as those described by *Duncan* and *Strong*, or the employment of special techniques such as dialysis sacs.

With an optimum growth temperature between 37° and 45°C. C. *perfringens is* mesophilic. The lowest temperature for growth is around 20°C, and the highest is around 50°C-Optimum growth in thioglycollate medium for six strains was found to occur between 30 and 40°C, while the optimum for sporulation in Ellner's medium was 37°—40°C. Growth at 45°C under otherwise optimal conditions leads to generation times as short as 7 min. Regarding pH, many strains grow over the range 5.5-8.0 but generally not below 5.0 or above 8.5. The lowest reported a_w values for growth and germination of spores flie between 0.97 and 0.95 with sucrose or NaCl, or about 0.93 with glycerol employing a fluid thioglycollate base. Higher a,, values appears to be required for the spore production than the above minima. *Labbe* and *Duncan* demonstrated growth of type A at pH 55, but no sporulation or toxin production occurred. A pH of 8.5 appears to be the highest for growth. *C. perfringens* is not as strict an anaerobe as are some other clostridia. Its growth at an initial Eh of + 320 my has been observed. At least thirteen amino acids are required for growth along with biotin, pantothenate, pyridoxal, adenine, and other related compounds. It is heterofermentative, and a large number of carbohydrates are attacked. Growth is inhibited by around 5% NaCl.

Some being typical of other mesophilic sporeformers and some being highly resistant the endospores of food poisoning strains differ in their heat resistance. A D 100°C value of 0. 31 for C.*perfringens* (*ATCC* 3624) and a value of 17.6 for strain NCTC 8238 have been reported. For eight strains that produced reactions in rabbits, D 100°C values ranged from 0.70 to 38.37: strains that did not prcduce rabbit reactions were more heat sensitive.

Several groups studied the heat destruction of vegetative cells of C. *Perfringens*, in view of the practice of cooking roasts in water baths for long' times at low temperatures (LTLT). For strain *ATCC* 13124 in autoclaved ground beef. D 56.8°C was 48.3 min, essentially similar to the D 56.8°C or D 47.9°C for phospholipase C.*Employing* strain NCTC 8798, D values for cells were found to increase with increasing growth temperatures in autoclaved ground beef. For cells grown at 37°C, D 59°C was 3.1 min ; cells grown at 45°C had D 59°C of 7.2; and cells grown at 49°C had D 59°C of 10.6 min. While the wide differences in heat resistance between the two strains noted may in part be due to strain differences, the effect of fat in the heating menstr un may also have played a role. With beef roasts cooked in plastic bags in a water bath at 60°-61°C, holding the product to an internal temperature of60°C for at least 12 min eliminated salmonellae and reduced the *C. perfringens* population by about 3 log cycles. To effect a 12-log reduction of numbers for roasts weighing 1.5 kg, holding at 60°C for 2.3h or longer was necessary. Respectively 25.4 and 23.8 min of the thermal destruction of C. *perfringens* enterotoxin in buffer and gravy at 61°C required.

Similar variations have not been recorded for C. *botulinum*, especially types A and B while the wide variations in heat resistance recorded for C. *perfringens* spores which may be due to many factors. The latter organisms have no history in the intestinal tract of man, while *C. perfringens* strains are common inhabitants of this environment as well as soils. Wide variations may be expected to be shown by organism inhabiting environments as diverse as these may be among its strains. Another factor that is important in heat resistance of bacterial spores is that of the chemical environment. *Alderton* and *Snell* have pointed out that spore heat resistance is largely an inducible property, chemically reversible between a sensitive and resistant state. By treating spores is Ca-acetate solutions. For example, 0.1 or 0.5 m at pH 8.5 for 140 h at 50°C, it has been shown that spores can be made more heat resistant, if this hypothesis is used. The heat resistance of endospores may be increased 5- to 10-fold by this method. On the other hand, heat resistance may be decreased by holding spores in 0.1 N HCI at 25°C for 16 h, or as a result of the exposure of endospores to the natural acid conditions of some foods. The high variability of heat resistance of *C. perfringens* spores may be a more or less direct result of immediate environmental history as it is not inconceivable.

Strong and *Canada* studied the freezing survival of *C. perfringens* in chicken gravy and found that only around 4% of cell survived when frozen to -17.7°C for 18 days. Dried spores, on the other hand, displayed a survival rate of about 40% after 90 days but only about 11 %, after 180 days.

Because of the many serovars there appears to be no consistent relationship between outbreaks and given serovars but serotyping has been employed for epidemiologic studies. The bacteriocin typing of type A has been achieved, and of ninety strains involved in food outbreaks, all were typable by a set of eight bacteriocins and 85.6% consisted of bacteriocin types 1-6.

The Enterotoxin

Enterotoxin is the causative factor of C. *perfringens* food poisoning. It is unusual in that it is a spore-specific protein; its production occurs together with that of sporulation. All known food-poisoning cases by this organism are caused by type A strains. An unrelated disease, necrotic enteritis is caused by beta toxin produced by type C strains and is only rarely reported outside of New Guinea. While necrotic enteritis due to type C has been associated with a mortality rate of 3 5-40%, food poisoning due to type A strains has been fatal only in elderly or otherwise debilitated persons. At this time the role of some type C strain in disease is unclear but is shown(to produce enterotoxin.

Duncan and *Strong* demonstrated the enterotoxin of type A strains. The purified enterotoxin has a molecular weight of 36,000 daltons and an isoelectric point of 4.3. It is heat sensitive (biological activity destroyed at 60°C for 10 min), pronase sensitive but resistant to trypsin, chymotrypsin, and papain. In one study. L-forms of *C. perfringens* which produces the toxin were shown to produce as much enterotoxin as classical forms.

In association with late stages of sporulation the enterotoxin is synthesized by sporulating cells. The enterotoxin is released along with spores and just before lysis of the cells sporangium's is the peak for toxin production. Conditions that favour sporulation also favour enterotoxin production, and this was demonstrated with raffnose, caffieine and theobromine. The latter two compounds increased enterotoxin from undetectable levels to 450 tg/lm of cell extract protein. The enterotoxin has been shown to be similar to spore coat. Cells sporulate freely in the intestinal tract and in a wide variety of foods. Enterotoxin is known to be produced by vegetative cells at extremely low levels but in culture media, the enterotoxin is normally produced only when endospore formation is permitted. A single gene has been shown to be responsible for the enterotoxin trait, and enterotoxin and spore-coat protein have been shown to be controlled by a stable mRNA.

For three stains of C. *perfringens in* Duncan-Strong (DS) medium after 24-36 h production of enterotoxin from 1 to 100 pg/ml has been shown and the enterotoxin may appear in a growth and sporulation medium about 3 h after inoculation with vegetative cells. It has been suggested that performed enterotoxin may exist in some foods and in infrequent cases contribute to the early onset of symptoms. Purified enterotoxin has been shown to contain up to 3,500 mouse LD/mg N.

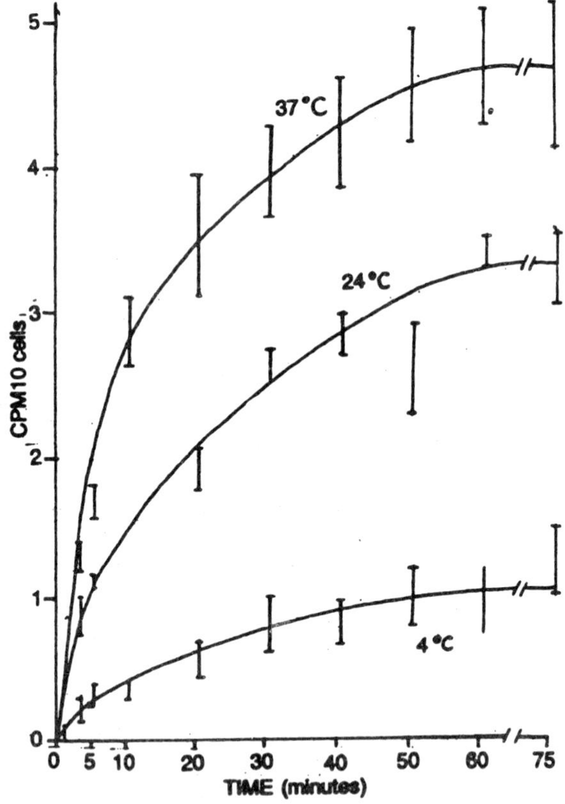

Fig. 9.1. Specific binding of (^{125}I) enterotoain to intestinal cells as a function of temperature and time. Error bars show standard error of the meanwhich if not shown was smaller than the symbol.

The enterotoxin may be detected in the feces of victims. From one case, 13-16 μg/g feces were found and from another victim with a milder case, 3-4 gg/g were detected.

For the expressidn of biological activity, it has been demonstrated that binding of the enterotoxin is necessary with respect to mode of action. The toxin has been shown to bind to isolated rabbit intestinal epithelial cells and tissue homogenates from liver and kidney but not to brain tissue. Its binding is specific, and time and temperature dependent, and it appears to be irreversible. The enterotoxin subseq-uently becomes trapped when once bound, it acts directly on the cell membrane via receptors and fluid accumulation results after its entrapments which causes loss of structured integrity and function. In rabbits the activity of enterotoxin was shown to affect the intestinal tract in the following order: ileum > jejunum: duodenum. According to *McDonel*, in the normal ileum, there is a net absorption of water, Na+, Cl^-, and glucose, while at the same time there is a net efflux of K^+ and bicarbonate ions. The net movement of water, Na^+, and Cl^- is reversed, while net movement of K^+ and bicarbonate is unaffected under the influence of enterotoxin. Rounding of cell inducing holes in outer cell membranes, inhibiting macromolecular synthesis and causes of cell death all is caused by the decrease is O_2 consumption by enterotoxin which is showed by the use of cell structure and isolated tissues. The toxin also causes erythema in test animals, increased capillary permeability, and exhibits parasympatho-mimetric properties. Its effect on rabbit ileum is presenteyi. These and other effects on tissue culture system and bioassays are treated further.

Vehicle Foods and Symptoms

The symptoms of contaminated foods are characterized by acute abdominal pain and diarrhea with nausea, fever, and vomiting being rare, upon its ingestion appear between 6 and 24 h especially between 8 and 12 h. Except in the elderly or in debilitated persons, the illness is of short duration, one day or less. The fatality rate is quite low and no immunity seems to occur, although circulating antibodies to the enterotoxin may be found in some persons with a history of the syndrome.

It is quite likely that only those outbreaks and cases that affect groups of people are ever reported and recorded because of the relative mildness of the disease the true incidence of C. *perfringens* food poisoning is unknown. The confirmed out- breaks reported to the U.S. Centers for Disease Control for the years 1973-75 totaled forty, with 2,706 cases.

The endospore germinate and grow upon cooling and remaining and the heat preparations of meat dishes; which is prepared one day and eaten the next, is presumably inadequte to destroy the heat resistant endospores, such food is involves *in. C. perfringes* outbreaks are most often the cause of this syndrome, although nonmeat dishes maybe contaminated by meat gravy. The greater involvement of meat dishes may in part be due to the slower cooling rate of such cooked foods and also to the higher incidence of food poisoning strains in meats. Strong *et al.* found the overall incidence of the organism to be about 6% in 510 American foods. The incidence for various foods was 2.7% for commercially prepared frozen foods, 3.8% for fruits and vegetables, 5% for spices, 1.8%, for homid-prepared foods, and 16.4% for raw meat, poultry, and fish. *Hobbs et al.* found that 14-24% of veal, pork, and beef samples examined contained heat-resistant endospores, but all 17 samples of lamb were negative. An *C. perfringens* has been demonstrated to grow in a large number of foods that's why in an outbreak of food poisoning involving 375 persons where 140 became ill, was shown to be caused by both *C. perfringers* and *Salmonella typhimurium. A* study of retail, frozen precooked foods revealed that one- half were positive for vegetative cells, while 15% contained endospores. The latter investigators inoculated meat products with the organism and stored them at -29°C for up to 42 days. While spore survival was high, vegetative cells were virtually eliminated during the holding period. Upon storing raw ground beef at temperature between 1° and 12.5°C led to the foundation that inoculated cells survived in decreased numbers, being studied by *Goepfert* and *Kim.* The raw beef contained a natural flora, and the above finding suggests that *C. perfringens is* unable to compete under these conditions. For the recovery of C *. perfringens* from foods, an appropriate reference in Table or the review by *Walker* should be consulted.

Prevention

Noted in the previous chapter, the leading causes of all types of food poisioning may be prevented by proper attention to the *C. perfringens* gastroenteritis syndrome. Since this syndrome often occurs in institutional cafeterias, some special precautions should be taken. Upon investigating *a C. Perfringens* food-poisoning outbreak in a school lunchroom in which 80% of students and teachers became ill, *Bryan et al.* constructed a time-temperature chart in an *effort* to determine when, where, and how the turkey became the vehicle. It was concluded that meat and gravy, but not dressing, were responsible for the illness. These authors suggested nine points for the preparation of turkey and dressing as a means of preventing recurrences of such episodes; which are summarized below:

1. Cook turkeys until internal breast temperature reaches at least 165°F, preferably higher.

2. Thoroughly wash and sanitize all containers and equipment that previously had contact with raw turkeys.

3. Wash hands and use disposable plastic gloves when deboning, deicing, or otherwise handling cooked turkey. 4. Separate turkey meat and stock before chilling.

5. Chill the turkey and stock as rapidly as possible after cooking.

6. Use shallow pans for storing stock and deboned turkey in refrigerators.

7. Bring stock to a rolling boil before making gravy or dressing.

8. Bake dressing until all portions reach 165°F or higher.

9. Just prior to serving, heat turkey pieces submerged in gravy until largest portions of meat reach 165°F.

Botulism

While growing in foods, the ingestion of highly toxic, soluble exotoxin is produced by the organism which is the cause of symptoms of botulism, unlike *C. perfringens* food poisoning, in which large numbers of viable cells must be ingested.

The first recorded case of botulism was in 1793, and the etiologic agent of the disease was first isolated in 1895 by E. *Tim Ermengen.* The outbreak studied by Van Ermengen, which occurred in Belgium, involved thirty-four cases and three deaths. The causative organism was named *Bacillus botulinus* from the Latin *botulus* meaning sausage. A gram-positive. anaerobic sporeforming rod with oval to cylindrical. terminal subterminal spores is certain strain ofclostridium botulinum which causes Botulism. On the basis of the serological specificity of their toxins, seven types are recognized A, B, C, D, E, F, and G. Types A. B. E, F, and G cause disease in man: type C causes botulism in fowls, cattle, mink, and other animals; and type D is associated with forage poisoning of cattle, especially in South Africa. The types are also differentiated on the basis of their proteolytic activity. Types A and G are proteolytic as are some types B and F strains. Type E is nonproteolytic, as are some B and F strains. The proteolytic activity of type G is slower than that for type A , and its toxin requires trypsin potentiation.

A vast literature exists on botulism, and the information that follows is no way meant to be complete. For more information, see Smith Sperber, and Sakaguchi.

Distribution of C. Botulinum

This organism is indigenous to soils and waters. In the United

States, type A occurs more frequently in soils in the western states, and type B is found more frequently in the eastern states and in Europe. Soils and manure from various countries have been reported to contain 18% type A and 7%, type B spores. Cultivated soil samples examined showed 7% to contain type A and 6% type B endospores. Type E spores tend to be confined more to waters, especially marine waters. In a study of mud samples from the harbor of Copenhagen, *Pederson* found 84% to contain type E spores, while 26% of soil samples taken from a city park contained the organism. From a study of 684 environmental samples from Denmark, the Farce Islands, Iceland, Greenland, and Bangladesh, 90% of aquatic samples from Denmark and 86% of marine samples from Greenland contained type E. This strain was not found in Danish soils and woodlands, while type B was. Disseminated by water currents and migrating fish, and proliferating in dead aquatic animals and sediments is the type E, a truly aquatic organism which was suggested by *Huss* based on these results. Type E spores have been known for some time to exist in waters off the shores of northern Japan. Prior to 1960. the existence of these organisms in Great Lakes and Gulf Coast waters was not known, but their presence in these waters as well as in the Gulf of Maine and the gulfs of Venezuela and Darien has been established. Ten percent of soil samples tested in Russia were found positive for *C. botulinumn*, with type E strains being predominant. The presence of types A and E spores in 4 of 33 samples was revealed in a study of sediment samples from the Chesapeak Bay area of the U.S. Atlantic Coast. The investigators believed these organisms to be randomly distributed in sediment and to be autochthonous. From Lake Michigan. 9% of fish caught contained type E spores, while from Green Bay 57% of fish contained these organisms. In another study 6.2% of 500 commercially dressed fish taken from Lake Michigan near the Two Rivers, Wisconsin, area yielded type E, while only 0.4% of 427 laboratory-dressed fish were positive. The authors found the type E organisms to exist in relatively low numbers on freshly caught fish but to increase after evisceration. The highest incidence (21%) at the brine tank processing stage was found in a study of the incidence of C. *botulinum* on whitefish chubs is smoking plants, Pace *et al.* The buildup of microorganisms on foods through successive processing stages is discussed more .fully.

It has been suggested that the numbers/g are probably less than one, as to the over all incidence of C. *botulinum* in soils. It appears that the non-proteolytic types are associated more with waters than soils and it may be noted from Table that the discovery of these types occurred between 1960 and 1969. The late recognition is probably a consequence of the low heat resistance of the nonproteolytics, which would be destroyed if specimens were given their usual heat treatment for spore recovery from vegetative cells.

In an outbreak of botulism, the first type F stains were isolated by *Moller* and *Scheibel* from a homemade liver paste incriminated involving one death, on the Danish Island Langeland. Since that time, *Craig* and *Pilcher* isolated type F spores from salmon caught in the Columbia River; *Eklund* and *Povsky* found type F spores in marine sediments taken off the coasts of Oregon and California; Williams-walls isolated two proteolytic strains from crabs collected from the York River in Virginia; and *Midura et al.* isolated the organism from venison jerky in California.

The type G strain was isolated first in 1969 from soil samples in Argentina by *Gimenez* and *Ciccarelli*, and it was isolated more recently from five human corpses in Switzerland. These deaths were not food associated. It has not been incriminated in food-poisoning outbreaks to date. and the reason for this might be due to the fact that this strain produces considerably less neurotoxin than type A. It has been shown that type G produced 40 LD_{50}/ml of toxin in media in which type A normally produces. 10,000 to 1,000,000 LD_{50}/ml, but that under certain conditions the organism could be induced to produce up to 90,000 LD_{50}/ml of medium.

Growth of C. Botulinum Strains

In table causes of botulism in man: which are some of the growth and other characteristics of the strains are summarized. The discussion that follows emphasizes the differences between the proteolytic and nonproteolytic strains irrespective of serologic type. The proteolytic strains, unlike the nonproteolytics, digest casein and produce H_2S. The latter, on the other hand, ferment mannose while the proteolytics do not. The proteolytics and non-proteolytics have been shown to form single groups relative to somatic antigens as evaluated by agglutination. Antibodies from all three of that group is removed by the absorption of antiserum by any one of a group. Proteolytic strains are placed in Group I, non proteolytic E, B, and F are placed in group III, and type G is placed in Group IV

Requiring B vitamins and minerals while amino acids is being complex with the nutritional requirements of these organisms. Synthetic media have been devised that support growth and toxin production of most types. The proteolytic strains tend not to be favoured in their growth by carbohydrates, while the nonproteolytics are. At the same time, the non-proteolytics tend to be more fermentative than the proteolytic types.

A few reports exist, in which proteolytics growth was detected at 10°C though generally they do not grow below 12.5 °*C.* The upper range for types A and proteolytic B, and presumably for the other proteolytic types, is about 50°*C.* On the other hand, the nonproteolytic strains can grow as low as 3.3°C with the maximum about 5 degrees below that for proteolytics. As is noted minimum and maximum temperatures of growth of these organisms are dependent upon the state of other growth parameters, and the minima and maxima noted may be presumed to be at totally optimal conditions relative to pH, a,,, and the like. In a study of the minimum temperature for growth and toxin production by nonproteolytic types B and F in broth and crabmeat both grew and produced toxin at 4°*C* in broth, but in crabmeat growth and toxin production occurred only at 26 °*C*and not at 12°C or lower. At 8° A type G strain did not grew and produced toxin both in broth and crabmeat but rather at 12°C.

The subject of many studies is the minimum pH that permits growth and toxin production of *C. botulinum* strains. It is generally recognized that growth does not occur at or below pH 4.5 and it is this fact that determines the degree of heat treatment given to foods with pH values below this level. Because of the existence of botulinal toxins in some high acid, home-canned foods, this area has been the subject of recent studies. One study reveals that when the product was inoculated with *Aspergillus gracilis*, toxin was produced at pH 4.2 in association with mycelial mat but no growth of types A and B did occurred in tomato juice at pH around 4.8. In another study with the starting pH of tomato juice at 5.8, the pH on the underside of the mold mat increased to 7.0 after 9 days. and to 7.8 after 19 days. The tomato juice was inoculated with type A botulinal spores, a *cladosporium sp* and *a penicillium sp*. The topmost 0.5 ml of product showed pH increases from 5.3 to 6.4 or 7.5 after 9 and 19 days, respectively. One type B strain was shown to produce gas in tomato juice at pH 5.24 after 30 days, and at pH 5.37 after 6 days. In food systems consisting of whole shrimp, shrimp puree, tomato puree, and tomato and shrimp puree acidified to pH 4.2 and 4.6 with acetic or citric acid, none of three type E strains grew or produced toxin at 26° C after 8 weeks. When citric acid but not acetic acid was used to control the pH of culture medium growth and toxin production of a type E strain at pH 4.20 and 26°C in 8 weeks was demonstrated. In general, the pH minima are similar for proteolytic and nonproteolytic strains.

0.94 value seems to be well established which is the minimum a_w that permits growth and toxin production of types A and proeolytic B strains. The minimum for type E is a bit higher around 0.97. While all strains have not been studied equally, it is possible that the other nonproteolytic strains have a minimum similar to that of type E. The way in which a_w is achieved in culture media affects the minimum values obtained. When glycerol is used as humectant, a_w value tend to be a bit lower then when NaCl or glucose is used. Salt at a level of about 10% or 50% sucrose, will inhibit growth of types A and B, and 3-5% salt has been found to inhibit toxin production in smoked fish chubs. When nitrites are present lower levels of salt are required.

The proteolytic strains are much more resistant to heat than the non-proteolytic. Although the values noted in the table suggest that type A is the most heat resistant, followed by proteolytic F and then proteolytic B, these data should only be taken as representative since heating menstra, previous history of strains, and other factors are known to affect heat resistance, as noted. Of those noted, all were determined in phosphate buffer. Among type E, the Alaska and Beluga strains appear to be more heat resistant than others, and in ground whitefish chubs, D 80°C of 2.1 and 4.3 have been reported, while in crabmeat, D 82.2°C of 0.51 and 0.74 have been reported, respectively, for Alaska and Beluga. In one study, mostly with the type E strains 10 or 1.2% of 858 freshly smoked chubs given the same heat treatment were contaminated, while in another study, it was determined that heating smoked whitefish chub to an internal temperature of 180°C for 30 min produced a nontoxigenic product.

With regard to type G, the Argentine and Swiss strains both produce two kinds of spores- heat labile and heat resistant. The former which are destroyed at around 80°C after 10 min. represent about 99% of the spores in a culture of the Swiss strains; while in the Argentine strain only about 1 in 10,000 endospores are heat resistant. The D 230° F of two heat-resistant strains in phosphate buffer was 0.45 to 0.54 min, while for two heat-labile strains, D 180°F was 1.8 to 5.9 min. The more heat-resistant spores of type G have not yet been propagated.

Unlike heat, rediation seems to affect the endospores of proteolytic and nonproteolytic strains similarly, with D values of 1.1 to 2.5 KGy having been reported. However, the D value of one nonproteolytic type F strain was found to be 1.5 kGy, which was similar to the D value for a type A strain; but a proteolytic type F strain produced a D of 1.16 kGy.

Ecology of C. Botulinum Growth

In competition with large numbers of other micro organisms it appears that this organism cannot grow and produce its toxins. Because of heat treatments toxin-containing foods are generally devoid of other types of organisms. In the presence of yeasts, however. C. *botulinum* has been reported to grow and produce toxin at a pH as low as 4.0. While a synergistic effect between clostridia and lactic acid bacteria has been reported on the one hand, lactobacilli will antagonize growth and toxin production-indirect evidence for this is the absence of boutulinal toxins in milk. Yeasts are presumed to produce growth factors needed by the clostridia to grow at low pH, while the lactic acid bacteria may aid growth by reducing the O/R potential or inhibit growth by "lactic antagonism." In one study, type A was inhibited by soil isolates of C. *sporogenes*, *C. perfringen.* and *B. cereus.* An inhibitor was produced by some C. *perfringens* strains that was effective on eleven type A strains, on seven type B proteolytic and one nonproteolytic strains, and on five type E and seven type F strains. It is possible for C. *botulinum* spores to germinate and grow in certain canned foods whose pH is < 4.5 when *Bacillus coagulans is* present. In a study with tomato juice of pH 4.5 inoculated with *B. coagulnns*, the pH increased after 6 days at 3.5°C to 5.07, and to 5.40 after 21 days, thus making it possible for C. *botulinum* to grow. *Kaunter et al.* found that type E strains are inhibited by other nontoxic organisms whose biochemical properties and morphological characteristics were similar to type E. Inhibition of type E strains were shown to be effected these organisms as the produced a bacteriocin-like substance desigenated "boticin E. In a more detailed study, proteolytic A.B, and F strains were found to be resistant to boticin ·E elaborated by a nontoxic type E. but toxic E cells were susceptible. The boticin was found to be sporostatic for nonproteolytic types B. E. F. and nontoxigenic type E.

It is shown that types A and E spores germinate and produce toxin in smoked fish whereas C. botulinum strains supported growth and toxin production of vacuum-packaged foods such as bacon without causing noticeable off odors. Fish inoculated with type A was offensively spoiled, while type F strains caused a less drastic type of spoilage. The proteolytic strains generally produce more offensive by-products than the nonproteolytics. In a study of type E toxin formation and cell growth in turkey rolls incubated at 30°C, type E spores germinated and produced toxin with in 24 h. Toxin outlasted viable cells as the appearance of toxin coincided with cell growth for 2 weeks. In the absence of type E cells it is possible to find type E toxin in foods as suggested by these findings. After 56 days of incubations toxin could not be demonstrated.

A report on the ecology of type F showed that the absence of this strain in mud samples during certain times of the year was associated with the presence of *Bacillus licheniformis* in the samples during these periods, when the bacillus was apparently inhibiting type F strains.

Nature of the Botulinal Toxins

Released upon autolysis and formed within the organism, the neuro toxins are produced by cell, growing unaer optimal conditions, though resting cells have been reported to from toxins as well. The botulinal toxins are the most toxic substances known, with purif ed type A reported to contain about 30,000,000 mouse FD_{19} mg. When grown in cellophane sacs suspended in culture media, higher yields may be attained. The first of these toxins to be purified was type A, which was achieved by C. *lamanna et al.* and byA. *Abrams et al.* , both in 1946. The purification of B. E. and F has been achieved.

With a molecular weight of about 150,000 daltons the neurotoxin as a single poly-peptide chain (unnicked) is synthesized by all botulinal strains, as it appears. The proteolytic strains A. B. and F produce endogenous proteases that cleave the 1,50,000 delton unit to form a heavy chain of about 1,00,000 daltons and a light chain of about 50,000, the two being held together by at least one disulfide bond. The nonproteolytic types B. E, and F release into the environment the 1,50,000 delton chain, which is referred to as *a progenitor* toxin. It is made toxic by treatment with exogenous proteases (nicking) such as trypsin in. Toxicity is lacked and neither is known to possess enzymatic activity, if the double-chained molecule is reduced to individual chains. In culture fluids, botulinal toxins actually exist as complexes with nontoxic culture proteins, which may be considered the natural state of botulinal toxins. The molecular weight of these complexes may be as high as 900.000 daltons.

Being the subject of many studies the botulinal toxin's specific nerve receptor as a prerequisite to its neurotoxic activity must attach to neural tissue. It has been demonstrated that treatment of botulinal toxin with formalin (toxoiding) results in the destruction of receptor-binding activity. The gangliosides have been shown to react with botulinal toxin and reduce its in vivo toxicity. It appears that for the binding of toxin, two sialic acid residues on the inner galactose of the gangliosides are essential, and an additional sialic acid at the nonreducing end of the ganglioside also aids toxin binding. The release of acetylcholine from cholinergic nerve endings is presynaptically blocked when toxin exerts its effects after being once attached.

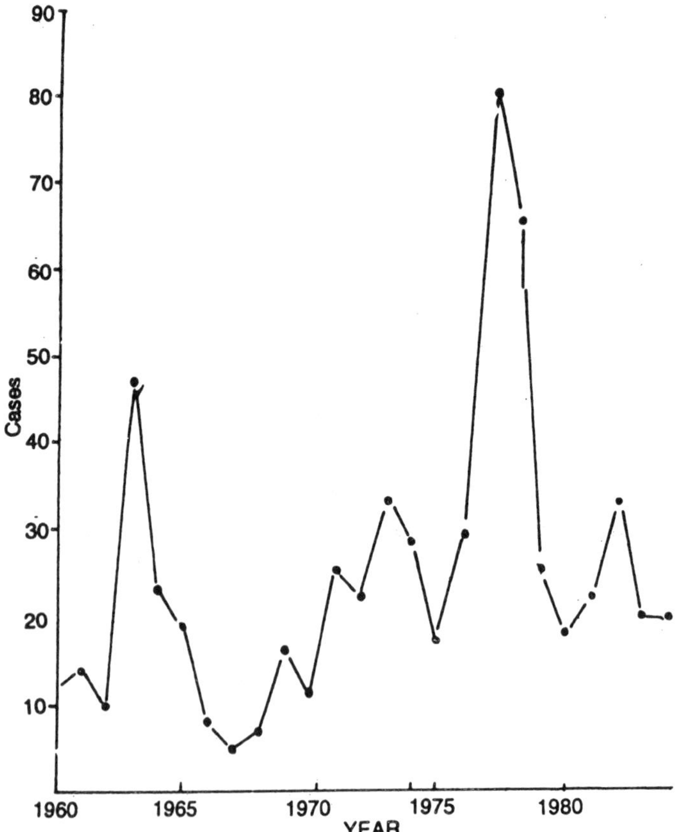

Fig. 9.2. Reported cases of food-borne botulism in the United States for the period 1960-84.

Type A toxin has been reported to be more lethal than B or E. Type B has been reported to have associated with it a much lower case mortality than type A, and case recoveries from type B have occurred even when appreciable amounts of toxin could be demonstrated in the blood.

By either parenteral or oral administration of the toxins, symptoms of botulism can be produced. Both through the respiratory mucous membranes as well as through the walls as the stomach and intestines they may be absorbed into the blood stream. The toxins are not completely inactivated by the proteolytic enzymes of the stomach, and, indeed, those produced by nonproteolytics may be activated. It has been shown that the high molecular weight complexes or the progenitor possess higher resistance to acid and pepsin. While the derivative toxin was rapidly inactivated, the progenitor was shown to be resistant to rat intestinal juice in vitro. The progenitor was more stable in the stomach of rats. Similar findings were made *by Ohishi et al* who showed that progenitor toxins of nonproteolytics were more toxic orally in mice than the dissociated toxic components of the derived toxins. The toxin activity as it appears is provided protection by the nontoxic component of the progenitor. After botulinal toxins are absorbed into the bloodstream, they enter the peripheral nervous system where they affect nerves as noted above.

Unlike the staphylococcal enterotoxins and heat-stable toxins of other food-borne pathogens, the botulinal toxins are heat-sensitive and may be destroyed by heating at 80°C (176°F), for 10 min- or boiling temperatures for a few min.

The Sdult Botulism Syndrome—Incidence and Vehicle Foods

Anywhere between 12 and 72 h later symptoms of botulism may develop after the ingestion of toxin-containing foods. Even longer incubation periods are not unknown. Symptoms consist of nausea, vomiting. fatigue. dizziness and headache; dryness of skin. mouth. and throat: constipation. lack of fever. paralysis of muscles. double vision and finally, respiratory failure and death. The duration of the illness is from 1 to 10 or more days, depending upon host resistance and other factors. The rate being generally lower in European countries than United States, the mortality rate varies between 30 and 65%. All symptoms are caused by the exotoin, and treatment consists of administering specific antisera as early as possible. Although it is assumed that the tasting of toxin- containing foods allows for absorption from the oral cavity. *Lamanna et al.* found that mice and monkeys are more susceptible to the toxins when administered by stomach tube than by exposure to the mouth. Irreversibly to nerves is attached by the botulinal toxins which are neurotoxins and prognosis is brightened with the early treatment by use of antisera.

Types A_2 B toxins where the causes of most cases of botulism in the United States in which the vehicle foods were identified were traced to home canned vegetable, as *prior* to 1963. In almost 70% of the 640 cases reported for the prior to 1899-1967, the vehicle food was not identified. Among the 640 cases, 17.8% were associated with vegetables, 4.1%, fruits, 3.6%, fish, 2.2%, condiments, 1.4%, meats and poultry, and 1.1 % for all others. Reported food-borne cases in the United States for the years 1960-84 are shown in Figure. The three largest U.S. outbreaks involved fifty-eight, thirty-four, and twenty-eight cases each. In 1977, fifty eight cases occurred is a restaurant in Pontiac, Michigan, following consumption of a hot sauce prepared from home-canned jalapeno peppers. No deaths occurred, and type B toxin was identified. The outbreak of thirty-four cases occurred in 1978 in New Mexico, with potato salad or bean salad incriminated. The outbreak of twenty-eight cases occurred in 1963 in the state of Illinois, with sauteed onions as the apparent food source. The total number of cases from all sources in the United States rately exceeds 50 per year, with the highest 10 year period being 1930-3 9, when 384 cases were reported from noncommercial foods. Between 1899 and 1963,1561 cases were reported from noncommercial foods, while 219 were reported from commercial foods between 1906 and 1963, with 24 in 1963 alone.

304% or 75% occurred in Japan of 404 verified cases of type E botulism through 1963, prior to 1951 no outbreak of botulism was recorded in Japan. For the period May 1951 through January 1960, 166 cases were recorded with 58 deaths for a mortality rate of 35%. Most of these outbreaks were traced to a home-prepared food called *izushi*, a preserved food consisting of raw fish, vegetables, cooked rice, malted rice (*koji*), and a small amount of salt and vinegar. Holded for 3 weeks or !onger to permit lactic acid fermentation, this preparation is packed tightly in a wooden tub equipped wifh a lid. The growth of anaerobes is thus allowed during this time when the O/R potential is lowered.

Prior to 1930 and during 1899 to 1973 sixty two out breaks of botulism resulting from commercially canned foods were recorded. Between 1941 and 1982, seven outbreaks occurred in the United States. involving commercially canned foods in metal containers, with seventeen cases and eight deaths. Three of these outbreaks were caused by type A and the remainder by type E. In five of the outbreaks. can leakage or under processing occurred. Canned mushrooms have been incriminated in several botulism outbreaks. A study in 1973 and 1974 turned up thirty cans of mushrooms containing botulinal toxin (twenty-nine were type B). An additional eleven cans contained viable spores of C. *botu/inurn* without preformed toxin. The capacity of the commercial mushroom (*Agaricus hisporus*) to support the growth of inoculated spores of *C. botulinium* was studied by *Sugiyama* and *Yang*. Following inoculation of various parts of mushrooms, they were sealed with plastic film and incubated. Toxin was detected as early as 3-4 days later, when products were incubated at 20°C. The type A strains appeared to be more active than type B, even though type B strains appear more often in canned products. The oxygen is apparently consumed by the fresh mushrooms for the respiration at a fester rate than it entered the film though the plastic film used to wrap the inoculated mushrooms for gas exchange. No toxin was detected in products stored at refrigerator temperatures.

One of the recorded outbreaks of botulism (five cases with one death) due to type F involved homemade liver paste. The only U.S. outbreak occurred in 1966 from home-prepared venison jerky, with three clinical cases.

Foods that are improperly handled or given insufficient heat treatments to destroy botulinal spores are the causes of the greatest hazards of botulism which as it is quite clear, comes from home prepared and home canned foods. Such foods are often consumed without heating. The best preventative measure is the heating of suspect foods to boiling temperatures for a few minutes, which is sufficient to destroy the neurotoxins.

Infant Botulism

Infant botulism has since been confirmed in most states in the United States and in some other countries though first recognized as such in California in 1976. Upon germination botulism is ingested is the intestinal tract, toxin is synthesized, while in infant botulism viable botulinal spores are ingested and in the adult form, preformed toxins are ingested. While it is possible that in some adults under special conditions botulinal endospores may germinate and produce small quantities of toxin, the colonized intestinal tract does not favour spore germination. Infants over one year of age tend not to be affected by this syndrome because of the establishment of a more normal intestinal flora. The disease is mild in some infants while in others it can be rather severe. During the acute phase of the disease high numbers of spores are found in the feces of infants and as recovery progresses. number of organisms abate.

By use of the mouse lethality test this syndrome is diagnosed by demonstrating botulinal toxins in infant stoods. Since *Clostridium difficle* produces mouse-lethal toxins in the intestinal tract of infants, it is necessary to differentiate between these toxins and that of *C. hotulinum*.

Infants get viable spores from infant foods and possibly from their environment. Vehicle foods are those that do not undergo heat processing to destroy endospores, and the two most common products are syrup and honey. Of ninety samples of honey examined, nine contained viable spores. Six of these had been fed to babies who developed infant botulism. Of the nine, seven were type B and two were type A. Of 910 infant foods from ten product classes, only two classes were positive or sproes- honey and corn syrup. Of 100 honey samples, two contained type A, while eight of forty corn syrup samples yielded type B. Reported cases in the United States through 1984 are shown in figure. Type A and B toxins equally are involved is the sixty one cases for 1982, which occurred among infants aged 2-48 weeks.

Animal models for the study of this syndrome involve 18-11 day old mice and 7-13 days old rats. In the mouse model, botulinal toxin was found in the lumen of the large intestine, and it was not associated with the ileum. The sensitivity of these animal models is noted.

Bacillus Cereus Gastroenteritis

Since at least 1906, *Bacillus cerr is;* an aerobic, sporeforming rod normally present in soil, dust and water, has been associated with food poisoning in Europe. Among the first to report this syndrome with precision was *U Plazikowski*. His findings were confirmed by several other European workers in the early 1950s. The first documented outbreak in the United States occurred in 1969, while the first in Great Britain occurred in 1971.

The minimum growth temperature of this bacterium ranges around 10°C-12° C and a maximum of 48°C-50° C and its growth has been demonstrated over the pH range 4.9-9.3. Its spores possess a resistance to heat typical of other mesophiles. It grows rapidly in foods held in the 30°-40°C range.

B Cereus Toxins

The following toxins and extracellular products like lecithinase, proteases, hemolysin, B-lactamase, mouse lethal toxin, cereolysin, emetic enterotoxin, and diarrheagenic enterotoxin are produced by food poisoning strains. The enterotoxins are responsible for the two food-poisoning syndromes caused by this organism.

Vascular permeability in the skin of rabbits is induced by the diarrheagenic toxin, elicits fluid accumulation in the rabbit ileal loop, and causes diarrhea in Rhesus monkey. It has been shown to be a protein of molecular weight' of about 50.000 with an isoelectric point of 4.9. Its production is favoured by low dissolved 0_2, and most is produced during the logarithmic phase of growth. It is heat labile and sensitive to trypsin and pronase. Produced over the temperature range 18-43°C and its production is favoured over the pH range 6.0-8.5, with the optimum between 7.0-7.5°*C. perfringens*, can be separated from phospholipase and the heat liable cereolysin and unlike the enterotoxin, it is a vegetative growth metabolit. The purified toxin shows mice lethality. It induces diarrhea apparently by stimulating the adenylate cyclase-CAMP system.

Being heat and pH-stable and having a molecular weight of 5,000 daltons, the emetic (vomiting type) toxin is distinctly different from the diarrheagenic. It is insensitive to trypsin and pebsin. The emetic toxin strains grow over the range 15°-50°C, with an optimum between 35°-40°C. While the emetic syndrome is most often associated with rice dishes, growth of the emetic toxin strains in rice is not favoured in general over other *B. cereus* strains, although higher populations and more extensive germination have been noted in this product.

Diarrheal Syndrome

Being rather mild, this syndrome symptoms develops within 8-16 h more commonly within 12-13 h and lasts for 6-12, consists mainly of nausea (vomiting being rare). Cramplike abdominal pains, tenesmus, and watery stools. Fever is generally absent. The similarity between this syndrome and that of C. *perfringens* food poisoning has been noted.

Vehicle fib consist of cereal dishes that contain corn and corn starch, mashed potatoes, vegetables, minced meat, liver sausage, meat loaf, milk, cooked meat. Indonesian rice dishes, puddings, soups, and others. Reported outbreaks between 1950 and 1978 have been summarized by *Gilbert*, and when plate counts on leftover foods were recorded, they ranged from 10^5 to 9.5×10^8/g, with many in the 10^7-10^8/g range. The first well-studied outbreaks were those investigated by *Hauge*, which were traced to vanilla sauce, and the counts ranged from 2.5 × 10' to 1 × 10^8/g. From meat loaf involved in a U.S. outbreak in 1969, 7 × 10^7/g were found. Serovars found in diarrheal outbreaks include types 1, 6, 8, 9, 10, and 12. Serovars 1, 8, and 12 have been associated with this as well as with the emetic syndrome.

Emetic Syndrome

Besides, as described above, this from of B. *cereus* food poisoning is more severe and acute, the incubation period ranging from 1 to 6 h, with 2 to 5 being most common. Its similarity to the staphylococcal food-poisoning syndrome has been noted. It is often associated with fried or boiled rice dishes. In addition to these, pasteurized cream, spaghetti, mashed potatoes, and vegetable sprouts have been incriminated. Outbreaks have been reported from Great Britain, Canada, Australia, the Netherlands, Finland, Japan, and the United States. In 1975, the first U.S. outbreak with mashed potatoes as the vehicle food was reported.

The numbers of organisms necessary to cause this syndrome seem to be higher than for the diarrheal syndrome, with numbers as high as 2 *x* 10^9/ g having been found, *B.cereus* serovars associated with the emetic syndrome include 1, 3, 4, 5, 8, 12, and 19.

Salmonella and Escherichia

Members of genus *Salmonella* are the most important among the gram negative rods known to cause food-borne gastroenteritis. This syndrome and those caused by *Escherichia* coli are presented in this chapter. The general incidence of these organisms in foods is discussed.

Salmonellosis

Indistinguishable from *E. coli* under the microscope or on ordinary nutrient media is the *Salmonellae* which are small, gram-negative, non-sporing rods. They are widely distributed in nature, with man and animals being their primary reservoirs. *Salmonella* food poisoning results from the ingestion of foods containing appropriate strains of this genus in significant numbers.

Salmonella's species and strains may be presumed to be pathogenic for man, and the disease syndromes divide themselves into several distinct clinical types. Typhoid fever, caused by *S. typhi*, *is* the most severe of all disease caused by this genus and a classic example of an enteric fever. In the same general category are the paratyphoid fevers caused by S. *paratyphi A*, *S. paratyphi* B, and others. The paratyphoid syndrome tends to be milder than that of typhoid. In the latter, the period of incubation is longer, a higher body temperature is produced, the organisms may be isolated from the blood and sometimes urine, and the mortality rate is higher. The etiologic agents of the typhoid and paratyphoid syndromes oftenly have positive blood cultures in them which are specifically pathogenic for man.

Gastroenteritis is the third disease entity caused by salmonellae. This syndrome differs from the enteric fevers in having an incubation period as short as 8 h, generally negative blood cultures, and a lack of host specificity among the numerous serovars (serotypes) capable of causing this disease. 'The largest number of gastroenteritis or food poisoning are identified or the basis of antigenic analysis through some of them can be identified on the basis of biochemical and cultural characteristics.

Based on host predilections the salmonellae may be divided into three groups, primarily adapted to man-the typhoid and paratyphoid agents are the prime examples of this group; primarily adapted to particular animal hosts-included in this group are S. *choleraesuis* and *serovars* of S. *enteritidis* such as S. *pullorum*, *S gallinasum*, *S.dublin and* so on; and unadapted this group includes over 2,000 serovars that may cause illness in man and other animals and generally do not show any host preference. Primarily members of this group causes food-borne gastroenteritis.

Salmonellae is divided into five subgenera by a more recent scheme as according to it, all but about 200 of the 2,000 or so serovars are placed in subgenus 1, which is characterized. largely, as follows : ONPG, lactose, and gelatinase negative; dulcitol and mucate positive: no growth in the presence of KCN; and natural habitat or warm-blooded animals.

Classification of Salmonella

The original work of *Kauffmann* and *White* is based upon the classification of these organisms by antigenic analysis and is often referred to as the Kauffmann White Scheme. Classification by this scheme makes use of both somatic and flagellar antigens. Somatic antigens are designated 0 antigens, while flagellar antigens are designated H antigens. The K antigens are capsular antigens that lie at the periphery of the cell and prevent access of anti agglutinins (antibodies) to their homologous somatic antigens. The K antigen differs from ordinary 0 antigens in being destroyed by heating for 1 h at 60°C and by dilute acids and phenol. The fact that each antigen possesses its own genetically determined specificity is based upon the use of H, 0 and K antigens as the basis of classification of *Salmonella* spp.

According to similarities in content of one or More 0 antigens species and serovars are placed in groups designated A, B. C and so on, when classification is made by use of antigenic patterns. Thus, S *hirschfeldii*, *S. choleraesuis*, *S. oranienberg*, and *S. montevideo* are placed in Group C, because they all possess O antigens 6 and 7 in common. S *new port* is placed in Group C_2 due to its possession of O antigens K and 8. For further classification, the flagellar or H antigens are employed. These antigens are of two types : specific phase or phase 1. and group phase or phase 2. Phase 1 antigens are shared with only a few other species or varieties of *Salmonella*, while phase 2 may be more widely distributed among several species. Organisms in only one phase or in both flagellar phases may be consisted by any given culture of *Salmonella*. The H antigens of phase 1 are designated with small letters, and those of phase 2 are designated by arabic numerals. 6 and 7 refer to O antigens, c to phase-I flagellar antigens, and 1 and 5 to phase-2 flagellar antigens. Thus, the complete antigenic analysis of S. *choleraesiun* is as follows 6, 7, c, 1, 5. *Scrovars* is being referred to by *Salmonella* subgroups of this type. With a relatively small number of O, phase-1, and phase-2 antigens, a large number of permutations are possible, allowing for the possibility of a large number of serovars. The number increases yearly, though over 2,000 *Salmonella* Serovars are presently known.

S london. *S. miami*, *S richmond*, and so on, are the names of a serovar which is named after the place where it was first isolated as under the system, naming of *Salmonella* is now done by international agreement. Prior to the adoption of this convention, species and subtypes were named in various ways- for example, S *typhimurium* as the cause of typhoid fever in mice. Most food-borne salmonellae are serovars of S. *enteritidis*.

Distribution of Salmonella

The intestinal tract of animals such as birds, reptiles, farm animals, man, and occasionally insects are the primary habitat of *Salmonella spp*. Although their primary habitat is the intestinal tract, they may be found in other parts of the body from time to time. As intestinal forms, these organisms are excreted in feces from which they may be transmitted by insects and other living creatures to a large number of places. As intestinal forms, they may also be found in water, especially polluted water. These organisms are once again shed through fecal matter with a continuation of the cycle when polluted water and foods that have been contaminated by insects or by other means are consumed by man and other animals. The augmentation of this cycle through the international shipment of animal products and feeds is in large part responsible for the present world-wide distribution of salmonellosis and its consequent problems.

TABLE 10.1 ANTIGENIC STRUCTURE OF SOME OF THE MORE COMMON SALMONELLAE

			H antigens	
Group	*Species/serovars*	*0 antigens]*	*phase 1*	*phase 2*
A	*S. paratyphi A*	1, 2, 12	a	(1, 5)
B	*S. schottmuelleri*	1, 4, (5), 12	b	1, 2
	S. typhimurium	1, 4, (5), 12	i	1, 2
C_1	*S. hirschfeldii*	6, 7, (*Vi*)	c	1, 5
	S. choleraesuis	6,7	(c)	1, 5
	S. oranienburg	6,7	m, t	—
	S. montevideo	6,7	g, m, s (p)	(1, 2, 7)
C_2	*S. newport*	6, 8	e, h	1, 2
D	*S. typhi*	9, 12, (Vi)	d	—
	S. enteritidis	1, 9, 12	g, m	(1, 7)
	S. gallinarum	1, 9, 12	—	—
E_1	*S. anatum*	3, 10	e, h	1, 6

Salmonella spp. incidence in various parts of animals has been shown to vary though they have been recovered from a large number of different animals. In a study of slaughter- house pigs, Kampelmacher found these organisms in spleen, liver bile, mesenteric and portal lymph nodes, diaphragm, and pillar, as well as in feces. A higher incidence was found in lymph nodes than in feces. The frequent occurrence of *Salmonella spp.* among susceptible animal populations is due in part to the contamination of *Salmonella-free* animals by animals within the population that are carriers of these organisms or are infected by them. A carrier is defined as a person or an animal that repeatedly sheds *Salmonella* spp., usually through feces, without showing any signs or symptoms of the disease. An intestinal carrier rate of 3-5% was found by *Sadler* and *Corstvet* upon examining poultry at slaughter. During and immediately after slaughter, carcass contamination from fecal matter may be expected to occur. In an examination of the rumen contents of healthy cattle after slaughter, *Grau* and *Brownile* found 45% to contain salmonellae. Some 57% of samples taken from the environment of' cattle in transit to slaughter were positive for these organisms. From 53.1 to 61.9% of inspected broiler carcasses have been found to be contaminated with *Salmonella spp*. Acquired from the environment via insects, rodents, feeds, other animals, and man as these organisms appear not to be normal flora as poultry.

The contamination of eggs and egg products is equally serious. Mostly S *typhinurium* contaminates 2.6-70% of eggs as indicated by reports from various countries. Duck eggs have been reported to have an even higher contamination rate, reaching 20%. Another common source of these organisms to animal populations is animal feed. In terms of the overall control of salmonellosis perhaps this source is the most important as felt by some investigators. In a study of animal reeds in England for the years 1958-1960, *Taylor* isolated *Sabnonella* serovars from meat and bone products 855 times. from mixtures. mashes, and the liked 58 times,; from fish products 100 times; and from vegetable products 1· times. *S. senftenberg* was isolated most frequently, followed by *S. anatum* and *S. cubana*. *S. senftenberg* has been shown to be the most heat-resistant of all *Salmonella* serovars, and its higher incidence in animal feeds may be due to the fact that most others are destroyed by heat in the processing of these products. *Taylor* found a very large number of different serovars in bile spleen, and lymph glands, of slaughter animals. Among the many serovars reported by this author. S *dublin* was found to be associated with bovines more than with any other animals. The presence of salmonellae in animal feeds has been shown by many investigators.

Eggs are the most common food vehicles of salmonellosis in man, poultry meat, and meat products. *Steele* and *Gallon* found in a study of sixty-one outbreaks of *Salmonella* food poisoning for the period 1963-65 that eggs and egg products accounted for twenty three, chicken and turkey for sixteen, beef and pork for eight, ice cream for three, potato salad for two and other miscellaneous foods for nine. The most common food vehicles involved in 12,836 cases of salmonellosis from thirty-seven states in 1967 were beef, turkey, eggs and egg products, and milk. Of 7,907 salmonellae isolations made by CDC in 1966, 70%, were from raw and processed food sources. Turkey and chicken sources accounted for 42%. Of the food borne disease outbreaks with known etiology traced to poultry for the period 1972-74, 44% were salmonellae. In a study of the incidence of salmonellae in sixty-nine packs of raw chicken pieces, 34.8% were positive and eleven serovars were represented with S. *muenchen* being the most common. From a study in \ nezuela, forty-one of forty-five chicken carcasses studied yielded salmonellae consisting of eleven serovars with *S anatum* being most frequently isolated. The wide distribution of these organisms among slaughter animals makes all meats potential sources as poultry products are important sources of salmonellosis outbreak. Even when such meats are cooked sufficiently to destroy salmonellae, in the raw state they may still serve as sources to other foods such as vegetables, salads, and the like by cross contamination.

Pork sausage is most likely to contain viable salmonellae which is among the fresh food item in a typical supermarket. A study of forty producing plants in 1969 revealed an overall incidence of 28.6% positive samples of 566 examined. Ten years later, the overall incidence of positive samples had decreased to 12.4% of 603 examined. The incidence remained the same in seven decreased in twenty and increased in thirteen of the forty matched plants. 17 of 247 examined salmonellae were found in commercially prepared and packaged foods. Among the contaminated foods were cake mixes, cookie doughs, dinner rolls, and cornbread mixes.

Foods of this type usually become contaminated from infected eggs, bulk egg products. or by contact with rodents, flies, or even man. Salmonellae have been found in coconut meal, salad dressing, mayonnaise, milk, and many other foods. None of plant origin yielded salmonellae as found from study of health foods, but from two of three lots of beef liver powder from the same manufacturer were isolated S, *minnesota*, *S anatum*, and *S. derby*. Salmonellae may be found in pet foods and on pets, especially pet turtles.

Throughout the world of the various seravors in food borne outbreaks, invariably the most commonly encountered is *S typhimurium*. Of 1,713 serovars isolated from foods during 1963-65. *Steele* and Galton found the following 5 to be the most common : S *infantis*, *S. oranienberg*, *S. lyphimurium*, *S. montevideo*, and S. *heidelberg*. In general, the incidence of *Salmonella* serovars in foods closely parallels their incidence in man and animals. On 1956-60 in England and Wales, the 7 most frequently isolated from man were as follows : S. *typhimurium*, *S. heidelberg*, *S. enteritidis*, *S*, *newsport*, *S thompson*, *S. saint Paul* and S *anatum*. For the period April 1962 to April 1963, the 9 most prevalent serovars identified from animal sources in the United States were: S *typhimurium*, *S. heidelbeig*, *S. anatum*, *S choleraesuis*, *S infantis*, *S*, *montevideo*, *S. derby*, *S.*

saintpaul, and *S. oranienberg*. Of 17 serovars isolated from 603 samples of fresh pork sausage in 1979, the 3 most frequently found were S. *derby*, *S anatum*, and S. *agona*. The 5 most frequently isolated from human sources in 1972 and 1980 are listed in Table. In figuge, for the period 1955 through 1982 in the United States is depicted the pattern of human isolation of salmonellae. Forty percent of the 34,766 reported cases for 1982 affected children < 5 years of age. By the consumption of improperly pasturized and raw milk increase in isolations from adults is accounted for in large part. The specific serovar associated with raw milk consumption (including certified raw milk) is *S. dublin*. Over the past 5 years or so, persons from whom this serovar was isolate was so old and had underlying illness requiring longer periods of hospitalization.

Decline in isolation of S. *thompson* and increase in *S. agona* isolates was noted among trends in the United States and Canada over the period 1969-77. The latter was first isolated from fish meal, and while no isolations were made in 1969, 1,461 were made in 1976. S. *eastbourne* is frequently isolated from an contaminated chocalate and example of incidence of some serovars which tends to be associated with single products. *Bryan* has noted the association of some serovars with animal sources. Frequently isolated from chickens and turkeys are .S. *heidelberg* and S. *saint-paul;* from cattel *S. dublin; S. johannesburg* from chickens and S. *choleraesuis* from swine.

From fifty two outbreaks in United States for the year 1971-83, were examined the antimicrobial resistant salmonellae.

TABLE 10.2. THE MOST FREQUENTLY ISOLATED SALMONELLAE FROM HUMANS IN THE UNITED STATES IN 1972 AND 1980.

	% of isolates	
Serovars	***1972***	***1980***
S. typhimurium	25.8	34.8
S. heidelberg	5.6	6.6
S. enteritidis	6.5	6.3
S. newport	8.4	5.5
S infantis	6.3	4.8

The case fatahly rate was higher for persons infected with antimicrobial-resistant strains than those with anitmicrobial sensitive strains, and food animals were the source of eleven of sixteen resistant and only six of thirteen sensitive strains. Raw milk was the source of resistant strains in four outbreaks and beef in another. S *typhimurium* were the resistant serovars is seven outbreaks and in two outbreaks is *S. newport*.

Growth and Destruction of Salmonellae

Well within 24 h at about 37°C, these organisms are typical of other gram-negative bacteria in being able to grow on a large number of culture media and produce visible colonies. They are generally unable to ferment lactose sucrose, or salicin, although glucose and certain other monosaccharides are fermented, with the production of gas. Although they normally utilize amino acids as N-sources, in the case of S. *typhimurium*, nitrate, nitrite, and NH, will serve as sole sources of nitrogen. Some serovars can utilize this sugar, though lactose fermentation is not usual for these organisms.

Being bactericidal with values above 9.0 and below 4.0, the pH for optimum growth is around neutrality. A minimum growth pH of 4.05 has been recorded for some (with HCI and citric acids), but depending upon the acid used to lower pH, the minimum may be as high as 5.5. The effect of acid used to lower pH on minimum growth is presented in Table. Aeration was found to favour growth at the lower pH values. The parameters of pH, a_w, nutrient content, and temperature are all interrelated for salmonellae as they are for most bacteria. For best growth, the salmonellae require pH between 6.6 and 8.2. The lowest temperatures at which growth has been reported are 5.3°C for S. *heidelberg* and 6.2°C for S. *typhimurium*. Several authors have reported that temperatures around 46°C is optimum to be the open limit for growth. Regarding available moisture, growth inhibition has been reported for a_w values below 0.94 in media with neutral pH, with higher a_w values being required as pH is decreased toward growth minima.

Brine above 9% is reported to be bactericidals as *Salmonellae* are unable to tolerate high salt concentrations, unlike the *staphylococel*. Nitrite is effective, with the effect being greatest at the lower pH values. This suggests that the inhibitory effect of this compound is referable to the undissociated HNO_2 molecule. The survival of *Salmonella spp. in* mayonnaise was studied by Lerche, who found that they were destroyed in this product if the pH was below 4.0. Destruction may be possible within 24 h for low number of cells but several days may be required if level as contamination is high. *S. thomption* and S. *typhimurium* were found to be more resistant to acid destruction than *S. senftenberg*.

TABLE 10.3. MINIMUM pH AT WHICH SALMONELLAE WOULD INITIATE GROWTH UNDER OPTIMUM LABORATORY CONDITIONS.

Acid	pH
Hydrochloric	4.05
Citric	4.05
Tartaraic	4.10
Gluconic	4.20
Fumaric	4.30
Malic	4.30
Lactic	4.40
Succinic	4.60
Glutaric	4.70
Adipic	5.10
Pimelic	5.10
Acetic	5.40
Propionic	5.50

At milk pasteurization temperatures all *Salmsonellae* are readitly destroyed with respect to heat destruction. Thermal D values for the destruction of S. *senftenberg* 775W under various conditions are given. Shimpton *et al.* reported that *S. sent enberg* 775W required 2.5 min for a 10^4-10^5 reduction in numbers at 54.4°C in liquid whole egg. This strain is the most heat-resistant of all salmonellac serovars. The above treatment of liquid whole egg has been shown to produce *a Salmonella-free* product and destroy egg alpha-amylase. As a means of determining the adequacy of heat pasteurization of liquid egg (compare with the pasteurization of milk and the enzyme phosphatase it has been suggested to use the alpha-amylase test). In a study on the heat resistance of S. *senftenberg* 775W *Ng et ul.* found this strain to be more heat sensitive in the log phase than in the stationary phase of growth. These authors also found that cells grown at 44° were more heat resistant than those grown at either 15° or 35°C.

It has been found by Beloian and Schlosser that baked foods reaching a temperature of 16°F or higher is the slowest heating region can be considered *Salmonella* free because *Salmonella* destroys in baked foods. These authors employed S *senftenberg* 775W at a concentration of 7,000-10,000 cells/ml placed in reconstituted dried egg. With respect to the heat destruction of this strain in poultry, it is recommended that internal temperatures of at least 160°F be attained. S. *typhimurium* has been found to be more resistant to dry heat than S. *senftemberg* 775W, though it has been reported to be thirty times more heat resistant than the former. These authors tested dry heat resistance in milk chocolate.

Rogers and *Gunderson* investigated the destruction of S. *pullorum* in turkeys and found that it required 4 h and 55 min to destroy an initial inoculum of 115,000,000 in 10-11-1b, turkeys with an internal temperature of 160°F, and for 18-lb. turkeys with an initial inoculu m of 320,000,000 organisms, 6 h and 20 min were required for destruction. The salmonellae are quite sensitive to ionizing radiation, with doses of 0.5 to 0.75 Mrads being sufficient to eliminate them from most foods and feed. It has been reported that decimal reduction dose range from 0.04-0.07 Mrad for *Salmonella Spp.* in frozen eggs. In a study *by Ley et al* the effect of various foods on the radio sensitivity of *Salmonellae* is shown. These investigators found that for frozen whole egg, 0.5 Mrad gave a 10^7 reduction in the numbers of *S. typhimurium*, while 0.65 Mrad was required to give a 10^5 reduction in frozen horsemeat, between 0.5-0.75 Mrad for a 10^5-10^8 reduction in bone meal, and only 0.45 Mrad to give a 108 reduction of S *typhimuriunn* in desiccated coconut.

When inoculated into dry milk, cocoa powder, poultry feed, meat, and bone meal *S. montevideo* was found to be more resistant than *S. heidelberg* in dry foods at a_w 0.43 and 0.52 than at a_w 0.75.

The Salmonella Food-Poisoning Syndrome

The ingestion of foods that contain significant numbers of non-host specific species or serotypes of the genus *Salmonella* causes this syndrome. Its symptoms usually develop in 12-14 h, from the time of ingestion of food, though shorter and longer times have been reported. The symptoms consist of nausea, vomiting, abdominal pain (not as severe as with staphylococcal food poisoning), headache, chills, and diarrhea. These symptoms are usually accompanied by prostration, muscular weakness, faintness, moderate fever, restlessness, and drowsiness. Symptoms usually persist for 2-3 days. The average mortality rate is 4.1%, varying from during the first year of life, to 2% between the first and fiftieth year, and 15% in persons over fifty. *S, choleraesuis* has been reported to produce the highest mortality rate-2 1%, among the different species of *Salmonella*. 5% of patients may become carriers of the organisms upon recovery from this disease, while these organisms generally disappear rapidly from the intestinal tract.

For salmonellosis, numbers cells on the order of 10^7-16^9 are generally necessary. That outbreaks may occur in which relatively low numbers of cells are found has been noted. From three outbreaks, numbers of cells found were as low as 100/100 g (S. *eastbourne* in chocolate) to 15,000/g (*S. cubana* in a carmine dye solution). In general, minimum numbers for gastroenteritis range between 10^5-10^6/g for S, *barilly* and S. *newport*, to 10^9-10^{10} for S. *pullorum*.

Salmonella Toxins

Two toxins-an enterotoxin and a cytotoxin, is involved in the pathogenesis of salmonellosis as it appears. In 1975 *Koupal* and *Deibel* demonstrates the enterotoxin for the first time. Using *S. enteritidis* and the suckling mouse assay, a difficult-to-separate cell envelope-associated toxin was prepared, producing results in the suckling mouse assay similar to those elicited by the heat-stable and heat-labile enterotoxins of *E. coli.* Inconsistent results were given by loop assays including the infant rabbit. Employing S. *typhimurium*, an enterotoxin was produced in BHI broth and a 2% Casamino acids medium and measured by the rabbit ileal loop assay. These two media were found to be the best of several that were tried. A toxin that induced rabbit skin permeability and acted in a manner similar to the enterotoxins of *Vibrio* cholerae and *E. coli* was recovered from salmonellae by another group of researchers in the meanwhile. The toxin in question produced positive responses in the rabbit ileal loop assay. It was later shown that the vascular permeability factor could be neutralized with monospecific cholera antitoxin, and that the toxin induced elongation in,Chinese hamster ovary (CHO) cells similar to the toxin of V *cholerae. Koo* and *Peterson* in their attempts to obtain larger quantities of *Salmonellae* enterotoxin, studied the influence of nutritional factors and found that glycerol, biotin, and Mn' enhanced production, while glucose was found to be a poor carbon source. It was later determined that more enterotoxin is produced during the stationary phase of growth, at pH 6-7 or higher, at 37°C, and with increased aeration. The enterotoxin was found to be heat-labile at 100°C, to have a molecular weight < 110,000 daltons, and an isoelectric point of approximately 4.3-4.8. Mitomycin C added 3 h after inoculation increased the quantities in culture filtrates due to bacteriophage induction and subsequent cell lysis. The weight of the evidence suggests that the salmonellae toxin described above is an enterotoxin that acts in a manner similar to those of *E. coli* by elevating intestinal cAMP Unlike the *E. coli* enterotoxins, it is produced in much ower quantities and is more difficult to separate from producing cells. In biologic and antigenic characteristics, the salmonellae ei rotoxin is quite similar to cholera toxin (CT). Heated CT (procholeragenoid) administered parenterally protects against loop fluid responses by viable salmonellae cells.

The intestinal toxicity associated with salmonellosis was not explained while the enterotoxin described above was shown to affect the adenylate cyclase system and fluid accumulation in animal models was induced. Although the enterotoxins of E. *coli* induce fluid accumulation, tissue toxicity that is normally associated with shigellosis and salmonellosis does not occur. Otherwise, we can say that more than the enterotoxin mediated *syndromes*, the pathogenes is of salmonellosis that of shigellosis. This led Koo *et al.* to examine salmonelleae extracts for a cytotoxin. Cytotoxin activity of salmonellae extracts were actually is shown first by some uropean workers as early as 1962. When extracts from salmonellae were added to isolated rabbit intestinal epithelial cells and to Vero cells, protein synthesis was inhibited. These investigators presented evidence to support the view that the cellular damage that occurs to the intestinal mucosa during salmonellosis is caused by a cytotoxin. Additional tissue damage can be brought about by the intestinal mucosa which is more easily invaded by the infecting organisms ifsonce damaged. While the pathogenesis of shigellosis and salmonellosis appear to be closely related, more tissue destruction occurs in the former than in the latter. This may be due to an additional toxin-one that is more destructive-or to other factors. When an anti-inflammatory agent (indomethacin) was employed both salmonellae enterotoxin and CT induced then synthesis in intestinal epithelial cells which is suggested by the finding that prostaglandins may play a role.

Virulence for mice by three serovars (S. *dublin*, *S. typhimurium*, and *S. enteritidis* has been associated with plasmids of 36 to 60 Mdal, but how virulence factors are controlled by plasmid genes is unclear. The pathogenic Mechanisms of *Salmonella* require much more study.

In chapter further description of animal models and tissue culture systems for the assay of salmonellae toxins ae given.

Incidence and Vehicle Foods

Since small outbreaks are often not reported to public health authorities so the precise incidence of salmonellae food poisoning is not known. Some authorities believe as many as 2 million human cases of salmonellosis may occur each year in the United States alone.

As is the case for staphylococcal food poisoning, the largest outbreaks of salmonellosis usually occur at banquets or similar functions. However, the outbreak that occurred during the spring of 1985 was exceptional. In at least four states over 15,000 cases of salmonellosis in traced to pasteurized milk produced at a plant in Illinois. Most of the milk contained 2% fat, and S. *typhimurium* was recovered from some unopened containers as well as from victims. Although the cause is still under investigation, it appears that the organisms entered the pasteurized product by cross contamination of raw milk. The next largest on record, which occurred in 1974 on the Navajo Nation Indian Reservation, affected an estimated 3.400 persons. The vehicle food was potato salad served to about 11,000 individuals at a free barbecue. It was prepared and stored for up to 16 h at improper holding temperatures prior to serving, and the serovar isolated was S *nexport*. Among the unusual outbreaks was one traced to marijuana in four midwestern states. From marijuana samples counts as high as 10'/g were obtained and S *muenchen* was the serovar isolated. Generally for staphylococcal food poisoning vehicle foods may also serve as sources of *salmonellosis*. Common to both are foods that are prepared by hand and consumed sometimes later without sub nt heating. Vehicle foods for salmonellae often contain uncooked eggs' eef, turkey, homemade ice cream (containing eggs), pork, and chicken are the five most common vehicle foods in the United States and Canada. Turkey is the most common source in Canada.

Kampebnacher addressed the reason for the increase of food borne salmonellosis which always continues : (1) the increase in mass food preparation. which favours spread of *Salmonella;* (2) inappropriate methods of storing food, which, because of modern living conditions, is sometimes accumulated in excessive amounts; (3) the increasing habit of eating raw or insufficiently heated foods, partly because of overreliance on food inspection; (4) increasing international food trade; and (5) decreased resistance to infection resulting from improved standards of general hygiene.

Recovery of Salmonella from Foods

A difficult problem to food microbiologists and food scientists is presented by the recovery of the presence of *Salm&nella spp. in* foods which in view of the federal regulation prohibits its presence. How can one be certain that a 1,000-lb, lot of powdered eggs is free of *Salmonella* if there might be only 1 organism/100 g ? The problem is made all the more difficult by the fact that foods normally contain larger numbers of microorganisms other than *Salmonella*, such as *Proteus*, *Pseudomonas*, *Acinetobactor* and *Allcaligenes* spp., all of which may develop on some of the media employed for the recovery of *salmonellae*. The problems encountered in the recovery of these organisms from foods are similar to those that one encounters in the recovery of staphylococci from foods; that is, a generally high ratio of total numbers of other organisms to pathogens. For recovering these organisms any one of a large number of media may be suitable especially where the ratio of total flora to salmonellae is rather low. Special methods are necessary, however, when few salmonellae exist in the presence of a high total count.

To inhibit or kill non salmonellae types it is necessary generally because of low ratio of salmonellae to total flora though to improve enough the chances of finding *salmonellae* on plates or in broth, they are allowed to increase to high numbers. The fluorescent antibody technique and other salmonellae methods are discussed. For a review of salmonellae methodology.

Prevention and Control of Salmonellosis

An overall view of the primary sources and transmission of *Salmonella spp*. to man is presented. The intestinal tract of man and other animals is the primary source of these organisms, as is previously noted. From human feces, salmonellae may enter water from which meats, poultry, and other foods may become contaminated when such water is used. With these organism from polluted waters insects and rodents may also become contaminated and then directly they are disseminated to either prepared or raw foods. Animal fecal matter is of greater importance than human, and it may be noted that animal hides and poultry products may become contaminated from this source. By means of nonsymptomatic animal infections, and by means of animal feeds, which have been shown by many investigators to harbor comparatively large numbers of these organisms are maintained salmonella spp. within an animal population. Both of these sources serve to keep slaughter animals reinfected in a cyclical manner.

The other more important means of transmission of salmonellae to man is these secondary contamination. The presence of these organisms on eggs, meats, and in the air makes their presence in certain foods inevitable through the agency of handlers and direct contact of non contaminated foods with contaminated foods. This secondary contamination may occur at various stages of food preparation, and is most frequently of animal origin, although human sources can be of some importance have been pointed at by *Prost* and *Riemann.*

Improper cooling of cooked foods, lapse of a day or more between preparation and serving of foods, inadequate cooking or heating ingestion of contaminated or raw ingradients, and cross contamination, are amongst the leading causes of outbreaks.

In view of the world-wide distribution of salmonellosis involving numerous serovars from many different animals, the ultimate control of this problem consists of freeing animals and man of the organisms. This is obviously a difficult task. It is not impossible, however, when it is considered that only 33 of the more than 2,000 species and serovars account for almost 90% of human isolates and approximately 80% of nonhuman isolates. To render themselves *salmonellae* free the reinfection of animals through animal feeds can be controlled by treatment of feeds. One of the more promising ways of achieving the latter consists of heat treatments.

How important it is not known though an important role is presumed to be played by *Salmonella* carrier at the consumer level. The proper cooking of vehicle foods, their proper handling, and subsequent storage at temperatures below the growth range of these organisms will obviously do a great deal to lessen the incidence of salmonellosis at this level. However, the potential hazards of salmonellosis in man will likewise remain as long as these organisms remain among the animal population.

E. coli Gastroenteritis Syndromes

Although sporadic reports of *Escherichia* coli-related gastroenteritis of food origin appeared prior to the 1970s, it was the 1971 outbreak in the United States traced to imported cheese that focused attention on this organism as a food-borne pathogen. This interest coincided with that of medical micro- biologists who were interested in *E. coli* as a cause of infant diarrhea. For assessing toxic components the latter work led to the development of specific and accurate in vitro and bioassay methods and of the virulence mechanisms of this organism to better understanding. Although only a relatively few food- borne outbreaks have been documented, more is known about the pathogenesis of *E. coli* gastroenteritis than that of salmonellosis *E. colt* as an indicator organism is discussed, culture and isolation methods are covered and chemical and bioassay methods for its enterotoxins arc covered. The early history of this syndrome can be found in *Bryan Sack* and *Mehlman et. al.*

Strains and Distribution

Mortality rate was brought as high as 50% by the first studies on *E. coli* which was associated by dian heal disease involving nursery epidemics in the mid 1940s. During the mid 1950s. some *E. coli* isolates were shown to produce responses in the rabbit ileal loop test similar to those of *V. cholerae*. These findings led to studies of *E. coil* as a possible etiologic agent of cholera-like diseases in India. The first reports of enterotoxigenic strains from young animals with diarrhea appeared in 1967, and in 1970 the production of two enterotoxins by virulent strains was reported.

The *EE coli* strains of importance as potential food-borne pathogens are among the fecals (with the possible exception of hemorrhagic colitis agents), and their incidence in some foods is noted. In general, these strains have a wide distribution in food environments in *low* numbers. The microbiological criteria for raw/uncooked foods acknowledges this fact. It should be recalled that as an indicator, *E. coli* in foods in sufficient numbers is taken to indicate the possibility of fecal contamination and the possible presence of other enteropathogens such as salmonellae. As a potential food-borne pathogen, the generally acceptable low numbers take on new meaning, especially when conditions permit their proliferation. While the latter can be said for coagulase-positive staphylococci, unlike fecal *E. coli*, they are not employed as indicators of sanitary quality

Enteropathogenic (EPEC), enterotoxigenic (ETEC), enteroinvasive (EIEC), and facultatively enteropathogenic (FEEC), are the four groups into which *E. coli* strains involved in gastroenteritis may be placed. EPEC strains usually do not produce either of the two enterotoxins but some do. Just how they cause disease is not entirely clear. Some EPEC strains produce a Shigalike (similar to that produced *by Shigella c4senteriae* 1) cytotoxin that can be demonstrated by the use of Vero cells, and the cytotoxin is produced more frequently by these strains than by other *E. coli* isolates. In one study, 79% of twenty-nine EPEC were positive for the Shigalike cytotoxin while only 24%, of eighty-three from healthy individuals were positive. ETEC strains produce one or both enterotoxins as well as colonizing factor antigens (CFA) represented by fimbriae (or. pili), which mediate binding of cells to epithelial cells. Of 240 *E. coli* isolates from cheeses, ground beef, seafood, and sausage, 19(8%) produced the heatlabile toxin, and of these, 8 also produced the heat-stable toxin while I 1 produced only the heat-labile toxin. FEEC strains are associated with sporadic diarrheal outbreaks.

Three antigens are employed to serotype these strains : 0 (heat-stable somatic .antigens); K (heat-labile somatic antigens); and H (heat-labile flagellar antigens). About 164, 100 and 56 of O, K, and II, respectively. are known. Only about thirty serovars have been associated with diarrheal disease, and the first was 0111, which was isolated from children with diarrhea and constituted as high as 80-100% of fecal flora. *E. coli* normally carried in the lower bowel consisted mainly about 1 % of the cultivable fecal flora of man while the upper bowel is colonized by the pathogens (except hemorrhagic colitis strains).

From individual to individual there appears to be little consistency with respect to serotype/serovars. A study of this organism in the fecal flora of thirteen healthy adults in England revealed wide variations in serotypes, with several individuals carrying one predominant type while several yielded as many as twelve different types. The 0 antigenic types carried by four to six persons were : 01, 02, 018,068, 088, 0107, 0116, 0126, and 0132. The serovars responsible for diarrheal disease in thirty-three children and adults varied rather widely, with only six being recovered from two to four individuals : 06, 015, 025, r/8,0126, and 0128. Some of the latter types are known to be nontoxic. In a study of the incidence of pathogenic strains among 219 food handlers. 14 (6.4%) were carriers of a total of eight different serovars. From other reports, the incidence in the feces of healthy adults and children range from 1.8 to 15.1%. Either enterotoxin is produced by only one of thirty-four of serotype 014%, nine of forty-five of serotype 0114; and eighteen of eighty two of serotype 0128, among EPEC strains. In one study, the most common serotype isolated from foods was 0149.

The K88-positive strain of porcine origin has been shown to effect surface colonization in piglets. and to be lethal to 50% of piglets while the K88-negative variant was lethal to only 3%. The K88 antigen is a short piluslike structure that is highly antigenic. K99 is similar but pathogenic in cows and lambs but not pigs. Although K88 produces the heat-labile toxin, it has been suggested that an immunofluorescence test for in vivo-produced pilus antigens be used for the diagnosis of ETEC infections. The K88 antigen is plasmid borne. It was observed by earlier investigators that a poor correlation exists between serotypes and ileal loop responses of E. *coli* strains. While serotyping is of value epidemiologically, it appears to be of little value as a predictor of *E. coli* virulence.

From any other bacteria plasmids from *E. coli* have been studied more. Strains from patients have been shown to contain more conjugative plasmids than those from healthy individuals. ETEC strains usually carry five or more plasmids with antibiotic resistance, enterotoxins, and adherence antigens on separate plasmids. Among specific plasmids in *E. coli* is Coly, which controls an iron-sequestering mechanism-possibly enterobchelin or enterobactin-and serum resistance.

The Enterotoxins

Heat labile (LT) and heat stable (ST) are the two enterotoxins produced by ETEC strains, as noted above. The maximum amount of ST was produced after 7 h of growth in one study in a Casamino acids yeast extract medium containing 0.2%, glucose. In a synthetic medium, ST appeared as early as 8 h but maximal production required 24 h with aeration. While they are generally produced under all conditions that allow cell growth, the release of LT in particular from cells in enriched media was favoured at pH of 7.5-8.5.

While most strains produce both enterotoxins, some are known that produce only one. Plasmid mediated enterotoxins are those which are along with the colourization factor antigen and hemolysin. The enterotoxins are encoded on Ent plasmids that also may carry genes for resistance to several antimicrobials. However, an LT-like toxin produced by E. *coli* strain SA53 is apparently controlled by chromosomal genes. EIEC strains apparently carry a 140-Mdal (megadalton) plasmid. In the case of ST_a, it is encoded within a transposon.

In about 30 min. at 60°C LT is destroyed while for 15 min. at 100°C the ST toxin is withstanded. In acid LT is labile while ST is resistant. LT is a protein with a molecular weight of about 91,000 daltons, and cistrons encoding for its production on plasmid DNA have been mapped. It is associated more with man and porcines than other animals. LT is composed of two protomers. The A protomer has a molecular weight of about 25.500 daltons and is synthesized as a single.Polypeptide chain that. when nicked (with trvpsin). becomes an enzymatically active A_1 polypeptide chain of 21,000 daltons linked by a disulfide bond to an A_2-like chain (compare with botulinal toxins. The B protomer has a molecular weight of about 59,000 and consists of five noncovalently linked individual polypeptide B chains of 11,800 daltons.

Heat stability is retained by both of the two types of *E. coli ST. ST* $_e$ (STI) has a molecular weight of 1,972, is methanol soluble, is an acidic polypeptide (lacks basic amino acids), is active in neonatal piglets 1-3 days old, and is active in infant mice but generally not in weaned pigs. Biological activity of ST is lost upon treatment with 2-mercaptoethanol or dithiothreitol, indicating the presence and need of disultfide bridges. ST.'S from human and bovine sources all contain ten different amino acids in a sequence of eighteen with the same C-terminal (tyrosine) and N-terminal (asparagine) groups, and antisera from one cross reacts with all. The same general properties is exhibited by those produced by *E. coli* which when compared with those as ST_e which has been chemically synthesized. The ST from human, bovine, and porcine sources is essentially similar and may have originated; from a single, 'widely disseminated transposon. There is some evidence that ST, may be a family of at least two peptide toxins.

Active in weaned pigs and rabbit ileal loop tests, but not in infant mice is ST_b (ST II) which is methanol insoluble. ST_e and ST_b are genetically and immunologically distinct.

E. coli LT has a molecular weight of 84,000-91,000 daltons. It possesses enzymatic activity similar to that of CT but ST does not. LT shares some features in commron with the enterotoxin of V *cholerae* (*CT*). In the rabbit ileal loop test antisera to CT neutralized LT from human and porcine strains and equal protection against subsequent challenges against both CT and LT and immunization with CT induced, thus establishing that the two toxins share common antigenic determinants. LT differs from CT in amino acid composition, but they do share many other common features.

Mode of Action of Enterotoxins

10^6-10^{10} viable cells/g colonizes the small intestines and produce enterotoxin(s) and causes the *E. coil* gastroenteritis syndrome. The colonizing factors are generally fimbriae or pili. The syndrome is characterized primarily by nonbloody diarrhea without inflammatory exudates in stools. The diarrhea is watery and similar to that caused by V *cholerae*. Diarrhea results from enterotoxin activation of intestinal adenylate cyclase. which increases cyclic 3'. 5'-adenosine monophosphate (cAMP). first shown for. *E. coli* enterotoxins by *Evans'ets al.*

With respect to LT, the B protomer mediates binding of the molecule to intestinal cells. LT binds to gangliosides, especially monosialogangliosides (GM,). CT also binds to GM, ganglioside, CT and LT are known to share antigenic determinants among corresponding protomers although they do not cross *act. Upon binding, the A polypeptide chain (of the A protomer) catalyses ADP ribosylation of adenylate cyclase, which induces increases in intracellular cAMP

Regarding ST, ST_a binds irreversibly to a specific high affinity nonganglioside receptor and initiates a transmembrane signal to active particulate guanylate cyclase. The increased levels of mucosal cGMP lead to loss of fluids and electrolytes ST differs from CT in that only the particulate form of intestinal guanylate cyclase is stimulated by ST. ST_a differs from LT in that the former stimulates guanylate cyclase while the latter and CT both activate adenylate cyclase. Stimulation of guanylate cyclase by ST_a is tissue specific, and only the intestinal form of the particulate enzyme responds to ST. Guanylate cyclase is not activated by ST_b though its precise role is not understood. Genes controlling its production have been genetically mapped and subcloned from its plasmid and sequenced.

Food-borne and Related Outbreaks

Dated from around 1900 and consisting of variety of foods such as cream pie; mashed potatoes, cream puffs, and creamed fish are the etiologic agent of reports incriminating *E. coli.'* The feeding of volunteers with serotypes 055 : B5, 01 11 : B4, and 0127: B8 at levels of 10^6-10^8 organisms was shown to produce gastroenteritis symptoms.

Most of the documented outbreaks are summarized in Table. Not included are four to six outbreaks reported from the USSR, Eastern Europe, and Japan. As noted above, the U.S. outbreaks in 1971 were well documented. An EIEC strain was the etiologic agent. The cheese involved was imported from France and sold under several names (Brie, Camembert, Coulommiers), but all had been made in the same way. The serovar was 0 124 : B 17. Median time for onset of symptoms was 18 h with a mean duration of 2 days. Common symptoms were diarrhea, fever, and nausea, in order of decreasing frequency. Less common symptoms included cramps, chills, vomiting, aches, and headaches. The attack rate was 91% among those who ate the soft-ripened cheese. A total of 107 outbreaks occurred in thirteen states and the District of Columbia. While some of the cheese contained 10^3- 10^5 coliforms/g, Enterobacteriaceae at levels of 10_6-10_7/g were found. Imported Brie cheese was the common source of the outbreak in 1983.

Hemorrhagic Colitis

At least forty seven individuals were affected by this syndrome which was first characterized in 1982 in outbreaks in the states of Michigan and Oregon. It was associated with eating any of three sandwiches at fast-food restaurants of the same chain in both states with all sandwiches containing ground beef. Of 43 patients studied, all had bloody diarrhea and severe abdominal cramps with 63%experiencing nausea. 49% vomiting, but only 7% fever. The mean incubation period was 3.8-3.9 days, and symptoms lasted for 3 to > 7 days From a frozen raw beef patty and nine of twelve stools collected within 4 days, a noninvasive, nontoxigenic *E. coli* serotype 0157 : H7 was recovered. This rare serotype was not recovered from stools collected 7 or more days after onset of illness. The only previous isolation of this serotype in the United States was from a sporadic case of hemorrhagic colitis in 1975. An outbreak of hemorrhagic colitis occurred in Ottawa, Canada, in November 1982, involving 31 of 353 residents of a home for the aged. The apparent source was Kitchen - prepared food having serotype 0.57 : H7.

Lack of production of LT or ST its lacks of invasiveness or toxigenicity be cell culture assays, are among the unusual features of *E. coli* 0157: H7, although it produces a Vero cell cytotoxin; and its site of pathology in the colon rather than the small intestines. It is more heat sensitive than salmonellae (D 69°C=45 sec. in ground beef) but it survived in ground beef for 9 months held at -20°C with little change in numbers. The organism grows poorly in the temperature range 44°-45°C with no growth at 45.5°C, suggesting that its presence may not be detected by fecal coliform assays. It is nonfluorogenic in the MUG assay. Its capacity to colonize chicken cecae suggests that chickens may serve as hosts or reservoirs. It has been shown that lysogenization by a bacteriophage resulted from cytotoxin.

Travelers' Diarrhea

Among new arrivals in certain foreign countries occurs acute watery diarrhea by E. *coli* which is well established as one of the leading causes. In a study of thirty-five Peace Corps volunteers during their first 5 weeks in rural Thailand, 57% developed the syndrome and 50% had evidence of infection by ETEC strains. The shipboard outbreak of gastroenteritis of 1976 was caused by serotype 025 : K98 : NM that produced only LT. Strains that produced only LT have been Isolated from victims traveling in Mexico. EPEC and ST - producing strains have been isolated from victims.

Rotaviruses are among other organisms associated with this syndrome. Norwalk agent (virus). *Entanioeba histolvtrca*, *Yersinia enterocolitica*, *Glardia lamblia*, *Campylobacter jejuni/coli*, *Shigella* spp., and possibly *Aeromonas hydrophila*, *Klebsiella pneumoniae*, and *Enterobacter cloacae*.

FOOD POISONING BY VIBRIO, YERSINIA AND CAMPYLOBACTER SPECIES

Vibrio parahaemolyticus

V parahaemolyticus gastroenteritis is contracted almost solely from seafood. While most other known food poisoning syndromes may be contracted from a variety of foods. When other foods are involved, they represent cross contamination from seafoods products. Another unique feature of this syndrome is the natural habit of the etiologic agent-the sea. In addition to its role in gastroenteritis. Extraintestinal infections in man is known to be caused by VV *parahaemolvticus.*

Table 10.4. Some Colonial and Biochemical Differences Between *V Parahaemolyticus* and Three Other *Vibrio* spp.

Species	V parehae -molytrcus	V algino -lyticus	V vuln- ificus	V chol- erae
Lateral Flagella on solid media	+	+	—	—
Rod shapeVP	S-	S+	C	d
Growth in 10% NaCl	—	+	—	v
Growth in 6% NaCl	+	+	+	—
Swarming	—	+	—	—
Production of acetioin/diacetyl	—	+	—	+
Surcose	—	+	—	+
Cellobiose	—	+	—	—
Utilization of putrescine	+	d	—	—
Colour on TCBS agar	G		G	Y

* 24 h.

S = straight, C = curved, G = green, Y = yellow, d = 11 to 90% of strains positive, v = variable; strain instability.ss

The genus 11 *brio* consists of at least twenty- eight species, and three that are often associated with *V. parahaemolyticus* in aquatic environments and seafood are *V. vulnificus*, 1'' *alginolvticus*, and *V. cholerae*. Some of the distinguishing features of these species are noted in Table and the syndromes caused by each are described below. Thorough reviews of these and related organisms have been provided by *Clowell* and *Joseph* et al.

V. parahaemolyticus is common in oceanic and coastal waters. Its detection is related to water *temperatures*, with numbers of organisms being undetectable until water temperature rises to around 19°-

20°C. A study of the Rhode River area of the Chesapeake Bay showed that the organisms survive in sediment during the winter and later are released into the water column, where they associate with the zooplankton from April to early June. In ocean waters, they tend to be associated more with shellfish that with other forms. They have been demonstrated to adsorb onto chitin particles and copepods, whereas organisms such as *Escherichia coli* and *Pseudomonas fluorescens* do not. This species is generally not found in the open oceans and it cannot tolerate the hydrostatic pressures of ocean depths.

Growth Conditions

In between 2-4% range the growth occurred best while in the presence 1-8% NaCI grows the *V. parahaemolyticus*. It dies off in distilled water. It does not grow at 4°C, but growth between 5° and 9°C has been demonstrated at pH 7.2-7.3 and 3%. NaCI, or at pH 7.6 and 7% NACI. its growth at 9.5-10°C in food products has been

TABLE 10.5. MINIMUM pH OF GROWTH OF VV PARAHAEMOLYTICUS ATCC 107914 IN TSB WITH 3% AND 7% NACI AT DIFFERENT TEMPERATURES.

Temp. (°C)	*Minimum pH at NACI conc.*	
	3%	7%
5	7.3	7.6
9	7.2	7.1
13	5.2	6.0
21	4.9	5.3
30	4.8	5.2

demonstrated although the minimum for growth in open waters has been found to be 10°C. The upper growth temperature is 44°C, with an optimum between 30° and 35°C. Growth has been observed over the pH range 4.8-11.0, with 7.6-8.6 being optimum. It may be noted from table that the minimum growth pH is related to temperature and NACI content, with moderate growth of one strain observed at pH 4.8 when the temperature was 30°C and NACI content was 3%; but minimum pH was 5.2 when NACI content was 7%. Similar results were found for five other strains. This organism has a generation time of 9-13 min (compared to about 20 min for *EE coli*) under optimal conditions. Optimum a_w for growth corresponding to shortest generation time was found to be 0.992 (2.9% NACI in tryptic soy broth). Employing the latter medium at 29°C and various solutes to control a_w, minimum values were 0,937 (glycerol), 0.945 (KCI). 0:948 (NaCI), 0.957 (sucrose), 0.983) (glucose), and 0.986 with propylene glycol. It is reported that the organism is heat sensitive, with D47°C values ranging from 0.8 to 65.1 min. With one, strain, destruction of 500 cells/ml in shrimp homogenates was achieved at 60°C in 1 min, but with 2 × 10^5 cells/ml some survived 80°C for 1 5 min. Cells are most heat resistant when grown at high temperatures in the presence of about 7% NaCl.

Virulence Properties

The most widely used in vitro test of potential virulence for V *parahaenrolvticus* is the Kanagawa reaction, with most all virulent strains being positive (K^+) and most avirulent strains being negati ue (K^-). About

1 % of sea isolates and about 100% of those from gastroenteritis patients are K^+. K^+ strains produce a thermostable direct hemolysin (toxin) K^- strains produce a heat-labile hemolysin, and some strains produce both. The Kanagawa reaction is determined generally by use in human red blood cells in Wagatsuma'sagar medium. In addition to human red blood cells, those of the dog and rat are lysed; those of the rabbit and sheep give weak reactions; and those of the horse are not lysed. To determine the K reaction, the culture is surface plated, incubated at 37°C for 18-24 h, and read for the presence of b-hemolysis. Of 2,720 *V parahaemolyticus* isolates from diarrheal patients, 96% were K' whereas only 1 % of 650 fish isolates were K'. In general, isolates from waters are K^-.

The thermostable direct hemolysin has a molecular weight of 42,000 daltons and is a cardiotrophic, cytotoxic protein that is lethal to mice and induces a positive response in the rabbit ileal loop assay. Its mean mouse LD_{50} by intrapertioneal (1P) injection is 1.5 μg, and the rabbit ileal loop dose is 200gg. The hemolysin is under pH control and was found to be produced only when pH is 5.5-5.6. That K^+ hemolysin may aid cells in obtaining iron stems from the observation that lysed erythrocyte extracts enhanced the virulence of the organism for mice. The membrane receptors of the thermostable direct hemolysin are ganliosided GT_i and GDI_a, with the former binding hemolysin more firmly than the latter. The resistance of horse erythrocytes to the hemolysin apparently is due to their absence of these gangliosides.

A synthetic mediugi has been developed for the production of both the thermostable direct and the heat-labile hemolvsins. and serine

TABLE 10.6. SUMMARY OF SOME OUTBREAKS OF E.COLI GASTROENTERITIS FROM FOODS AND OTHER SOURCES.

Year	*Location*	*Vchicle food/soruce at risk*	*No victims/no. type*	*Toxin/strain*	*serotype*
1947	England	Salmon (apparently)	47/300		0124
1961	Romania	Substitute coffee drink	10/50		086: B7:. H34
1%3	Japan	ohagi	17/31		
1966	Japan	Vegetables	244/435		
1967	Japan	Sushi	835/1.736		027
1971	14 American	Imported cheeses	387/7	EEC	0124: B17
1980	statesWisconsin	Food handler	500/23,000	L.TST	06: H16
1981	Texas	Not identified	28213,000	L.T	025: H+
1983	4 American states	Imported Brie cheese	15/?	ST	027: H20

TABLE 10.7. SYNOPSIS OF SOME OUTBREAKS YERSINIOSIS

Year	*Location*	*Vehicle*	*Characteristics of outbreaks*	*Serovar*
1972	Japan	Unknown	47% of 182 school children and 1 teacher infected	0.3
1972	Japan	Unknown	53% of 993 children and adults at a primary school affected	0.3
1972	Japan	Unknown	198 of 1,086 junior high school publis infected	
1972	North Carolina	Dog/puppies	16 of 21 persons in 4 afamilies were infected	
1975	North Carolina	Food handler	Two common-source outbreaks occurred in nursery schools. The children also ate snow covered with maple syrup	
1975	Montreal	Raw milk	57 elementary school children and 1 adult infected. Serover 0 : 5, 27 was recovered from milk; 0 : 6,30 from victims.	
1976	New York	Chocolate milk	Some 218 school children were infected. Chocolate syrup added to pasteurized milk in open vat was the appearent vehicle.	0 : 8
1981	New York	Powdered milk	About 35% of 455 teenage compars and staff were infected from dissolved powdered milk and/or chowmein. Five had appendectomies.	0:8
1982	Washington state	Commercial tofu	Of the 87 victims. 56 had positive stools. Water used in processing was the apparent source of the organisms	o 0 : 8 0 : Tacoma
1982	Connecticut	Pasteurized mills	53 of 300 became victims with the attack rate being greatest among the 6 to 13-year-olds. Twenty of 52 stools were positive for the serovar noted.	0:8
1982	Tennessee, Arkansas, Mississippi	Pasteurized mills	More than 172 victims resulted from milk pasteurized in Tennessee. Seventeen patients underwent appendectomies, and 41% of victims were under age 5.	0:13,0:18

and glutamic acid were found to be indispensable. The heat stability of the thermostable direct hemolysin is such that it can remain in foods after its production. In Tris buffer at pH 7.0, D 120°C and D 130°C values of 34 and 13 min, respectively, were found for semipurified toxin; whereas in shrimp $D_{120}$and D_{130}values were 21.9 and 10.4 min, respectively. Hemolysin was detected when cell counts reached 10^6/g. and its heat resistance was greater at pH 5.5-6.5 than at 7.0-8.0.

The thermostable direct hemolysin gene (*tdh*) is chromosomal, and it has been cloned in *E. coli*. When the *tdh* gene was introduced into a K^-strain, it produced extracellular hemolysin. The nucleotide sequence of the *tdh* gene has been determined, and a specific *tdh* gene probe constructed, which consists of a 406-base pair. Employing this probe, V *parahaemolyticus* strains were tested. All K+ strains were gene positive - 86%. of them were weak positives-and 16% of K^- strains reacted with the probe. All gene-positive strains produced the thermostable direct hemolysin as assessed by an ELISA method. Of 129 other vibrios tested with the gene probe including 19 named *irbrio spp.*, only *V hollisae* was positive. The transfer of R-plasmids from *E. coli* to *V parahaemolyticus* has been demonstrated.

At least twelve O-antigens and fifty-nine K-antigens have been identified, but no correlations have been made between these and KK and K^- strains, and the value ofserotyping as an epidemiological aid has been minimal.

Since not all K^+ strains produce positive responses in the rabbit ileal loop assay, and because some K^- strains are associated with gastroenteritis and sometimes are the only strains isolated, the precise virulence mechanisms of this organism are not known. The thermostable direct hemolysin undoubtedly is responsible for the deaths that occur, but it plays no role in the diarrhea that characterizes the syndrome. While it has been shown to penetrate the intestinal epithelium of suckling rabbits. It is nuclear whether this occurs in adult animals. *Twedt et. al.* have noted that pathogenicity depends upon something other than the thermostable direct toxin, but the identity of that factor(s) is not known at this time.

Gastroenteritis Syndrome and Vehicle Foods

The identity of V *parahaemolyticus* as a food-borne gastroenteritis agent was made first by *Fjinomir*, 1951. While the incidence of this illness is rather low in the United States and some European countries, it is the leading cause of food poisoning in Japan. accounting for

24% of bacterial food poisoning for 1965-74. In 1973-75. three outbreaks were recorded in the United States, with 224 cases. A synopsis of some outbreaks is presented in Table. Among the more than 81,000 cases reported during this period, thirty-one deaths were recorded.

With regard to symptomatology, findings from the Louisiana outbreak illustrate the typical features. The mean incubation period in that outbreak was 16.7 h, with a range of 3-76 h. The symptons lasted from 1 to 8 days, with a mean of about 4.6 days. Symptoms (along with percent incidence of each) were diarrhea, cramps, weakness, nausea, chills, headache and vomiting. Both sexes were equally affected, the age of victims ranging from 13 to 78 years.

TABLE 10.8. SYNOPSIS OF SOME GASTROENTERITIS OUTBREAKS CAUSED BY V PARAHAEMOLYTICUS.

Year	*Location/incidence/comments*
1951	Japan. The outbreak occurred following consumption of *shirasu* (boiled and semidried young sardines). There were 272 victims, including 20 deaths.
1956	Japan. Salted cucumber was involved in a hospital outbreak with 120 victims.
1960	Japan. An explosive outbreak affecting thousands of people occurred along the Pacific coast. Horse mackerel was thought to be the vehicle.
1971	Maryland. Steamed crabs and crab salad were incriminated in 3 outbreaks in which 425 of about 745 people became ill. Isolations from food and victims revealed K' strains 04 : K 11 as the causative agent. This was first documented out-break in America.
1974	Mexico. K' strains were recovered from two victims who ate raw fish.
1976	Guam. Some 122 cases developed from eating octopus aboard a ship.
1976	Louisiana. Some 100 cases resulted from eating boiled shrimp at a picnic.
1978	Louisiana. Boiled shrimp was the vehicle food in this out-break involving about 67% of 1.700 persons at risk. K' strains were recovered from leftover shrimp and other foods as well as foods the stools of 7 of 15 victims.

No illness ocurred among fourteen voluntreers who ingested > 10^9 cells. but illness did occur in one person from the accidental ingestion of $\sim 10^7$ K^+ cells. In another stud). 2×10^5 to 3×10^7 K^+ cells produced symptoms in volunteers, whereas 10^{10} cells of K^- strains did not. As noted above, some K^- strains have been associated with outbreaks.

Vehicle foods or outbreaks are seafood, such as oysters, shrimps, crabs, lobsters, clams, and related shellfish. Cross contamination may lead to other foods as vehicles.

For the recovery and enumeration of V *parahaemolyticus* from foods, an appropriate reference from Table should be consulted.

OTHER VIBRIOS

Vibrio cholerae

The *V cholerae* that cause epidemic cholera belongs to serovar 0 group 1. The strains of *V cholerae* that are biochemically similar to the epidemic strains but that do not agglutinate in V *cholera* 0 group 1 antiserum and are not associated with the epidemic disease are reffered to as non-01 or nonagglutinating vibrios (NAGs). The non-01 strains have been shown to cause gastroenterities, soft-tissue infections, and septicemia in man. As in the case of V. *parahaemolyticus*, they are found in barckish'surface waters during the warm weather months, *Kaper et. al.* consider them to be autochthonous (indigenous) estuarine bacterial bacterial species in Chesapeake Bay waters.

Among the earliest information linking non-01 *V cholerae* to gastroenteritis in the United States are findings from twenty six of twenty-eight patients with acute diarrheal illness between 1972 and 1975. While some had systemic infections, 50% of the twenty-eight yielded non-cholera vibrios from stools and no other pathogens. In another retrospective study of non-01 *V cholerae* cultures submitted to the U.S. Centers for Disease Control (CDC) in 1979, nine were from domestically acquired cases of gastroenteritis and each patient had eaten raw oysters within 72h of symptoms. One of these isolates produced a heat-labile toxin, whereas none produced heat-stable toxins.

With regard to distribution, non-0 1 strains of *V cholerae* have been found in the Orient and Mexico in stools of diarrheal patients along with enteropathogenic *E. coli*, *V cholerae* non-01 was isolated from 385 persons with diarrhea in Mexico City in 1966-67. The organism causes diarrhea by an enterotoxin similar to cholera toxin (CT) and perhaps by other mechanism. A strain isolated from a patient produced a CT-like toxin, positive responses in the Chinese hamster ovary (CHO) and skin permeability assays. was invasive in rabbit ileal mucosa. but was Sereny-test negative.

From Chesapeake Bay, sixty-five non-01 s were isolated in one study. Throughout the year their numbers in waters were generally low, from 1 to 10 cells/1. They were found only in areas where salinity ranged between 4 and 17%. Their presence was not correlated with fecal E. coli, whereas the presence of the latter did correlate with Salmonella. Of those examined, 87% produced positive responses in Y-1 adrenal, rabbit ileal loop, and mouse lethality assays. Investigations conducted on waters along the Texas, Louisiana, and Florida coasts reveal that both 01 and non-01 *V. cholerae* are fairly common. Of 150 water samples collected along a Florida estuary, 57% were positive for *V. cholerae*. Of 753 isolates examined, 20 were 01 and 733 were non-01 types. Of the 20 01 strains, 8 were Ogawa and 12 were Inaba serovars, and they were found primarily at a sewage treatment plant. The highest numbers of both 01 and non-01 strains occurred in August and November. Neither the fecal coliform nor the total coliform indecx was an adequate indicator of the presence of *V. cholera*, but the former was more useful than the latter. Along the Santa Cruz, California, coast, the highest numbers of non-01 s occurred during the summer months and were associated with high coliform counts.

Vibrio Vulnificus

This organism is found in seawater and seafood. It is isolated more often from oysters and clams than from crustacean shellfish products. It has been isolated from seawater from the coast of Miami, Florida, to Cape Cod. Massachusetts, with most (84%) isolated from clams. Upon injection into mice, 82% of tested strains were lethal. Like *V. alginolyticus*, it caused soft-tissue infections and primary septicaemia in man. The strains are highly invasive and produce hemolysin and a cytotoxin. Infections have been seen in the United States, Japan, and Belgium of those seen in the United States all but three occurred between May and October, and most patients were males over 40 years of age. This organisms is believed to be a significant pathogen in individuals with higher than normal levels of iron (as, for example, in hepatitis and chronic cirrhosis), although its virulence is not explained entirely by its capacity to sequester iron.

Vibrio Alginolyticus

This species is a normal inhabitant of seawater and has been found to cause soft-tissue and ear infections in man. Human pathogenicity was first confirmed in 1973, although its possible role in wound infections was noted by Twedt *et. al.* in 1969. Extraintestinal infections have been reported from several countries including the United States. Wound infections occur usually on body extremities, with most patients being males with a history of exposure to seawater.

The prevalence of *V. alginolyticus* along with that of *V. parahaemolyticus* was studied in coastal waters of the state of Washington *by Baross* and *Liston*, who found higher numbers of organisms in invertebrates and sediment samples than in water where the numbers were quite variable. Number found in oysters correlated with the temperature of overlying waters, with highest numbers associated with warmer waters. Whether of not this organism is of any significance as a food-borne pathogen is not clear at this time.

For more information on *vibrio* infections, see the reviews by *Blake et al. Colwell* and *Joseph yet al.*

YERSINIA ENTEROCOLITICA

In the genus *Yersinia*, which belongs to the family Entero bacteriaceae, seven species and five biovars are recognized, including *Y pestis*, the cause of plague. The species of primary interest in foods is *Y. enterocolitica*, First isolated in New York state in 1933 *by M. B. Coleman* this gramnegative rod is some-what unique in that it is motile below 30°C but not at 37°C. It produces colonies of 1.0 mm or less on nutrient agar, is oxidase negative, ferments glucose with little or no gas, lacks phenylalanine deaminase, is urease positive, and is unique as a pathogen in being psychrotrophic. It is often present in the environment with at least three other yersiniae noted in Table. The early history of *Y. enterocolitica* was reviewed by *Bottone*. General reviews relative to foods have been published by *Stern* and *Pierson*, *Swaminathan et al.* and *Zink et a!.*

Growth Requirements

Growth of *Y. enterocolitica* has been observed over the temperature range of -2°-45°C, with an optimum between 22°C and 29°C. For biochemical reactions, 29°C appears to be the optimum. The upper limit for growth of some strains is 40°C, and not all grow below 4°-5°C. Growth at 0°-2°C in milk after 20 days has been observed, Growth at 0°-1 °C on pork and chicken has been observed and three strains were found to grow on raw beef held for 10 days at 4°-1°C. The addition of NaCI to growth media raises the minimum growth temperature. In brain heart infusion (BM broth containing 7% NaCl, growth did not occur at 3° or 25°C after 10 days. At pH 7.2, growth of one strain was observed at 3°C and very slight growth at pH 9.0 at the same temperature, while no growth occurred at pH 4.6 and 9.6. Although 7% NaCI was inhibitory at 3°C, growth occurred at 5%NaCl. With no salt, growth was observed at 3°C over the pH range 4.6-9.0. Clinical strains were less affected by these parameters than were environment isolates.

TABLE 10.9. SPECIES OF *YERSINIA* ASSOCIATED WITH *Y ENTEROCOLITICA* IN THE ENVIRONMENT AND IN FOODS, AND MINIMUM BIOCHEMICAL DIFFERENCES BETWEEN THEM.

Species	*VP*	*Sucrose*	*Rhamnose*	*Raffinose*	*Melibiose*
Y enterocolitica	+	+	—	—	—
Y kristensenii	—	—	—	—	—
Y frederikensii	+	+	+	—	—
Y intennedia	+	+	+	+	+

VP = Voges-Proskauer *reaction*
\+ = positive reaction
— = negative reaction

Y enteroc·litica is destroyed in 1-3 min at 60°C . It is rather resistant to freezing, with numbers decreasing only slightly in chicken after 90 days at 18°C. The calculated D62.8°C for twenty-one strains in milk ranged from o.7 to 17.8 seconds, and none survived pasteurization.

Distribution

Y enterocoliltica and the related species noted in Table are widely distributed in the terrestrial environment and in lake, well, and stream waters, which are sources of the organisms to warm-blooded animals. It is more animal adapted and is found more often among human isolates than the other species in Table. Of 149 strains of human origin, 81,12 5.4, and 2% were, respectively, *Y enterocolitica, Yersinia intermedia, Yersinia frederiksenii, and Yersinia kristencenii. Y intermedia and Y. federiksenii;* are found mainly in fresh waters, fish, foods, and only occasionally are isolated from man. *Y. kristensenii* is found mainly in soils and other environmental samples as well as in foods but rarely isolated from man. Like *Y. enterocolitica,* this species produces a heat-stable enterotoxin. Many of the *Y. enterolitica-like* isolates of *Hanna et.* al. were rhamnosepositive and consequently are classified as *Y. intermedia and/ or Y. frederiksenii;* and all grow at 4°C. Rhamnose positive yersiniae are not known to cause infections in man.

TABLE 10.10. SYNOPSIS OF SOME OUTBREAKS OF COMPYLOBACTER ENTERITIS

Year	Location	Vehicle	Synopsis
1938	Illinois	Contaminated	This presumptive outbreak involved 357 cases at 2 institutions.
1978	Vermont	pasteurized milkWater	The outbreaks stopped after milk was boiled.The town's water supply was contaminated. About 2,000 of 10,000 persons were infected. Swabs from 5 of 9 victims releaved the agent.
1978	Colordo	Raw milk	There of 5 family members were infected. Organism was recovered from stools of all victims as well as from cow feces.
1979	Iowa	Barbecued	There were 8 victims of 11 who ate undercoocked barbecued chicken.
1979	Scotland	chickenRaw milk	There were 648 cases fdllowing an electrical failure at the dairy plant.
1981)	England	Raw milk	The incnbation period ranged from 1 to 13 days.About 75 of 300 college students were affected. The organism was found in milk samples, and 46 students had antibodies to C jejuni.
1981	Kansas	Raw milk	There wee over 264 cases. Fifty-two percent of 116 persons in households
1981	Oregon	Raw milk	that had one of more ill family members yielded the agent.Of 167 who drank infected milk, 77 became ill. Agent was found in stools.
1981	Georgia	Raw milk	There were 50 victims in 30 households but the organims was not found in milk
1982	Connecticut	Cake icing	C jejuni was isolated from 16 to 41 victims.
1984	California	Raw milk	Twelve of 35 children and adults became infected after drinking certified raw milk.

Animal from which *Y. enterocolitica* has been isolated include cats, birds, dogs, beavers, guinea pigs, rats camels, horses, chickens, raceoons, chinchillas, doer, cattle, swine, lambs, fish, and oysters. It is widely believed that swine constitutes the single most common source of *Y. enterocolitica* in humans. Of forty-three samples of pork obtained from a slaughterhouse and examined for *Y. enterocolitica, Y. intermedia, V. kristensenii and Y. frederiksenii.* eight were positive and all four species were found. Along with *Klebsiella pneumoniae, Y. enterocolitica* was recovered from crabs collected near Kodiak Island, Alaska, and was shown to be pathogenic.

Serovars and Biovars

The most commonly occuring *Y enterocolitica* serovars (serotypes) in human infections are 0 : 3, 0 : 5, 27, 0 : 8, and 0 : 9. Each of forty-nine isolates belonging to these serovars produced a positive HeLa cell response while only five of thirty-nine other serovars were positive. Most pathogenic strains in the United States are 0 : 8 (biovars 2 and 3); and except for occasional isolations in Canada, it is rarely reported from other continents. In Canada, Africa, Europe, and Japan, serovar 0.3 (biovar 4) is the most common. The second most common in Europe and Africa is 0.9, which has been reported also from Japan. Serovar 0.3 (biovar 4, phage type 9b) was practically the only type found in the province of Quebec, Canada, and it was predominant in Ontario. The next most common were 0 : 5, 27 and 0: 6, 30,. From human infections in Canada, 0 : 3 represented 85% of 256 isolates, whereas for nonhuman sources, 0:5,27 represented 27% of 22 isolates. Six isolates of 0.8 recovered from procine tongues were lethal to adult mice, and only 0 : 8 was found by *Mora* and *Pai* to be Sereny positive. Employing *HeLa* cells, the follwing serovars were found to be inliective : 0 : 1, :2,0:3,0:4,0:5,0:8,0:9, and 0:21. Serovar 0:8 strains are not only virulent in man but they possess

TABLE 10.11. THE FOUR COMMON BIOVARS OF *V ENTEROCOLITICA*

	Biovars			
Substrate/product	***1***	***2***	***3***	***4***
Lipase (Tween 80)	+	—	—	—
DNAse	—	—	—	+
Indole	+	+	—	—
D-xylose	+	+	+	—

mice lethality and invasiveness by the Sereny test. The four most common biovars of *Y enterocolitica* are indicated in Table. It appears that only biovars 2. 3, and 4 carry the virulence plasmid.

Virulence Factors

Y enterocolitica produces a heat-stable (ST) enterotoxin that survives 100°C for 20 min. It is not affected by proteases and lipases and has a molecular weight of 9,000-9,700 daltons. and biological activity is lost upon treatment with-2 mercaptoethanol. When subjected to isoelectric focusing, two active fractions with pl's of 3.29 (ST- 1) and 3.00 (ST-2) have been found. Antiserum from guinea pigs immunized with the purified ST neutralized the activity of *Y enterocolitica ST* and *E. coli* ST. Like *E. coli* ST, it elicits positive responses in suckling mice and rabbit ileal loop assays. It is methanol soluble and stimulates guanylate cyclase and the cAMP response in intestines but not adenylate cyclase. It is produced only at or below 30°C and its production is favoured in the pH range 7-8. Of forty-mix isolates, only three produced ST in milk at 25°C and none at 4°C. At 25°C, > 24 h were required for ST production. It appears to be chromosomal rather than plasmid mediated.

In a study of 232 human isolates, 94% produced enterotoxin, while only 32% of 44 from raw milk and 18% of 55 from other foods were enterotoxigenic. Of the serovars 0:3, 0:8, 0:5 27, 0:6, 30 and 0:9, 97% of 196 were enterotoxigenic. Ninety percent of the rhamnose- positive strains studied by *Pal et al.* produced enterotoxin, indicating that not all isolates were *Y. enterocolitica* and that some of the other species produce enterotoxin, as previously noted. It has been found that most natural waters in the United States contain rhamnose-positive strains that are either serologically untypable or react with multiple serovars. In another study, forty-three strains of *Y. enterocolitica* from children with gastroenteritis and eighteen laboratory strains were examined for ST production and all clinical and seven laboratory strains produced ST as assessed by the infant mouse assay, and all were negative in the Y-1 adrenal cell assay.

Although pathogenic strains of *Y. enterocolitica* produce ST, it appears that this agent is not critical to virulence. Some evidence for the lack of importance of ST was provided by *Schiemann*, who demonstrated positive HeLa-cell and Sereny test responses, with a 0:3 strain that did not produce enterotoxin. On the other hand, each of forty- nine isolates belonging to serovar 0:3 and the other four virulent serovars produced ST. **Virulence appears to be a result to** tissue invasiveness for this organism. The latter has been shown to be mediated by a 40-48 Mdal plasmid. The 44-Mdal plasmid of *Y. enterocolitica* and a 47- Mdal plasmid of 1: *pestis* strain have been shown to share 55% DNA sequence homology over about 80% of the plasmid genomes. In addition to tissue invasiveness, the 40-45 Mdal plasmids are responsible for calcium dependent growth at 37°C, autoagglutination in tissue culture medium, adult mouse lethality for serovar 0:8 strains suckling mouse lethality, HEp-2 cell adherence, and adherence in at least three outer membrane proteins. The plasmids appear not to be responsible for enterotoxigenicity. HEp-2 cell invasiveness, or expression of fimbrial proteins. Other plasmids exist in ygrsiniae ranging from 3 to 36 Mdal. but they are not virulence associated. Often strains representing six serovars that contained 42-44 Mdal plasmids, all were lethal to suckling mice, whereas those without these plasmids were not. The feeding of virulence plasmid-bearing strains to thirst stressed mice was found to be lethal, while plasmidless strains had no effect on mice. The same plasmid is responsible for other virulence-associated properties of this organism, including autoagglutionation calcium-dependent growth, production of V and W antigens and serum resistance. The V and W antigens of 0:8 (biovar2) were immunologically identical to those of *Y. pestis* and *Yersinia pseudotuberculosis*. The serum resistance factors encoded for by the virulence plasmid consist of outer membrane proteins synthesized when cells are grown at 37°C but not at 25°C. The letter cells adhered more to Henle monolayers than the 37°C-grown, thus making the latter more resistant to serum killing.

Although its role in virulence is unclear, some strains of *Y. enterocolitica* have been shown to produce a broad-spectrum mannose-resistant adhesion at 20°C that agglutinated erythrocytes of at least ten animal species. The hemagglutination is associated with fmbriae, which were not produced when cells were cultured at 37°C. Of 210:3 and 0:8 serovars, 7 produced the agglutinating fimbriae, while only 46 of 115 from a variety of sources did.

To determine which of three in vitro tests best correlated with virulence, thirty-four strains were tested for calcium dependency, autoagglutination, and the presence of 40-48 Mdal plasmids. With Ca^{2+} dependency, twenty-nine of thirty one strains were positive, whereas all of thirty-four were positive by the other two tests. These authors favoured autoagglutination in tissue culture medium at 35°C as being perhaps the single best test. *Prpic et al.* also found autoagglutination to be the best in vitro method, followed by Ca^{2+} dependency. In addition to *Y. enterocolitica* strains, virulent *Y. pestis* and *Y. pseudotuberculosis* autoagglutinate in tissue culture medium, whereas avirulent strains do not. *Schiemann* and *Devenish* have suggested that the two most important factors involved in virulence of this organism are the presence of V and W antigens and the presence of an invasive factor demonstrable by *HeLa* cell infectivity, but general support of this position is wanting.

When iron-dextran was administered IP to mice, the median lethal dose of *Y. enterocolitica* serovars 0:3 and 0:9 was reduced by about tenfold, while Desferat (desferrioxamine B mesylate) reduced the lethal dose> 100,000 fold. The 0:8 strains were less affected by these compounds, suggesting their lower requirement for iron.

Incidence of Y Enterocolitica in Foods

This organism has been isolated from cakes, vacuumpackaged meats, seafood, vegetables, milk and other food products. It has been isolated also from beef, lamb, and pork. Of all sources, swine appears to be the major source of strains pathogenic for man.

From thirty-one procine tongues from freshly slaughtered animals, twenty-one strains were isolated and represented six serovars with 0:8 the most common and 0:6, 30 the second most commonly isolated. The other serovars recovered were 0:3, 0:13, 7, 0:18, and 0:46. Of one hundred milk samples examined in the United States, twelve raw and one pasteurized yielded *Y. enterocolitica*. In eastern France, 81% of seventy five samples of raw milk contained *Y. enterocolitica* following enrichment, with serovar 0:5 being the most predominant. In Australia, thirty-five isolates were recovered from raw goat's milk, with 71% being rhamnose positive.

Gastroenteritis Syndrome and Incidence

In addition to gasteroenteritis, this organism has been associated with human pseudoappendicitis, mesenteric lymphadenitis, terminal ileitis, reactive arthritis, peritonitis, colon and neck abscesses, cholecystis, and erythema nodosum. It has been recovered from urine, blood, cerebrospinal fluid, and the eyes of infected individuals. It is, of course, recovered from the stools of gastroenteritis victims. Only the gastroenteritis syndrome is addressed below.

There is a seasonal incidence associated with this syndrome, with the fewest outbreaks occurring during the spring and the greatest number in October and November. The incidence is highest in the very young and the old. In an outbreak studied by *Gutman et al.* the symptoms (and percent complaining of them) were fever, diarrhea, severe abdominal pain vomiting, pharyngitis and headache. The outbreak led to two appendectomies and two deaths.

A synopsis of some outbreaks in which *Y. enterocolitica* was shown or suspected as being the etiologic agent is presented in Table milk (raw, improperly pasteurized, or recontaminated) was the vehicle food in most. The first documented outbreak in the United States occurred in 1976 in NewYork state, with serovar 0:8 as the responsible strain, and chocolate milk prepared by adding chocolate syrup to previously pasteurized milk was the vehicle food.

Symptoms of the gastroenteritis syndrome develop several days following ingestion of contaminated foods, and are characterized by abdominal pain and diarrhea as noted above. Children appear to be more susceptible than adults, and the organisms may be present in stools for up to 40 days following illness. As noted above, a variety of systemic involvements may occur as a consequence of the gastroenteritis syndrome.

Campylobacter jejuni

The genus *Campylobacter* is composed of organisms once classified as *vibrio* spp. and known primarily to veterinary microbiologists until recent years. The genus contains at least eight species, and the interest of veterinarians in this group stems from the role of these organisms in spontaneous abortions in cattle and sheep and other animal pathologies.

This bacterium is microaerophilic, requiring small amounts of oxygen (3-6%) for growth. Growth is actually inhibited in 21% oxygen. Carbon dioxide (about 10%) is required for good growth. Its metabolism is respiratory. In addition to *C. jejuni*. *C. coli* and *C. intestinalis* are infectious for man. More detailed information on the campylobacters can be found in Smibert.

The species of interest in foods is *C. jejuni*, and to a lesser extent C. *coli*, which, lake all members of the genus, are slender, spirally curved rods that possess a single polar flagellum at one or both ends of the cell. They are oxidase and catalase positive, will not grow in the presence of 3.5% NaCl do not grow at 25° but do at 42°C, and are inhibited by nalidixic acid. *C. jejuni* will hydrolyze hippurate. They grow best at 42°C but grow slower than the Enterobacteriaceae. Because of their small cell size, they can be separated from most other gram-negative bacteria by use of a 0.65 μm filter. *C. jejuni* is heat sensitive, with D 55°C for a composite of equal numbers of five strains being 1.09 min in peptone and 2.25 min in ground, autoclaved chicken. With internal heating of ground beef to 79°C, 10^{7} cells/g could not be detected after about 10 min. It appears to be sensitive to freezing, with about 10^{4} cells/chicken carcass being greatly reduced or eliminated at-18°C, and for artificially contaiminated hamburger meat, the numbers were reduced by 1 log cycle over a 7 day period.

Distribution

Unlike *Y. enterocolitica* and *V. parahaemolvticus*, *C. jejuni* is not an environmental organism but rather is one that is associated with warm-blooded animals. A large percentage of all major meat animals have been shown to contain these organisms in their feces, with poultry being prominent. A synopsis of some reports on their prevalence in some animal specimens as well as in poultry edible parts is presented in Table. Its prevalence in fecal samples often ranges from around 30 to 100%. Reports $_0$n isolations by various investigators have been summarized by *Blaser*, and the specimens and percent positive for *C. jejwii* are as follows: chicken intestinal contents, swine feces, sheep feces (up to 73), swine intestinal contents, sheep carcasses, swine carcasses, eviscerated chicken, and enviscerated turkey, The prevalence of C. *jejuni* and C. *colt* in 396 frozen and 405 fresh meats was examined. About 12% of fresh meats were positive but only 2.3% of the frozen, suggesting the lethal effects of freezing on the organisms. A higher percentage of chicken livers was positive (30% of fresh and 15% of frozen) than any of the other meats, which included beef, pork and lamp livers as well as muscle meats from these animals. Over, 2,000 samples of a variety of retail-store meats examined for *C. jejuni/coli* and *C. coli* by nine defferent laboratories. The organisms were found on 29.7% of chicken samples, 4.2% of pork sausage, 3.6% of ground beef, and about 5.1% of 1,800 red meats. Only *C. coli* was recovered from pork products. A higher incidence was noted in June and September (8.6%) than in December and March (4.5 and 3.9% respectively).

Fecal specimens from humans with diarrhea yield *C. jejuni*, and this bacterium may be the single most common cause of acute diarrhea in man. Of 8.097 specimens submitted to eight hospital laboratories over a 25 month period in different parts of United States, this organism was recovered from 4.6% salmonellae from 2.3%, and shigellae from 1%. The peak isolations for *C. jejuni* were in the age group 10-29 years. Peak isolation occur during the summer months, and it has been noted that 3-14% diarrheal patients in devel-oped countries yield stool specimens that contain *C. jejuni*. Peak isolations from individually caged hens occurred in October and later April-early May. In the latter study, 8.1% of the hens were chronic excreters of the organism, whereas 33% were negative even though they were likely exposed.

The prevalence of *C. jejuni* on some poultry products is noted in Table. The numbers reported range from log 2.00 to 4.26/g. Once this organism is established in chicken house, most of the flock becomes infected over time. A recent study revealed that the organism appeared in all chicken inhabitants with in a week once it was found among any of the inhabitants. In addition to poultry, the other primary source of this organism is raw milk. Some recorded outbreaks of *C. jejuni* enteritis from raw milk are noted in Table. Since the organism exists in cow feces, it is not surprising that it may be found in raw milk, and the degree of contamination would be expected to vary depending upon milking procedures. In a survey of 108 samples from bulk tanks of raw milk in Wisconsin. only 1 was positive for *C. jejuni*, whereas the feces of 64% of the cows in a grade A herd were positive.

Virulence Properties

At least some strains of *C. jejuni* produce a heat-lablile enterotoxin (CJT) that shares some common properties with the enterotoxins of *V. cholerae* (CT) and *E. coli* (*LT*). CJT increases cAMP levels, induces changes in CHO cells, and induces fluid accumulation in rate ileal loops. Maximal production of CJT in a special medium was achieved at 42°C for 24 h, and the amount produced was enhanced by polymyxin. The quantities produced by strains varied widely from node to about 50 ng/ml CJT protein. The amount of toxin was doubled as measured by Y-1 adrenal cell assay when cells were first exposed to lincomycin and then polymyxin. CJT is neutralized by CT and *E. coli* LT antisera, indicating immunological homology with these two enterotoxins. The *C. jejuni* LT appears to share the same cell receptors as CT and *E. coli* LT, and it contains a B subunit immunologically related to the B subunits to CT and LT of *E. coli*.

C. jejuni enteritis appears to be caused in part by the invasive abilities of the organism. Evidence for this comes from the nature of the clinical. symptoms, the rapid development of high agglutinin titers after infection, recovery of the organism from peripheral blood during the acute phase of the disease, and the finding that *C. jejuni* can penetrate *HeLa* cells.

Plasmids have been demonstrated in *C. jejuni* cells. Of seventeen strains studied, eleven were found to carry plasmids ranging from 1.6 to 70 Mdal, but their role and function in disease is nuclear.

A serotyping scheme has been developed for *C. jejuni.* From chickens and humans; 82 and 98%, respectively, of isolates belonged to biovar 1.

Enteritis Syndrome

About 2,000 individuals contrated infections, the symptoms (and percent of individuals affected) were as follows: abdominal pain or cramps diarrhea, malaise, headache, and fever, which were traced to a water supply, from the first U.S. outbreak of *C. jejuni.* Symptoms lasted from 1 to 4 days. In the more severe cases, bloody stools may occur, and the diarrhea may resemble ulcerative colitis, while the abdominal pain may mimic acute appendicitis. Highly variable, usually 48 to 82 h even may be as long as 7 to 10 days, or more is the incubation period for enteritis.

Prevention

Heat-sensitive bacteria that are destroyed by milk pasteurization temperatures are *V parahaemolvticus*, *Y enterocolitica*, *C. jejuni.* The avoidance of raw seafood products and care in preventing cross contamination with contaminated raw materials will eliminate or drastically reduce the incidence of food-born gastroenteritis caused by *V. parahaemolyticus* and 1. *enterocolitica.* Seawaters entry should be avoided to prevent wound infection by vibrios, through individuals with body nicks or abrasions. Yersionsis can be avoided or certainly minimized by not drinking water that has not been purified and by avoiding raw or underprocessed milk. By not eating undercooked or unpasteurized foods of animals origin, especially milk, campylobacteriosis can be avoided.

SPIROCHAETACEAE

The term *spirochete* refers to a class of bacteria that characreristically possess flexible, helically coiled cell walls. The diverse organisms making up the family Spirochaetaceae are divided into five genera, but the pathogenic spirochetes are found only in the genera *Treponema, Borrelia, and Leptospira.*

Structurally, the spirochetes have a gram-negative-type cell wall composed of an outer membrane, a peptidoglycan layer, and a cytoplasmic membrane. Interestingly, bactericidal antibody appears to be directed toward determinants in the outer membrane of the spirochetes.

Immediately beneath the outer membrane lies one or more axial filaments that, because of their similarity to other bacterial flagella, are termed flagella, or by some, endoflagella. The spirochete flagella are attached subterminally at one end of the cell and extend toward the opposite pole. These flagella are apparently responsible for the rapid motility of the spirochetes, but, since they lie beneath the outer membrane, the mechanism by which they achieve this motility is not entirely clear.

Many spirochetes are present as normal flora in the digestive tracts of both ruminant and nonruminant animals, as well as in the human oral flora where they can be found in subgingival plaques. It has been suggested, but not established, that spirochetes may be involved in periodontal disease. Their role, however, as etiologic agents of other human diseases is well known, and a discussion of that role comprises the remainder of this chapter.

Spirochetes are slender, undulating, cork-screw-like, relatively flexible, filamentous organisms. They are ubiquitous, occurring in nature in soil, water, and decaying organic materials and in the bodies of plants, animals, and man. Some of the spirochetes are saprophytes, some are commensals, and others are pathogens, causing a number of severe diseases of human beings and of the lower animals. The first disease- producing spirochete was discovered by Obenneier in 1873 is the blood of patients with relapsing fever. *Treponema pailidum* was not discovered until 1905, and the discoverers, *Schaudinn* and *Hoffmann* believed the organism was a protozoan.

MORPHOLOGY

The spirochetes have short or long spirals with the coils in three dimensions. The size varies greatly, from 2 to 500 *t* in length. They multiply slowly in Noguchi's ascitic fluid-rabbit kidney medium and in embryonated eggs.

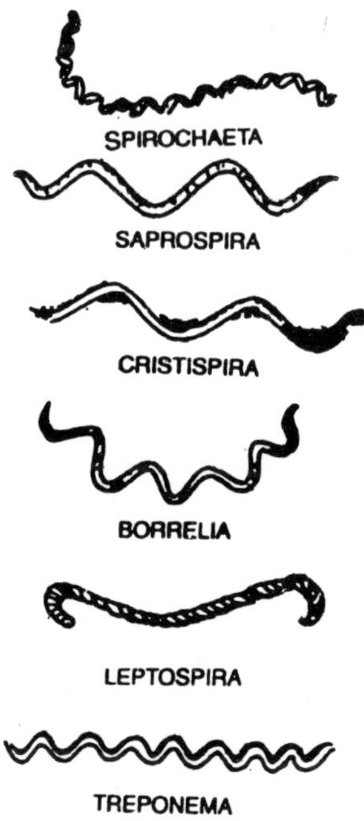

Fig. 11.1. Morphological characters of various Spirochaetes.

Flexibility

All spirochetes are more flexible than bacteria, but flexibility of these organisms varies with different species.

Filtrability

Treponema pallidum, the spirochete which causes syphilis, passes through membrane filters with some difficulty. Chandler and Clark found that none pissed through membranes of 0.22 mμ pore size, but did pass through as the pore size was increased up to 14mμ. With this size pores 78 per cent of motile and 50 per cent of nonmotile *?ieponema* passed through *the* filters.

Motility

Spirochetes are motile. They progress by sinuous and rotating movements of the body. External flagella are not found on organisms examined directly from living man or animals. However, after tryptic or peptic digestion for 10 minutes, 3 axial filaments can be seen *in* the body of *T pallidum*, and 8 to12 in *Borr recurrentis*. After 20 minutes' digestion, the filaments are freed from the body and appear as flagella. The contractile material in the *Leptospira* is wound around the outside of the organism. The organism *Spirillum minus*, which causes rat bite fever, resembles a spirochete in many ways but has a tuft of flagella at each end.

Division

Spirochetes usually divide by transverse fission, but they may have a more complicated method of reproduction. The very beautiful electron micrographs made by *Listgarten* and *Socransky* show that the division of *Treponema microdentium* is by transverse fission with the outer envelope being the last to divide.

Resistance

Since these organisms do not form endospores, their resistance to injurious substances and physical agents is similar to that of the nonsporogenous bacteria. Susceptibility to chemotherapeutic agents is notable among the organisms in this group, and the spirochetes differ from the bacteria in being especially susceptible to destruction by arsenic, antimony, bismuth, mercury compounds, and penicillin when they are within the bodies of animals.

Staining Reactions

Some spirochetes stain readily with the ordinary aniline dyes, but most of the pathogenic varieties are difficult to stain. Such stains as those of Wright. Giemsa. and the ones based upon Romanowsky's method give the best results. Spirochetes which can be stained by Gram's method are gram-negative. Impregnation of the organisms with silver nitrate, followed by reduction of the silver in the organism, is a procedure of great utility in the demonstration of spirochetes in tissue and smears. The Levaditi method usually is applied to tissues ; the Fontana- Tribondeau method is employed in staining smears.

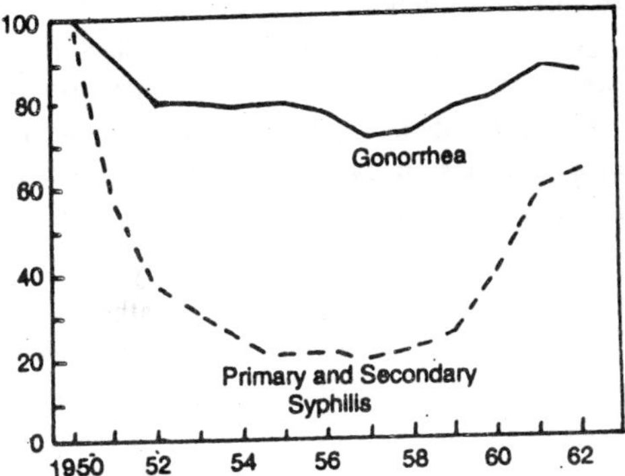

Fig. 11.2. Graph showing the increase of syphilis in the leen-age population from 1956 to 1962.

The pathogenic spirochetes, 0.1 to 0.2 μ in thickness, are seen best in the living state by darkfield illumination. Darkfield illumination is and should be a routine procedure in the examination of material for spirochetes.

Cultivation

Geiman has reviewed the nutritional requirement and metabolism of the spirochetes which can be cultivated. The *Leptospira* and many of the free-living forms are aerobic and can be cultivated without much difficulty. The *Borrelia* are anaerobic or microaerophilic. They survive and multiply slowly in Noguchi's ascitic fluid-rabbit kidney medium and in embryonated eggs. Investigators agree that the pathogenic *Treponema* from syphilis, yaws, and pints have not been cultivated.

Hardy, *Lee*, and *Nell* succeeded in cultivating 14 strains of treponemas and one of *Borrelia vincentii* in colony form on agar plates inoculated under ordinary atmospheric conditions but incubated anaerobically.

Rosebury and *Reynolds* have grown colonies of spirochetes directly from human gingival scrapings after passage of such scrapings through guinea pigs.

CLASSIFICATION

1. *Spirochaeta.* These are large, spiral organisms with flexible

undulating membranes and the protoplast is wound spirally round the axial filament like a staircase. Type species *Spirochaeta plicatalis.*

2. *Saprospira.* It consists of spiral protoplasm divided by septa but without any axial filament or crista. They are free swimming, aquatic organisms. Type *species-Saprospira grandis*

3. *Cristispira.* Ftexuous cell bodies in coarse spirals are characterised by a thin band-like undulating membrane or crista, found as parasites in the intestinal tracts of moluscs.Type *species-Cristispira balbiannii.*

4. *Borrelia.* (Spironema). They are usually 8 to 10μ in length, spirals are coarse, open, irregular. Some are pathogenic for man and others for mammals and birds and found either in the blood or in the mucous membrane. Type species *Borr recurrentis*, *Borvincenti etc*

5. *Leptospira.* Finely coiled organisms, 6 to 20tt in length, have closely set primary coils, which are difficult to observe and Secondary, larger coils in the form of C, S, or W, ends being hooked; some are pathogenic for man or animals.Type species- *Leptospira icterohaemorrhagiae.*

6. *Treponema.* Protoplasm often shows regular, close spirals with pointed ends; pathogenic and parasitic for men and animals. Type species-*Treponema pallidum.*

SYPHILIS

Syphilis is an infectious disease with protean manifestations caused by a spirochete, *Treponema pallidum.* Under natural conditions syphilis occurs only in man, and the infection usually is transmitted from one human being to another by direct contact, generally through sexual intercourse.

Beginning about 1936, a major effort was made to control syphilis in the United States. Moderate success was being obtained before the introduction of penicillin therapy in 1945. The combination of control measures and penicillin therapy reduced the number of cases of primary and secondary syphilis by 85 percent between 1947 ands 1955. Unfortunately, the rap4elimination of federal and state funds for control measures forced the abandonment of organized control programs. This was followed by the elimination of routine serologic tests for syphilis in many clinics and hospitals. This period of neglect is now bearing bitter fruit. Syphilitic psychotics in tax-supported mental institutions still cost $50 million per year. The low point in the incidence of new infections was reached in 1955. with a rise beginning in 1956. From 1959 to 1963 each year has shown 50 percent increase in incidence over a previous year. The most rapid increase has been in homosexuals and in teenagers. Between 1956 and 1960 there was an increase of more than 130 percent in the 15 to 19 year age group. About 124,000 cases of syphilis of all ages were reported in 1962. It is known that general practitioners and specialists, outside of well-organized hospitals and clinics, report only from 10 percent to 50 per cent of the actual cases seen.

TABLE 11.1. CLASSIFICATION OF SPIROCHAETES

Family	*Genus*	*Species*	*Pathogenicity*	*Vector or Reservoir*
Spirochaetaceae	Pirochaeta		Non pathogenic	
	Saprospira		"	
	Cristispira			
Tepenematacease	Borrelia	Bor. recurrentis	Relapsing fever (Europe)	Louse
		Bor. carteri	Relapsing fever (India)	Louse
		Bor. duttoni	Relapsing fever (Africa)	Ticks
		Bor. vincenti	Vincent's angina	
	Leptospira	L. icterohaem-orrhagiae	Weil's disease	Rats
		L.hebdomadis, etc	Japan seven-day fever	Field mice (voles)
	Treponema	Tr. pallidum	Syphilis	
		Tr. pertenue	Yaws	
		Tr. carateum	Pinta	
		Tr. micro-dentium	Commensals, mouth	
		Tr. macro-dentium	Commensals, mouth	

After the return of Columbus' sailors to Europe in about1494, syphilis became almost epidemic and was one of the great scourges of the next century. There is disagreement among authorities about the origin of this sudden explosion. Some believe that syphilis has been smouldering in the population for centuries and became epidemic about the time Columbus' sailors returned from the New, World. Others believe that syphilis evolved in the New World and was introduced into Europe by the returning sailors.

The contagiousness of syphilis was apparent to those who contracted it, and in the eighteenth and nineteenth centuries *John Hunter*, *Ricord*, and other physicians proved that syphilis was infectious by inoculating nien with material from syphilitic sores. *Treponema pallidum* was discovered in 1905 by *Schaudinn* and *Hoffnann*.

MORPHOLOGY AND STAINING

Treponema pallidum is delicate in form and resistant to staining by the methods usually employed for staining bacteria. It is readily visualized by the darkfield technique, or by coating of the organism with reduced silver nitrate after the method of Fontana-Tnbondeau. It was demonstrated first in tissue sections by Levaditi's silver impregnation method.

Deacongnd his associates found that *T pallidum* could be identified in smears on slides by the new fluorescent antibody technique. Later studies by *Edwards* have shown that the method is about as accurate as a dark field and has the advantage that slides may be made in any part of the world and mailed to a central laboratory for staining. By appropriate absorption of the testing serum the various species of *Treponema* can be identified. This should make it possible to identify the *Treponema* of yaws, pinta, and bejel.

Treponema pallidum has a cylindrical, flexible body 5 to 20 i in length and abort 0.2 tt in diameter. The ends are pointed and sometimes prolonged in delicate, terminal filaments. The body is coiled in 8 to 14 regular, rigid, sharp spirals, with a spiral amplitude of about 1 It. Living organisms rotate rapidly but progress slowly. The rotation continues as the organism bends in 8 and circular shapes without losing its coiled shape. The beautiful electron micrographs of Swain reveal an outer periplast which covers the entire organism. Neither axial fib ments nor flagella are visible. After 20 minutes of tryptic digestion the periplast is dissolved to reveal three twisted axial filaments. The fibrils, 14 to 17 μ in diameter, may become detached from the body at one end to spread out on the film to simulate flagella.

Multiplication is usually by transverse fission, with a division time of 30 hours calculated from direct enumeration of organisms in experimental chancres in rabbits. The division time for the cultural form of the nonpathogenic Reiter strain of *Treponema* averages 10 hours. *T pallidum* cannot be differentiated morphologically from *T pertenue* or from such nonpathogenic spirochetes of the mouth and genitalia as *T microdentium* or *T mucosum.*

Cultural Characteristics

There is general agreement among investigators that the pathogenic treponemas, *T pallidum*, *T pertenue*, and *T carateum*, have not been cultivated. The organisms are anaerobic, and although they grow readily in the tissues of man and in the testicles of experimentally inoculated rabbits, they do not grow in tissue cultures, in embryonated eggs. or *in* artificial media. even when the latter are under anaerobic conditions.

The cultured treponemas such as the strains isolated by Noguchi, Zinsser, Nichols, Reiter, and Kazan, were originally isolated from syphilitic lesions, but were probably contaminating saprophytes.

Resistance

These delicate organisms are immobilized and killed by contact with oxygen, saponin, distilled water, soap, mercuric ointment, and other common bacterial agents. *Carpenter*, *Boak*, and *Warren* found that *T pallidum* in infected testicular tissues of rabbits was destroyed by a temperature of 39°C in 5 hours, of 40°C in 3 hours, of 41°C in 2 hours, and of 41.5°C in 1 hour. These observations form a rational basis for the treatment of syphilis with fever, whether induced by malaria or high frequency electric currents.

Since *T pallidum* dies in three days in blood stored in the refrigerators of blood banks, there is little danger of transmitting the disease by a routine blood transfusion from banked blood, although the infection may be transmitted by fresh blood.

Antigenic Structure

Information concerning the antigenic structure of *T Pallidum* is incomplete, primarily because of the difficulty in obtaining enough treponemas free of tissue proteins for chemical study. Limited studies have shown the presence of proteins, polysaccharides, and two different lipids. Although clinical evidence of immunity had been demonstrated in experimentally infected rabbits and in man, nothing was known about the nature of this immunity, and it was assumed, until about 1950, that the classic type of antibodies associated with immunity in bacterial diseases was absent in syphilis. The first breakthrough on this problem was achieved by *Nelson* and *Mayer* in 1949 when they described the "treponema pallida immobilization test" (TPI). The serum of patients showing evidence of clinical immunity was able to stop the motility of living *T pallidum* obtained from primary experimental testicular lesions in rabbies. The improved methods of harvesting and freeing the living treponemas from rabbit tissue protein supplied the material with which precipitins, agglutinins, and complement-fixing antibodies have been demonstrated. In the presence of complement the treponemas are not only immobilized but are eventually killed With the immobilization test (TPI) there are cross-reactions between *T pallidum* from different patients and between *T pallidum* and *T pertenue*, but none between the nonpathogenic cultured strains of *Treponema*, such as the Reiter. Kazan and S26. There was no cross-immobilization with *T cuniculi*, which causes veneral spirochetosis *in* rabbits. or with pathogenic *Leptospira* or *Borrelia*.

The Wassermann Reaction

The complement-fixation test for syphilis, introduced by *Girsserm-ann* and his associates in 1906, uses a nonspecific lipoid antigen and measures an antibody known as reagin which is not protective. The nonspecific antigen is distributed widely in mammalian tissues and even in some plants. The cultivated strains of nonpathogenic *Treponema* also contain an antigen which will react with the reagin. Although the reagin is not a protective antibody and is measured with a nonspecific antigen, this antibody is produced by practically every patient who becomes infected with *T pallidum. Sachs*, *Klopstock*, and *Weil* suggested in 1925 that an infection with *T pallidum* damages the tissues of the host and splits of a lipoidal fraction which, acting as a hapten, combines with the protein of the treponema and then stimulates the production of antibodies (reagin) which can be measured in the complement -fixing reaction with the lipoid antigen.

Numerous precipitin tests have been evolved for the rapid and economic detection of antibodies in patients suspected of having syphilis. . The best of these is the VDRL developed in the Venereal Disease Research Laboratory. When used as an eliminating test it was found to give a fairly high percentage of biologically false tests.

In 1957, *Deacon* and his co-workers introduced the fluorescein treponemal antibody test (FTA) as a substitute for the very expensive *Treponema pallidum* immobilization test (TPI)'. The new FTA test was very sensitive but gave some false positive tests because it detected some antibodies produced in man by the essentially nonpathogenic Treponemas. *Hunter*, *Deacon*, and *Meyer* absorbed the cross-reacting antibodies from the serum by treatment with the Reiter treponemes. After this absorption the new test FTA-ABS was found to be both sensitive and specific for the staining of *T. pallidum*, the Nichols strain, and *T pallidum* from man.

The use of the FTA-ABS test has been recommended by *Olanskv and Norins* and by *Mackev* and his associates as the most specific test for syphilis. The FTA-ABS should be used on sera giving positive test to the eliminating VDRL.

Logan aid *Cox* reported good progress in the development of a quantitative automated microhenragglutination assay for antibodies to *T. pallidum*.

Antibodies

Both 19 S (IgM) and 7 S (IgG) antibodies are made in man to the nonspecific cardiolipin-like antigen. A series of studies on the specific antibodies made to the antigen of *T. pallidum* showed that IgM, IgA, and IgG globulins were produced. The 1gM globulins occur early in infection. Later IgM, IgA, and IgG globulin appear, but only IgG globulins persist in late infection. These studies were confirmed and extended by *Tulian*, *Logan* and *Norins* in 1969 and by *Julian* and his associates in 1971.

Allergic Reactions

The destructive lesions in late syphilis seem to be analogous to those in tuberculosis, which are known to be the result of hypersensitivity. Patients with destructive lesions usually give strong local dermal reactions 24 to 48 hours after the intracutaneous injection of 'organic luetin" which is prepared by extracting mature syphilomas from the testicles of rabbits, or of *T. pallidum*, freed of tissue by centrifugation and preserved with 1 percent formalin This latter preparation is called "treponemin".

Clinical observations suggest that some strains of *T pallidum* are more virulent than others and that some are more neurotropic than viscerotropic, but this variation may be in the patient rather than in the spirochete. Rabbits do show varying degree of resistance to homologous and heterologous strains of *T pallidum.*

Toxins

Neither exotoxins nor endotoxin have been demonstrated and the minimal amount of reaction to the primary infection suggests the absence of toxin.

The typical local primary lesion is circumscribed, indurated. superficially ulcerated, relatively avascular, and painless. It is frequently called a hunterian chancre in honor of *John Hunter*, or a hard chancre, to distinguish it from the chancroid caused by infection with *H. ducrevi*. The primary lesion unfortunately, is not always characteristic or detectable and may be so insignificant that it is overlooked by the patient. Thus, in the female the chancre may be located on the cervix of the uterus, and in the male it occasionally occurs in the urethra. where it cannot be seen by a casual inspection. Infections have been produced in rabbits without the development of observable local lesions, and presumably similar infections occur also in man. The regional lymph nodes usually arc swollen. hard. and rubbery.

A clinical diagnosis of primary syphilis always should be confirmed by the demonstration of the spirochetes in the secretions from the lesion. It is important that the specimen be examined before the administration of arsenicals or penicillin, because the treponemas usually disappear from the local lesion within 6 to 24 hours after the first treatment.

No detectable antibodies appear during the incubation period of the disease or even during the early days after the appearance of the chancre. Usually within40 days and always within 30 days after the appearance of the primary lesion an antibody appears in the serum ; it can be detected by any one of the various serologic tests for syphilis.

The primary lesion invariably heals, even without treatment, within a period of 10 to 40 days. The mechanism by which the spirochetes in the local lesion are destroyed is not understood, but it is presumed to be of the nature of a local tissue immunity rather than a humoral immunity, because ann unhindered multiplication of the organisms in the skin and the mucous membranes preparatory to the explosive onset of the secondary lesions occurs simultaneously with the elimination of the spirochetes from the local lesion.

Secondary Syphilis

Following the healing of the primary lesion, the patient is asymptomatic for a period varying from two to six months, with an average, of three months, before the appearance of multiple secondary lesions in the skin or mucous membranes or both. Often secondary manifestations develop concurrently with the healing of the primary lesion, The patient may have some constitutional symptoms at the time, such as fever, headache, and malaise, but the, symptoms are minimal in view of the multiplicity of the lesions and the enormous numbers of spirochetes present in each individual area. Usually there is a generalized enlargement of the lymph nodes at this time. The lesions generally disappear without treatment and within minimal scar formation after intervals of 3 weeks to 3 months, but may recur after a latent period of 3 to 12 months, In some instances, latent periods alternate with recurrences for as long as four years, although" the latent periods become materially lengthened and the recurrences correspondingly shortened. During the period of secondary recurrences the serologic tests for syphilis practically always are positive.

Tertiary or Late Latent Syphilis

After an interval of about four years the mucosal and cutaneous recurrences no longer appear, but lesions of the cardiovascular and nervous systems make their appearance. Lesions in these systems are indolent and slowly progressive and stimulate no violent tissue reaction. This is sometimes described as the anergic type of reaction. *Lawton Smith* and his associates have demonstrated actively motile *T pallidum* in indolent lesions of the aqueous humor of the eye, and in the cerebrospinal fluid and liver of patients with late ocular and neurosyphilis. These treponemas were identified as *T pallidum* by their reaction to fluorescein tagged anti-*Treponema pallidum* globulin.

Pathogenicity

Syphilis is seen in man only, but primary, secondary and tertiary stages are seen after experimental inoculation in chimpanzees. Experimental inoculations are produced in monkeys, rabbits and mice by intratesticular, intradermal or corneal inoculation of tissue containing the spirochaetes. Monkeys often show a primary lesion only. In rabbits, the infection is readily obtained and comparable to the human disease. Inoculations into the anterior chamber of the eye produces keratitis and iritis. In an intratesticular inoculation after an incubation period of 2-3 weeks, the testis becomes swollen, indurated, the lymph nodes are later involved and a generalised infection follows (analogous to secondary stage in man). *Mice.* Inoculation of the syphilitic material causes infection without any symptom and the organism may be recovered from the lymph node, spleen and brain after any length of time.

In man, *Trr pallidum* causes syphilis.

SYPHILIS

Syphilis is a specific, contagious, venereal disease caused by *Trr pallidum*, marked by lesions on the skin and other organs of the body. The name of the disease is derived from the name of a shepherd, called "Syphilus" from the Latin poem of *Fracastorius*, published in 1530.

Transmission

It is customary to divide syphilis into two; namely, *acquired* and *congenital*. The disease is generally acquired through sexual intercourse. The infection occurs through some abrasion on the skin or through mucous surface. The spirochaete can enter through the intact mucous membrane. *Extragenital infection* may occur by kissing ; or doctors, nurses and midwives may acquire the disease by handling cases of syphilis. Infection may occur by *blood transfusion*, in which case, however, the primary lesion is absent.

Congenital

Syphilitic women can transmit congenital syphilis to the offspring and the organism in this case passes through the placenta from the maternal blood to the foetal circulation. In this case, the infection is generalised from the time of manifestation without any primary stage. After infection through an abrasion, the organism multiplies locally and is also carried to the regional lymph node along the lymphatics within a very short time. During the early period of infection, the organism rapidly enters into the blood and tissues without, however, producing any clinical sign of the disease at that,time.

Course

Primary stage

After an incubation period of 2-6 weeks, a hard sore or "chancre" develops at the site of infection. This is accompanied by enlargement of the regional lymph nodes. The chancre exudate teems with *Trr pallidum* and is highly contagious. It usually heals up in 3-8 weeks.

Secondary stage

This begings 6-12 weeks is characterised by malaise, slight fever and generalised lesions on the skin and mucous membrane, sore throat, generalised enlargement of the lymph nodes and affections of the bones, eyes and other organs. Late in the secondary stage, condylomas in mucocutaneous areas are common and the lesions show a large number of the organisms in the serous secretion.

Tertiary stage

It may soon follow the secondary stage or be delayed for many years. The commonest lesions are gumma in various internal organs (visceral syphilis) and skin syphilitic aortitis and meningeal involvements. The organisms are scanty in the tertiary lesions.

Quarternary Syphilis (Parasyphilitic Affections)

It is characterised by involvement of the central nervous system showing infections like *tabes dorsalis* and general paralysis of in some of these usually appear many years after the infection.

Each of these stages is separated by a period of remission or a quiescent interval, when the symptoms disappear.

Congenital Syphilis

This is trasmitted through the placenta of a syphilitic mother an4 the infection of the foetus usually occurs in the second half of pregnancy. There is no primary stage and the secondary and late secondary stages are mixed up. When the infection is heavy during pregnancy the child is stillborn with an enormous number of spirochaetes in the viscera like liver. spleen, lung, suprarenal, etc. But a child born many years after the mother's infection may show little evidence of syphilis except some stigma.

Pathogenesis of Syphilis

Primary Syphilis

Following initial contact, the organisms penetrate the mucous membranes and enter the lymphatics. Regional lymph nodes become enlarged, and a blood-stream invasion results in the dissemination of the organisms throughout the body. A primary lesion, called a chancre, usually occurs about 3 weeks after contact at the site of the initial entrance of organisms, although it may appear at any time between 1 and 12 weeks after initial contact. The lesion is teeming with treponemes, and a dark-field examination of the fluid from the chancre provides the most fundamental laboratory method for an immediate clinical diagnosis.

Secondary Syphilis

After several weeks, the chancre spontaneously heals, leaving little or no scar and suggesting a spontaneous cure. However, the swollen lymph nodes may persist somewhat longer, and, at about the time the chancre heals (and occasionally before its disappearance), the widespread lesions of secondary syphilis appear. Because of the appearance of lesions, syphilis was originally given the name, "the great pox," to differentiate it from smallpox. The lesions are most commonly recognized on the skin and mucous membranes; when hair follicles are involved, a loss of hair, eyebrows, or beard results. These lesions are filled with spirochetes, easily visualized by dark-field microscopy; because they are highly infectious, the organisms can be spread by contact in a nonvenereal manner. During this stage, essentially any organ of the body may be involved (including the central nervous system, eyes, bones, and internal organs), leading to a wide variety of clinical manifestations. Immune-complex glomerulonephritis and arthritis are commonly seen, and, for this reason, syphilis has been referred to as "the great imitator".

After a period of 4 to 8 weeks, the lesions disappear and the disease appears to become latent. During the subsequent 3 or 4 years, however, relapses may occur, resulting in mucocutaneous lesions, which eventually disappear. Approximately one fourth of these cases appear to be true cures. based on the observation that such persons will lose their antibodies to the treponemes. Another one fourth apparently retain a latent infection for life because they maintain antibody to the organisms but remain asymptomatic. However. about half of the spontaneous remissions of secondary syphilis become reactivated as tertiary syphilis. Recent data support the concept that the long duration of the secondary disease before it culminates in latency occurs because the treponemes are able to suppress a cellular immune response, and that it is only after the host is able to overcome this suppression that the disease is cured or enters a latent state.

Tertiary Syphilis

Tertiary syphilis may occur 5 to 40 years after the initial infection. Lesions may occur in the central nervous system, causing paresis, or in the cardiovascular system, resulting in aortic aneurysms. They may also arise in the eyes, skin, bones, or viscera. Tertiary lesions, called gummata, develop as painless swellings that enlarge and later rupture, resulting in ulcers. These lesions contain very few organisms, and the remarkable severity of the lesion is attributed to an intense cellular immune response to the organisms and their products.

Congenital Syphilis

T. pallidum can pass across the placenta to infect the fetus, and if the infection does not kill the fetus, the newborn will have congenital syphilis. Such newborns appear to have a common cold, but a maculopapular rash soon develops, resulting in a sloughing off of the epithelium, particularly on the palms and soles. Bone involvement frequently affects the nose, and liver damage often results in jaundice. Untreated survivors usually become latent after about 1 year, but subsequent tertiary disease may result in a wide variety of clinical entities, including blindness, deafness, neurosyphilis, and severe bone involvement.

Congenital syphilis can be avoided if the mother is adequately treated during the first 4 months of pregnancy.

Laboratory Diagnosis of Syphilis

Because direct observation of spirochetes is possible only during the active primary or secondary stage of the disease, serologic techniques are the major diagnostic tools.

Nonspecific Tests

The original antigen used by *A. P von Wassermann* was an extract from fetal liver obtained from fetuses that had died from congenital syphilis. Wassermann mixed this material with dilutions of the patient's senun and fresh guinea pig serum, and observed for complement fixation. It subsequently was found that it is not necessary to use liver or other organs that have been infected with *T pallidum* and that extracts of normal beef heart serve equally well. It is now known that the actual antigenic substance involved in' the Wassermann test is a normal constituent of tissues called cardiolipin, which is diphosphatidylglycerol. Over the years, a number of modifications of this test using the same antigen have been devised. These modifications employ flocculation rather than a complement-fixation test and are known by the names of their originators.

Some of the more common ones are the Kolmer. Kline, Hinton, and Kahn tests. One test that is frequently used is the Venereal Disease Research Laboratory (VDRL) test ; this test mixes a buffered saline suspension of cardiolipin, plus lecithin and cholesterol, on a slide with the patient's serum. The slide is agitated on a mechanical rotor for several minutes, and a positive test is noted by a clumping of the cardiolipin. Another widely used nonspecific test is the rapid plasma reagin (RPR) card test. The RPR is performed by adsorbing the VDRL antigen on carbon particles and mixing this modified antigen with the patient's serum on a card. In a positive test, the flocculation of the carbon particles is visible to the naked eye. None of the tests employing cardiolipin as an antigen is completely specific, and about 1% of normal adults will give rise to antibodies resulting in false-positive reactions. A more specific test to evaluate positive results is essential.

The microhemagglutination test for *T. pallidum* (MHA-TP) also assays for specific treponemal antibodies. This method employs specially treated sheep's eythrocytes that have been coated with antigen from *T pallidum.* The test has been automated and adapted to a microvolume procedure. A positive result is signified by the agglutination of the red cells.

There are a number of other procedures for determining specific treponemal antibodies, such as the *T pallidum* agglutination (TPA), *T pallidum* immune adherence (TPIA), and whole body *T pallidum* complement fixation tests. None of these, however, is used in diagnostic laboratories ; they serve primarily as research tools.

The choice of which test to use may, in part, be dictated by personal preference. The VDRL or RPR test is less expensive than procedures for determining specific antibodies and should, therefore, be used in screening low-risk populations such as persons having premarital serologic testing. Positive results can be confirmed with one of the specific tests. When it becomes possible to grow the pathogenic treponemes in an artificial medium, the availability of an inexpensive antigen will undoubtedly influence the choice of tests- used to diagnose syphilis scrologically.

Treatment and Control of Syphilis

Before the turn of the century, there was no treatment for syphilips, but at that time *Paul Ehrlich* was carrying out his. systematic search for a "magic bullet" that would selectively attack microorg- anisms without undue toxicity to the host. Although Ehrlich never found his universal weapon, he did develop an arsenical compound, arsphenamine, that, together with bismuth, was relatiyely effective in treating syphilis. Such treatment was long and painful and has not been used since the advent of penicillin.

Syphilis could, theoretically, be eradicated because the organism is sensitive to low levels of penicillin. Even the tertiary stage may be arrested with adequate penicillin therapy, but, in these cases, therapy must be prolonged for several, weeks, probably because the organisms are growing so slowly. Erythromycin and tetracycline are also effective antibiotics, but they do not cross the placenta in sufficient concentrations to cure congenital syphilis. However, in spite of the cease with which the disease may be cured, public health authorities have: reported a rising incidence since 1960.

An interesting phenomenon called the Jarisch-Herxheimer reaction occasionally occurs 1 to 2 hours after treatment with penicillin. This systemic reaction results from the release of endotoxin following lysis of the spirochetes. It is self-limiting and persists for only 12 to 24 hours.

Humoral antibodies to syphilis appear several weeks after the occurrence of the primary lesion, but it is believed that a cellular immune response causes the eventual regression of the lesions of secondary syphilis. Persons with a latent infection cannot be reinfected, and, even if treated, persons with very long-standing infections appear to retain their immunity. It would, therefore, seem theoretically possible to produce an effective vaccine, and considerable effort is being expended toward this objective. Initial attempts with rabbit-grown treponemes indicate that vaccines may be effective but that the antigen which induces immunity is probably quite labile. Undoubtedly, the ability to grow the pathogenic organisms in culture would improve the potential for developing a vaccine.

Bejel (Endemic Syphilis)

Bejel is a nonvenereal disease occurring in Africa and the Middle East. The etiologic agent is similar (or identical) to that causing syphilis and is called *Treponenta pallidum* subspecies *endemicum.*

The disease occurs primarily in rural children living under poor standards of personal hygiene and is spread from person to person. usually through the use of common drinking and eating utensils.

Initial lesions are most common in the oral mucosa, followed by additional, secondary lesions on the oral mucosa and at the corners of the mouth. Tertiary lesions are more widespread and consist of syphilitic gummata on the skin, bone, and nasopharynx.

The infection can be eliminated by a single injection of long-acting pencillin, and it seems probable that this disease may one day be eradicated.

Treponema Pertenue

Treponema pertenue, the etiologic agent of yaws, is morphologically indistinguishable from *T. pallidum*, and it is likely that they are closely related organisms.

Epidemiology and Pathogenesis of Yaws

Yaws is restricted to the tropics, where it seems to 'be spread from person to person either by direct contact with open ulcers or by vectors such as flies. An initial lesion occur 3 to 4 weeks after exposure, and, after ulcerating, spontaneously heals. Several months later, secondary lesions appear, which ulcerate, heal, and reappear in crops over a period of several years. The disease may become quiescent, only to reappear as tertiary lesions of the skin and bones-frequently resulting in considerable disfigurement of the face.

Laboratory Diagnosis, Treatment, and Control of Yaws

In all likelihood, the average diagnosis is based on the clinical picture occurring in an area where yaws is endemic. However, all of the serologic tests for syphilis described above will yield positive results. *T. pertenue is* very sensitive to penicillin, and, like syphilis, this severely disfiguring disease could be easily controlled if it were possible to give adequate penicillin therapy to infected persons. Such eradication programs have been under way in the Western Hemisphere since 1950. At that time, Haiti was estimated to have one million cases of yaws. After a house-to-house survey and treatment of infected persons, the disease has been essentially eliminated from that country A similar program was undertaken in Brazil and in the Lesser Antilles, leaving very few infected areas in the Americas.

Treponema Carateum

Pinta is a disease that occurs mainly in Central and South America. *Treponema carateum*, the etiologic agent, also is indistinguishable from *T. pallidum*, but the skin lesions produced are flat red or blue areas that do not ulcerate and ultimately become depigmented. Lesions are usually confined to the skin.

Transmission appears to require direct person-to-person contact, and, like the other species of *Treponema, T carateum* is very sensitive to penicillin. Eradication programs in Mexico and Colombia, similar to those for yaws, have considerably reduced the incidence of pinta in these areas.

Treponema Vincentii

Treponema vincentii (the older name was *Borrelia vincentii*) and *Bacteroides melaninogenicus* have been thought to be involved in a fusospirochetal (caused by both fusiform bacteria and spirochetes) disease. It is commonly referred to as Vincent's angina, an acute necrotizing ulcerative gingivitis, or "trench mouth" because it was prevalent among the infantry during World War *I.T.vincentii* is an active, motile spirochete, and *B. melaninogenicus* is a non-motile.

GONOCOCCUS

The name gonorrhea was introduced by Galen about 130 A.D. Neisser in 1879 described diplococci, which he found consistently in the purulent secretions of acute cases of urethritis and vaginitis and in smears made from the acute conjunctivitis of the newborn. *Neisseria gonorrhoeae* was cultivated by Leistikow in 1882 and by Bumm in 1885. The latter maintained pure cultures of the organism by serial transfers on coagulated human blood serum and established its etiologic significance by reproducing the disease in human volunteers.

Both gonorrhea and syphilis declined precipitously after the introduction of penicillin, but this dramatic success led to complacency and a reduction in appropriations for the control of venereal disease. It has been estimated by the officials in the Public Health Service that 1.7 million new cases of gonorrhea occur each year in the United States, although only about one sixth of these are reported to Public Health authorities.

MORPHOLOGY AND STAINING

In smears from urethral discharges the gonococcus is seen as an oval or spherical coccus, 0.8 g by 0.6 g. The organisms, found frequently in pairs with the adjacent sides flattened, usually are intracellular. The gonococcus is nonsporogenous, nonmotile, does not have a capsule except in its mucoid variant phase.

N.gonorrhoeae stains readily with aniline dyes. Good results are obtained with methylene blue alone or eosin followed by methylene blue. Excellent preparations also may be made with polychrome stains, such as Pappenheim-Saathoff methyl green-pyronine. The, gonococcus in gram-negative. The presence of gram-negative intracellular diplococci in smears of pus from the male urethra is presumptive evidence of gonorrhea. In exudates from the vagina or from the eye, however, the morphologic picture is less reliable. since other gram-negative cocci are present frequently in these regions. In staphylococcal infections of the conjuctivas, dead organisms may fail to retain the blue dye and by taking the counterstain they may appear in the smears in the form of gram-negative intracellular cocci; hence, considerable emphasis must be placed on the shape of the cocci as well as on their staining reactions.

Cultural Characteristics

The gonococcus is a delicate aerobic but facultative anaerobic organism which usually requires an atmosphere of 2 to 10 present CO_2, an optimal temperature of 35° to 36° C, and a pH of 7.2 to 7.6 Growth ceases below 30° and above 38.5°.

On chocolate agar, after 48 hours incubation, round, convex, smooth, grayish-white colonies 0.5 to 1 mm in diameter appear. On further incubation, the colonies-may increase in size and develop a roughened surface with crenated edges. The colonies are soft and somewhat slimy when touched with a platinum loop.

Colonies of gonococci, meningococci, and other bacteria synthesizing indophenol oridase turn bright purple when a plate is flooded or sprayed with a 1 per cent solution of tetramethyl-p-phenylenediamine. The excess dye should be removed quickly by tilting or inverting the plate. The organisms are not killed by this short exposure and may be subcultured during the next 30 minutes. The oxidase reaction may be prevented by acid formed from the oxidation of glucose but becomes positive with the addition of a neutralizing reagent.

The introduction of the Thayer-Martin selective medium has revolutionized the cultural methods. This is particularly true for women where the disease is often asymptomatic and where the few gonococci in cervical secretions cannot be recognized in smears and could not be cultivated by previous methods. The Thayer-Martin selective medium contains vancomycin, colistimethate, and nystatin. Inhibition of saprophytic *Neisseria* is nearly complete, and *Mima polymorpha var. oxidans* another organism that might be mistaken for the gonococcus, is also inhibited. An organism which grows on this medium, which has the typical morphology of a *Neisseria* and gives a gonococcus confirmatory test such as sugar fermentations or fluorescent staining may be used for conformation.

The chief cause of ncoative cultures in worr .n with asymptomatic gonorrhea was the death of the organisms between the time the material was removed from the patient and when it reached the laboratory. This problem has apparently been solved by Martin and Lester who made a transport medium by modifying the Thaver-Martin medium. They added more agar and dextrose and tubed the medium in screw-cap bottles which contained a mixture of air and CO_2. The gonococci may actually grow while being transported to the laboratory. Only a short period of additional incubation will be necessary before smears can be made.

Resistance

Gonococci succumb to drying within 1 to 2 hours. Moist heat kills them at 55°C in less than 5 minutes and at 42°C in 5 to 15 hours. They are very susceptible to the usual antiseptics, especially to $AgNO_3$, which, in a 1 : 4,000 dilution, destroys gonococci in 2 minutes. Cultures maintained at room temperature die in 1 to 2 days and after 4 to 6 days at 37°C.

Gonococei are very susceptible also to sulphonamides and pennicillin. Resistant strains, however, developed rapidly as each new sulphonamide, in succession, was introduced in treatment. Penicillin on a weight for weight basis is from 10 to 25 times as effective as the other available antibiotics.

There has been a steady increase in resistance to penicillin. This has necessitated a steady increase in the doses required for a cure.

Kellogg and Thayer recognized four colony types. Types I and 2 were virulent while types 3 and 4 were not virulent. However, when human volunteers were inoculated with type 1 and 2 infection occurred with the inoculated type but as the disease progressed type 1 was replaced by type 2 or *vise versa.*

The term *entericfever* is frequently used in Britain to include typhoid and the paratyphoid fevers caused respectively by Salmonella typhi and *S paratyphi* A, B or C : typhoid fever was confused with typhus fever until 1850 when Jenner, having examined 66 fatal cases of the two diseases both clinically and at postmortem examination, clearly differentiated them before the causal agents of either had been discovered. Though the Portal of entry and exit of the infecting bacilli is the intestinal tract, the enteric fevers are septicaemia infections with wide- spread involvement of tissues throughout the body.

Typhoid and the paratyphoid fevers are clinically similar and the assumption that cases of typhoid fever are invariably more severe is not always true. Also, the gross pathology of the enteric fevers is similar regardless of the causal organism and only bacteriological examination can differentiate between them. In Britain, typhoid fever is now relatively rare and the majority of recorded cases are imported from other countries. A significant endemic level of infection with *S. typhi* persists in the warm climate countries of Southern Europe. Outbreaks of infection due to S. *paratyphi B* outnumber other causes of enteric fever in Britain: *S.,paratyphi* A infections are uncommon in this country but are frequently encountered in Eastern Europe, the Americas, India and the Middle East; *S. paratyphi* C, as a cause of paratyphoid fever is largely restricted to Eastern Europe and Asia.

Antigenic classification

Neisseria gonorrhoeae, routinely called the gonococcus, appears to consist of an antigenically heterogenous group of organisms, and no successful immunologic classification is available. Serotypes have, however, been proposed based on different ectrophoretic mobilities of their major outer membrane protein. The organisms are also divided into four types based on their colonial appearance, but these morphologic variations are a result of mutations occurring within a single strain. Thus, types 1 and 2 are pathogenic for humans, but, after growing on laboratory media overnight, at least half of any culture will show the colonial morphology of types 3 or 4, and, after more prolonged cultivation, all organisms will appear as the avirulent types 3 and 4.

Pili

On a microscopic level, the most obvious difference between the various colonial types is that the virulent types 1 and 2 possess pili, whereas the avirulent types 3 and 4 do not. Since it is well established that pill are involved in the attachment of microorganisms to cells, it appears quite probable that the gonococcus requires close attachment to produce disease. Furthermore, the pili are antiphagocytic, perhaps in part because the organisms are so intimately attached to host cells. Removal of pili from virulent cells by treatment with trypsin results in their phagocytosis and destruction.

Because pili not only mediate the attachment of the gonococci to epithelial cells but are also instrumental in preventing their phagocytosis, one might postulate that purified pili could serve as an effective vaccine for the prevention of gonorrhea. Unfortunately (for humans), pili isolated from different strains of gonococci display a wide variation in their amino-acid composition and, as a result, display extensive antigens heterogeneity. Moreover, it has been conclusively shown that even a single strain of the gonococcus possesses multiple genes for pilus production, resulting in many antigen i.e., types within a given clone. These genes, as characterized by Per Hagblom and co-workers, consist of two expression loci designated *pil* E_1 . and *pil* *E*,. Both genes carry intact pilin-coding sequence and their own promoters. As a result of single or multiple recombination events between repeated sequence that exist within these loci, deletions occuring in either of those genes convert the organism from a p' to a p^- cell, even though the other pilin expression gene remains unchanged.

In addition to the pilin expression genes, the chromosome of the gonococcus also contains multiple silent sequences (*pil S* loci), which lack their own promoters and, hence, are not expressed. These silent loci, however contain multiple sequences, which correspond to the variable part of pilin and it appears that the antigenic diversity of the pilus is not due to recombination events between the two expression genes, $PilE_1$ and $pilE_2$, and between the expression genes and the silent loci. Thus, the gonococcus not only changes from p^+ to p^- but also switches from p- back gonococcus to a different p^+. That such events happen in nature was clearly demonstrated by an analysis of pilin genes obtained from origin could be traced to a single source during an epidemic of gonorrhea.

But, all is not hopeless for the construction of an effective pilus vaccine. Recombinant DNA techniques have shown that the pilus is made up of three general regions. The first 53 amino acids at the amino terminal end are highly conserved and are, therefore, constant in all strains of gonococci. The second region. comprises amino acids 54 to 114, and it has.been termed semi-variable because it represents a small number of amino-acid changes. The carboxy terminal portion of the protein is highly variable. Antibodies to whole pilin are directed primarily at this hypervariable region. If, however, one uses synthetic peptides representing will the constant region of the pilin protein, antibodies are induced thacellst prevent heterologous strains of gonococci from binding epithelial Because binding to such cells is an absolute requirement for gonococcal pathogenicity, such peptides may one day be used to induce an active immune response to the gonococcus in humans.

Outer Membrane Proteins

The three major outer membrane proteins of the gonococci have been named proteins I, II and III. Protein I is the predominant species in the outer membrane and although antigenically constant within a given strain, varies considerably among the diverse strains of gonococci. It appears to act as a porin and serves as a basis for serotyping the gonococci.

Protein II consists of a large, related family of proteins that appears to be associated with the adherence of the gonococci to various types of host cells. The ability of the gonococcus to survive in normal human serum as well as its cytotoxicity to host cells have also been with the presence of protein II in the outer membrane. Protein II has also been termed the *opacity protein.* because its presence is correlated with a dark. opaque colony: most light. translucent colonies of gonococci lack protein II.

Because antibodies induced by protein II act as opsonins, it would appear that this protein might serve as an effective vaccine. But, alas. the gonococcus has evolved mechanisms to circumvent this event. Thus, a strain of gonococci may produce I or 2 types of protein II simultaneously; it may cease to produce protein II or, as described for gonococcal pili, it may switch to form an antigenically different protein II- As many as six antigenically distinct types of protein II have been found within a single strain of gonococci. It has been estimated that about one cell in each thousand generations will switch to make a different protein 11, probably through a gene rearrangement within the chromosome. It thus appears that the gonococcus has evolved some very complex genetic mechanisms to ensure its survival.

Protein Ill appears to be identical in all gonococci, and, as yet, it has not been associated with any specific virulence factor.

Epidemiology and Pathogenesis of Gonorrhea

Gonorrhea is a venereal disease that, with few exceptions, is acquired through, sexual contact with an infected individual.

The organisms penetrate the mucuos membranes of the gential tract, causing a localized infection initially. In the male, the infection may be asymptomatic, but it usually causes an acute urethritis, resulting in a purulent dischange and painful urination. The gonococci may also infect the prostate gland and epididymis. In the female, the infection is much more likely to be asymptomatic or accompained by a minor discharge that may go unnoticed. The organisms, however, may infect the urethra, vagina, cervix, and fallopian tubes, causing a pelvic inflammatory disease resulting in sterility. Disseminated gonococcal infection may also occur, leading to lesions in the skin, heart, eye, meninges, or joints. resulting in gonococcal arthritis.

Until recently, there was no explanation as to why some individuals succumbed to the disseminate disease. It now appears likely that the strains of gonococci capable of hematogenous spread are resistant to phagocytosis in the absence of specific antibodies, whereas those organisms causing local infections are more readily phagocytosed in the presence of normal human serum. The difference between such strains appears to reside in the ability of the serum-sensitive strains to directly activate complement, whereas the serum-resistant stains *will* do so only in the presence of specific antibodies. As a result, virtually all gonococci isolated from the blood are resistant to phagocslosis in the absence of specific opsonic antibodies.

Ophthalmia neonatorum is a gonococcal infection of the eye acquired by a newborn during passage through the birth canal of an infected mother. Such infections often result in blindless but have been largely eliminated by the legal requirement that silver nitrate, bactericidal for these bacteria, be dropped into a baby's eyes at birth.

Laboratory Diagnosis

In acute infections this evenly spread smears are made from the discharge. In men, specimens are taken from the urethral dischare; the meatus should be cleansed with sterile gauze soaked in saline solution, and specimens are taken either with a wire loop from within the meatus or drops of the discharge are taken directly on to slides. In women specimens are taken from the urethra and cervix uteri with a wire loop or swab and a vaginal speculum. Specimens may also be taken from the rectum and from the orifice of the greater vestibular gland.

Separate films are stained by methylene blue and Gram's method, (with neutral red or Sandiford's stain as the counter stain). In the acute stage, both in men and women, the occurrence of the *characteristic Gram-negative intracellular, diplococci* is strongly suggestive of gonorrhoea. However, intracellular cocci may be scanty and pleomorphic, particularly if the patient has already received treatment; or only extracellular cocci are seen.

In *chronic infections*, the cocci may be relatively scanty in films and difficult to identify accurately among the secondary infecting organisms which may include Gram-negative commensal diplococci. In the male the 'morning drop' of secretion from the urethra should be examined, or films are made from a centrifuged urinary deposit or from any discharge after prostatic massage. In the female, secretion from the cervix uteri, and not vaginal discharge, should be examined.

Any vaginal discharge should, however, be examined as a wet prepatation for *Trichomonas vaginalis*.

Recently, fluorescent techniques for the identification of gonococci in smears have come into use but this 'on-the-spot' diagnosis must be confirmed by cultural and biochemical characters. Where there is a mixed infection, isolation of the organism may be technically difficult and a selective medium, e.g., that of Thayer and Martin or *Transgrow* containing trimethoprim should be used. Inoculation of material to be cultivated if possible, be made directly from the patient on to a suitale medium pre-warmed to 37°C, and the culture should be incubated at once, or at least within an hour or two, since the gonococcus may die quickly in an adverse environment.

When it is impracticable to make direct cultures, the specimen is taken with a charcoal-impregnated swab on a wooden applicator which is broken into a tube of start's holding medium for transport to the laboratory. Cultures are incubated at 35° to 36°C. For 1 to 2 days in an atmosphere of 5 to 10 percent CO_2. In mixed culture, e.g., from cases of chronic or symptom infection in females, the oxidase reaction (q.v.) is useful in detecting colonies of the gonococcus, which quickly develop a purplish colour.

Serology

The complement-fixation test has been used with varying degrees of success, and is most useful for the diagnosis of chronic infection in females and for suspected gonococcal complications such as salpingitis and arthritis. Considerable care and experience are needed in the preparation of the gonococcal antigen to ensure maximum specificity without non-specific sensitivity. The degree of specificity of the test increases with increased positivity of the reaction but, with present procedures, both false-positive and false-negative reactions may be reported. Cross-reactions occur in patients with meningococcal infection and may be found in patients with chronic bronchitis and bronchiectasis related, perhaps, to antibody responses to commensal neisseriae. The test is, therefore, of doubtful value and not recommended for routine use.

Chemotherapy

The gonococcus is ordinarily sensitive to a wide range of antimicrobial drugs (e.g., MIC of penicillin=0.005 units/ml) but a proportion of strains have developed resistance to those drugs which have been most commonly used in therapy, viz., the sulphonamides, penicillin and streptomycin. In many countries the proportion of strains highly resistant to sulphonamides increased from less than 10 per cent to 80 to 90 per cent between 1936 and 1946, by which time penicillin became generally available and replaced sulphonamide in the treatment of gonorrhoea. After use of sulphonamide had became infrequent, the prevalence of sulphonamide-resistant strains declined and these strains are now a small minority. Penicillin-resistant strains were not encountered until 1957 and althoughthe incidence of penicillin-resistant strains has increased in the past decade to 10 to 20 per cent in some areas, the degree of pcnicillin-resistance is not very high (MIC= 0.1 to 1.0 units/nil) and infection may be susceptible to cure by treatment with high dosage. Crystalline penicillin (5 mega units) or procaine penicillin (1.2 to 2.4 mega units) is still the drug of first choice.: The dose should be repeated on three successive days for women with chronic infection and for cases of proctitis. In patients that do not respond to such therapy, the additional use of probenecid (0.5 to 1 g) to delay renal excretion has given good results. Alternative drugs that have been used successfully are tetracylines, spiromycin and kanamycin. The combination of trimethoprim and a sulphonamide, suggested by Garrod and Waterworth because of the *in-vitro* synergistic action of this combination, may indicate the usefulness of contrimoxazole.

EPIDEMIOLOGY

Sources and Modes of Transmission

Patients with clinically apparent or chronic inapparent infection are the only sources, and the infection is transmitted from person to person almost exclusively by sexual contact, so that gonorrhoea is classified as a venereal disease. The reason why the gonorrhoea is mainly dependent on sexual contact for its transmission transmission are firstly that its main portal of entry and exit from the body is through the urogenital tract and that the coccus is so exceptionally susceptible to killing by the conditions of the extracorporeal environment, e.g., drying, cold, exposure to air, absence of nutrients, that it can only very rarely survive transmission by means less direct than the immediate transfer from the urogenital tract of one person to that another. There is evidence to suggest that occasionally it may survive rapid transfer of exudate on the fingers to the conjunctiva or on damp towels as in the spread of gonococcal vulvo-vaginitis institutions.

Gonorrhoea has been increasing at an alarming rate in most of the world during the past decade. Its global incidence in 1970, estimated at 16 million new cases, makes it, one of the commonest specific infectious diseases. In the U.S.A.Jwhere there were about 2000,000 cases in 1970, giving a rate of 2000 per 100,000 of population over 15 years of age; the present prevalence is, therefore, regarded as being epidemic. In Britain, after a peak incidence immediately after the Second World War and relatively low levels in the early 1950s, probably as a result of effective chemotherapy, the annual returns from venereal diseases clinics in England and Wales have shown a steady increase since 1954 (17536 cases) and had reached 53525 cases in 1970. This number does not include patients treated privately or in the Armed forces. Concomitat with the increasing incidence, a larger proportion of the diagnosed cases are occurring among teenagers with more girls than boys affected. The rate for girls under 16 years is about 4'/$_2$, times that for boys of the same age group. This sex ratio may be contrasted with that for adults which ranges from 3:14: 1, males to females, due partly to reservoir of promiscuous women and prostitutes and partly to the difficulties of recognition of infection in the female. In recent years, a high proportion of the male cases in England and Wales have been immigrants, mostly from the West Indies and Asia whereas less than 20 per cent of the female cases were born abroad.

The processes of modern life which have led to earlier maturity, greater mixing of the sexes, economic freedom for the young and increasing facilities for travel tend to lead to promiscuity. Thus, factors that contribute to the mounting incidence of gonorrhoea are (a) an apparent inerase in promiscuity, both heterosexual and homosexual, in a permissive society; (b) the easy availability of birth control methods and of effective chemotherapy for the infected; (c) difficulties in recognition (and therefore of treatment) in women and in passive male homosexuals; (d) greater population mobility within and between countries for cultural, commercial, touristic or military purposes; and (e) high infectiousness and short incubation which make the chain of infection difficult to break; to which may be added the development of drug resistance in the gonococcus which accentuates the need for-accurate diagnosis, elective treatment and tests for cure.

Control Measures

Control measures are aimed at the early recognition and effective treatment of clinical cases, tracing of infected contacts and bringing them in for treatment, use of physical and/or chemical barriers during intercourse, and health education. Treatment of venereal diseases in

Britain is free and confidential at 'special clinics' (perhaps better renamed 'departments of genitourinary diseases') which are usually sited in the out patient department of large general hospitals. These clinics deal with a wide range of sexually transmitted and related conditions besides venereal diseases which affect only about one-quarter of all the patients who attend. Many of the clinics have attached social workers who help to tackle the problems of young people, unmarried mothers, unstable marriages, etc. A most important function of the clinics is contact tracing, which means seeking information from the patient about possible sources or recipients of infection and, hopefully, persuading them to attend the clinic for examination and treatment. There is, of course, no legal compulsion for prostitutes or promiscuous to seek examination and treatment but most of those that are traced attend regularly. General practitioners may prefer to treat their own patients and if so, they, too, must endeavour to trace infected contacts. More health education is needed to warn the community that promiscuity carries a real risk of acquiring venereal diseases which, in women, may be easily missed and may be followed by serious sequelae. There is, for example, evidence of an increasing incidence of salpingitis which can lead to sterility.

Future developments may include greater emphasis On contact-tracing, better serological tests for the detection of symptomless infections in women, a combined birth control and antimicrobial substance to be applied locally, and the selective use of prophylactic vaccines..

Treatment

In 1937 Dees and Colston reported the successful use of sulphan-ilamide in the treatment of gonorrhea. In the first series of reports there was a rapid and complete cure in more than 90 percent of the patients. Each new sulphonamide was. highly successful when first introduced, but its effectiveness was lost as resistant strains appeared. Penicillin was then discovered and found to be effective against sulphonamide-resistant strains.

Penicillin remains the drug of choice for the treatment of gonorrhoea although there has been a slow but progressive increase in the resistance of the organism to penicillin. The average sensitivity of gonococcus strains from treatment failures has increased from 0.1 units per ml in 1954 to 0.5 units per ml in 1969. The minimal resistant gonococcus has shifted from a high of 0.2 units per ml to 3.5 units per ml in the past 15 years. In the 1940s 100,000 units of penicillin, in one dose, were curative and now 4.8 million units are required.

Tetracycline is frequently used as a substitute for penicillin when penicillin allergy is present. A number of new analogues of tetracycline are effective but much more expensive. Ampicillin and cephaloridine are effective in 2- to 3-gram single doses but are expensive. Kanamycin is also curative with a single dose but neither kanamycin nor cephaloridine should be used when the kidney function is impaired.

Prevention

Man is the only known host for N. *gonorrhoeae*, and the organism may survive for years in the genitalia of the female without any symptoms suggesting its presence.

Pseudogonorrhea

Strains of"*N. gonorrhoeae*" reported as highly resistant to penicillin when studied in a central laboratory have all been instances of infection with organisms belonging to the genus *Herellea*, which is grain-negative and frequently occurs in a diplococcal form resewbling *Neisseria;* and if isolated from the genitalia are naturally assumed to be N. *gonorrhoeae*, De-Bord described the *Mimeae* and distinguised three genera; *Mimea*, *Herellea*, and *Colloides.*

Colloides has been shown to be synonymous with *Escherichia Jreundil.* The unusual characteristics of *Mimeae-Herellea* are: (1) the appearance as a gram-negative coccus on solid media but; (2) a grain-negative bacillus in broth; with (3) a capsule. It cannot (4) reduce nitrates; or (5) form indol; (6) give the methyl-red and Voges-Proskauer reaction; (7) form hydrogen sulphide; (8) grow or, Scagar; and (9) is nonmotile. These features serve to distinguish this tribe from *Pseudomonas alcaligegnes*, *Bord. bronchisepticas*, and *Laplomonaso* with which they have been confused in the past.

Green and his associates have found tetracycline ineffective in treatment but have had reasonably good success with sodium, colistimethate, kanamycin sulphate. raethenamine *mandelate*, and polymycin-B sulphate.

Nonspecific Urethritis

When *N. gonorrhoeae* cannot be isolated from a case of urethritis after repeated attmepts at culture on suitable media the case is diagonsed as non-specific urethritis. Gram-positive cocci of various kinds and pleuropneusmonia-like organisms, have been isolated from some of these patients, but their etilogic significance has not been established.

A special strain of mycoplasma designated the ·r· strain has been isolasted from 60 to 93 per cent of young men with nongonococcal urethritis by Shepard.

Nonspecific urthritis of all types has reached a rate in some areas of 23.9 cases per 1,000 per annum. Cases usually recover following intense therapy with sulphadiazine-and penicillin, urethral irrigations, and sounding.

GONORRHOEA

Gonorrhoea is a venereal disease caused by N. *gonorrhoeae* and the infection occurs directly from person to person by sexual intercourse. Mechanical infections may take place in some cases particularly in cases of conjunctivitiis. Vulvovaginitis in young female children is occasionally seen due to sleeping in the same bed and spread in such cases occurs often through fomites.

Pathogenesis and Pathology

The organism has predilection to infect the columnar epithelium: the stratified and the squamous epithelia are resistant to this infection Even in the earliest stage of disease the organism may pass to distant parts of the body by the lymphatic channel. Haematogenous transmission may occur in certain cases quite early in the infection. In the mucous membrane, as a result of infection acute catarrhal inflammation develops, producing congestion, oedema and leucocytic infiltration. This is associated with increase of secretion. The discharge is at first mucoid and later mucopurulent and then purulent. The acute stage may pass off in a few days' time and subcute stage ensues. As the infection persists, a chronic condition of gleet supervenes. In the earliest stage, the discharge is glairy and the organism is found in the exudate, but as the discharge becomes purulent it is loaded with leucocytes containing the organism within a few days of infection secondary organisms appear; namely, streptococci, *staph. pyogenes*, *Esch coli* and diphteroids. They help in maintaining the irritation and are responsible for secondary complications. Lesions may be divided into early primary lesions and secondary lesions.

Early Primary Lesions

In males the infection of anterior urethra is associated with an acute catarrhal inflammation, producing anterior urethritis. *In females* urethritis is soon followed by inflammation of the cervix uteri (Endocervicitis). In *children* it occurs as an anterior urethritis in males, and vulyo-vaginitis in females. In the *niew born infants* infection occurs at birth producing a condition of purulent conjunctivitis (ophthalmia neonatorum).

Secondary Lesions

These are due to spread by : (*a*) *direct extension*, (*b*) *lymphaties*, (*c*) *bloodstream*, (*d*) *mechanical means.*

In Males

The infection is characterised by acute urethritis affecting the anterior urethra. The acute catarrhal inflammation is associated with congestion, oedema and leucocytic emigration. On the third day of the disease, the smear shows gonococci and pus cells when the discharge is purulent.

(a) Direct Extension

This occurs by continuity and contiguity and the infection spreads to the paraurethral ducts, Littre's and Cowper's glands and their ducts. It also extends through the external urethral sphincter to the prostate, causing a condition of prostatitis. Prostatic utricle is; involved later and it may further extend to the common ejaculatory ducts, seminal vesicles, vas deferens and epididymis producing inflammatory condition of the affected areas. It the epididymis. the lumina of the tubules are filled with leucocytes causing extensive destruction of the lining epithelium and resulting in ulceration of the surrounding tissues and fibrosis. Bilateral epididymitis produces permanent aspermia and sterility. Once the inflammation has extended to the posterior urethra, as a result of chronic gonorrhoeal infection, healing is more difficult.

(b) Lymphatics

In males epididymitis might Occur as a result of lymphatic spread; but in chronic cases of gonorrhoea, conditions of cystitis, pyelitis, pyelonephritis are due to ascending infections caused by the secondary organisms. These are due to intercommunication between the lymphatic, of the bladder and pelvis of the kidney through periureteral lymphatics. Obstruction due to stricture or the urethra, helps the spread by direct continuity through the lumen as a result of back pressure. Inguinal bubo may arise as a complication due to secondary infection through the lymphaties.

(c) Blood Spread

Generalised blood infection is common in males due to prostatic infection and this haematogenous spread is explained by the high vascularity of the organ at the primary site of infection. Rarely the organism may produce a condition of septicaemia which results in a condition of *ulcerative endocarditis*. The diagnosis in such a case depends on the isolation of the organism from the blood stream in a patient clinically presenting a condition of septicaemia. Vegetations found in the endocardium are luxuriant and friable and the condition ends fatally. Arthritis and iritis are other metastatic lesions that may occur in a case of gonorrhoea.

Gonorrhoeal arthritis

Gonorrhocal rheumatism is the result of gonococcal pyaemia. There is a sexual preponderance of 2:1 in men. It is found in all stages of gonorrhoea, namely acute, subacute and chronic. The synovial membrane, ligainents, fibrous aponeurosis, and tendon sheaths may be involved producing arthritics, fibrositis, tenosynovitis and allied conditions. Gonorrhoeal arthritis may be monoarticular or polyarticular and joints like temporo-rnandibular, sterno-clavicular or vertebral joints are commonly affected. Fluid collects in the joint with inflammation and swelling of the part and the organisms may be isolated from the fluid aspirated from these joints. *Spondvlitis deformans* has been traced to an old gonococal infection.

Gonorrhoeal irnitis

Gonorrhoeal conjunctivitis is caused by mechanical infections due to the transfer of the organism from the anterior urethra; but the gonorrhoea] iritis is a metastatic lesions due to haemalogenous transmission and in certain cases the whole of the uveal tract may be affected. *Acute gonococcal meningitis. This* is extremely rare and postmortem findings are similar to those in other types of bacterial meningitis.

Complications

Urethral stricture, chronic prostatitis, vesiculitis are complications of gonorrhoea. Ascending pyelitis and secondary infection with*Esch. coli* of the urinary tract are often seen as late results of infecon. But all these complications are rare nowadays owing to the discovery of antibiotics.

Urethral Stricture

The commonest site of stricture is at the junction of the bulbus with the membranous part of the urethra as it is the most dependent part and pus tends to accumulate there owing to insufficient drainage. The presence of the sphincter adjacent to this area also helps in the process, as during the contraction of the sphincter, the inflamed part is subject to injury, resulting in the rupture of the granulation tissue and subsequent formation of excess of fibrous tissue producing stricture.

Females

In this case, urethritis is associated with burning pain during micturition due to inflammation of the external urethral orifice and the urethra is red, swollen, everted and prominent. It may cause inflammation of Bartholin's gland and Skene's gland, as these are lined by columnar epithelium. The vagina escapes infection as the organism cannot multiply in the squamous cells. This is further prevented by acid pH of the vagina. The cells moreover have high glycogen content and as soon as they are desquamated, the Deoderlein's bacillus produces acid by fermentation of the carbohydrate. The organism infects the cervix uteri causing a condition of cervicits. There again, the organism multiplies in the columnar cells lining the cervical glands. Here it forms a chronic nidus and the infection may pass to the uterus causing endometritis, salpingitis. pyosalpinx. coophoritis, tubo-ovarian abscess and pelvic peritonitis with plastic inflammatory changes. The mucous membrane of the anus and rectum is usually involved in the females and in such a case purulent proctitis is common.

Salpingitis

The weight of evidence goes in favour of direct spread of the organism than by the lymphatics to produce this condition. The tube is red and swollen and fimbriae are prominent. From the abdominal ostium, yellow pus may be expressed. The rugae of the mucous membrane are swollen. oedematous and with the organisation of the exudate, plicae become adherent to one another. Thus, in a chronic case, there are irregular isolated spaces lined by epithelium. Chronic salpingitis is the commonest cause of sterility in women, as the pathway of the ovum from the ovary is blocked. In this way it is also a predisposing factor in tubal pregnancy. When both the ends of the tubes are obliterated by fibrous tissue, the lumen is distended with pus, resulting in pyosalpinx; and subsequently, during resolution, the pus is converted into a thin colourless fluid producing the condition of hydrosalpinx. *Tubo-oi'arian abscess*. In some cases, the free extermity of the Fallopian tube' becomes adherent to the adjacent part of the ovary. Abscesses form within the ovary and communicate with the tube by a large cavity representing the lumen of the tube. This is known as tubo-ovarian abscess. The wall of the abscess consists of loose fibroblastic tissue infiltrated with mononuclear cell and plasma cells. Many of the mononuclear cells are found distended with vacuoles.

Sterility

Sterility is more common in females than in males. The spread of infection to Fallopian tubes and ovaries precludes all possibility of conception. Similarly, in males, inflammation of the seminal vesicles, epididimis and the testes may lead to sterility.

Abortion

Implantation of the ovum is not possible in a chronically inflamed endometrium and this is the cause of repeated abortion in females suffering from gonorrhoeae endometritis.

Laboratory diagnosis

Diagnosis is based on direct and indirect methods.

Direct Method

This is done by finding of the organism by : (*a*) *microscopic* examination of the smear; (b) cultural method which is chiefly applicable to both acute and chronic cases.

(*a*) *Microscopic examination of smear.* It is very useful in acute cases. The smear shows Gram-negative intracellular *Diplococci* in pus cells having characteristic morphology. Secondary organisms and epithelial cells may also be present. In chronic cases in man. the smear should be examined. In chronic cases, a provocative method may show positive smearsafter a big dose of vaccine or after irritation produced by application of sliver salts in the male urethra.

(*b*) *Culture.* The culture should be made as soon as the swab is taken. The material is inoculated into fresh blood agar and chocolate agar at 37°C without delay. If inoculation is not done at once, the organism may die at room temperature. It is better to cultivate in an atmosphere of 10 per cent CO_2 for 48 hours and the colonies should be isolated. In sulphonamide treated cases media containing PABA (5 mg per 100 ml) should be used. Colonies should always be examined with hand lens. *Oxidase reactin* is helpful in detection of colonies.

Indirect Method

The diagnosis by this method is based on : (a) Complement fixation test and (b) agglutination test; the latter is not very useful.

Complement fixation test

This test is useful in chronic cases, when the organism cannot be . demonstrated in smear or culture. A polyvalent antigen should be used for the test. The antibody does not appear in the blood until two weeks after infection. But it may be delayed when the disease is confined to the anterior urethra. The test is done by making 2 fold serial dilutions (i.e., 2, 4, 8, 16 and so on) of the serum and using an antigen containing gonococci. The. test is usually positive complications like prostatitis, arthritis, iritis, etc. A single negative test does not exclude gonorrhoeal infection and the test should be done twice or thrice at intervals of 3 weeks and repeated negative result give a strong evidence against the infection. A Positive reaction becoming negative in 3 months after a course of treatment is a strong evidence of cure of a case. It should be remembered that the test is valueless in vaccine treated patients.

Pseudogonorrhoea

Gonorrhoea-like condition is caused by highly penicillin resistant strains of organisms of the *genus Herellea*, which are Gram-negative diplococci resembling Neisseria. When isolated from the genitalia, they are naturally confused with N. gonorrhoeae. According to DeBord *Mimeae* were distinguished into 3 genera : Mimea, Herellea and Colloides. Two thirds of the penicillin resistant cases of gonorrhoea in Italy are caused by *Mimea*. The infection with these organisms are not limited to the urethra only but may be isolated from blood and produce characteristic symptoms of Waterhouse-Frideriuhset;; yndrome caused by *meningitis*. These organisms appear to be related to *Diplococcus mucosus* as shown by Seelinger or identical with *B. anitratum*. According to Daly *et al.*, 7 types of organisms, e.g., *D. mucosus*, *B. anitratum*, B5W, Moraxella Iwoffivar. glucidolytica, Mimea glucidoiytica, *Actineo batter anitratum* and N. winogradoski are all identical with *Herellea vaginicola*. of these, type I appears to be most common and resistant to penicillin, streptomycin and tetracyclines.

Mima polymorpha

It is a Gram-negative, plcomorphic bacillus, 'Which is easily confused with members of the Neisseria group, from which it can be separated by failure to give (i) a positive oxidase reaction or (ii) specific typing serum. Meningitis caused by *Mima polymorpha*, closely resembles meningitis caused by more common pathoggens and can not be differentiated from them on clinical grounds. *Mima polymorpha* is often resistant to penicillin and sulphonamides and responds only to tetracyclines.

NON-SPECIFIC URETHRITIS

In recent years, cases of nonspecific urethritis appear to have increased in frequency. They are not of gonococcal origin but their precise nature is not definitely known. They have been suggested to be caused by pleuropneumonia-like organism (PPLO) and suggestive evidences have been obtained in certian cases. It is possible that the disease may have multilple aetiological factors. It may be a part of a generalised disease of undetermined aetiology, known as Reiter's disease in which the joints and conjunctiva are also involved in addition to urethritis.

Genus: (II Veillonella)

Veillonella are anaerobic strains of the family. Nisseriaceae and includes genus: II Veillonella Prevot.. 1933. The Type species is i *Pan'ula* (Veillon and Zuber) Prevot.

They are Gram-negative cocci. 0.30μ in diameter, anaerobic grow best at 37°C . Six species are recognised. The species are recogngized by colony characterse and biochemical reaction 1 *pan'ula* are characterized by formation of H_2O. CO_2, H,S and indole from polypeptides and fermentation of glucose and certain other sugars. haemolytic action and reduction of nitrtate to nitrite.

The organisms are commensals in the natural cavities of man and animals, particularly the mouth and alimentary canal and are considered to be opportunists.

Treatment

Supiphonamide therapy. It is effective in this infection and drug like, sulphadiazine is the drug of choice; whereas sulphmezathine which passes slowly through the blood-brain barries is not effective. For an adult, 3 gm a sulphadiazine should be administered immediately after the diagnosis, followed by a daily dose of 9 gm for 3 days, then a daily dose of 3 fo 6 gm for 4 days. In unconscious patients, the drug must be administered intravenously. *Penicillin therapy.* It give an equally good resuslt as sulphonamide therapy, and both the drugs are combined with advantage in severe cases. Waterhouse-Friderichsen syndrome is succesfully treated with corticosteroid, transfusion of blood and plasma, combined with sulphonamide.

NEISSERIA CATARRHALIS

These are the commensals of the nasopharynx and it is difficult to differentiate them morphologically from *N. meningitis.*

Cultural Characters

They glow on nutrient agar and the colonies are larger, thicker and more opaque than those of meningococcus. The colonies are sticky and do not emulsify easily.

Biochemicol Reactions

They do not ferment dextrose and other sugars.

Antigenicity

They differ antigenically from *N. meningitis.*

Pathogenicity

They sometimes cause catarrhal inflammation of the nasopharynx.

STAPHYLOCOCCUS

The genus *Staphylococcus* consists of cluster-forming Grampositive cocci. It is important because it includes the common and versatile pathogenic species *Staphylococcus aureus* (syn. *Staph. pyogenes*). This staphylococcus is the cause of a wide range of different kinds of major and minor pyogenic infections, and also occurs harmlessly as a commensal parasite in the anterior nares and on moist areas of skin in 20 to 30 percent of healthy persons ('carriers'). Other staphylococei, called *Staph. album* (*syn. Staph epidermidis*), are harmless commensals that grow on the whole surface of the skin and in the nostrils and mouth of all persons throughout their life, but they occasionally act as opportunistic pathogens in persons with defective antimicrobial defences, e.g., damaged heart valves or urinary tract anomalies. The staphylococci can survive and grow in high salt concentrations, e g., in drying sweat and pickled meat, and produce lipases and esterases that enable them to utilize the lipids of sebaceous secretion as a source of carbon and energy. The *albus* variety is frequently found in acne lesions, though its role in acne is doubtful.

Definition of the Genus Staphylococcus

Gram-positive cocci that grow in irregular, grape-like clusters, are facultatively anaerobic, form acid from glucose under either aerobic or anaerobic conditions, produce catalase, and occur as parasites on the skin in man and other vertebrate animals.

Other genera of cluster-forming Grain-positive cocci are harmless saprophytes that live in soil, water and foodstuffs : *Micrococcus* differs from *Staphylococcus* in being strictly aerobic. Sarcina differs in forming cubical packets of eight cocci, and *Aerococcus* in not producing catalase. *Peptococcus* consists of strictly anaerobic cocci that live as harmless commensals in the throat, intestine and vagina.

DEFINITION OF THE TWO SPECIES OF STAPHYLOCOCCUS

Staphylococcus Aureus

Coagulase-positive. toxin-forming, pathogenic staphylococci. Most strains form golden-pimented (aurens) colonies: some form white or cream coloured colonies.

Staphylococcus Albus

Coagulase-negative. non-toxin-forniing and non-pathogenic staphylococi. Most strains form white (albus) colonies, but a few form pigmented ones (lemon, yellow, red).

History

Koch (108) observed micrococcus like organisms in pus; Pasteur cultivated these cocci in liquid media. Ogaston, a surgeon in Aberdeen, found it to be constantly present in the pus of acute and chronic abscesses. The organism was cultivated by him in eggs and he found it to be pathogenic for mice and guineapigs. In 1883, he distinguished cocci in groups from cocci in chains. Julius Roseanbach made a through study of the organism, obtained pure culture of staphylococci on solid media and divided them according to their pigment production into *Staphylococcus pyogenes* aureus and *Staphylococcus pvogenes albus* and Passet added Staphylococcus pyogenes citreus.

MORPHOLOGY AND STAINING

Staphylococcus aureus is a typical sphere, although one side may be somewhat flattened when the cells are grouped in the irregular grape-like clusters which gave to the organism its generic name. The average diameter of the sphere is 0.8 μ, but individual organisms or entire strains occasionally vary between the extreme limits of 0.4 and 1.2 g. In smears from pus the cocci are seen singly, in pairs, in clusters, and even in short chains. The irregular clusters are found characteristically in smears from cultures grown on solid media. In both cultures short chains and diplococcal forms occur so frequently that it often is impossible to distinguish between staphylococci and streptococci by their morphology alone.

Staphylococci are nonmotile, although they may exhibit marked brownian motion when examined in a hanging drop. They are non-sporogenous and gram-positive, but a few gram negative forms may occur in the center of clusters, in organisms phagocytozed by cells, and in old, dying cultures.

No definitive statement can be made in respect to then presence or function of a capsule. An obvious capsule on a few specific strains was reported by Lyons in 1937 and Price and Kneeland in 1956.

CULTURAL CHARACTERISTICS

Laboratory strains of staphylococci grow equally well on meat extract or meat infusion media at a temperature of 37°C. The optimal temperature for growth lies at or about 35°C. although growth occurs readily at temperatures as low as 15°C and as high as 40°C.

The most characteristic and luxuriant growth occurs under aerobic conditions. but staphylococci are facultatively anaerobic and *will* grow in an atmosphere of hydrogen. The optimal reaction of the medium is pH 7.4.

On nutrient agar plates the colonies are usually round. I to 2 mm in diameter, convex. opaque. glistening, with an entire edge and soft or butter-like consistency. Typical growth is golden yellow, but this colour may vary in shade and intensity.

On blood-agar plates the colonies are usually larger, and certain varieties are surround by zones of hemolysis. Primary cultures should be planted by streaking or pouring petri dishes ofblood-ager medium. Young colonies in the depth of the medium develop no pigment and, because they often are surrounded by a zone of hemolysis and are extremely small. may be confused with colonies of beta-hemolytic streptococci.

Staphylococci can be grown in a synthetic medium if both thiamine and nicotinic acid are included: however. uracil is necessary y for anaerobic growth.

Pathogenic strains usually oxidize mannitol, and all strains oxidize simple sugars without gas. Litmus, methylene blue, and rosaniline are decolourized, and nitrates are reduced to, nitrites, but indol is not formed in peptone water.

The growing importance of *Staphylococcus* in hospital infections, in food poisoning, and in mixed infections with gramnegative bacilli in man has forced our attention on a more selective medium for the differentiation of these organisms from others in pus with a mixed flora, from foods of all kinds, and from the dust from the air, floors, and furniture in, hospitals. Chapman's alkaline brom-thy mol-blue agar containing potassium tellurite for the isolation of staphylococci from-the feaces was followed by Maitland and Martyn's salt agar with salt as the inhibitor and mannitol as a differential.

Pigment Production

Very young colonies of *Staphylococcus aureus* are always colourless. but as growth takes place. a pigment is elaborated' which is soluble in alcohol. ether, chloroform, and benzol and has been classified as a lipochrome. The pigment remains in the colony and does not diffuse into the medium, but its solubility in tissue exudates gives pus and sputum a faint, golden yellow colour which should suggest the possibility of this type of infection. Transferring colonies to plain agar or- Loffler's medium and incubating at room temperature results in maximum production of pigment.

Virulence and the ability to produce coagulase is associated with. but does not depend upon. the colour of the colony. Only a few of the very yellow *S. aureus* isolates fail to produce coagulase, while only a few of the *S. epidermidis* colonies do, produce coagulase.

Resistance

Staphylococci are among the most resistant of all the nonsporulating bacteria. On agar slants cultures remain alive at room temperature or in the icebox for months.

A strain of *Staphylococcus* aureus, which is killed in 10 minutes but not in 5 by phenol diluted 1 : 90, is used U. S. Food and Drug Administration as a standard organism for evaluating other antiseptics. Abraham et. al. employed a standard strain of this organism to establish the unit of penicillin.

Penicillinase-producing strain were in antibiotic penicillin was discovered. As a rule, susceptible strains do not develop penicillinase or resistance when exposed to the drug either in the test tube or by treatment.

Penicillinase is an enzyme that destroys penicillins breaking the b-lactam ring. Its production is extrachromosomal plasmids which can be transferred by bacteriophages.

Resistance to streptomycin and to novobiocin transferred by lysogenic phage. Both streptomycin resistance and free coagulase production have been transduced by specific phase types. Patte and Baldwin employed phage 80 to transfer resistance to chlorotetracycline and noyobiocin and also the ability to synthesize penicillinase. Blair and Carr have induced penicillinase synthesis with a phage and have conferred toxin production upon certain nontoxigenic strains by lysogenization with a phage derived from a toxigenic strain.

The synthesis of 6-aminopenicillamic acid was followed by the production of a number of penicillin homologues which are not susceptible to penicillinase.

The best-known are methicillin, oxacillin, and ancillin, new ones seem to appear each month. All of the new penillines are much more expensive and somewhat less against penicillin-susceptible strains than old Penicillin G. hence they should be reserved for serious infections with penicillin-resistant staphylococci.

Resistance and even dependence develop with great rapidity to streptomycin, dihydrostreptomycin, and erythromycin. Cross-resistance also occurs between erythromycin and catbomyein. Resistance is building up to neomycin, bacitracin, and to a lesser degree, chloramphenicol. Ristocetin. kanamycin. and vancomycin are effective with penicillin-resistant organisms but are rather toxic. Resistance to kanamycin in a single phagc type. type 54.

Another, but less important. type of resistance to penicillin occurs in association with the appearance of G type and L form colonies.

Variability

The golden yellow staphylococci may give rise to white or translucent. colourless colonies with or without a corresponding change in colony formation and virulence.

Antigenic Structure

Rantz and his associates discovered an antigen which was common to all the gram-positive cocci and to a number of gram-positive bacilli. The Rantz antigen has been extracted by treatment with lysozyme from certain strains of staphylococci and used to sensitize erythrocytes which in turn could be used as an antigen to detect hemagglutinins in serum. Neter and his associates found that this hemagglutinin reaction was inhibited by human and animal serum and that the serum factor was heat-stable at 75°C.

Polysaccharide A

In 1935 Julianelle and Weighard isolated a species-specific polysaccharide. A from virulent strains of staphylococci and a polysaccharide B from strains which were not pathogenic. More recent studies, summarized by McCarty and Morse, have shown that polysaccharide A is a component of the cell wall of S *aureus* and belongs to the bacterial polyolphosphate polymers called teichoic acids, The polysaccharide A is easily extracted from the cell wall with trichloracetic acid. The antigenic specificity of the teichoic acid depends upon the N-acetylglucoamine moieties. The amino sugar my have either the a or the β-glycoside linkage and each may confer immunologic specificity. Antibodies against polysaccharide A apparently do not result in the agglutination of the whole intact coccus but may be required for effective phagocytoses.

Low levels of antibodies which precipitate polysaccharide A may be present in the serum of normal adults and at much higher levels in patientts with severe stphylococcal disease. A few children, but more adults, give an immediate type skin test when injected with polysaccharide A. Sensitivity to staphylococcal filtrates has been transferred passively to normal animals by white blood cells but not by serum.

Protein Antigen A

This component was isolated by Verwey in 1940 and studied in more detail by Jansen in 1958. Antigen A can be released from the cell wall by the by action of deoxyribonuclease. It is a basic protein with a molecular weight of about 13,000 and can be destroyed by trypsin or chymotr psin.

More recent work has shown that protein A does not function as an antigen in the reaction with human gamma globulin.

Polyglycerophosphate

This glycerol teichoic acid is not found in the cell wall and hence is assumed to be an intracellular constituent. It was isolated by McCarty in 1959 from streptococci but was found. later in other gram-positive organisms including the staphylococci.

Agar gel diffusion studies have shown that *S. aureus* contains at least seven antigens of which at least two are in the cell wall, and cell wall antigens would be involved in grouping staphylococci by agglutination. When grown in the presence of acridine orange, coagulase-positive *S. aureus* exhibits change in the number and shape of the precipitin bands, which suggest loss of the virulence factors coagulase and hemolysins.

Phage Typing

Fisk found that most strains of *S. aureus* were lysogenic; that is to say, they carry phages to which they themselves are immune but which will lose some other members of the same species. Fisk developed a primitive method of typing by cross culture, in which a spot of inoculum of sonic staphylococcus strain was superimposed upon a lawn of a second strain, and the appearance of plaques of lysis indicated that one of the pair carried a phage virulent for the other. The current phage typing method is a direct descendant of the scheme proposed by Wilson and Atkinson in 1945. Each specific phage was propagated on a specific susceptible strain of staphylococcus until it developed a high titer, and then the virus was separated by filtration and added in the proper dilution to one spot on a test plate. Usually about 25 phages are used, since this is a practical number to add to a single plate culture.

The phage groups, as defined by Parker, are shown in Table. The production of enterotoxin is confined primarily to phage groups III and IV In phage group I the 52, 52A. 80, 81 complex of strains predominate in hospital infections. In phage group II strains which react only with phage 71 appear to be specifically associated with vesicular skin lesions, such as staphylococcal impetigo, and pemphigus of the newborn.

Table : 13.1. The Lytic Groups The Lytic Groups of Staphylococcus Typing Phages Which are Included in the Internationally Agreed Set of Basic Typing Phages

Lytic Group	*Phages in Group*								
I	29	52	52A	79	80				
II	3A	3B	3C	55	71				
III	6	7	42E	47	53	54	75	77	83A
IV	42D								
Not allowed			81	187					

The study of phage typing is not complete, since many strains which cannot be typed by this method have been isolated.

Zabriskie has reviewed the existing evidence that toxin production may be mediated by a lysogenic phage. The Communicable Disease Center, U.S Public Health Service. Atlanta, Georgia is now the centeral laboratory for phage typing.

Bacterial Metabolites

Bernheimer and Schwartz studied the metabolites of four well-known coagulase-positive, virulent strains of *S.aureus*, and of three coagulasenegative, saprophytic strains of *S.epidermidis*. The coagulax positive styphylococci showed 15 different products, or about twice as many as the coagulase negative strains. Using commercial antitoxin prepared against the Wood strain, staphylococci isolated from lesions in man produced, on the average, six to seven lines of precipitate, while coagulase-negative strains formed none. The number of lines is directly related to virulence for the mouse. The materials of the diffusible product were different from the best- known staphylococcal enzymes and toxins.

The known, metabolites can be clsassified as follows: I, nontoxic metabolites. II, exotoxins, and III, enterotoxinss.

Nontoxic Metabolites. These are shown in Table, with an indication of their antigenicity.

TABLE : 13.2. NONTOXIC METABOLITES

1.	Surface antigen	Protective antibodies
2.	Coagulase (3 antigen types)	Anticoagulase
3.	Hyaluronidase	Antihyaluronidase
4.	Staphylokinase	Antifibrinolysin
5.	Gelatinase	
6.	Protease (2 anatigen types)	Antiprotease
7.	Lipase	Antilipase
8.	Egg-yolk factor (Tributyrinase)	Anti-egg-yolk factor
9.	Phosphatase	
10.	Lysozyme	
11.	Penicillinase	

The Coagulase

The first three antigenic types of coagulase were isolated by Rammelkamp and his associates in 1950. The Japanese investigators have brought the number up to seven. There is a fairly good correlation betty cell the coagulase type and the bacteriophage *type* but poor correlation with serologic type of organism. The ability of indent strains of staphylococci to coagulate plasma was noted by Leo Loeb in 1903, but worked out in detail by Much in 1908. This coagulase has been purified by Blobel and his associates and others by paper and starch electrophoresis. Staphylocoagulase is certainly an antigenic protein, but in the form in which it occurs in the organism it will not clot fibrinogen. The actual coagulative principle, coagulase-thrombin, is an enzyme which is activated by the action of coagulase and its plasma factor (CRF).

Bound Coagulase

Two methods for testing for the presence of coagulase have been evolved. The first was performed with plasma in a test tube. The second was the slide test where *S. aureus* cells were mixed with plasma on a slide and thick clumps of fibrin were deposited about the organisms. There was very good correlation between the results of the tube test and the slide test so it was assumed that both were measuring the same coagulase. Dothic found that bound coagulase was responsible for the slide test but not for the tube test. Antibodies to bound coagulase prevented the clumping in the slide test while antibodies to the free coagulase did not. Mouse plasma is readily coagulated by the bound coagulase while it is not coagulated by the free product. Furthermore, bound coagulase converts fibrinogen directly into fibrin without requiring an accessory plasma factor. There seems to be only one antigenic type of bound coagulase.

A number of other organisms can produce an enzyme which can coagulate plasma. These include group *D. streptococci*, *S. pyogenes*, *E. coli*, *and Serratia marcescens.*

The exact contribution of coagulase to the pathogenicity of staphylococci has not been determined. It is know however, from the work of Yotis and Ekstedt that a component in normal human serum which prevents the multiplication of coagulase-negative strains of staphylococci can be neutralized by the addition of purified coagulase. This suggests that coagulase may protect, at least temporarily, the staphylococci which are invading the tissues.

Hyaluronidase

Coagulase-negative strains of Staphylococci do not produce lryaluroidase, but the enzyme is produced by 93.6 per cent of coagulase-positive strains. Duran-Reynals concluded from his studies that the invasive properties corresponded to the amount of "spreading factor" (hyaluonidase) present in the filtrate.

Strain SaB, of*S.aureus* synthesizes hyaluronidase in a defined medium only in the presence of tyrosine and trvptophan. even though these amino acids are not required for optimal growth. Glycine is necessary for growth: glycyl-i-tryosinc and glycyl-i-tryptophan enhance both growth and hyaluronidasc production.

There is evidence that staphyococci produce at leat one other mucin-splitting enzyme which is active against vaginal mucin and is capable of destoying the Francis inhibitor.

There is only one antigenic type of hyaluronidase. and this

produces a specific type of neutralizing antibody. Hyaluronidase from the rabbit's testicle is different antigenically from that made by the staphylococci against the toxins producedd by staphyococci.

About 81 percent of the coagulase-positive strains of taphylococci from man produce staphylokinase, but it is produced by 30 percent of the coagulase-negative strains isolated from animals. Lack found that the mechanism of staphylococcus fbrinolysin was similar to that of streptococcus fibrinolysin, and that the agent acted as an activator of plasma and serum enzyme precursor to yield the lytic agent. Staphylokinase activates the plasma plasminogen to the fibrinolytic enzyme plasmin but unlike streptokinase it can activate the plasminogens from many species and does not require a plasma proactivator. Specific antibodies to staphylokinase inhibit its action on plasminogen.

Muelliers phenomenon was readily explained by Quie and Wannamaker as a manifestation of staphylokinase.

Gelatinase

Gelatinase is produced by 47 percent of staphylococci from Human lesions and by 98 percent of those from animal lesions, but also from 60 percent of the coagulase-negative, saprophytic staphylococci. Gelatinase production bears no relation to coagulase production hemolysis, or virulence. The antigenicity of gelatinase has not been demonstrated.

An enzyme distinct from gelatinase is responsible for the softening of inspissated serum. Indeed, Elek and Levy have identified two apparently distinct proteases, one of which was and the other of which was not inhibited by antitoxins made to the Wood 46 strains. The second one may be antigenic, but this particular one was not being produced by the Wood 46 strain.

These proteolytic enzymes may explain the rapid necrosis of tissues. including bone, which is characteristic of staphylocoal infections.

Lipase

Over 99.5 percent of coagulase-positive strains of staphylococci from man are lipolytic, and 75 percent of the strains from animals are lipolytic, while 30 percent of coagulase- negative, saprophytic strains also produce the enzyme. Lipase is antigenic, and commercial antitoxins contain appreciable amounts of antibody. There is no evidence that lipase plays a specific role in the pathogenicity of staphylococci.

Phosphatase

Barber and Kuper reported an excellent correlation between acid phosphatase activity and pathogenicity as well as between phosphatase activity and coagulase production. But testing for acid phosphatase is not only more difficult but a less specific indicator of virulence than the coagulase test.

Lysozyme

Jay studied 126 coagulase-positive strains of*Saureus* for their ability to produce lysozyme. He found that 120 or 95.2 percent produce lysozyme. 117 or 92.9 percent produced (x-hemolysis,108 or 85.7 percent precipitated egg yolk, and 102 or 81 percent produced sheep hemolysins. Only 4 or 49 coagulase-negative strains produced lysozyme. He concluded that lysozyme production was a better ancilary test for pathogenicity than either the a-hemolysis or egg yolk precipitation.

Penicillinase

This enzyme may appear as either an endocellular or an exocellulalr product. It acts by opening up the β-lactam ring of penicillin and hence destroys it activity. Many strains of *Staphylococcus aureus* have become resistant to penicillin by this mechanism. The resistance is most striking in strains from group I and III which are typed by bacteriophages.

Exotoxins

The exotoxins produced by virulent strains of *S. aureus* are shown in Table. It should be noteds that the enterotoxin which causes food poisoning has not been included. This toxin, which resists boiling and in other ways does not crrespond to either typical exotoxins or endotoxins. will be discussed later in this chapter.

α-hemolysin

This is the most common and best studied of all the exotoxins produced by virulent human strains of staphylocococci. This toxin. 1) hemolyzes red cells of the rabbit, sheep. cow. and goat. but not those of man: 2). produces necrosis in the skin of man and animals: 3) in a large dose can kill man or animals: 4) destroys the blood cells of rabbits bait not of man: 5) destroys the platelets of rabbits: and 6) is cytotoxic for cultured mammalian cells. All of these effects are neutralized with IgG antibody globulin but not with IgA or 1gM. The effect may be to release anions from phospholipids in the cell membrane.

The α-hemolysin can be separated from the δ-hemolysin and the S-hemolysin by electrophoresis localization. The chemical studies of α-hemolysin and β-hemolvsin were reviewed by Gow and Robinson in 1969.

This toxin is antigenic and toxoid can be formed by treating crude filtrates with formalin.

β-Hemolysin

The only property of β-hemolysin which is universally accepted is the "hot cold" lysis of sheep or bovine red blood cells which was described by Glenny and Stevens in 1935. Very little lysis occurs during primary incubation at 37°C but appears after subsequent storage at cold teinperatures.This hemolysin is found most frequently in staphylococcus strains isolated from animals.

δ-Hemolysin

Williams and Harper discovered a third type of hemolysin in 1947, which was not neutralized by either a or β antitoxin. This hemolysin produced a narrow but well-defined zone of baking around the colonies when exposed to human, rabbit, sheey, horse, rat, mouse, and guinea pig red cells. The association of α-lysin with human pathogenicity is at least as high as that of α-lysin, and it does not occur in coagulasenegative staphylococci.

Leukocidins

There are three distinct types of leukocidins produced by or another strain of S *aureus*. The first recognized is an old friend, the α-hemolysin, which hemolyzes the red cells of rabbits, sheep, cows, and goats, but not the red cells of man. The second leakocidin is apparently identical with the S-hemolysin, is thermostable, and causes marked morphologic changes in all types of leukocytes except those of sheep. The third leukocidin described by Panton and Valentine in 1932 is not associated with hemolytic activity. It occurs in 40 to 50 percent of strains and acts on human and rabbit leukocytes only. Woodin and his associates found that this leukoeidin was- formed of two protein components, named F and S, and both were necessaary for the toxic action. Gladstone found that an antibody to either F or S protected against each. Woodin found that this leukocidin, in the presence of calacium ions, destroyed the granules of the cells and produced cytoplasmic vesicles. A toxoid was prepared frrom this leukocidin by Gladstone which Mudd and his associates showed would produce antitoxin to botth the F and S fraction in normal ands in infected subjects. There was some local inflammation at the site of injection. There was definite clinical improvement in some patient with chronic osteomyelitis who were treated with the new toxoid but it would be difficult to say whether the improvement was the result of the increase of antibodies in the sermn or a decrease in the degree of allergy in the patient.

Staphylococcal Leukocyte Cytotaxin

The name cytotaxin ws proposed by Keller and sorkin for agents which act directly upon leukocytes, resulting intheir directional migration. Walker and his associates have isolated a heat-stable materil from a strain of *Staphylococcus aureus* which has this effect on leukocytes Cytotaaxins are formed under two other conditions. They appear (1) when antigenantibody complexes generate a trimolecular complex from complement coos isting of *C*'5, *C*'6 and *C*'7 and (2) when streptokinase converts plasminogen to plasmin which in turn reacts with C'3 to give a chemotactically active split product of C'3.

In hereditary chronic septic granulomatous disease the staphylococcus is often the infecting agent. The white cells can phagocytize the staphylococci but cannot digest them. A review of this disease can be found in the chapter on heritable disorders of immunity and in the review by Philippart and his associates.

Enterotoxin

At least three emetic toxins are produced by certain strains of staphylococci. They are distinctive proteins which are nonheniolytic, non-dermonecrotic, nonpar ic, and unlike lysins, resistant to both the beat of boiling for 30 minutes and the proteolytic action of pepsin and trypsin. They are rather weak antigenically, but can be detected by precipitation reactions, hemagglutination, gel diffusion, and colony-halo reactions. It is important for the student to remember that these endotoxin-producing strains usually, but not always; produce a full complement of the standard toxic and non-toxic metabolites discussed in the preceding pages.

Man is the best test animal for enterotoxin assay, followed by the monkey and the cat. Custard-filled puffs and eclairs, potato salad, chicken salad, egg salad, and sandwiches are particularly dangerous. Two large epidemics occurred in 1959 from infected ham. In the first epidemic 1,000 individuals were ill, and the organism was identified as phage type 6147153. In the second 216 persons were ill and a phage type 7 was recovered.

The incubation period is short, 2 to 6 hours, and the onset. of symptoms is sudden and violent, with nausea, vomiting, diarrhea. and sometimes sudden collapse, suggesting the onset of cholera. Death rarely, it ever, occurs, and recovery is usually complete in 24 to 48 hours. This is the most common type of food poisoning in this country. exceeding the combined cases of salmonella and clostridia poisoning.

EPIDEMIOLOGY OF STAPH. AUREUS INFECTIONS

Sources of Infection

1. Patients with Lesions Discharging Staphylococci into the *Environment.* Especially large numbers of cocci are disseminated in pus and dried exudate discharged from large infected wounds and burns and secondarily infected skin lesions, e.g. psoriasis, eczema and dermatitis, and in sputum coughed from the lung of a patient with bronchopneumonia. Small discharging lesions, e.g. pustules and paronychiae, on the hands of doctors and nurses are a special danger to their patients.

2. *Healthy Carriers. Staph. aureus* grows harmlessly on the moist invaginated, skin in the nostrils in 10 to 30 per cent of healthy persons and, on that of the perineum in about 10 per cent. The cocci are spread from these sites into the environment by the bands, handkerchief, clothing and dust (consisting of skin squanies and cloth fibres). Some carriers, called 'shedders', disseminate exceptionally large numbers of cocci comparable to the numbers disseminated by patients with large superficial lesions or lower respiratory tract infections.

During the first day or two of life the body surfaces of most babies become colonized by staphylococci acquired from their mother, nurse or environment. In babies born in hospital, the nose, umbilical stump and moist areas of skin are commonly colonized by *Staph. aureus*, often by a virulent multi-antibiotic-resistant strain. Nasal carriage in babies, as in older persons, is usually long-lasting. When a particular strain of *Staph. aureus* has colonized a carrier site in an individual, it tends to persist in that site for many months or several years, and to prevent colonization of the site by other strains. whether more or less virulent (bacterial interference). In babies who are nose carriers the occurrence of an intercurrent viral infection of the respiratory tract greatly increases the dissemination of staphylococci into the environment ('cloud babies'). Babies with skin infections or who are carriers of an 'epidemic' strain of staphylococcus may bring infection into the household from the hospital.

Animals of domesticated and some wild species may disseminate *Staph. auteus* from infected lesions or carriage sites and so cause infections in man, *e.g.* a dairy cow with staphylococcal infection of the udder may give infected milk which can cause staphylococcal food poisoning.

Modes of Infection

The modes of acquisition of an infection may be either (1) *exogenous. i.e.*, directly from a source in another person or animal; *e.g.* the operation wound of a patient may be infected from hand-carriage by a surgeon who sweats the organisms through glove punctures or by a nurse who is a nasal carrier; or (2) *endogenous i.e.*, from a source, either carriage site or minor lesion, elsewhere in the patient's own body. e.g., a boil may be caused by cocci transferred on the fingers from a carriage site in the nostrils to a hair follicle on the back of the neck, and a surgical wound may be infected post-operatively by contaminated fingers or by dust-borne staphylococci derived from the patient's nostrils or perineum.

The relative importance of erogenous and endogenous infection in the causation of surgical sepsis with Stoph. aureus appears to vary from hospital to hospital. In some studies a much higher incidence of sepsis (e.g. 8 per cent) has been found in patients who were nasal or perineal carriers than in those who were not (e.g., 2 per cent), but in other studies the incidence has been similar in the carriers and non-carriers.

Viability *Outside the Bodv*. Staphylococci do not grow outside the body except occasionally in moist nutrient materials such as meat, milk and= dirty water. They are, however, very hardy and, though not- spore-forming, may remain alive in a dormant state for up to several months when dried in Pus. sputum, clothing or dust. They are fairly readily killed by heat. e.g., by moist heat at 65°C in 30° min, by exposure to light and by strong disinfectants.

Mechanisms of Transmission in Cross-infection

These include:

1. Contact

The readist method of spread is thought to be direct contact (touching) with the contaminated hand or clothing of an infected person, e.g., with a hand on which there is a septic sore, or the band of a nasal carrier who has picked his nose.

Hundreds of staphylococci may pass in a drop of sweat exuded from the hand of a carrier surgeon through a puncture in his rubber glove or from his forearm through the moistened sleeve of his gown. Moderate numbers of staphylococci may be transmitted indirectly on the hands of non-carrier nurses who have contaminated their hands by touching infected patients or babies. Small nurrbers of staphylococci are likely to be spread by contact with objects, such as furniture, clothing. bedding, towels, hand-basins and baths, that have been contaminated by a patient or carrier. Staph. aurcus is commonly present on such foinites. Newborn babies have been shown to become colonized with Staph. aureus by contact with infected shirts, napkins and blankets. though less frequently than by contact with infected hands.

2. Air-borne Dust

Staphylococci carried on fragments of desquamated keratin. fibres of cloth and particles of powdered dried pus or sputum are readily shed into the air from the skin, handkerchief. clothing. bedding and surgical dressings of patients and carriers when these objects are disturbed or moved even slighly. For example, several thousand*Staph. aureux* carrying particles may be shed into the air by a carrier shaking open his handkerchief, changing his clothing or making his bed; most (e.g., 90 per cent) of these particles will fall out of the air within 15 to 20 min, but a few will remain air-borne for up to 2 hours or more *Staph. aureus-carrying* particles are likely to be present in considerable numbers in the air of occupied rooms and hospital wards during periods of activity such as bed, making, sweeping, dusting, etc. They may fall on to the body surfaces, surgical wounds or vehicles of infection such as surgical instruments, or they may be inhaled into the respiratory tract.

3. Droplet-spray and Air-borne Droplet-nucle

Which are freely disseminated in speaking, coughing and sneezing by healthy nasal carriers and patients with bronchopneumonia, are probably the least important of the diterent methods of spread, since relatively few of the droplet or droplet nuclei contain *Staph. aureus.*

Transmission of infection to Newborn Babies in Hospital

The circumstances that babies are born free from bacterial colonization and are highly susceptible to colonization with *Staph. aureus* have made it possible to compare the relative importance of different sources and mechanisms of transmission of *Staph. aureus* in the nurseries of maternity hospitals. Studies in which strains of *Staph. aureus* were distinguished by phage-typing suggest that it is usually a carrier nurse or a nurse with a septic lesion that introduces an epidemic strain into a nursery, that thereafter the colonized babies serve as the main source of that strain for other babies, and that the main means of transmission between the babies is by contact with the hands and clothing of the nurses that attend them. However, in a number of studies, measures taken to exclude the possibility of contact spread by nurses, e.g., disinfection or gloving of the bands, wearing of masks, and change of gown between babies have failed appreciably to reduce the rate at which the babies became infected, and there is evidence that infection has been transmitted by air and by fomites. The practice of nursing the baby alongside its mother instead of in a communal nursery or the use of several small nurseries in which successive cohorts, of babies are nursed has helped to reduce *staphylococcal* infection among neonates.

PATHOGENICITY IN MAN

Occurrence

Staph. aureus and less frequently *Staph. albus* are pathogenic to man. Staphylococci may produce either local or generalised infections. Local infections which are limited to the skin and subcutaneous tissues cause boils. sycosis barbac. pustular acne. localised abscesses. carbuncles, cellulitis, wound, suppuration, pemphigus neonatorum. When generalised, they may. cause septicaemia, cellulitis, acute osteomyelitis and pyaemic abscesses. Some strains growing in food containing milk or cream, produce enterotoxin causing purging and vomiting in man. Numerous staphylococcal strains are found in air, dust, clothings and fomites. They are commensals of a number of animals, e.g., dogs, cats, sheep, horses. They may be pathogenic to newborn babies from fomites.

Portals of Entry

These are normally present in the skin, nose, mouth and throat and when the normal barrier is broken, they produce pathogenic lesions. The organisms enter the skin through the hair follicles, sebaceous glands, sweat ducts or through some cracks, abrasion or injury to the skin.

Boils or Furuncles

These are infection of hair follicles and pilosebaceous glands. Initially, induration of the part occurs with formation, of a mass due to acute inflammation of the dermis; this is followed by infiltration of polymorphonuclear neutrophils with dilatation of blood vessels. The centre of the swelling undergoes necrosis and becomes inspissated to form a core. The cavity round the core is lined by granulation tissue and contains liquid pus and the mass points to the surface of the skin to form a boil. Formation of summer boils in the tropics is a special feature, in which there is soddening óf the skin and the local resistance of the skin is lost due to excessive perspiration. In such a case, the infection with syaphylococei is common along the hair follicles and pilosebaceous glands.

Carbuncle

Thís is characterised by formation of groups of boils deeply seated, which may cause necrosis of the subcutaneous tissues. It starts as a focal' indaration of the subcutaneous tissue; increases in size and spreads rapidly, resulting in a large, red, indurated and painful area with a diameter of several centimetres. In the course ofa few'days, necrosis and sloughing, of the part ensues, resulting in an ulcer with indurated base. In other cases, when the infection is relatively superficial, multiple follicular openings are seen giving a cribriform or honeycomb appearance. This is due to the formation of multiple boils, separated- by connective tissue trabeculac and subcutaneous fat. The site of election is the nape of the neck, where the skin is coarse and ilinourished due to poor blood supply of the part. Sometimes. lesions are seen on the face. when there is danger of thrombosis of the cavernous, sinus. Predisposing aetiological factors are diabetes mellitus. amoebic infection, chronic nehritis. anaemia and avitaminosis. Transient glycosuria however, may result in a case of carbuncle. Local lymph nodes show hyperplasia and inflammatory swelling.

Pemphigus Neonatorum

This is a pustular condition of the skin seen in newborn babies, specially on the palm of the hand and sole of the foot.

Mastitis

It is a condition of inflammation of the breast produced by staphylococcal infection, particularly during the period of lactation.

Whitlow (Paronychia)

The infection of the tip of the finger by staphylococci produces an extremely painful condition of acute inflammation resulting in suppuration commonly known as whitlow. It is often limited to the finger tip, but may spread along the tendon sheath into the palm of the hand, producing a condition of tenosynovitis and spreading upto the forearm.

Cellulitis

It is an inflammation of subcutaneous tissues of those areas, which are loose and traversed freely by lympbaties. The infection is characterised by spread of staphylococei along the tissue spaces where the barrier is poor. They are often mixed with streptococcal infection. The infection may be localised and form abscesses.

Generalised Lesion

In this, the infection tends to be generalised by the escape of the organism into the general circulation, producing a condition of septicaemia. This is seen in boils, wounds, or cases of puerperal sepsis. It is associated with a sustained rise of temperature, increased pulse rate, leueocytosis and toxaemia. The infection may cause a pyaemic condition resulting from the dislodgement of septic emboli after thrombophlebitis. In such a case, the infection spreads to the internal organs causing multiple abscesses of the heart and pericardium, lung, brain, meninges, kidney or spleen. The predisposing factors, which favour generalisation are : (*a*) *Lower resistance* of*the individual;* ,*e.g.*, diabetes, albuminuria, alcoholism, prolonged illness, anaemia, overwork, sedentary habits or avitaminosis; (*b*) *local trauma* like squeezing or untimely surgical interference before localisation.

Facial Cellulitis

This is a common complication of a pimple or furuncle of the face or lip and looks like erysipelas, accompanied by cellulitis and oedema of the face of the affected side. There is often a history of squeezing a boil or pimple. The organism in such a case is virulent and when the barrier is broken, a fulminating septicaemia occurs. A faulty or untimely surgical interference may act in a similar way. The prognosis in these cases is very grave and the case ends fatally within a few days, if chernotherapoutics like penicillin or tetracyclines are not administered. The infection may spread by a process of septic thrombophlebitis of the smaller veins, namely, angular or anterior facial vein. Due to the absence of valves in these veins and constant contraction of facial muscles, thrombi are carried onward. These veins directly communicate with the cavernous sinus and the infection may result in thrombosis of the cavernous sinus. Owing to this reason, area of the face drained by the angular vein and anterior facial veins is called "the dangerous area of the face".

Ulcerative Endocarditis

It occurs usually after an attack of infection of the skin, resulting in septicaemia with localisation of the organisms in the valvular endocardium. The infection causes rapid destruction of the affected valves, producing ulcerative valvular endocarditis ending fatally.

Brain

Abscesses of the brain may result from the direct extension of the infection from the middle ear or mastoid abscess; or the organism may reach the brain in the form of an infected embolus usually from the lung.

Meningitis

A condition of leptomeningitis may arise as a result of- generalised septicaemia; but as a rule, it occurs as an extension from otitis media or traumatic osteomyelitis of the skull.

Osteomyelitis

Haematogenous osteomyelitis is caused by a group of Organisms. In a study of 400 cases, the incidence was found to be staphylococcal in 78 per cent, pneumococcal in 14 per cent and streptococcal in 6 per cent of cases. Besides these, *Salm. typhosa* and *Esch. coli* are rarely found as the infective-organisms. Acute osteomyelitis is an acute inflammatory condition of the bone-marrow, caused by staphylococei and usually seen in childhood. Exanthematous lesions like measles, scarlet fever or similar conditions are often predisposing. factors. *Acute haemalogenous osteomyelitis* is common in unhealthy children with poor resistance. It starts as an acute condition with rigor and high fever, pain and tenderness, usually near the knee joint but it may become chronic, when the condition persists for some years. The lesion starts in the metaphysis. From this primary focus, the infection may spread outwards to the cortex forming a sub-periosteal abscess or along the medullary cavity destroying the structures in it and enclosing the bone into a case of pus. The cause of localisation in the metaphysis are fourfold, namely : (i) Frequent minor trauma to which the part is exposed. Even slight trauma, which injures the vessels cause haematoma and if, often determines the site of acute osteomyelitis. The haemorrhage is followed by formation of a thrombus, which acts as a medium for the growth of the organism; (ii) rich supply of blood; (iii) peculiar bending of the arteries (hair- pin bends), supplying the metaphysis and (iv) less phagocytic activity of the cells of the marrow at that part. The affected portion of the bone undergoes necrosis and forms *a sequestrum* (dead bone), often enclosed in a pool of rus. When the main nutrient vessel is thrombosed the major part of the shaft may form a sequestrum. The surface of the sequestrum in that case is smooth, as the periosteum does not get any chance to form new bone. The sequestrtun is often a rough, eroded, porous spicule of bone. In a subacute or chronic case, the periosteum surrounding the sequestrum is lifted up and begins to lay down new bone, forming a covering of granulation tissue around the sequest strum, known as involucrum. The sequestrum encased in the involucrum comes out through an opening called cloaca. Chronic osteomyeliti. in adults may produce localised abscess Gear the metaphysis, the so called Brodle's abscess. It is often seen in the proximal end of the tibia and the humerus or lower end of the Femur, and staphylococcus or other organisms can be isolated from pus. Septic thrombi may be dislodged from a focus of osteomyelitis and emboli, resulting in pyaernic condition in various organs.

Lungs

Staphylococci are commensals of the throat and do not, usually affect the mucous membrane of the respiratory tract. Bronchop-neumonia may develop (9 per cent) in the course of staphylococcal septicaemia or as a secondary complication in cases of influenza. Pyaemic abscess of the lung may result after staphylococcal infection due to lodgenient of septic, emboli in the capillaries. Staphylococcal pneumonia is specially seen in newborn children.

Genito-urinary Tract

In the course of septicaeniia, or pyaemia, acute focal glomerulo-nephritis, perinephric abscesses or multiple abscesses of the kidney may develop. In such a case, urine will contain pus cells and the organism may be. cultured from urine. Ascending infection of the kidney (Surgical kidney) may occur producing pyelonephritis or diffuse suppurative nephritis. It is often seen as secondary infection associated pith gonorrhoea or cystitis. The prostate may be the site of a primary or a metastatic focus of an abscess.

Food Poisoning

Staphylococci often produce bacterial food poisoning, arising from ingestion of milk or cream products, not properly refrigerated and handled by individual who is a carrier of pathogenic staphylococei or is suffering from an open staphylococcal skin lesion. It may be pointed out that the incubation period in this case is short and symptoms usually appear in 2 to 6 hours after the contaminated food is taken. But this period is about 12 to 24 hours btemore in typical 'botulism or salmonella food poisoning. The symptoms are nausea, followed by sudden *paroxysm* of vomiting, accompanied by abdominal cramps, acute diarrhoea and prostration. The symptoms persist for several hours and the patient feels normal after 24 hours. Fatalities are rare. The organism can be isolated from the vomitus or food products.

Laboratory Diagnosis

Staphylococci are identified by their morphological characters, staining reaction in mear preparation, and cultural characters on nutrient agar. The pathogenic strains give a positive coagulase test and the colour of the colony helps in the diagnosis of the variety of Staph. aureus, showing golden yellow colour. This is the common pathogenic variety. Sometimes, Staph. albiis is coagulase positive. The coagulase positive strains are called Staph. *pyogenes.T hey* produce toxins (haemolysin and leucocidin, etc.), ferment mannite, liquefy gelatin and are pathogenic to rabbits. Thus the pathogenic strains are differentiated from *Staph. epidermidis.* When the organism is isolated from a case of food poisoning (vomitus, istools or milk products), it is cultivated in Walbaum's medium under CO_2 tension and the fluid containing the enterotoxin may be administered to a monkey, kitten or human volunteer for typical symptoms.

PREVENTION OF STAPHYLOCOCCAL INFECTION IN HOSPITAL

Prevention is very difficult.The measures that may be attempted include the following:

1. Measures Against the Sources of Infection

(a) Patients with discharging lesions should be neutralized as sources of infection by the use of antibiotic therapy, occlusive dressings, barrier nursing and, where possible, isolation in Fingle-bed rooms with exhaust ventilation to the outside. Particular attention should be paid to patients with large septic wounds or burns, large areas of infective dermatitis, staphylococcal pneumonia or any open infection with a known epidemic strain.

(b) Surgeons. nurses. anaesthetists and surgical orderlies who have an open infected lesion on any part of the body. even if this lesion is small. *e.g.*, paronychia, a discharging pustule, or a patch of secondarily infected psoriasis, or who have a lesion of the hand or arm even if it is not discharging, should not attend patients until healing is complete. Covering the lesion with an occlusive dressing is not an adequate safeguard.

(c) Carriers among patients and staff may be detected by nasal and perincal swabbing and treated with twice-daily application of neomycin chlorbexidine cream to the carriage site. Carriers are generally numerous among the hospital staff and they should not be removed from duty unless they are known to be carrying a strain of a phage type that is currently causing an outbreak of clinical infection. Since bacteriolggical screening for carriers in a large staff is very laborious, it is usually not done unless there is a serious out- break of sepsis.

2. Measures Against Spread through the Environment

Mostly these are measures that are generally applicable in the control of hospital infection. They include recognized aseptic and antiseptic procedures during operations; aseptic and antiseptic techniques applicable in the wards for post- operative patients and for the impediment of nursing care (batbs, basins, weighing baskets, etc.) in infant nurseries; early recognition and isolation of any infected case and special protection of highly susceptible patients such as premature babies in special units or single rooms; and measures against the hazards of airborne infection from infected dust, etc. in, operating theatres, wards, dressing stations and special units.

3. Antimicrobial Prohylaxis

It is generally undesirable to give antibiotics to patients, with the object of preventing their acquiring a staphylococcal, infection. The antibiotic thus used will tend to eliminate the sensitive members of the body's commensal bacterial flora and, by removing competitors, facilitate infection with a hospital strain of Staph. aureus or another species that is resistant to the. antibiotic. If it is decided to attempt prophylaxis, the topical. application of a drug is preferable to systemic application, since it is possible to use the more toxic drugs, e.g., a mixture of polymyxin, neomycin and bacitracin, which are not used for systemic therapy; or a chemical antiseptic e.g. bexachlore phone may be applied. If systemic prophylaxis is required it is preferable to use a narrow-spectrum antibiotic such as, cloxacillin rather than a broad-spectrum one.

4. Bacterial Interference

This method for the control of staphylococcal infection in the newborn has been applied successfully in trials in several American hospitals but because of its hypothetical dangers is unlikely to come into general use. Its effectiveness however is of considerable interest because it demonstrates the marked ability of established commensal cocci to prevent the colonization of carriage sites by other, more virulent or antibiotic resistant strains and thus to reduce the likelihood of endogenous septic infections. A strain of Staph. aureus, chosen for its low virulence, may readily be inducedby the deliberate inoculation of bacteria from a culture to colonize the nasal and umbilical carriage sites in newborn babies who have not yet. acquired a staphylococcal flora by natural infection. Colonization with the inoculated strain is only rarely achieved in older babies and aftults already carrying another strain of Staph. atireus unless the resident strain is first eliminated by topical treatment with antibiotics. Carriage of *Staph.* album has some protective effect against the inoculation of *Staph. aureus*, but the degree of interference is less than that between two different strains of *Staph. aureus.*

In the American trials, a special strain of Staph. auretis of low pathogenicity, no. 502A, was able to establish itself when applied to the nostrils and umbilicus in doses of 10° to 10^6 cocci in 95 per cent of babies without previously resident staphylococci but only in 55 per cent of those already colonized by *Staph. albzis* and in 12 per cent of those carrying another type of *Staph. aureus*. The value of this 'prophylactic' procedure was tested in infant nurseries where epidemics of staphylococcal infection were occurring. Only 5 per cent of babies successfully colonized with the special strain, 502A, became carriers of the epidemic strain compared with 40 per cent of the uninoculated babies, and in a follow-up period only 9 of 96 inoculated babies developed septic infections compared with 26 of 45 babies who had acquired the epidemic strain type 80/81 and 10 of 54 babies who had become carriers of other strains of *Staph. aureus.*

STAPHYLOCOCCUS ALBUS

Staph. album is defined as consisting of the coagulase- negative staphylococci. It receives its name from the fact that most strains form white (albus) colonies. It differs from Staph. aureus in not forming toxins or other aggressive factors, so that it is devoid of primary pathogenicity. It is a constant, harmless commensal which grows on all areas of skin and in the nostrils mouth, external car and urethral meatus throughout life. By contact with the skin and by the shedding of skin squames large numbers of the cocci are disseminated on to clothing and fomites and into dust and air. For this reason the organism is a common accidental contaminant of clinical specimens and laboratory cultures, and in most cases its finding in such specimens may be regarded as being without any clinical significance.

Occasionally, however, *Staph. albus* acts as an opportunistic pathogen and causes infection in persons with defective resistance.

e.g.. cystitis in persons with urinary-tract abnormalities, septicaemia or endocarditis in patients after cardiac surgery meningitis with bacteriaemia in patients fitted with ventriculovenous cerebrospinal fluid shunts, and septicaemia in iinmunosuppressed and immunodefective patients. These cases are recognized by the finding of significantly large numbers of cocci (e.g.101 per ml in urine, 5 per ml in blood) in repeated specimens and the infections should be treated with an antibiotic indicated by the results of sensitivity tests on the infecting strain.

OTHER GRAM-POSITIVE CLUSTER-FORMING COCCI

The distinguishing characters of the other Gram-Positive, cluster-forming cocci are given. They are harmless comrnensals and saprapbytes that very rarely cause even opportunistic infections. One variety of Micrococcus (subgroup 3) has, however, been implicated as the cam of a number of urinary tract infections.

Staphylococcus Epidermidis

Staphylococcus epidermidis can be differentiated fromS. *aureus* in the following ways: S. *epidermidis* has white colonies; it possesses a glycerol-type teichoic acid, called *polysaccharide B;* and it does not produce coagulase. It also lacks the alpha toxin and protein A and is unable to ferment mannitol.

S. epidermidis exists as normal flora on the human skin and ingeneral, is not problem for the normal, healthy individual. However, it has now become an apportunistic pathogen, causing nosocomial infections in joint and vascular prostheses. It is also a cause of urinarytract infections, particularly in children and in elderly male patients who have undergone urethral instrumentation.

Staphyloccus Saprophyticus

There is some disagreement as to whether *staphylococcus saprophvticus* presents a new species or is merely a variant of S. *epidermidis. S. saprophvticus* is characterized as being coaglase-negative. DNase negative. unable to ferment glucose. and resistant to novabiocin.

S. saprophvticus is a frequent cause of urinary tract infections in women. particularly in those between the ages of 16 and 30 years. It is seldom observed in males. In one study it was reported tobe psesent in 42.3°7 of all females 16 to 25 years of age who had bacteriurea (*hacteria in the urine*).

The source for these infections is obscure, because this organism is only rarely isolated from the urine. recttun, or skin of uninfected individuals. It can, however, be isolated from the skin of a variety of animals and from lesions on the hand & of persons handling animals.

S. saprophvticus is routinely resistant to novobiocin but sensitive to a wide variety of antibiotics such as penicillin, ampicillin, methicillin, and erythromycin.

NEISSERIA

The neisseriae are Gram-negative diplococci of which the pathogenic members, meningococcus and gonococcus, are found inside the polymorphonuelear pus cells of the inflammatory exudate. Although difficult to differentiate on morphological and cultural characters, these two pathogens are associated with entirely different diseases. *Neisseria* meningitidis is the cause of an acute purulent meningitis, variously called epidemic cerebrospinal meningitis, cerebrospinal fever or, because of a purpuric rash which is sometimes present, 'spotted fever'. It may also cause a subacute septicaemia with a petechial rash but without meningitis, particularly during epidemics of meningococcal meningitis. The term meningococcal infection is used to embrace these two syndromes. *Neisseria gonorrhoeae* is the cause of a sexually transmitted or venereal disease, gonorrhoeo, a purulent infection of the mucous membrane of the urethra and also of the cervix uteri in the female; there may be rectal infection and secondary local and metastatic complications e.g. epididymitis, salpingitis and arthritis may occur if the primary infection is not promptly treated. A purulent conjunctivitis of the newborn, ophthalmia neonatorum, and a vulvovaginitis in young girls also occur as primary gonococcal infections.

The non-pathogenic or potentially pathogenic members of the neisseria genus are common commensals of the upper respiratory tract, which is also the reservoir of the meningococcus. They include :VV *catarrhalis*. *N. flmva* and *N. sicca*.

Morphology and Nutrition of the Neisseria

Bacteria in the genus *Neisseria* are nonmotile, gram-negative diplococci whose stained cells appear characteristically kidney-shaped with their concave sides adjacent to each other. As a result. the pairs of diplococci sometimes look like small doughnuts.

The nonpathogenic *Neisseria* (part of the normal flora of the nasopharvnx) are slightly larger and considerably easier to grow than the pathogenic species; they are able to multiply at 22°C on ordinary laboratory media such as nutrient broth, whereas the pathogens do not grow well below 37° C and not at all at 22°C. Furthermore, the pathogens are extremely sensitive to fatty acids and trace metals present in peptones and agar. This inhibitory effect can be eliminated by the additional of serum or blood to the growth medium. Moreover, if the blood is heated to 80°C for 10 minutes, it is even more effective. This procedure turns the agar medium a dark brown, and the resulting medium is commonly called *chocolate blood agar*. The pathogens also require a higher concentration of CO_2 for optimal growth than is present in the atmosphere. It is customary, therefore, to culture newly isolated pathogenic *Neisseria* either in a special incubator containing excess CO_2 or in ajar in which a candle has been lit before it is closed. The candle uses about half of the oxygen and releases CO_2, resulting in a final concentration of about 10% CO_2.

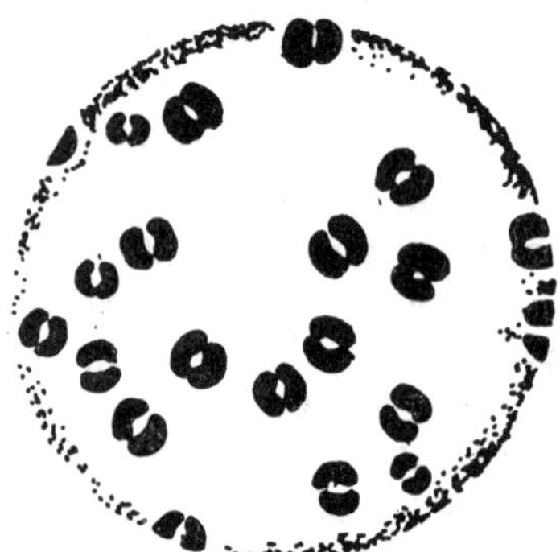

Fig. 14.1. Drawing of "doughnut-shaped" diplococci of Neisseria gonorrhoeae as they sometimes appear under the micorscope.

The pathogenic *Neisseria* are fragile organisms and will, readily autolyse unless their autolytic enzymes are destroyed by heating at 65°C for 30 minutes or by the addition of formalin. These techniques are used to preserve cell suspensions for serologic tests.

Another unusual property of the pathogenic *Neisseria* is their ability to secrete a protease whose only known substrate is human immunoglobulin of the IgAl subclass. This protease has no effect on the IgA2 subclass of antibodies. Its role in the pathogenesis of infection is unknown, but the observation that all strains of *N. meningitidis* and *N. gonorrhoeae* secrete, this protease suggests that it may be of value to the invading. organism.

All *Neisseria*, including the nonpathogens, are oxidase positive, that is, they are able to oxidize dimethyl-and tetramethyl-paraphenylene diamine. This property can be used to distinguish colonies of*Neisseria* from colonies of other bacteria growing on the same plate. The oxidase test may be carried out by spraying either dimethyl or tetramethyl-paraphenylene diamine onto the colonies and observing colour changes. Colonies that are oxidase-positive turn pink, then dark red, and finally black oxidase-negative colonies are unchanged. The reagent eventually kills the cells, but, if the colony is restreaked on fresh media before it turns dark, it can be grown again. A piece of filter paper may be wetted with the reagent, and part of a suspected bacterial colony can be smeared on the wet filter paper. A positive reaction will be indicated by the development of a dark purple colour within 10 to 15 seconds: It should be noted that although the oxidase test is an aid in the isolation and identification of *Neisseria*, any organism that possesses cytochrome oxidase in its respiratory chain will be oxidase positive.

Neisseria Meningitides

Neisseria meningitidis, commonly called the meningococcus, was first described in 1887 as occurring in the spinal fluid of patients with meningitis. Subsequently, it has been shown to be the etiologic agent for epidemic meningitis in humans and also to cause a fulminating, frequently fatal septicemia resulting in lesions, primarily of the skin, bones, and adrenal glands.

Antigenic Classification

Meningoeocci can be classified into a number of groups based on common antigens. Current serogroups are designated A, B, C, D, X, Y, Z, 29E, W-135, H, I, K, and L. Members of groups X and Y have been isolated from cases of meningitis, but X, Y, and Z are frequently found in carriers and have not been involved in large epidemics of meningitis. Interestingly, group Y meningoeocci have become the predominant meningococcal serogroup causing disease in United States Air Force personnel, but the disease most often caused by these organisms is pneumonia, not meningitis. Thus, it is groups A, B. and C that are the causes of epidemics of meningitis.

The group-specific antigen for the meningoeocci is a polysaccharide capsule that surrounds the organisms. The capsular polysaccharides occurring on groups A B, C, X, Y, W- 1 35. and L have been purified. and their chemical composition is listed in Table.

TABLE : 14.1 CHEMICAL COMPOSITION OF MENINGOCOCCALB CAPSULAR POLYSACCHARIDES.

Serogroup	*Chemical Composition*
A	N-acetyl O-acetyl mannosamine phosphate
B	2-8-a-acetyl neuraminic acid
C*	2-9-a- N-acetyl neuraminic acid
X	2-acetamide- 2deoxy-D-glucose 4-phosphate
Y	D-glucose and N-acetylneuraminic acid 1:1
W-135	D-galactose and N-acetyl neuraminic acids 1:1
L	N-acetyl glucosamine-phosphate

**In Some variants* of *Group C, the neuraminic acid is partially* 0-acetylated

Each group of meningococci can be further subdivided into, distinct serotypes based on the antigenicity of their major outer membrane proteins.

CULTURAL CHARACTERISTICS

N. meningitides is a strict aerobe, which grows best in a rich medium, at pH 7.4 to 7.6 and at 37°C. It can be cultivated in synthetic media.

After 24-hour incubation on a suitable medium, smooth, moist, elevated, bluish-gray colonies appear. They are somewhat larger than colonies of pneuomococci and less opaque than those of micrococci and have no effect on the blood cells in the medium. Autolysis occurs even during development of the colonies, which explains the appearance of swollen and poorly stained cocci in smears. The growth is augmented by incubating the culture in an atmosphere of 10 percent carbon dioxide Meningococcus colonies give the characteristic oxidase test upon the application of a solution of tetramethyl-p-phenylene diamine, but the reaction does not differentiate meningococci from gonococci and other members of the *Neisseria* group.

Two types of isolation media are being employed in the study of the meningococcius carriers. These are : (1) the Mueller-Hinton agar; and (2) the Thayer-Martin medium. The Thayer-Martin medium contains polymyxin B and ristocetin.

RESISTANCE

Meningococci are very delicate organisms and are killed in, 24 hours by drying or exposure to sunlight. During World War II. Levine and Thomas devised a growth. shipment. and maintenance medium which preserved the viability of the organism for five to eight weeks.

ANTIGENIC STRUCTURE

Meningococci and gonococci are known to share eight heatstable antigens. The meningococci also contain a somatic polysaccharide which is common to all *Neisseria*, pneumococci, and some strains of *Klebsiella*.

A genus specific complement fixing antigen has been reported by Edwards and Devine.

Subgroups can be detected by agglutination. The most common subgroups are A, B, D, C. Strains not typable as A, B, D, C were collected and restudied at the Communicable Disease Center in Atlanta and designated as E, F, and G.

During World War 1191.6 percent of typable strains were found to be type A. Since World War II the endemic B strains have practically replaced A but are in the process of being replaced by type C.

BACTERIAL METOBOLITES

Potent endotoxins are found in the bodies of dead meningococci. The active endotoxin of meningococci of group C is a lipopolysaccharide with about 20 percent lipid, less than 1 percent protein, and less than 1 percent nucleic acid. Sialic acid forms an integral part of the lipoprotein polysaccharide complex.

Shwartzman Phenomenon

In 1929 Shwartzman demonstrated a necropurpurogenic factor in meningococci. Black-Schaffer, Hiebert, and Kerby in 1947 made a comparative study of 8 strains of *N. meningitides* isolated from patients with the characteristic purpuric skin lesions, and 10 strains from patients who had no demonstrable skin lesions. Although the Shwartzman materials were produced by all strains, regardless of origin, in general, the more potent filtrates wore from cultures derived from patients with purpuric spots.

A small proportion of the patients with purpuric meningococcemia develop hemorrhages and necrosis of the adrenal glands, resulting in collapse and death with characteristic symptoms known as the

Waterhouse-Friderichsen syndrome. Adrenal damage was found in two rabbits in the series studied by Black-Schaffer et. al.

The clinical syndrome known as the Waterhouse-Friderichsen syndrome can occur in the absence of gross hemorrhage in the adrenal glands. The same syndrome can be produced, by septicemia with *dime polvmorpha.*

MENINGOCOCCAL INFECTION

Pathogenesis

The natural habitat of the meningococcus is the nasopharynx of man. Surveys of normal populations will demonstrate a carrier rate around 5 to 10 per cent. In communities in which outbreaks of cerebrospinal meningitis are occurring, the carrier rate of the epidemic strain may range from 20 per cent to 80 to 90 per cent and certain studies have shown that a sharp increase in the carrier rate of group A or other pathogenic groups of meningococci precedes the occurrence of clinical cases. However, this carrier case ratio is variable in different outbreaks.

The route of spread of the meningococcus from the nasopharynx to the meninges is a controversial matter; the organism may either spread directly through the cribriform plate to the subarachnoid space by the perineural sheaths of the olfactory nerve; or, much more probably, it may be blood-borne. In favour of the latter route are the frequent positive blood cultures in the early stages of infection, the purpuric rash in many cases with the isolation of meningococci from the skin lesions, and the occurrence, particularly during epidemics, of meningococcal septicaemia with rash but no clinical meningitis.

It is important to realize that infection of the meninges is 'opportunistic' and irrelevant to the survival and spread of the meningococcal species. The bacterium spreads to other hosts from its site of carriage in the nasopharynx and never from the blood or meninges. In cases where the meningitis is fatal its production is disadvantageous to the causal strain of meningococcus by terminating its opportunities for dissemination from the nasopharynx.

The problem of main concern in pathogenesis is the occurrence of cerebrospinal meningitis among only a limited proportion of the population at risk. Recent studies have confirmed some early observations that the absence of bactericidal antibody in the blood is the factor most closely related to susceptibility to clinical infection. Evidence in support of this relationship is : (1) the age-distribution of meningococcal disease which has its highest incidence in infants and young children, from 3 months to 3 years of age, amongst whom humeral meningococcicidal antibodies are rarely found : the analogy with haemophilus meningitis is obvious; (2) the recip- rocal relationship in the appearance of these bactericidal antibodies in older children and adults with the decreasing incidence of cerebrospinal meningitis, except when it occurs in outbreaks among adults brought together for special reasons. e.g.. in service training centres and in earlier days, in ships and jails; (3) prospective studies among military recruits which showed that whereas only 1 per cent of the total popula-tion at risk became clinically affected, 38.5 per cent of those lacking specific bactericidal antibody to meningococcus and who became infected with the epidemic group C strain developed meningococcal meningitis; and (4) patients convalescent from meningococcal infection develop typical immunoglobulins and bactericidal antibody to the infecting strains Goldschneider, Gotschlich and Artenstein.

It is clear, nevertheless, from the relatively low incidence of meningitis in young children and the absence of meningitis in a large proportion of adults lacking specific antibody that in most persons the first infection of the nasopharynx with meningococcus leads to antibody production without the development of meningitis. Presumably non-specific defence mechanisms are generally successful in preventing infection of the blood and meninges.

Laboratory Diagnosis

Lumbar puncture should be done as soon as meningitis is suspected. In a case of meningococcal meningitis the spinal fluid is under pressure and is turbid in appearance due to the large number of pus cells present. In the early stages of infection the Gram-negative diplococci are present usually in considerable numbers in the purulent cerebrospinal fluid and can be recognized by microscopic examination of the centrifuged deposit. At a later stage they may be scanty and even apparently absent.

Films made from the sediment are stained by methylene blue and Gram's method (with Sandiford's counterstain). In the early untreated case, Gram-negative diplococci are seen, filling a limited number of the pus cells but also extracellularly; if the organisms are scanty, they may be more easily demonstrated in the smear stained with methylene blue. Cultures are made on blood or 'chocolate' (heated blood) agar and incubated for 18 to 24 hours in an atmosphere of 5 to 10 per cent CO_2. If Gram-stained films from the resulting growth show typical Gram-negative cocci, subcultures for biochemical tests are made by picking off single colonies on to sugar-containing serum agar slopes. The serological group may be identified by agglutination tests with the appropriate antisera.

For quick differential diagnosis, which is essential for early effective chemotherapy, micro-scopic examination is often sufficient. However, in the later stages of infection, or if sulphonamides have been administered, the organisms may be scanty or undetectable in the centrifuged deposit. In such cases a method sometimes successful is to add an equal volume of glucose broth to the cerebrospinal fluid, incubate the mixture for 18 hours, and subculture on blood agar; or the supernatant fluid, after centrifugation, may be layered on to the specific antiserum in a capillary tube, in search of a precipitin reaction. A retrospective diagnosis of meningococcal meningitis may be made by demonstrating the development of complement-fixing antibodies in the patient's blood serum.

Chemotherapy

The meningococus is ordinarily sensitive to the sulphonamides (80 to 90 per cent of strains) and to many other antimicrobial drugs. Because the sulphonamides diffuse readily into the cerebrospinal fluid, a sulphonamide compound, e.g. sulphadiazine given orally (or intravenously in comatose patients) is the best drug for proven cases of meningococcal meningitis except in areas where it is known that the meningococcus has become sulphonamide-resistant (MIC > 0. 1 mg/ml). For these latter infections, benzyl penicillin or ampicillin parenterally should be used in addition to a sulphonamide; these drugs pass from the blood through inflamed, though not through normal, meninges into the cerebrospinal fluid. Otherwise chloramphenicol may be given orally since it diffuses even more readily into the cerebrospinal fluid. Prompt chemotherapy can be life saving and has reduced overall case-fatalities from a level of 20 to 40 per cent in untreated cases to 5 to 10 per cent. Fulminating infections, particularly in infants, sometimes with haemorrhagic involvement of the adrenals (Waterhouse-Friederichsen syndrome), may, despite treatment, end fatally within 24 hours of onset.

Epidemiology

The recorded number of meningococcal infections (mostly meningitis) in England and Wales fell from 1390 in 1951 to 293 in 1967. From October 1968 all forms of 'acute meningitis' became statutorily notifiable in England and Wales and it is hoped that doctors will specify . the infecting agent, where known, in the certificate of notification. Meanwhile it should be noted that the number of cases of meningococcal meningitis reported by the Public Health Laboratory Service has risen steadily from 358 in 1967 to 556 in 1970. About two-thirds of the cases occur in the first five years of life and in this age group more than half the cases are in infants under 1 year of age. Incidence is considerably higher in males than in females. Because of the greater frequency and severity of meningecoccal meningitis in early life, the death rate from this disease for the 5 years 1960-64 in England and Wales was around 70 per million in infants. 13 per million in 1 to 4-year-old children.. 1.0 per million in the age range 5 to 14 years and less than 1 per million in adults.

The spring plateau of cerebrospinal meningitis that used to occur in Britain has now virtually disappeared and the infection occurs sporadically throughout the year. Widespread epidemics of infection with serogroup A, sweep through the dry belt of Africa below the Sahara, e.g. in Sudan and northern Nigeria, rising to a peak in the dry months, February to May, and ending. abruptly with the onset of the rainy season. Whether crowdi indoors during the hot, dusty weather or the effect of inhaled dust and dry air on the nasopharynx is responsible for the timing of these epidemics is unknown. Outbreaks have frequently occurred among young adult populations recently recruited to live together in semi-closed communities and what might have been limited epidemics in Britain were fanned into great conflagrations of cerebrospinal meningitis among troops in training in the early years of both world wars. In recent years, localized outbreaks have been a regular occurrence in some American Army base camps; the epidemic strains have been groups B or C, not group A. Intensive studies of the infection in these training centres have added much to our knowledge of the natural history of the disease. A high proportion of the recruits become meningococcus nasopharyngeal carriers and if the carrier strain is relatively avirulent, it induces bactericidal antibodies to virulent strains without causing clinical disease. On the other hand, clinical infection may occur in a high proportion of susceptible individuals who acquire the epidemic strain. The natural acquisition of immunity with increasing. age from early childhood in civilian communities is therefore likely to be due, to asymptomatic infection with avirulent strains.

Outbreaks of meningococcal meningitis require at least three factors : the presence in the population of a proportion of susceptide individuals who lack bactericidal antibodies to the current strains, a high transmission rale from person to person, and a virulent meningococcus. The first stage is the carrier epidemic which requires close personal contact although the large crowded barrack which seemed to be a dominant factor in the occurrence of outbreaks among troops in training in the first world war is not nowadays regarded as so important; nor is physical or emotional stress. The important factors that determine virulence and communicability of the meningococcus are still not understood.

Control Measure

In the control of outbreaks, mass chemoprophyl axis with sulphadiazine given orally, or inhaled like 'snuff into the nose. for 2 to 3 days proved to be very effective in reducing carrier and case rates until the emergence of sulphonamide resistant strains of meningococcus, initially in U.S.A and more recently in Britain and other European countries. A satisfactory alternative drug for large scale chemoprophylaxis has not yet been found.

Since resistance to meningococcal meningitis is closely related to the possession of bactericidal antibodies, whether transiently derived from e mother or actively acquired by latent infection, the possibility of ducing immunity by vaccination has been explored from time to time and has. now become reality with the separation from the epidemic serogroups A and C of high molecular specific polysaccharides which have been shown to be good immunizing agents. Vaccine trials with a group C polysaccharide vaccine in U.S. Army Training Centres have resulted in effective protection, not only against clinical infection, but also against the carrier state with the epidemic strain. However, the protection was group-specific and there were compensatory increases in both carrier rates and clinical. disease with group B meningococci. Controlled vaccine trials in civilian communities are in train.

OTHER GRAM-NEGATIVE MICROCOCCI

Neisseria Catarrhalis

This organism is a diplococcus described first by R. Pfeiffer, who found it in the sputum of patients suffering from catarrhal inflammations of the upper respiratory tract.

Culturally *N. catarrhalis* grows more readily than the meningococcus upon ordinary culture media. The colonies of *N. catarrhalis* are coarsely granular and distinctly white, in contradistinction to the finely granular, grayish meningococcus colonies. *N. catarrhalis* will develop at temperatures below 20°C, while the meningococcus will not grow at temperatures below 25°C. No acid is produced from any of the carbohydrates. Baumann, Doudoroff and Stanier have suggested that *N. catarrhalis* should be classified with the old *Moraxella group as* a new genus.

N. catarrhalis can produce an infection which duplicates the signs and symptoms of an infection with *N. meningitidis*. Infections of the meninges with *N. subflm'a* are being found with greater frequency.

Neisseria Sicca

This organism, described by von Lingelsheim, is a grain-negative diplococcus often found in the normal pharnyx which can be recognized by its dry, crenated colonies on simple media. According to Elser and Huntoon. it sediments spontaneously in salt solution. and this, together with the fact that the colonies are formed in a way almost impossible to break up. makes it easy to distinguish from the meningococcus. This organism produces acid in glucose, fructose, maltose, and sucrose.

Neisseria Haemolysans

N. haemolvsans was named by Thjotta and Boe in 1938. Colonies are delicate and grow slowly but are characterized by a large zone of beta hemolysis by the second or third day. Acid is produced from glucose, fructose, maltose, and sucrose.

Neisseria Flavescens

During an epidemic of meningitis in Chicago, Branham isolated *N. Jlm'escens* from the spinal fluid of a number of patients. The organisms grew poorly on glucose agar but very well on blood agar and semisolid agar. A golden yellow pigment was produced in the colonies. The various strains were homologous but did not agglutinate in antimeningococcal serum. *N. flavescens* lacks the ability to oxidize the usual charbohydrates.

Neisseria Caviae

This organism was isolated from the pharyngeal region of the guinea pig by Pelozar in 1953. Colonies are a light caramel to dark brown colour. Some strains are weakly hemolytic against rabbit's blood. No acid is formed from carbohydrates.

Neisseria Subflava

This is the yellow colony type from Elser and Huntoon's chromogenic group III. The colonies are yellowish-gray and adhere to the medium. Sugar reactions, like with *N. meningitidis*, produce acid from glucose and maltose. The colonies are differentiated by colour and growth at 22°C and have been divided into seven serologic groups by Rogosa.

Neisseria Flava

This is from Elser and Huntoon's chromogenic group II and is more definitely yellow than V *subflava*. Acid is produced from glucose, fructose, and maltose. This organism has produced endocarditis.

Neisseria Perflava

This bright yellow *Neisseria* is from Elser and Huntoon's chromogenic group I. The yellow pigment can stain the sputum yellow, as does the pigment from *S. aureus*. *N. perflava* produces acid from glucose, fructose, maltose, and sucrose.

Veillonella

These are the anaecrobic strains of the family *Neisseriaceae* which include genus *Veillonela* Prevot 1933. The type species is *Veillonella parvula* (Veillon and Zuber) Prevot. Six species are recognized in the seventh edition of *Bergen's Manual*. They may be associated with disease as opportunists and secondary invaders but rarely, if ever, as primary invadlrs in healthy tissues. The species are differentiated by colony morphology and chemical reactions.

Vibrio Cholerae and Asiatic Cholera

No infection except plague arouses such panic as cholera. This disease apparently evolved in ancient tiines in the Bengal area of India which is now Bangladesh and the West Bengal Province of India. It remained endemic here for centuries except for some spread to China, presumably by overland trade routes.

Felsenfeld has reviewed the various pandemics of cholera. There have been six pandemics since 1817. The change from endemic to pandemic was made possible by the development of worldwide transportation.

In the past, cholera was ascribed to air, water or soil contaminations. In 1883, Robert Koch came to Egypt and India as the head of the German Cholera Commission. He discovered a living organism in cholera patients in Alexandria, when the Egyptian epidemic was declining. After studying 12 clinical cases and 10 autopsies in Egypt, the Commission came to India, and Robert Koch studied more cases in the Calcutta Medical College. He found that the same organism was responsible for cases in Calcutta as in Egypt. In Calcutta, he discovered the same organism in tanks, which were used for washing and drinking purposes. In Berlin Conference, he announced the discovery of the vibrio as the causative organism of the disease. By a specific aerological method, Pfeiffer and his associates finally established that, the bacterial agent was the real cause of cholera. Kraus and Pribram found out the haemalytic property of *El Tor* vibrios.

Taxonomy

Choleragenic vibrios, as suggested by Hugh , and Fenselfeld consists of *L: cholerae* and *F. cholerae biotype El Tor* causing classic cholera and cholera-like symptoms respectively. It is hoped that International Conunittee of Bacterial Nomenclature will accept this proposal.

MORPHOLOGY AND STAINING

Vibrio cholerae is a small, curved or rather helicodal-shaped, organism which varies from 1 to 3 μ in length and from 0.4 to 6.6 μ in width. The degree of curvature varies from the short, comma-shaped forms to definite spirals with one or two turns. The comma-shaped organisms predominate in fecal specimens and in young cultures, and the longer forms are found in older cultures.

Vibrios possess terminal flagella which are thicker than those of most bacilli. *V. cholerae* is actively motile but nonsporogenous and non-encapsulated, stains readily with the aniline dyes, and is gram-negative.

Spheroplasts can be produced by lysozyme treatment combined with freezing and thawing. The cholera vibrio is one of the few bacteria which are killed and lysed by the combined action of homologous antibody and complement. The sequence of events is death and then lysis. The very clever studies of Freeman, Burrows, and their associates have shown that the true sequence of events is the formation of spheroplasts by the action of antibody and complement. The delicate spheroplast, in the prdinary osmotic environment, dies and subsequently ruptures.

Cultural Characteristics

Vibrio cholerae is aerobic and grows poorly, if at all, tinder anacrobic conditions. The isolation of *V cholerae* front acute cases of cholera where the vibrios are present in enormous numbers presents no problem. But the isolation from inapparent infections and healthy carriers recommends the so called Thiosulphate (TCBS) agar introduced by Kobayashi and his cd-workers. This medium contains thiosulphate, citrate, bile salts, and: sucrose in an agar base and is available in dehydrate form. The colonies are low, convex, translucent flat domed structures with entire edges which are about 1 to 2 mm.

in size after 24 hours. Suspicious colonies should be testes by slide agglutination and subcultured for *confirmation* by the tests shown in Table.

TABLE 15.1. LABORATORY TESTS THAT HAVE BEEN USED TO DISTINGUISH "CLASSICAL" FROM "EL TOR" BIOTYPES OF V. CHOLERAE

Test	*Classic Cholera Vibrios*	*El Tor Vibrios*
Haemolysis (Sheep or goat cells)	Negative	Positive
Hemagghttination (Chicken cells)	Negative	Positive
Phage susceptibility (Mukerjee's phage IV)	Susceptible	Resistant
itoges-Prosskauer (Barritt)	Negative or weakly positive	Positive
Polymyxin B	Suseeptibe	Resistant

Vibrio cholerae and *V. cholerae* biotype El Tor do not produce hydrogen sulphide or decompose urea, but indole is formed and gelatin is liquefied in a characteristic manner. Nitrates are reduced to nitrates, and when sulphuric acid is added to a culture grown in nitrate-peptone broth a red colour develops. This is the classic cholera red or nitroso-indole reaction which once was thought of be diagnostic of cholera but now is known to be produced by any organism that produces indole and reduces nitrate.

Glucose, sucrose, and mannitol are among the carbohydrates which are fermented with the production of acid without gas. Lactose is fermented after two to eight days, while dulcitol and salicin are not fermented.

Resistance

Vibrio cholerae dies in a few hours in fecal specimens at room temperature. Organisms from broth cultures are killed in two hours by drying on a slide but may be preserved for four years when frozen, dried, and stored in vacuo. *Vibrios*, are destroyed readily by the usual chemical antiseptics and by the chlorination of water. The organisms are quite susceptible to heat, being killed in 10 minutes by a temperature of 55°C. Pasteurization or boiling therefore insures the safety of both milk and water. Survival in water or soil is short because of competition with other fecal organisms, but the vibrios may remain viable for four to seven days on the surfaces of fresh fruits and vegetables which have been stored in a cool, moist *environment*. They live only three or four days when frozen in ice.

Variability

Variations in colony form were observed by Baerthiein and Eisenberg. These studies on variations were continued by Balteanu and later brought to completion by White. White described four distinct forms which can be recognized as M, S. R, and p. A different polysaccharide occurs in each of then first three variants. The S form, isolated frequently from cases of cholera is virulent and agglutinable in specific antiserum. The p variant is a more degenerate form of the R phase and is similar to it except that it lacks the surface polysaccharide. The S form is relatively stable and persists unaltered in some strains after years of subculture on artificial media.

Antigenic Structure

The antigenic structure of the vibrios has been investigated by Gardner and Venkatraman who differentiated the various strains into O groups I.11. III, IV. V and VI. All pathogenic strains belonged to O group I. The H or flagellar antigens show such extensive overlapping in antigenic structure that all vibrios, whether pathogenic or not, agglutinate in anti-H senim.

Serologic studies showed that the 0 antigen A is common to all strains of *V. cholerae*, B is specific for Ogawa, while C is common to all Inaba types and the S_1-lacking subtype of Ogawa. The heat-stable K antigen S_1 common to all Asiatic cholera vibrios, while S_2 is specific for Inaba type. The heat-labile K antigen is common to all strains of *V Cholerae* a Feeley presented evidence for intermediate strains between *V. cholerae* and the El strain, and suggests five types.

An interesting and rather surprising by- product of the cholera vaccinations during World war II war the discovery that soldiers receiving the cholera vaccine had agglutins for *Brucella* in their serum for at least two years. Feeley has shown that the cross reaction was caused by specific O antigen shared by V *cholerae* and *Brucella* and not by flagella R antigens.

Another surprising discovery was made by Sack and Miller in 1969. When germ-free mice were fed the standard Ogawa and Inaba serotypes, the specific serotypes colonized the intestinal tract but did not produce disease. However, antibodies specific for the specific serotype appeared in the serum of the mice. The antibodies did not eiminate the *V chollerae* but caused them to change serotypes.

Biochemical reactions

Gelatin is lilquefied in a funnel-shaped manner in a few days. Modem agar media contain gleatin to make the colonies prominent.

Nitroso Indolel Reaction

(Cholera-red reaction) can be demonstrated by putting a drop of H_2SO_4 in 2 days' old culture in peptone water. This gives a red colour. V-P *reaction* is positive in case of *El Tor Vibrios* but negative for V. Cholereae.

TABLE 15.2. BIOCHEMICAL REACTION OF V.CHOLERAE

Lactose	Dextose	Mannose	Mannitol	Sucrose	Maltose	Arabinose	Xylose	Ducitol
—	A	A	A	A	A	—	—	—

A = Acid; — = No fermentation.

Haemolysin (Greig) Test

This is useful for distinguishing *V. cholerae* from El Tor vibrios; the latter shows a positive haemolysin test. Take equal parts of 2 days' old culture and 5 per cent goat's cell suspension in saline. Incubate for 2 hours at 37°C in a water bath; take the reading and let it stand overnight in the ice box. Read the result again next morning. VF *cholerae* does not produce soluble haemolysin in blood agar plates but causes haemodigestion, which is attributed to a proteolytic enzyme.

Because of variable results obtained by Greig's test for haemolysis, the method of Feeley and Pittm, which gives more uniform results is recommended now a days as follows:

Method. To 0.5 ml of a 24 hour heart infusion broth culture of vibrios at pH 7.4 grown at 35°C in a 16 min by 150 mm tube containing 10 ml of medium, equal volume (0.5 ml) of I per cent sheep cells is added. The mixture is incubated for 2 hours at 35°C to 37°C and kept overnight at 4°C after which reading is taken for haemolysis.

Viability

The vibrios are very susceptible to heat, desiccation, disinfectants and acids; 0.5 per cent solution of phenol kills the organism in a few minutes. Direct sunlight and a thorough desiccation kill the organisms. They die at 55°C in 15 minutes. They can, however, remain alive for some days at a temperature below freezing point. Ice prepared from contaminated water or drinks are dangerous. The vibrios remain alive in natural water, commonly used for drinking, but die rapidly in distilled or sterile water. In linen, contaminated with faecal matter and vomitus of cholera patients, the organism may remain alive for some time and may cause outbreaks of the disease by handling infected clothes. When stools are kept at room temperature in a noise place, the organism may remain alive for 7 to 8 days in cold weather but for 1 to 2 days in hot weather (Greig). Sunlight has lethal effect on the organism.

Food

In onion, garlic, orange, grapes and dates, the organism may remain alive for 3 days. In sour nlilk, it is killed within a few hours; but in sterile milk the organism remains viable, up to 3 weeks.

Flies

Under experimental conditions, vibrios survive for a period of 5 days and in a laboratory-bread fly, experimentally fed on cholera stools; the vibrio could be recovered 14 days after the feed.

Virulence

Freshly isolated strains are more virulent than those maintained in the laboratory. Virulence can be increased by intraperitoneal injection into a guineapig to which it is fatal in 24 hours. The virulence of the organism for mice is enhanced by injecting the organisms in 5 per cent gastric mucin suspension.

Toxin

It is an endotoxin, liberated after disintegration of the bacillus. Burnet and Stone demonstrated that, filtrates of *V. cholerae* contain enzymes, which caused desquamation of intestinal mucosa of the guine apig *in vitro* experiment. One of these enzymes has been demonstrated to be *mucinase*. These enzymes may be responsible for the pathogenesis of cholera. Burnet, McCrea and Stone demonstrated an enzyme in cholera, which destroyed the receptors on the surface of the red blood corpuscles for virus particles. The enzyme is best known *as receptor destroying enzytne* (RDE). Receptors help to elucidate the phenomenon of haemagglutination of viruses. An exotoxin has been claimed to be isolated from *V cholerae* but it waits confirmation.

Description

The vibrios are allocated to tile family Spirillaceae and are .characterized as Gram-negative motile rods, usually curved (the comma bacillus), with a single polar flagellum. They are non-sporiug, non-capsulated, facultative anaerobes, fermenting glucose without gas, hydrogen sulphide negative, and with enzyme activities on certain aminoacids (lysine+, ornithine+, arginine-for vibrios) which serve to distinguish them from two closely related genera, *A eromonas* and *Plesiomonas*. Indeed, it has been suggested that these three genera should be grouped in a new family Vibrionaceae. Only two vibrios, the classic and El Tor biotypes of *Vibrio cholerae*, are associated with the cholera syndrome but other vibrios may be causally related to diarrhoea disease. Reference is made in Vol. II to *Vibrio parahaemolyticus* which causes a form of acute food-poisoning, in Japan, S.E. Asia, U.S.A. and possibly elsewhere. Many non-pathogenic vibrios are found in nature, mostly in water and in fish. All vibrios, being motile, have 0 and H antigens the cholera vibrios can be differentiated from other vibrios on the basis of a somatic antigen, 01 which is specific to the classical and El Tor biotypes of V *cholerae* so that othei vibrios that lack this antigen are sometimes called non-aggultinating (NAG) or non-cholera vibrios (NCV). The two pathogenic biotvpes may each be divided into two serological subtypes, called *Inaba* and *Ogawa*, based on the presence of a subsidiary 0 antigen. The El Tor biotype was first differentiated from the classical biotype by its production of haemolysin; other distinctive characters are its resistance to one of the four cholera phages (group IV) which Mukerjee has used to sub-divide the classical vibrios. resistance to polymyxin B (50 units) and haemagglutination of chicken or sheep red cells. However, the haemolytic test may give variable results and most of the recently isolated El Tor strains arc non-haemolytic; differentiation should therefore be based on reliable tests such as resistance to group IV phage at routine test dilution. resistance to polymyxin B and direct haemagglutination of chicken or sheep red blood cells.

Clinical Infection

Cholera is typically characterized by the sudden onset of effortless vomiting and profuse watery diarrhoea. Vomiting is a common feature but the rapid dehydration and hypovolaemic shock which may cause death in 12 to 24 hours are related mainly to the profuse 'rice water' stools-watery, colourless with floeks of mucus and distinctive sweet, fishy odour (-) which, contain little protein (<0.1 per cent) and are very different from the mucopurulent blood(-) stained stools of classical dysentery. Anuria develops, muscle cramps occur and the patient quickly becomes weak and lethargic with loss of skin turgor, low blood pressure and absent or thready pulse. But there are all grades of severity and the milder cases of cholera, which are more common in El Tor infections, cannot be distinguished clinically from non-vibrio diarrhoeas. Symptomless infections are common.

Pathogenesis: Pathophysiology

The sequence of events leading to cholera are basically simple and confined to the gut. The cholera vibrios are ingested in drink or food and, in the natural infection, the dosage must often be very small; after passing the acid barrier of the stomach juices, the organisms begin to multiply in the alkaline medium of the small intestine. As they multiply, they produce a potent exotoxin, called *enterotoxin*, which stimulates a persistent outpouring of isotonic fluid by the gut mucosal cells. The toxin is thought to react with a receptor in the membrane of the intestinal epithelial cell, then to activate adenylcyclase in the membrane and thereby raise the intracellular level of cyclic adenosine monophosphate (CAMP) which induces increased secretion of water and electrolytes into the intestinal lumen. There is no convincing evidence of any inflammatory reaction involving increased capillary permeability. Obviously a number of factors. some still unknown, must contribute to the occurrence of clinical cholera in any infected person; for example, cholera strains vary in toxigenicity, and variations in host resistance probably explain the infrequency of more than one case in a family.

Much new knowledge about the pathogenesis of cholera has come from experimental studies in animals, e.g. baby rabbits (10 to 14 days old) in which a syndrome resembling cholera can be produced, localized infection in isolated intestinal loops (rabbit, fowl. etc.) characterized by outpouring of isotonic fluid, and experimental cholera in dogs after neutralization of the stomach acids.

It is now generally accepted that there is no inflammatory denudation of the bowel mucosa in cholera and no invasion the intestinal wall, deeper tissues or blood although the gall bladder may become a reservoir. The pathophysiological changes are directly related to the massive loss of isotonic fluid with excess of sodium bicarbonate and potassium through the gut, leading to hypovolaemic shock. acidosis and haemo concentration with a consequent sharp rise in plasma proteins. Delay in rehydration may result in renal failure due to acute tubular necrosis; hypokalaemia from excess loss of potassium is likely to occur in children.

Immunity

More than one attack of clinical cholera is rare but reinfections are not uncommon in endemic areas where evidence from serological surveys indicates that from infancy to adulthood an increasing proportion of the population have vibriocidal antibodies, presumably related to repeated exposure and the occurrence of symptomless or mild infections; this phenomenon has been called 'salting' of the population. After a clinical attack, specific antibodies (agglutinins, vibriocidal antibodies) are demonstrable in the blood within a few days, reaching a peak in 7 to 74 days and thereafter declining to low levels after about 3 months. The antibody responses are poorer in preschools than in schoolchildren or adults. The vibriocidal antibody titre correlates well with resistance to infection so that in endeniie areas the incidence of clinical cholera falls progressively with age; two-tbirds of the cases may be children under 15 years of age.

Despite the important part played by ente pathogenesis of cholera, the role of antitoxin against the infection has not yet been elucidated.

Laboratory Diagnosis

In the acute stage of cholera, vibrios are abundantly present in the watery stool (10^1 to 10^9/ml) which is best collected with a no. 24 to 26 rubber catheter into a test-tube or screw-capped container; or a rectal swab may be used. Collection from a bedpan should be avoided because of the risk of contamination or the presence of antiseptic. In the examination of contacts and possible carriers, the rectal swab is most convenient. or the specimen may be collected from a stool passed on to clean paper or a large leaf. If there is likely to be delay in examination of the faecal specimen, a transport medium such as salt sea water or its equivalent (Venkatraman- Ramakrislman fluid) or alkaline taurocholate tellurite liquid medium may be used: or strips of thick blotting paper may be soaked in the stool and wrapped in plastic or other impervious material to prevent leakage or evaporation.

Where there is urgency in making the bacteriological diagnosis of a case, a vibrio-immobilization test with dark field microscopy using two drops of the fresh fluid specimen on a glass slide or two drops of a young peptone water culture may be used. After the remarkable motility of the vibrios (like a cloud of gnats) has been seen, a drop of either Inaba or Ogawa antiserum is added to the bacterial suspension and specific immobilization can be, demonstrated in 60 to 80 per cent of acute cases of cholera.

In the early stages of infection. the stool is plated directly on to one or more selective solid media. From bile salt agar typical bluish grey colonies can be picked off, with or without the use of a stereo-plate microscope, after overnight incubation or as early as 5 to 6 hours. Precise identification of biotype and serotype depends on further biological, aerological and phage-sensitivity tests. Serological examination of paired serum samples taken within 48 hours of onset and after 7 to 10 days will usually show a significant rise of agglutinatting and vibriocidal antibodies and may be used to check the reliability of bacteriological diagnosis aerological micro-techniques using very small amounts of the reagents give satisfactory results so that finger-prick specimens of blood are adequate.

In epidemiological investigations for the detection of contact or convalescent carriers when the number of vibrios in the stool may vary fron, 10^1 to 10^1, per g, inoculation of a large sample (2 to 3g) of stool into 50 to 100ml alkaline peptone water will give best results although moistened rectal swabs have often to be used for convenience. More than one subculture after 6 hours incubation in alkaline peptone water or other enrichment medium may be necessary when the vibrous are scanty. Induced purging sometimes reveals a hidden carrier of El Tor vibrous and duodenal incubation has helped in detecting persistent carriers of El vibrios after clinical infection.

Bacteriophage Typing

Classic *V. cholerae* and El Tor stains can be separated by bacteriophage typing. Mukerjee and Guha Roy identified 4 phage groups. Groups III and IV included all the classic *I : Cholerae* strains but none of the El Tor strains. Group I and II included all the *T". cholerae* strain but also some hemolytic and nonhemolytic E Tor strains. Takeya and Shimodo bnfinned the findings of Mukerjee and Guha Roy and found that none of their 83 strains were susceptible to the group IV phage.

Bacterial Metabolites

V chloerae has an endotoxin, three antigentic types of mucinase and both of the Shwarthzan factors. However, the metabolites important in the pathogenesis of the disease have most of the characteristic of exotoxins. They are heatlabile and antigentic, can be converted to toxids, and can be neutralized by antitoxins.

Most preparations of the "choeragen" exotoxin also have a "permeability effect" which produces delayed-positive skins tests when injected into the skin of normal men and guinea pigs. This factor has been studied in detail by Craig. Feeley has suggested that the peremeability factor Craig is identical with Finkelstein's chloeragen. Recently Riichardson and Evans have reported the separation of the two factors by dextran sulphate precipitation and Lewis and Freeman have presented biologic evidence for two factors.

The classic endotoxin has been definitely eliminated as the cause of the permeability defect in clinical cholera. Freter and Gangarosa fed large doses of heat-killed V *cholerae* to human volunteers over a period of many days without producing intestinal symptoms. Seventy-five percent of the volunteers developed good titers of coproantibodies but very low titers of serum antibodies.

THE PATHOGENESIS OF CHOLERA

The cholera vibrio does not invade the blood like Salmonella ryphi or ulcerate the intestinal mucosa as do the Shigella. It does invade the mucosa and produce some erythema and edema. This irritation results in an enormous amount of fluid and electrolytes being poured into the lumen of the gut and expelled as stools. The alteration seems to be a dilatation of the smallest venuies which pick up the blood after it leaves the capillaries.

As the kbrios grow in the lumen of the small intestines they produce the labile exotoxin "choleragen" which causes the outpouring of more fluid in which the vibrios increase their multiplication and toxin formation. The process can bes stopped by vibriocidal antibodies killing the vibrios, or by antitoxin neutralizing the toxin formation, or by a combination of both. Passively transferred antitoxin can stop the fluid loss without killing the vibrios.

Pathology

In cholera, the vibrios reach the small intestine, where they multiply rapidly. The toxin irritates the wall of the intestine with great outpouring of exudative fluid causing purging and vomitting and this leads to profound dehydration. Stools are rice-water in appearance and contain flakes of mucus, floating, on the surface. The organism remains localised to the intestinal tract and does not escape into the blood stream. The endotoxin liberated by the dead and autolysed vibrios causes denudation of the epithelium of the intestine and increases its permeability, so that, there is loss of plasma and electrolytes of the blood. The tissue changes are, therefore, chiefly due to dehydration resulting in haemoconcentration, toxaemia, fall of blood presure and finally shock. The changes are, therefore, clinico-pathological in nature.

Pathogenesis

The the old concept that, profuse diarrhoea in choelra is due to an exudate through the denuded intestinal mucosa is no logner tenable due to the facts that: (1) biopsies from the patient show intact mucosa; (2) the protein content of bacteria-free cholera stool contains only 0.1 gm of protein per 100 ml; (3) iodine tagged polyvinyl pyrroldone (PVP) did not show any greater concentration of PVP in stools than in the control. According to phillips and other workers, the fluid loss in cholera is isotonic with excessive loss of bicarbonate and potassium. The excessive loss of fluid from bowles is due to the metabolite of the V. cholerae, which acts as an inhibitor of transport of sodium ion by the cells of the intestinal mucosa the so-called "sodium pump". There is a thermolabile inhibitor in cholera stools. As the fluid loss is isotonic with excessive loss of bicarbonate and potassium, hydrations should be restored by intravenous normal saline and bicarbonate solution (added separately) in a ratio of 3:1.

Post-mortem Changes

In persons, who die in the collapse stage of the disease, post-morten appearances are characteristic but typical changes are not seen nowadays due to the adminstration of saline.

External Appearance

Body is wel nourished but eye- balls are sunken in the socket, fingers and toes are shrunken like those of a washerwoman; cyanosis of face and blue discolouration of the nailbed are common features. *Rigor mortis*. Extermities are stiff and fixed firmly, as rigor mortis sets in early all over the body and persists for a longer period.

Internal Examination

On opening, the muscles are found to be firmer, darker and some fibres are seen to be torn off *Serous cavities*. The pericardium is dry without may any fluid in the sac; it often shows petechial haemorrhage. *Heart*. Right and systemic veins contain dark, tarry and imperfectly coagulated blood. Pleura is dry: *lungs* are shrunken, light in weight, vessels at the base contains thick dark blood. *Stomach*. It is extremely congested and may how petechial haemorrhage. Peritoneal cavity is dry without any exudate.

Small intestine. There is marked vascular engorgement with denudation of the epithelial lining and this accounts for the electrolytes, which are passed with the rice-water stools. The peritoneal surface is congested and shows a ground glass appearance. The mucous membrane of the ileum may often show hyperplasia of the Peyer's patches and solitary lymphoid follicles are prominent.

Microscopical. The small intestine is hyperaemic with loss of the epithelium. There is little cellular reaction in this infection. Vibrios are present in large numbers on the lining mucous membrane of the gut. *Large intestine* shows congestion specially of the caecum with petechial haemorrhage.

Gallbladder. The organism reaches the galibladder from the duodenum via the common bile duct and causes catarrhal inflammation of the duct. Epithelial cells are swollen and desquamated with production of excess of mucus. Along with this, there is a rapid multiplication of the organism in presence of bile. The gall-bladder is almost always full and distended with dark, green, thick bile and the duodenum and the small intestine do not contain any bile. Stools are rice-water in appearance without any trace of bile. This is due to closure of sphincter of Oddi and also inflammation of the biliary passage. The duodenum is congested at the opening of the bile duct. The organism is discharged intermittently from the infected gallbladder, which may act as a focus for a carrier. Liver. There is reduction of glycogen of the liver cells. *Mesenteric lymph* nodes. These are enlarged and hyperaemic with marked hyperplasia of the *lymphoid tissue*.

Kidney. Typical changes are not seen nowadays, as dehydration is combated by injection of saline. So after saline injection, cholera kidney comes under the category of extra-renal failure. The organ is swollen. enlarged and the capsule is stretched and pinkish red in colour. *Cut section*. The cut surface is pink with injected blood vessles passing towards the cortex; pyramids are intensely red, congested and haemorrhagic at the base. *Microscopically*, the appearance varies according to intensity of toxaemia. In very acute cases, tubular necrosis with congestion of glomerular and intertubular vessels are seen. Glomeruli are swollen and capsular spaces are filled with albuminous exudate. Thickening, of the basement membrane of the glomerular capillaries are often seen. Tubular epithelium is swollen with varying degrees of granular, fatty or hyaline degeneration. The tubules are often completely blocked with coagulated material, causing obstruction and resulting in suppression of urine. The pathological changes in the kidney resemble one of acute nephrosis rather than acute nephritis. This is due to overwhelming, excretion of toxin, which produced a functional paralysis of the organ. The degenerative changes is further helped by loss of tone of the vasomotor system. Kidneys usually heal up from acute nephrosis during convalescence.

Blood changes

In the blood, loss of fluid produces haemoconcentration, plolycythaemia (7-8 million of RBCs per cmm) and a relative increase of WBC (15 to 20 thousand per cmm) with a decrease in the percentage of lymphocytes and a rise of mononuelear cells, so that the ratio of the two is altered. Inorganic salts escape from the serum more than organic salts, chlorides before phosphates, sodium before potassium. Chloride is very much reduced in the serum.

Reaction of *blood* There is reduction of alkalinity of blood indicating acidosis and in these cases, injection of alkaline, saline is indicated; this reduces the danger of post-choleraic uraemia. When the reduction of alkalinity reaches a degree higher than N/100, fatal, irreversible uraemia ensues and no amount of alkali would averturaefnia in such a case.

Complications and Sequelae

Recovery is generally complete and sequelae are rare in a later stage of the disease, complications may arise: (i) Anuria. This is due to fall of blood pressure as a result of functional paralysis of the organ with loss of tone of the vasomotor system, particularly of the splanchnic areas. Loss of fluid, haernoconcentration, congestion of the kidney and anoxia due, to stagnation of circulating blood, low filtration head in the vessels of the glomeruli aggravate anuria and suppression of urine during the collapse stage of the disease. It is the most frequent and fatal of all complications. (ii) *Hiccupl.* This is a very persistent and annoying condition. (iii) *Cholecvstitis.* It is mild and eventually subsides. It is often associated with pain in the right hypochondriurn. *(iv) .Jaundice.* It is a rare and dangerous complication. *(v) Eve.* Secondary conjunctivitis and, corneal ulcers are due to the dryness of the cornea. (vi) *Parotitis.* This is due to secondary septic infection of a serious nature and may lead to abscess formation. (vii) Pneumonia and bronchopneumonia. Pneumonia and bronchopneumonia develop in 3-4 per cent of cases and prove fatal. (viii) *Gangrene.* Gangrene of the fingers, toes and genitalia are seen in patients following prolonged unrelieved collapse. These complications are rare nowdays due to early administration of saline. In pregnant women abortion and miscarriage invariably occurs and the foetus shows evidence of cholera infection.

Carriers

Patients in the stage of convalescence pass vibrios in stools for sometime. The carrier stage is a temporary one as 99 per cent may last for one month and in the remaining I per cent the organism disappears in 3 to 4 months. *pseudocarriers* The carrier of El Tor vibrios may be considered as pseudo *carriers. Incubation carriers.* During the incubation period of the disease, the subject may pass the organism in the stools and act as a carrier. The period is usually 1 to 2 days but it may prolong to 18 days. *Health carriers.* Contacts may pass *V.. cholerae* without any symptoms of the disease. The period is usually 5 to 10 days but it may last as long as 19 days, or according to Topley, it may be one month.

EPIDEMIC CHOLERA

Cholera is endemic in the Bengal area of India and present a different picture from the classic epidemic cholera. When the vibrios are carried by man into nonendemic areas the total population is found to be susceptible and the route of sprea is usually by contaminated water. Severe cases of cholera are dramatic; they alarm the physicians and terrify the community.

The incubation period is short, from six to eight hours to two or three days, depending upon the size of the infecting dose. The vibrios multiply at a prodigious rate in the smal intestine.

The onset of symptoms may be gradual, but more often it is sudden and explosive. Severe gripping pains appear in the abdomen, followed by almost contiuous vomiting and diarrhea The patient may have 20 to 30 stools per day, losing liters of water. The watery stools at first contain some fecal material, but this is soon evacuated and the clear opalescent discharges contain nothing but small balls of mucosa. which give the characteristic "rice water" appearance. With the excessive loss of body fluids and electrolytes. the patient exhibits symptoms of extreme dehydration. The urine is suppressed, the skin becomes wrinkled, the nose pinched, the eyeballs sunken, and the voice is weak and husky. The blood pressure falls, the heart sounds and barely audible, and the pulse becomes rapid and weak; the rate of respiration increases, and the mucous membranes become cold and cyanotic, although the rectal temperature may be normal or elevated. Severe cramp-like pains develop in the extremities. The loss of fluids causes extreme hemoconcentration, slowing of the circulation, and'finally coma and death.

ENDEMIC CHOLERA

Our present understanding of endemic cholera and the basis for treatment of cholera has been learned over the past six years by investigators in the Pakistan-SEATO Cholera Research Laboratory in Dacca, the Calcutta School of Tropical Medicine, and the Calcutta Infections Disease Hospital. By serial test for the appearance ofvibriocidal antibodies in the serum and improved methods of cultivation it was learned that an epidemic could occur with few, if any, patients ill enough to require hospitalization.

The major infections occur in December and January with an occasional second epidemic in May, June and July. The attack rate is higher among Hindus than Muslims. Mild cases occur most often in children under five years. Some degree of immunity is acquired with vibriocidal antibodies and antitoxins for the labile cholera exotoxin in the serum, presumably from one or more mild attacks of cholera.

The organisms survive between outbreaks in convalescent, intestinal carriers or chronic gallbladder carriers and possibly in the local water tanks.

Treatment

The death rate from cholera can approach zero, even without the use of antibiotics, when the loss of water and electrolytes is replaced. However, tetracycline therapy can reduce the period of hydration by 50 percent.

The degree of dehydration can be estimated from the blood pressure and pulse rate or determined accurately by plasma, specific gravity or central venous pressure. Over-hydration can be detected by the fullness of the veins in the neck.

A new replacement fluid has been recommended by Gutman and his associates. It is called pediatric cholera replacement solution-PCRS. It is supposed to be superior to the standard lactated Ringer's solution. The PCRS contains magnesium and dextrose, and less sodium but more potassium and bicarbonate than lactated Ringer's solution.

Harper and his associates reported in 1970 that cycloheximide, a rapid-acting inhibitor of protein synthesis, will prevent fluid production in loops of bowel of rabbits stimulated by fluid-producing exotoxins. No reports of the use of this agent in man have appeared.

Laboratory diagnosis

Finding of *V cholerae* is important for the diagnostic and-, epidemiological purposes and care must be taken in collection of specimen of stools.

Collection. The stool should be fresh or collection by the introduction of a rectal catheter; rectal swab is less satisfactory but has the advantage of being soaked in a tellurite solution for transport. Stools should be collected before administration or antibiotics.

Preservatives. When there is delay in sending the specimen from the field to the laboratory, it should be sent in (a) Venkataraman's preservative,* or (b) bile peptone transport medium, preferably with potassium tellurite (1 in 200,000), in which vibrios remain alive, preventing the growth of other organisms, and sub cultures are made within 6 hours in Monsour's (GTTA) medium.

Smears. Direct smears from stools or smear from the surface of peptoria water can be examined after staining with Zielh's fuchsin (1:20 aqueous solution of carbol fuchsin) and examined for typical "fish in stream" appearance.

Enrichment. It is done before isolation in peptone water (pH 8.4) or bile alt peptone water. In enrichment, the vibiros overgrow other organism in alkaline peptone water and come to the surface, being aerobic, form a pellicle, from which subcultures are made for isolation and smear.

Motility under Dark Ground Illumination.Typical motility of the organism like 'a swarm of gnats or mosquitoes" is characteristic; addition of specific antiserum stops the motility. This procedure is hopeful in more than 80 percent cases for immediate diagnosis.

Fluorescent Antibodv Method (*Immunoelurescence*). This has been applied for the rapid diagnosis. The method is particularly useful in rural outbreaks of cholera, where within an hour of receiving the specimen a smear May be sent to the laboratory for diagnosis by this method.

Isolation. Modern method is to utilize plates containing gelatin; *r:Cholerae* spilts gelatin and make the colonies conspiceous, forming haloes round the colonies. The colonies are moist, translucent and bluish in appearance. Media that may be used are : (1) bile salt (0.5%) agar, (2) bile gelatin agar, (3) Monsur's (GTTA) medium or (4) TCBS agar of Kobayashi et al. 1963).

Streaks are made direct from fresh material or from enrichment media.

Pure colonies growing on plates are studied for morph4 logical, cultural, biochemical characters including V-P (-ve) reaction, phage sensitivity and finally for agglutination with specific 0 type sera. Inaba and Ogawa types are dignosed monospecific sera. *V cholerae* should then be differentiated from *El Tor vibrios* by the haemolysin production, and phage insensitivity of the latter. Other differentiating points are stated under *El Tor vibrios.*

Isolation of V. Cholerae from Water

To 100 ml of a sterile 10 per cent alkaline (pH 9) peptor solution containing 5 per cent sodium chloride, are added 900 ml of the sample of water and the mixture is then distributed in sterile flasks. After 24 and 48 hours, inocula are taken frol the surface growth and the inoculated in a suitable medium and the organism is isolated as mentioned before. Large quantities of water may be tested by filtering it through Scitz filter and then using the disk as an inoculum in peptone wate for culture.

Differential Diagnosis

There is no difficulty in the clinical diagnosis, when the epidemic is on; but it is difficult to diagnose mild sporadic cases and bacteriological examination only is confirmatory. The following diseases are often confused with cholera : (a) acute gastroenteritits, (b) choleraic form of algid malaria, (c) fullminating bacillary dysentery, (d) food poisoning, (e) arsenical poisoning.

Immunity. During convalescence the scruni may show the agglutinin titre as high as 1::1,000 but agglutinin does not appear early to help in the diagnosis of the disease. Carriers may show a high agglutinin titre. Active immunisation is produced by prophylactic vaccine, which protects for about six months to one year.

Prophylaxis. It consists of mass inoculation of cholera vaccine durilo) epidemics. *For primary immunisation* two doses are assumel be more effective than one. Pre-existing copro antibodies may be an essential feature of antibacterial immunity. The artificial immunity of cholera gives protection ranging from 40-80 per cent only for 3 to 6 months or so and boosting is before epidemic outbreaks. The vaccine is prepared 24 hours' culture of h: *cholerae* grown on nutrient agar. the suspension being phenol (1 per cent) killed. and phenol per cent) preserved and standardised to contain 8,000 million organisms per ml. It is desirable that, local strains should be included. Both Inaba and Ogawa-Hikojmia strains are included in the vaccine. Judged by mouse inoculation. this vaccine should protect against the infection with El Tor vibrios as well. However, Boseca Savilla et al. reported that, in comparison with *V cholerae* vaccine, the one prepared from El Tor vibrios is more antigenic in human subjects and more potent in protecting mice against challenge doses of both V. .chclerae and biotype *El Tor*.

Personal Prophylaxis. Fatigue, overwork, mental worries or any apprehension or indignation of any kind should be avoided.The diet should be plain and simple and easily digestible. Raw fruits and vegetables should be washed in a solution of pot. permanganate. Water should be taken after boiling and food should be taken warms, so that, no fly could contaminate the food, milk, etc. Acid and acidulated drinks are useful as acids are injurious to; *V. cholerae.* Administration of hydrocholoric acid ms 10 in a glass of water, thrice daily is useful.

Long purified water supply must be ensured and it must be free from the risk of contamination by carriers. Wells and storage tanks may be treated with bleaching powder. In absence of a safe supply of drinking water, water must be boiled. *Chemoprophylaxis.* For rapid elimination of vibrios from faeces, cases must be treated with tetracycline, which reduces the duration of infectivity of cases and thus diminish the community spread. It is more useful for the contacts but should not be used for the mass population for several reasons : (i) antibiotic agents cause changes in the intestinal flora of healthy individuals and (ii) there is danger of emergence of resistant strains.

Bilivaccine

This Was introduced by Besredka, who propounded the theory that, actual protection against cholera or intestinal organisms could be had only, when the resistance the of intestinal epithelium was increased by a process of immunisation of the local cells (local immunity). The vaccine is administered as a tablet and it is preceded by a dose of bile. Preliminary administration of bile increases subsequent action of the vaccine. Both the bile and the vaccine are given in the empty stomach in 3 to 5 doses. The vaccine gives immunity of local cells without the appearance of demonstrable antibody in the blood.

Chemotherapy

The first and essential requirement in the treatment of cholera is rehvdration but chemotherapy plays a useful support ing role. The cholera vibrios are sensitive to the tetracyclins chloramphenicol. streptomycin, furazolidone and other chemotherapeutic drugs active against most Grain-negative organisms In practice. dosage with 2 g daily or tetracycline or furazolidone (in divided doses) for 2 to 3 days quickly eliminates the vibrioi from the stools and sharply reduces the duration of the diarrhoea and associated loss of fluid.

Epidemiology

Man is the only natural host of the cholera vibrio and the spread of infection is from person to person with contaminated water or certain foods such as uncooked seafoods (shrimps etc.) or vegetables as the most common vehicles. cholera is characteristically an infection of crowded poor class communities living in low lying areas and it tends to persist in such communities which share communal water supplies such as 'tanks', ponds, canals or rivers for bathing, washing of lines and household uses. Outbreaks occur either as explosive epidemics, usually in non-endemic areas, or as protracted epidemic waves in endemic areas. The seasonal incidence is; fairly consistent in different endemic regions but the climatic conditions during epidemic waves may be distinctive for each region. For example, in Bangladesh the cholera season (November to February) follows the monsoon rains and ends with the onset of the hot, dry months; across the Bengal delta the main epidemic wave in Calcutta (May to July) rises to its peak in the hot, dry season and ends with the onset of the monsoon but extends inland to neighbouring states during the rainy season. In endemic areas, clinical infection is most common among the 'unsalted' pre-school children although it is rare in infancy. In explosive outbreaks, often associated with fairs, festivals and pilgrimages, or in non-endemic areas, adults are more commonly affected. In rural India infection spreads along lines of human village just as it does on the global scale.

Spread is probably facilitiate by the high ratio of symptomless carriers to clinical cases, varying from 10 : 1 to 100 : 1 depending on living conditions as well as on biotype. Symptomless carriers occur much more frequently in *El Tor* than in classical cholera infections. Although the clinical disease is similar after infection with one' or other of the two biotypes, the epidemiological features may be distinctive, related to the high infectivity, low virulence and greater hardiness of the El Tor biotype which facilitates more direct person-to- person spread (e.g. by formites and feeding utensils) than is the case with the classical biotype, for which water is the most likely vehicle. The symptomless carrier probably plays an part in spreading *El Tor* infection into new communities.

In non-epidemic periods in endemic areas, carriers or mild missed cases are essential links in maintaining the reservoir of infection since the vibrios do not multiply or survive for long on possible vehicles such as water, food, fniit, vegetables. After an acute attack of cholera, the vibrios may be excreted for a few weeks in convalescence although more persistent *El Tor* carriers have been reported. Maintenance of the reservoir of infection seems to depend on the chain infected case—water-infected case plus more direct person-to-person spread with the resistant El Tor biotype. Detection of human reservoirs may be attempted by the bacteriological examination of sewage, e.g. collected night soil as has been done in Hong Kong or bucket latrines as in Calcutta.

Phage-typing has not yet contributed much information about the epidemiology of cholera, mainly because only types 1 and 3 of the five phage-types of classical *V cholerae* are commonly found and because there is some instability among the provisional six El Tor phage-types.

Control Measure

It seems unlikely that cholera can be controlled in the endemic areas until good water supplies are installed in individual houses, better provision is made for sewage disposal and the necessity or habit in certain countries of using communal water in ponds, canals and rivers for washing of bodies and linen as well as for household use can be abolished. A most disturbing feature of the seventh pandemic is that the number of affected countries in Asia and Africa has been rising steadily in the past decade and in India the infection is more widespread than it has been for many years. A number of European countries have also been invaded. This wide geographic dissemination is wholly due to the El Tor biotype which, because of its greater hardiness and higher infectivity/ virulence ratio than the classical biotype, is likely to establish endemic foci in many crowded centres in African and Asian countries with poor standard of environmental sanitation and household hygiene. It is noteworthy that Japan has resisted invasion despite several introductions of cholera and it seems unlikely that cholera will become endemic in countries with good environmental sanitation and high public health standards.

A number of controlled trials in different countries to test the efficacy of prophylactic vaccination has shown that with the presently available killed whole cell vaccines, protection of about half of the inoculated community lasts for only 3 to 6 months. In an endemic area, one dose of vaccine is more effective when given to the 'salted' school children than are two doses given at 4 to 6 weeks' interval to the highly susceptible pre-school children Controlled trials with monovalent antigens have indicated that protection is specifically against the infecting serotype. Mass immunization of schoolchildren with one dose of vaccine at the beginning of the *epidemic period* in endemic areas might be practicable and help to control the spread of infection. Mass immunization of pilgrims on their way to Mecca and of those attending religious festivals, and perifocal inoculations during a localized outbreak, e.g. in a refugee camp, may also be useful prophylactic measures. However, it has been concluded that cholera vaccination as a general public health measure is ineffective in preventing the introduction of cholera into a community, in containing its spread or in reducing mortality where adequate treatment facilities are available. The possible usefulness of cholera toxoid, whole cell vaccine plus toxoid, purified antigens with or without adjuvant, and live attenuated oral vaccines are presently under consideration.

Meanwhile, there is evidence that in some areas where cholera is now endemic, e.g. the Philippines, improved sanitation in the shape of readily available water supplies and/or cheap privy construction will reduce the incidence of cholera and presumably other diarrhocal diseases, and will,. in the long term, be economically preferable to repeated mass vaccination.

Control of incipient outbreaks in non-endemic areas requires prompt recognition of suspected clinical cases and quick laboratory confirmation so that early treatment and suitable preventive measures, e.g. chemoprophylaxis among close contacts, are put in train. Unfortunately such facilities are not usually available in developing countries but W.H.O. has been active in fostering training courses and laboratory services in countries where the risks of importation seem greatest. A rational use of the international Health Regulations, which aim at combining a maximum of safety with a minimum of interference in international traffic and trade instead of unnecessarily, restrictive quarantine and trade measures against countries reporting cholera, would help to minimize economic and political upheavals. Health administrators must know, and make it known, that cholera, if promptly recognized, is certainly curable if not yet preventable. Measures against the importation of cholera to European countries are discussed in a memorandum 'Cholera Control in the European Region issued by the European Regional Office of World Health Organization.

OTHER CHOLERA-LIKE VIBRIOS

In addition to V. cholerae. 33 other species are recognized in the seventh edition of *Bergev'sAlanual.* One species. *Vibrio piscium,* causes disease in fresh water firm. Another. Vibrio. fetus, is definitely pathogenic for cattle, sheep, and man. V1 *coil* causes dysentery in swine, and VV *jejuni* causes dysentry in cattle, and related animals; these two species may produce enteritis in children. *V fetus, V jejuni* and *V coli* are microacrophilic. Two species, *V. niger* and *V. sputorum,* are strict anaerobes. Both are found in gangrenous lesions to the mouth and lungs.

Bergey', Manual (seventh edition) lists *V. sputigenus,* which occurs normally in the mouth, as an aerobic species; but then studies by Loesche and his co-workers have shown that it is microaerophilic.

Rosebury considered both the vaginal and oral vibrios to be *V. sputorum*. No primary pathogenicity has been demonstrated, but Smith found that vibrio was a part of the fusospirochetal symbiotic mixture.

An aerobic species, *V. protects*, has been isolated from then faces of children with severe diarrhea. A third aerobic species, *V. leonardii*, *is* highly pathogenic for certain species of insects. The remaining species are apparently saprophyte isolates from soil, salt and fresh water, and pickling brines.

VIBRIO FETUS INFECTION IN ANIMALS AND MAN

Vlbrio fetus was isolated from cases of infectious abortion cattle by Theobald Smith in 1918. It is now recognized as second only to brucellosis as a cause of economic loss to the farmer. This infection is truly a venereal disease in cattle, since. the organism may be carried in the testes of the bull for lift without causing signs or symptoms of disease. This vibrio not, only causes recognized abortions but reduces the conception, rate of the herd *V. fetus* causes abortion in sheep, but the ram is not involved in the transmission of the disease. Presumably the *vibrio* is transmitted by contaminated food and water.

BORDETELLA

The genus *Bordetella* belongs to the family Brucellaceae, small, ovoid to rod-shaped Gram-negative bacilli; two of its members,. *Bord. pertussis* and *Bord. parapertussis*, cause one of the most frequent bacterial respiratory infections of childhood in communities not effectively protected by vaccination. The name whooping-cough is given to this infection because of the tendency for a paroxysm of coughing to end with a long inspiratory high-pitched note or whoop. The disease in its typical form is prolonged and debilitating and may affect 70 to 80 per cent of unprotected children with a high incidence and severity of attack in infants under 2 years of age.

Available bacteriological and serological methods of laboratory diagnosis fail to demonstrate bordetella infection in a substantial proportion of cases diagnosed clinically as whooping-cough. Probably most of the cases giving negative. results are bordetella infections that are not demonstrated by the laboratory tests because the methods used are insufficiently sensitive or because the time or method of collection of the specimens is unsuitable. Some of the 'negative' cases, however, may be due to infection with other kinds of microorganisms and there is evidence suggesting that a clinical syndrome stimulating whooping-cough may be caused by adenoviruses of types 1, 2 and 5 some other respiratory viruses, *and Mycoplasmapneumoniae*.

DESCRIPTION

Bord. pertussis used to be classified with *Haemophilus* because a culture medium rich in blood was needed for its primary isolation. But the bordetellae are not dependent on nutritional factors in blood for growth and the other two members of the genus, *Bord. parapertussis* and *Bord bronchiseptica* are less exacting in their growth requirements than *Bord. pertussis.*

Bord. pertussis is a small. Gram-negative coccobacillus uniform in size and shape in primary culfure but definite bacillarv forms occur on subculture and become more numerous in 'rough' cultures. The organism is non motile and nonsporing; capsules are demonstrable in young cultures. In culture films, the organisms-tend to form loose clumps with clearer spaces between, giving a 'thumbprint' distribution.

Bord. pertussis is an aerobe and grows best at 35° to 36°C. Catalase and a substance, e.g. albumin or charcoal, which will absord toxic products (possibly unsaturated fatty acids) are essential for growth. For primary culture the special medium of Bordet and Gengou containing 33 per cent fresh blood or a modification of it should be employed. On this medium, which should be kept moist, growth occurs slowly and after two or three days or even longer there appear small raised greyish white colonies which are highly refractile to light, resembling a bisected pearl or a mercury drop. The colonies are cohesive and may be picked off entire for slide-agglutination. Penicillin (0.25 units per ml) is usually incorporated for the suppression of commensal bacteria and diamidine (M and B 938) may also be included to make the medium more selective.

Bord. pertussis differs from *Haemophilus influenzae* in its continued viability at low temperatures (0° to 10°C). It is killed by heat at 55°C for half an hour. It has no fermentative properties.

Recently isolated strains appear to be closely related in antigenic characters antigenic characters and react with the same agglutinating and complement-fixing antisera. There are, however, a number of surface agglutinating factors, numbered 1 to 6, of which I is. common to all strains. Thus, agglutination with absorbed, single factor sera distinguishes three common serotypes, type 1,2, type 1,2,3, and type 1,3, according to their content of agglutinating factors, 1, 2 and 3.

A number of other distinguishable antigenic fractions have been isolated from *Bord. pertussis*, e.g. haemagglutinin. protective antigen, histamine-sensitivity fraction, and endotoxin. It is difficult to assess the significance of these and other factors in the pathogenicity or toxicity of the organism.

Bord. parapertussis is related antigenically to *Bord. pertussis* but produces a milder form of whooping-cough which is rare in Britain but common in some other European countries, e.g. Denmark and Czechoslovakia. It differs from *Bord. pertussis* in its more rapid growth so that the pearly colonies are well developed after two days' incubation on Bordet-Gengou medium. The underlying medium becomes greeny-black due to the production of a brown pigment. *Bords* parapertussis actively Produces catalase and on subculture grows readily on ordinary culture media. It can be specificall% identified by agglutination with an absorbed antiserum.

Cultural Characteristics

The medium of choice for the isolation of Bord, pertussis is the original glycerine-potatoblood agar of Bordet and Gengou. Material may be collected from the nasopharynx by swabbing with a specially prepared curved wire swab, or the patient may cough directly on a Bordet-Gengou plate.

Penicillin can be used to prevent or reduce the number of contam-inating organisms. Bradford and his associates suggest that one drop. of penicillin solution containing 1,000 units per ml be added to the surface of the plate. The nasophary ngeal swab from the patient is passed through this drop several times before streaking the plate. Kendrick and her co-workers suggest that 0.5 units of penicillin per ml of medium be added, after the addition of the blood and before pouring plates.On these plates colonies barely visible to the naked eye appear after 24 hours' and they slowly increase to their maximum size after 48 to 72 hours incubation. The colonies are smooth, glistnning, and somewhat domeshaped, and the edges are entire. They are more opaque than the colonies of H.: inf uenaae and have a grayish colour suggesting a bisected pearl. A chase teristic "fuzzy" zone of hemolysis develops about the colony.

Bord Pertussis is aerobic. It grows at 37°C but will multiply slowly at lower temperatures. It does not oxidize carbohydrates, reduce nitrates, or produce indol.

Resistance

Bord. pertussis is killed readily by drying, by the usual antiseptics, and by heating for 30 minutes at 55°C. The organism is resistant to the action of sulphonamides and penicillin but is susceptible to tetracycline, chlortetracycline, and chloramphenieol.

VARIABILITY

In 1931 Leslie and Gardner showed that there was a four phase dissociation, described as types 1. II, III; and IV. In general. the colonies in phases III and IV were larger and rougher and had dense, elevated centers.

Animals immunized with phase IV vaccines showed no resistance to challenge doses of Bord. pertussis in phase I.

Bord. pertussis has a non-toxic surface agglutinogen and a hemagglutinin. The cell wall contains: 1) the protective antigen; 2) a heat stable toxin; and 3) a histamine-sensitizing factor. Munos and Bergman have reviewed the characteristics of the histamine-sensitizing factor.

Antigens

It has been demonstrated (*Keogh et al.*) that the cultures of smooth strains of *Bord. pertussis* contain haemagglutinin for rats and human red cells. *Anderson* described two antigens of *Bord. pertussis;* one thermostable 0 and the other thermolabile K antigen. 0 antigen is common to this and other species of the genus, namely; *Bord. parapertussis* and *Bord. bronchiseptica :* latter possesses more antigen of *Bord. pertussis.* K antigens ar species specific.

Four antigenic components of S form of *Bord. pertussis* are now recognised in relation to O antigen, namely :(1) agglutinogen, (2) toxins (heat labile and heat stable), (3) haemagglutinins and (4) protective antigen.

(1) Agglutinogen is on the surface, nontoxic, water soluble and can be liberated by breaking the cell with sonic vibration and acid extraction. It produces high titre of agglutinin in rabbits.

Toxin (Evans and Maidand)

A toxin has been extracted from *Bord. pertussis* by disruption of the organism. It is destroyed at 55°C for 30 minutes. When mixed with formalin it can be transformed into toxoid, which is antigenic. Though thermolabile, it resembles an endotoxin but it is like an exotoxin in its ability to stimulate antitoxin, either in its toxin or toxoid form. The toxin is antigenic, when combined with agglutinogen but not so, when separated from it. The toxin has a dermonecrotic action in rabbits and is lethal to these animals and guineapigs, when injected intravenously in small doses. When injected intratracheally, it produces severe oedematous reaction of the lung followed by accumulation of macrophages the alveoli and lymphocytic infiltration iround the blood, vessels and bronchi similar to changes produced in the lung of whooping cough c ases.The intravenous injections of anti toxin 24 hours before the intratracheal injection protect rabbits from these effects. The lethal effect of pertussis, toxin in mice could be prevented by antitoxic serum but not by antibacterial serum; whereas, when mice were injected intravenously with *Bord. pertussis*, antibacterial serum was effective but the antitoxin did not reprevent the infection.

(2) Haemagglutinin

It is an antigen which agglutinates rat, mouse and human red cells and agglutination is observed at 42° to 50°C. The haemaggl-utination depends on a water soluble substance removable by washing. It is antigenic and the antigen is extracted from freshly isolated organisms. The antibody present in the serum neutralises the laemagglutination and can be measured by haemagglutination inhibition test. Like the toxin and type specific antigen, it is lost in the S®R variation.The relation of virulence haemagglutinin is indefinite, but resistance to infection may be parallel to antihaemagglutinin, production.

(3) Protective antigen

The role of protective antigen of *Bord. pertussis* is rather controv-ersial, as the protective effect may be associated with the agglutinogen.

Serology

Bord. pertussis is identified serologically by the agglutination test using antisera prepared in the rabbits with strains representing various phases of the organism.

Immunity

The relative importance of humoral and cellular immunity is not clearly defined. Humoral antibodies are measured by agglutination and complement fixation. All these circulating antibodies appear as a result of infection or inoculation. But immunity has been found to exist in individuals with little or no demonstrable circulating antibody and, therefore, it is probable that cellular mechanism is also concerned with the local tissue resistance of the respiratory tract.

Pathogenicity

Effects of intraperitoneal injections into rabbits and guineapigs are similar to those of *H. influenzae*. The action is toxic rather than invasive and the minimal lethal doses of phase III and IV organisms are many times higher than those of phase I or phase *II. Intranasal instillation* of *Bord. pertussis* in anaesthetised mice produces lesions in the lung resembling those of human *pertussis*. *Intratracheal inoculation* in monkeys produces the catarrhal stage of the disease after an incubation period of 10 days. Many workers produced lesions in monkeys like those of human pertussis with interstitial pneumonia and mononuclear celll reaction accompanied by lymphocytosis, but none of the monkeys developed cough. In man, *Bord. pertussis* produces whooping cough.

WHOOPING COUGH

Whooping cough is an infection caused by *Pordd pertussis,* characterised by fits of whoops, common in children below the age of 10 years but most common up to the age of 5 years.

PORTAL OF ENTRY

Infection occurs either by direct contact or droplet infection. The droplets are excreted during whoops and contain a large number of the organism. The organisms multiplies rapidly upon the epithelial cells of the respiratory tract and spreads to alveoli and their walls.

Symptoms

The incubation period is 1 to 2 weeks. Clinical course of the disease consists of three stages. (*a*) *Catarrhal stage.* Cough, sneezing, etc. in the stage last for about 1 to 2 weeks. It is characterised by infiltration with polymorphonuclear leucocytes. (*b*) *Paroxysmal stage.* The stage of paroxisin with distressing cough and whoops lasts for about 3 to 4 weeks. Whoops consist of a paroxysm of cough followed by a long drawn inspiratory phase and often associated with vomiting. (*c*) *Convalescent stage. This* stage lasts for 1 to 3 weeks, when intensity of whoops is reduced and convalescence follows.

Pathology

The infection affects the mucosa of the upper respiratory passage with hyperaemia and catarrhal inflammation causing laryngitis, tracheitis, bronchitis. The organisms rapidly multiply and destroy cilia with interference of their function. As a result, secretion accumulates, forms plugs of mucous to obstruct the air passage resulting in spasmodic cough. Peribronchial lymph nodes are hyperaemic and show hyperplasia. The infection spreads to the bronchioles and may produce peribronchiolitis; and interstitial pneumonia is due to direct infection caused *by Bord. pertussis.* Secondary infections with streptococci, staphylococci, pneumococci and influenza bacilli may cause alveolar exudate and produce complication like bronchopneumonia

Complications

Respiratory. Laryngitis in the catarrhal stage but later bronchopneumonia at any stage are the usual complication. Bronchopneumonia is caused by the secondary organisms present in the throat, e.g., *Str.*

heamolyticus. In interstitial pneumonia, oedema and haemorrhage are present in the lung parenchyma. Mucous plugs may obstruct the lower air passage and produce atelectasis. Anoxaemia produced by interstitial pneumonia may be responsible for convulsion T he attack may open up latent focus. of tuberculosis with softening of the bronchial nodes and may show flare-up of an old focus.

Gastrointestinal. Acute gastroenteritis may occur at any stage of the disease. either by swallowing of sputum or due to secondary organisms or dvseptery bacilli.

Nervous system. Bulbar paralysis or cerebral haemorrhage are serious complications of whooping cough. Cerebral haemorrhage is often accompanied by death, hemiplegia or other permanent neurological changes. Pertussis encephalitis is, occasionally seen but its mechanism is not fully understood.

Renal. True nephritis is rare but transient albuminuria may appear.

Special senses. Subconjunctival haemorrhage is common, due to . whoops. Otitis media is caused by secondary organisms spreading from the throat via the Eastachian tube.

Laboratory Diagnosis

The diagnosis is based on : (a) examination of stained smear, which may show chains of small Gram-negative bacilli; (b) isolation of H. *pertussis* from the sputum early in the disease, when organisms are present in large numbers but they become scanty and cannot be isolated after the 3rd week. (c) Agglutinin and complement fixing antibodies appear in blood after the third 'week. (d) Other tests.

I. Isolation of the organism

(a) *Cough plate method.* It is done on Bondet-Gengou medium plate. Penicillin is spread on the surface of the plate and for this 10 units of penicillin are used in 4 drops, for a plate 4 inches in diameter, containing 12 ml of agar. The plate is then dried before use. During. a paroxysm of cough, the plate is exposed by holding in close to the mouth (6" of) and this is incubated for 48 hours or 72 hours. Silvery or aluminium paint like streaks are seen after incubation, indicating the growth of the organism. Darkening of the blood agar plate occurs around the colonies. After isolation, the organism is identified by staining and by agglutination reaction with specific antiserum.

(b) *Post-nasal swab.* This is a better method. A swab is taken from the nasopharynx and streaks are drawn on the penicillin plate prepared, as mentioned before.

(*c*) *A prenasal swab* may be obtained, passing the swab along the floor of the nose to the nasopharynx. The swab is inoculated into the penicillin plate as described above.

(*d*) *Laryngeal swab* may also be taken' for culture.

II. Serum Diagnosis

Agglutination and complement fixation tests are useful for diagnosis in the later part of the disease, when these become positive. They are done by using bacterial suspension of Phase I as antigen. *Agglutination reaction is* less reliable than isolation of the organism but a prompt and complete reaction with patient's serum in a title of 1:100 to 1 : 200 is of some diagnostic value. *Complement fixation test.* The test is not useful for diagnostic purpose in the early stage of the disease. In convalescence, a positive test only confirms a past infection.

III. Pathogenicity test

It. is done by instillation of the material into the nose of anaesthetised mice, in which fatal interstitial pneumonia is produced by the organism.

IV Clinical Pathology

Leucocyte count. Total leucocyte count may rise as high as 20,000 per c mm and this is of diagnostic value in the later stage of the disease, when a positive culture cannot be obtained. Absolute increase in the *lymphocytic count* is very characteristic of this infection. ESR Retardation of ESR is peculiar to whooping cough.

EPIDEMIOLOGY

Source and Transmission of Infections

Patients with clinical whooping-cough appear to be the only significant sources of infection. Healthy carriers are probably rare but a few subclinical infections have been detected by culture in healthy home contacts of patients. The bacillus is not very resistant to drying or other environmental conditions and transmission probably takes place mainly by contact with fingers and other objects contaminated with sputum or saliva, or by direct spraying of the eyes, nose or mouth with cough droplets.

Incidence

Mortality from whooping-cough has declined dramatically over the past half century. Whereas this infection killed some 40,000 children in England and Wales in the decade 1921 to 1930, there were only 279 deaths in the 10 years 1959 to 1968; 216'or 77 per cent of these occurred in thc:first year of life and 171, or 4 out of 5 of these 216 deaths were in infants under 6 months of age. The recorded incidence of Whooping-cough has been falling in the past two decades but notifications give a gross underestimate of total morbidity because of poor reporting. However, the data indicate that the national use of pertussis vaccines has reduced the incidence of the disease because the epidemic waves, which used to have a biennial periodicity, now occur at 3 to 4 year intervals and with decreasing amplitude: but the health administrator must be cautious about attributing the downward slope of the epidemic wave to the introduction of some new preventive measure like prophylactic vaccination.

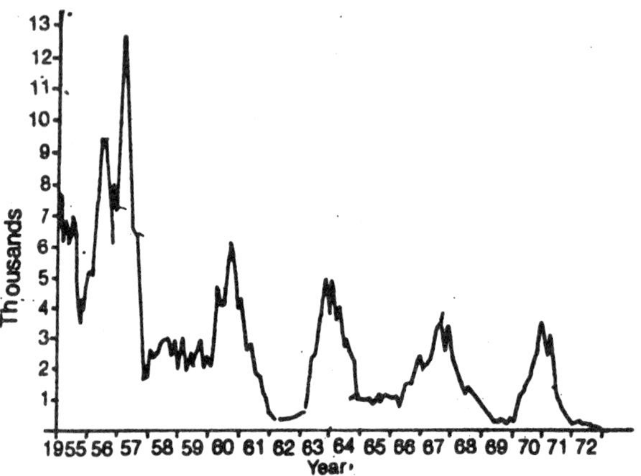

Fig. 16.1. Whooping -cough notification : England and Wales: 1955-1972. (Pertusis vaccination of young childern came into geral use about 1957.)

Whooping-cough is essentially a disease of early childhood. There is little or no transfer. of passive immunity from mother to offspring so that infections occur in early infancy and some 10 per cent of unprotected infants in urban areas develop whooping-cough in the first year of life. The attack rate is about the same for each of the next 4 years of life so that half the child population has been affected by the age of 5 years. Morbidity and mortality rates are rather higher in females than in males in contrast to most other specific childhood fevers. One attack does not necessarily confer long-lasting immunity and clinical infections, often unrecognized, may occur in adults, e.g., parents of affected children.

Transfer of infection requires fairly intimate contact. Thus, the secondary attack rate is 80 to 90 per cent among susceptible siblings (home exposures) but much lower for contacts outside the home; in day and residential nurseries the infection may spread in a slow and smouldering fashion in contrast to the explosive outbreaks of measles. A child with whooping-cough is most infectious in the first 2 to 3 weeks after onset before any whoop develops; duration of convalescent carriage of the pathogen i s probably shortened by early chemotherapy or previous vaccination.

Control Measures

Whooping-cough due to *Bord pertussis* can be controlled, if not wholly prevented by prophylactic vaccination. After encouraging results reported by the *Danes* in the epidemics on the Faroe Islands and by *Kendrick* and *Eldering* in Grand Rapids, Michigan, a series of controlled trials of different vaccines was carried out in Britain during the 1950s under the sponsorship, of the Medical Research Council. In all, some 50,000 children, mostly in the age range 6 months to 2 years, were involved and 25 different vaccines were tried. The main findings as summarized in the final Medical Research Council Report were

The results of the trials clearly showed that it was possible by vaccination to produce a high degree of protection against the disease, as shown by the substantial reduction in the attack rate amongst home contacts, and, in those cases where vaccination failed to give complete protection, to reduce the severity and duration of the disease. The results also showed that the different vaccines employed varied a great deal in their protective action; the poorest gave an attack rate in home contacts of 87 per cent, and the most effective an attack rate of 4 per cent.

The protective *efficacy* of different vaccines was checked against a number of laboratory tests of which the mouse protection test was found to correlate best with the results of the field trials. But sometimes there was considerable divergence between the mouse test and the clinical results. In a recent reassessment, pertussis vaccines that had passed the laboratory test failed to give any significant protection to vaccinated children exposed to infected siblings. Thus, the attack rate among fully vaccinated children under 5 years after exposure in the home to a bacteriologically proven case was 56 per cent and the corresponding rate for nonvaccinated children was 67 per cent. The poor protection in the vaccinated children was not apparently affected by the age of the child, the interval since vaccination or the absence of a booster dose. It was, however, noted that the serotype of the strains in the vaccines used in the late 1950s was type 1, 2 whereas the infecting strains in the late sixties were predominantly type 1,3.. *Preston* has attributed the inadequacy of these vaccines to the appearance of new antigenic variants but Pittman believes that the total amount of immunizing antigen is the critical factor in the prophylaxis of whooping.. cough. Improved methods for testing the antigenic potency of pertussis vaccines and ensuring better protection have been proposed, but despite improved modifications in British vaccine production since 1968, notifications of whooping-cough again reached a high level in 1970 to 1971. Obviously, more determined efforts to improve antigenicity and reduce toxicity of pertussis vaccines are needed.

There is conflicting but mostly negative evidence about the protective value of seroprophylaxis with human immunoglobulin given to intimately exposed contacts.

Early recognition and isolation of an infected child in a day or residential nursery may help to limit the spread of infection to other children.

RICKETTSIACEAE AND CHLAMYDIACEAE

The family Rickettisiaceae includes the causative organisms of the two forms of typhus, and those of spotted fevers and trench fever, together comprising the genus *Rickettsia;* also that of Q fever, now placed in a separate genus: *Coxiella*

Rickettsiae have a very wide host range in nature and have been found in lice, fleas, ticks, mites, birds and in many species of mammals. With the exception of epidemic typhus, maintenance of the organisms is enzootic and man is infected by accidental intrusion into cycle of transmission between arthropod and vertebrate hosts, or those between vertebrate hosts.

In past times epidemic typhus has been one of the great, lethal, infective scourges of man accompanying war, revolution and poverty. No doubt it remains in the wings to return in any period of social disruption; its last appearance in Europe was during the second World War in the eastern theatre, in and subsequently around the Nazi concentration camps and in North Africa and Italy (Naples) *Zinsser* has chronicled the earlier social and political effects of typhus in *Rats*, *Lice* and *History*. Although foci of rickettsial disease remain in various areas of the world at present in developed western nations, given stable social circumstances, rickettsial diseases are uncommon. Only infrequent sporadic, imported. murine typhus, Brill-Zinsser disease, and sporadic cases or small outbreaks of Q fever are likely to be encountered in Europe with Boutonneuse fever in the Mediterranean littoral.

CLASSIFICATION AND BIOLOGICAL PROPERTIES OF RICKETTAIAE

Rickettsiae are small prokaryotic cells that, with one exception. have an obligate intracellular existence.The exception is *R. quintana*, which grows extracellularly in the louse gut and has been cultivated on modified blood agar. The rickettsial cells are pleomorphic and. on light microscopy. are rod-shaped. coccal. or occasionally filamentous organisms some 200 to 500 nm in diameter and 800 run to 2.0 gm or more in length. They are Gram-negative in the main but *Coxiella burnetii* is Grain-positive with alcoholic iodine as a mordant.

The established rickettsiae making up the typhus, spotted fever, scrub typhus, trench fever and Q fever groups are given in Table. Some other rickettsiae-R. *sennetsu*, *R. montana*, *R. parkeri* and R. *canada*-of uncertain significance for man, have been described recently. On the basis of cross protection and serological tests the spotted fever group have been arranged in 4 subgroups-(A) R. *rickettsii* and R. *sibirica : (B) R. conori* and *R. parkeri;* (C) R. *australis* and R. *akari* (D) R. *montana. R. canada* appears to be related to the typhus group and may be maintained in a bird-tick cycle.

The genus Rickettsia differs in a number of ways from that of *Coxiella.* All species of pathogenic rickettsia release a 'soluble' CF antigen when shaken with ether; this is probably derived from a capsule. Similar material is not extractable from C. *burnetii* with ether. C. *burnetii* exists in two antigenic forms as detected with CF reaction : phase 1 in arthropod and vertebrate hosts and phase 2 on passage in the chick embryo yolk sac. This is a host-controlled variation resembling smooth-rough variation in bacteria. Phase 1 antigen can be removed by treatment with trichloracetic acid revealing phase 2. The phase 1 antigen of C. *burnetii, a* lipopolysaccharide, is heat-stable (resisting autoclaving at 121°C for 15 min) and the organism itself is more resistant to drying, to storage for long periods at room temperature, to heating at temperatures up to 60°C, and to exposure to phenolic disinfectants than most vegetative bacteria. Rickettsiae, on the other hand, are easily inactivated by these treatments. Studies of the nucleic acid base composition of C. *burnetii* and R. *prowazekii* indicate that the G+C percentage of the two organisms are quite different thus substantiating the separation of the former into a separate genus. *Ormsbee* lists further differences between C. *burnetii* and other rickettsiae and concludes that the two genera may be of very different origins with similarities resulting from convergent evolution in the selective circumstances of arthropod and animal cells. Studies of the fine structure of the rickettsial cell show that it is rod-shaped, 300 to 700 nm in diameter, and 0.8 to 2.0 μm or more in length. There is a thin multi-layered cell wall, about 7-1 0 min thick, and an underlying cwtoplasmic membrane, 6-8 mn, with the characteristic 'unit' membrane structure found in bacterial cell. Some rickettsiae, such as *R. prowazekii*. display the ether-soluble capsule. Internally there are ribosomes. 7-20 nm in diameter and presumably of the baccterial t pe.

The nuclear material inay be organized in a central body with radiating fibres (C. *burnetii*) or dispersed as a network of fibrils; a double-stranded DNA has been extracted from *C. burnetii.*

Cell walls of rickettsiae contain two amino sugars, glucosamine and muramic acid, and sensitive to lysozyme. Diaminopimelic acid, an amino acid found in the cross-lying peptide chains of the cell walls of Gram-negative bacteria, is also found in rickettsiae including C. *burnetii*. These features, together with the general amino acid composition and the absence of techoic acid, a cbr3cteristic component of the cell walls of Gram-positive bacteria, all underline the resemblance between rickettsiae and Gram-negative bacteria. This lends some credence to the notion that rickettsiae evolved from the intestinal flora of arthropods.

Rickettsiae, other than C. *burnetii*, are unstable outside of host cells and their cytoplasmic membranes readily leak macromolecules such as RNA and intracellular ions into aqueous media. Consequently, special suspending media with sucrose, glutamate, bovine serum albumin and K+, Mgr* are used; this may be further supplemented with ATP, coenzyme 1 and coenzyme A, perhaps mimicking the intracellular environment found to be favourable by an organism with an especially permeable cell membrane. Significantly, *R. quintana* does noll have a requirement for the intracellular ion, K+

With the exception of R. *quintana* the rickettsiae multiply intracellularly and by binary fission. Most form colonies of organisms in the cytoplasm, but R *rickettsii* and R. *canada* may also be found in the nuclei of infected cells. C *burnetii* probably also multiplies by binary fission although *Kordova* and associates have suggested a mode of division involving smaller, filterable forms.

Rickettsial suspensions outside of cells have a variety of enzymes connected with metabolic pathways for the breakdown of carbohydrate or for the generation of energy (ATP) from some steps in the Krebs cycle; enzymic equipment varies from species to species, C. *burnetii* being the more active. Pathways for the synthesis of lipid and protein are also present. *Moulder* provides a useful discussion of the metabolic basis for the intracellular parasitism of rickettsia, chlamydia and malaria.

Ormsbee suggests that the host cell contribution may include primary substrates such as glutamate and pyruvate factors such as ATP, NAD and coenzyme A; perhaps also nucleoside triphosphate precursors and other cell pool components such as amino acids.

Rickettsiae have been propagated in mouse fibroblasts. Detroit 6 cells. HEp2. HeLa and other continuous cell lines. Multiplication is slow and growth of rickettsia in the cell causes little obvious damage until numbers increase to a point at which the cell bursts: there is no nuclear 'switch off or rearrangement of cell metabolism as observed with viruses.

At the level of the whole animal concentrated suspensions of typhus rickettsiae, some spotted fever rickettsiae and scrub typhus rickettsiae will kill mice within a few hours of intravenous injection; *C. burnetii* does not do this. This toxic effect is neutralized by specific antiserum and the reaction is of value in subdividing rickettsial groups and measuring the potency and antigenicity of rickettsial vaccines.

RICKETTSIAL INFECTIONS IN MAN AND ANIMALS

Pathogenesis and Clinical Aspects of Human Infection

Human rickettsial infection results mainly from exposure to the various species of infected arthropod involved in the maintenance of the organisms in nature. Q fever differs in that although a few instances of human infection from tickbite have been described, man is infected from the cycle of maintenance in domestic animals by inhalation of aerosols of *Ci burnetii* from the products of conception of infected cattle, sheep or goats, or from the consumption of their milk or milk products. These modes of infection resemble those of brucellosis.

The tick-borne and mite-borne rickettsiae (spotted fever group and scrub typhus; Table are inoculated into the skin through the mouth parts of the arthropod after a period of feeding; a lesion (eschar) may from at the site and is of clinical diagnostic import in scrub typhus, rickettsial pox and some other members of the spotted fever group. With the louse-borne and flea-borne rickettsioses, i.e. epidemic and murine typhus and trench fever. infection follows when the infected insect faeces is rubbed or scratched into abraded skin at the site of the bite or, conceivably, contaminates the conjunctiva or respiratory mucosa.

The rickettsiae probably multiply at the site of inoculation and from there are disseminated throughout the body. However, events during the 10-20 day incubation periods of the rickettsioses and of Q fever are unclear except that there is a rickettsiaemia during the latter part of the incubation period and early febrile phase of the illness. The typhus and spotted fever groups of organisms parasitize the endothelial cells of the small blood vessels. Experiments with non-human primates show that R. *rickettsii* will also multiply in the alveolar cells of the lung and in organs such as the spleen. The clinical aspects of the diseases, particularly the various forms of rash. may be understood in terms of the vascular involvement. In Q fever there is less clear-cut involvement of the vascular endothelium although peripheral thrombosis is one of the sequelae of the disease. There is a rickettsiaemia in Q fever and, as with the other rickettsioses, infection may involve any organ system. A substantial proportion of Q fever patients have pneumonia, often of a lobar type. There may be hepatitis with small foci of necrosis. These modes of presentation often dominate the clinical picture. Pneumonia also occurs in the other rickettsioses but is overshadowed by the other signs and symptoms.

This variation aside, the general features of the rickettsial infections are broadly similar. Onset of illness is often abrupt and may be recorded to the hour. Headache-frontal or retroorbital-is often very severe and resistant to analgesics. Fever (100-104°F), rigors and sweating, myalgia and arthralgia, anorexia, nausea and vomiting are all found, as in many other acute infections. 'Sore eyes' or photophobia with severe headache is a memorable feature of many Q fever cases and a useful differential point in history-taking. The rash of the typhus-spotted fever groups of infections appears four to seven days after onset of illness, first as macules or papules, that progress in severe cases (e.g. spotted fever) to petechial or haemorrhagic lesions, or in rickettsial pox, to vesicular lesions that simulate chickenpox. A small proportion of patients with epidemic or murine typhus do not have a rash, and a rash is very uncommon in Q fever.

The course and case fatality of the various rickettsioses,without chemotherapy, differs from group to group. Epidemic typhus, scrub typhus and the Rocky Mountain spotted fever group display an overall case fatality of 10-20 per cent or more with substantially higher rates in the over 50 age group. These rates are effectively reduced by treatment with tetracycline or chloramphenicol. Murine typhus, and trench fever have a negligible case fatality; likewise, although Q fever may be severe and very debilitating on occasion, it is rarely fatal.

The duration of disease varies from 2-5 weeks with stupor, delirium or coma and uraemia as complications of severe typhus or spotted fever. Although the heart, kidneys and brain bear the brunt of acute typhus, sequelae are uncommon.

This composite account of the clinical features of the rickettsioses is necessarily superficial; admirable detailed accounts of the diseases are given by Snvder on epidemic and murine typhus; by tt'oodward and Jackson on the spotted fever group: by Sinadel and Elisberg on scrub typhus: by Derrick. Clark et al. and Powell on Q fever. In Q fever a small proportion of clinical or subclinical infections particularly in persons with pre-existing rheumatic heart disease, may lead to a chronic, 5ubacute endocarditis with features resembling those of subacute bacterial endocarditis. The mitral or aortic valve may be involved with small compact vegetations containing microcolonies of *C. burnetii* A substantial nwilber of cases of Q fever endocarditis have now been described in the United Kingdom and recently chronic liver disease has been recognized as a complication in some of the patients. Treatment is by prolonged aritihiotic therapy (tetracycline and lincomycin) with valve replacement to correct mechanical defect or extension of the lesion. Q fever may also present as a pericarditis, meningoencephalitis, uveitis and optic neuritis. The organism has also been isolated from the human placenta but, as with cattle, sheep and goats, is not a significant cause of abortion.

It might be expected that other rickettsiae would give rise to chronic endocarditis; French workers have produced some interesting but not entirely conclusive evidence. Chronic infection with rickettsiae does, however, occur elsewhere, probably in the reticulo-endotheliat system, and is exemplified by Brill-Zinsser disease or recrudescent typhus; a condition of considerable epidemiological importance and immunological interest. In the early 1900s *Brill* described a form of typhus in migrants to New York who had come from areas of eastern Europe where there had been outbreaks of epidemic typhus. *Zinsser* showed that R. *prowazekii* was present in the blood of these cases and that the condition was a relapse of ari infection acquired many years previously. These cases have now been described in most parts of the world that have received migrants from eastern Europe or other endemic areas and substantial numbers have alse been recognized in the residents of countries (e.g. Yugoslavia) that had epidemic typhus in the Second World War.

Details of rickettsial infection in animals and of the veterinary aspects of Q fever are outside of the scope of this text. The general point may be made that rickettsial infections in animals are rickettsiaemic but usually trivial and that the vector arthropod mainly suffers no ill effects while transmitting infection transovarially or interstadially. Head and body lice, however, are killed as a result of infection with *R. prowazekii.*

Laboratory Diagnosis of Rickettsial Infections

The approach in laboratory diagnosis is the same, in principle, as with many viral and bacterial infections, viz. the organism may be isolated or the serological response to infection may be measured with antigens prepared from prototype strains of the organisms.

Isolation of rickettsiae in laboratory animals should not be attempted except in laboratories equipped with safety cabinets and other facilities, segregated animal accommodation and with staff who have been vaccinated against the rickettsiae to be handled, the processing of infected yolk sac material is a particular hazard for laboratory workers. Epidemic and murine typhus rickettsiae, and the majority of the spotted fever rickettsiae can be isolated in guinea-pigs; cotton rats are highly susceptible to *R.prowazekii.* White mice are used for scrub typhus and the vesicular rickettsioses such as rickettsialpox. C. *burnetii* readily infects guinea-pigs and hamsters. The larger animals are bled before inoculation, their temperatures are taken for 3 weeks after inoculation and they are bled again 4-6 weeks after inoculation. The pre- and post-inoculation sera are tested with known antigens to ascertain the type of infecting organism and to detect a non-febrile infection. The inoculum, given intraperitoneally, is usually the clot from a blood specimen collected during the rickettsiaemia,and ground in sterile skimmed milk or in a special suspending medium without antibiotics. Febrile animals are bled, or killed and the brain, spleen or liver used for passage material for fresh animals or, after a few passages, to establish the rickettsiae in the yolk sac. A good account of the practical details is given by *Elisberg* and *Bozeman*.

With Q fever it is considered that the demonstration that a guinea-pig has seroconverted to CF antibody positive after inoculation constitutes an 'isolation' of C. *burnetii;* visualization of the organism in impression smears of liver or spleen or adaptation of the strain to the yolk sac is not required for routine diagnosis and is a hazardous procedure.

Examination of patients' sera is based on specific CF reactions with purified rickettsial antigens extracted from infected chick embryo yolk sacs, and on the Weil-Felix reaction. The latter depends on fortuitous similarity of serological specificities of carbohydrate haptens found in certain rickettsiae and in non-motile, '0' variants of *Proteus vulgaris* and *Protects mirabilis*. Patients infected with *R. prowazekii*, *R. mooseri*, some of the spotted fever group and scrub typhus rickettsiae may develop agglutinins to the various proteus strains; those with Brill-Zinsser disease, rickettsial pox and Q fever generally do not. The antibodies concerned are in line IgM class, heatlabile at 56°C, and develop rapidly. It is important to demonstrate a changing titre; false positive reactions in liver disease and other conditions are characterized by lower, unchanging levels.

The CF tests commonly utilize the group-specific, ether soluble heat-stable antigens for, respectively, epidemic and murine typhus and for the spotted fever group. A positive reaction does not distinguish between infection with various members of the group; for this purpose washed rickettsial suspensions for CF or agglutination tests are required; now difficult to obtain. Antibody may also be measured by immunofluorescence with slide preparations of the appropriate rickettsia, also microagglutination.

In suspected Q fever, patients' sera are tested with suspensions of C. *burnetii* in phase 2 and if positive also with a phase-1 antigen. Patients with the acute, self-limiting form of Q fever show rising antibody levels to phase 2, usually over a titre of 80, and no or only low antibody levels to phase-1 antigen. In Q fever endocarditis the phase 1 CF antibody titres are of the same order or higher than those for phase 2 and are mostly over 1,000. Attempts should be made to isolate C. *hurnetii* in suspected cases of subacute endocarditis that have only low titres of phase 2 antibody as the serological result alone is inadequate to sustain the diagnosis. Patients with Q fever endocarditis have raised IgM levels and this may differentiate them from subacute *bacterial* endocarditis. All cases of subacute endocarditis, with or without bacteria in blood culture, should be tested for

Q fever CF antibody as double infections with bacteria and rickettsiae have been observed and C. *burnetii* does not respond clinically to penicillin.

Previous exposure to C. *hurnetii* may be detected by skin tests with purified, inactivated vaccine; reactions give a typical delayed type hypersensitivity response. Antibody may also be detected by double antibody radio immunoassay with suspensions of C. *hurnetii* tagged with (131)I or (125)T The results of skin testing and radio immunoassay reveal a much wider experience of subclinical infection with C. *burnetii* than is found in surveys with the CF test.

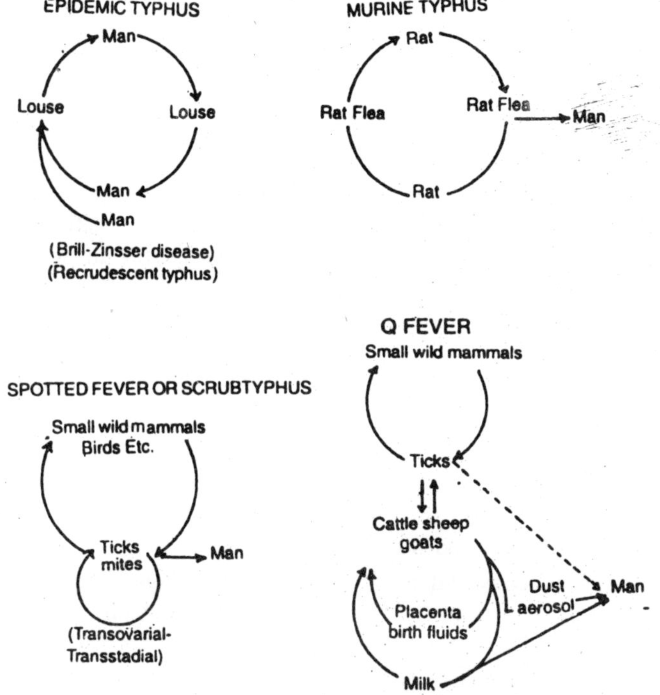

Fig. 17.1. Diagram of ecosystems for maintenance of rickettsiae.

The differential diagnosis of typhus, spotted fever and Q fever is clearly a complex matter. Early smallpox, enteric fever. meningococcal septicaemia, chickenpox (with the vesicular, rickettsioses), leptospirosis. brucellosis and other medium term fevers may be confused with the condition and can be resolved by systematic testing along the lines described in other chapters.

Epidemiology of the Rickettsioses

The ecosystems responsible for the maintenance of the various groups of rickettsiae in nature are summarized in Figure. The interaction of these with human social patterns determines the prevalence of disease in man.

The geographical distribution of the rickettsioses is outlined in Table. In general terms it was noted that Q, fever had virtually a world-wide prevalence corresponding to the distribution and movement of infected domestic animals. The wide distribution of rats and their ectoparasites, particularly rat fleas, determines the prevalence of murine typhus. Scrub typhus is more sharply limited to the S.E. Asian subcontinent, Oceania and Australasia and similarly the location of the various members of the spotted fever group is determined by the distribution of the arthropod hosts, small wild animals. Epidemic typhus (*R. prowazekii*) is dependent on man for survival and is transmitted by head and body lice in circumstances of poverty and social disintegration that favour louse infestation - crowding, cold climate, lack of fuel and water for washing, no change of clothing. Lice are infected by feeding on a person with rickettsiaemia; consequently the patient with recrudescent typhus, Brill-Zinsser disease, plays a central role in initiating an epidemic. Although there have been claims to have demonstrated antibodies to *R. prowazekii* in domestic animals and to have isolated the rickettsia from them, experimental inoculations have not supported the concept of an alternative vertebrate host.

Discussion of the ecology of vertebrate hosts and arthropods, vectors for murine typhus, spotted fever rickettsiae and scrub typhus are given *by Snyder*, 1965; *Woodward* and *Jackson*, 1965; *Smadel* and *Elisberg*, 1965, and *Audy*, 1961.

In the United Kingdom Q fever is the only significant rickettsial infection; in the period since 1940 there have been rare episodes of murine typhus on visiting ships and some indigenous cases of Brill-Zinsser disease; vesicular rickettsioses have not been observed. Cattle and sheep in many parts of the U.K. are infected with C. *burnetii* and the prevalence of infection in these animals and in man is greater in areas where both are present. Limited surveys of chickens and other birds and small wild animals did not reveal infection. The organism has been isolated from one species of native tick (*Dermacentor punctata*). Serological surveys of rural populations in England showed that infection is widespread and Q fever is a significant cause of illness in the fanning community and persons associated with it. Prevalence in urban communities is generally small. Exposure to cattle or sheep at parturition, or consumption of infected raw milk was a satisfactory explanation for many of the cases observed. Puzzling outbreaks occur as a result, no doubt, of the prolonged survival of C. *burnetii* on fomites.

Treatment and Control

Chemotherapy with tetracycline or chloramphenicol has radically improved the treatment and prognosis of all the rickettsial infections.

Treatment of Q fever endocarditis is less satisfactory although the use of tetracycline combined with lincomycin or trimethoprim-sulphonamide (cotrimoxazole) is reported to be effective, greater experience is required.

Effective vaccines are available for epidemic and inurine typhus, spotted fever and Q fever, but the indications for their detail by the now limited. General hygienic control measures are described Public Health Association, 1960.

Clostridium : II : Cl. Tetani : Cl. Botulinum

Tetanus occurs in man and animals when a wound is infected with *Clostridium tetani* under conditions that allow the organism to multiply and produce toxin. Absorption of the toxin to the central nervous system leads to hyper-excitability of voluntary musculature and the disease is characterized by increased muscle tonus and exaggerated muscular responses to trivial stimuli. Trismus occurs when the muscles of the jaw are affected and, as this is quite frequently an early sign of tetanus in man, the disease is sometimes called lockjaw.

History

Cl. tetani was first isolated by *Nicolaier* but the relationship .of the organism to tetanus was definitely established by *Kitasato*, who isolated the organism in a pure culture from wounds and experimentally reproduced the disease; proving that, it is *the* causative organism of tetanus. *Behring* and *Kitasato* produced antitoxin by injection of exotoxin into animals.

Habitat

The organism is widely distributed *in* nature and found as saprophytes in the intestine of man and animals particularly horses and present in their excreta. It is also present in the cultivated and manured soil.

Lockjaw or tetanus, though a comparatively infrequent disease, has been recognized as *a* distinct clinical entity. for many centuries. The infectious nature of the disease, however, was not demonstrated until 1884, when Carlo and Rattone produced tetanus in rabbits by the inoculation of pus from the cutaneous lesion of a human case. In 1889 *Kitasato* definitely solved the problem of etiology by isolating. from cases of tetanus. pure cultures of bacilli with which he was able to reproduce the disease in animals.

Kitasato succeeded because of his use of anaerobic methods and his elimination of nonspore-bearing contaminants by means of heat. The tetanus bacillus occurs in the superficial layers of the soil and is especially frequent in the earth of cultivated and manured fields, probably because of its presence in the feces of some of the domestic animals.

MORPHOLOGY AND STAINING

The tetanus bacillus is a slender rod 2 to 5 p in length and 0.3 to 0.8 *g* in width. The vegatative forms,which occur primarily in young cultures, are slilghtly motile and possess numerous peritrichal flagella. After 24 to 48 hours' incubation, the length of time depending some what on the nature of the medium and the degree of anaerobiosis, the bacilli develop spores which are characteristically located at one end, giving the bacterium the diagnostic drumstick appearance. As the cultures grow older the sporebearing forms completely supersede the vegetative ones.

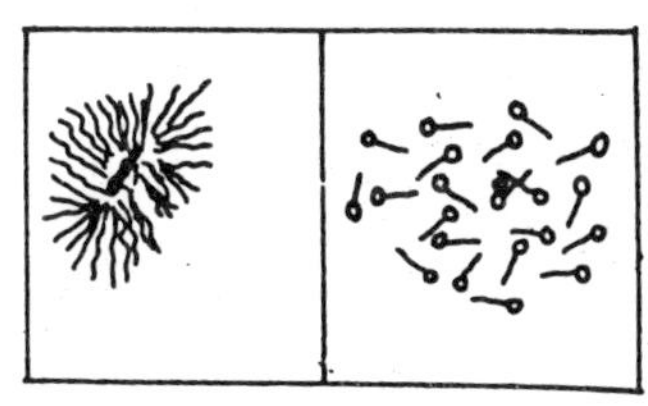

Fig. 18.1. Peritrichate flagella and spores of Cl. tetani.

The tetanus bacillus is stained easily by the aniline dyes and is gram-positive after 24 hour's incubation, but may appear as gram-negative after that time. Flagellar staining is successful only when very young cultures are employed.

Culture

Cl. tetani are obligatory anaerobes and usually cultivated in McIntosh and Fildess' jar at an optimum temperature of 37° C, the range for growth being 14 °*C* to 48 ° but the growth is poor at 20 °*C*. The growth is slow and it requires 3 to 4 days for a good growth. Spore formation commences within 2 days at 37°C.

Blood agar

The medium usually used for the growth is the blood agar prepared by addition of the Fildes' peptic digest of blood. They produce haemolvsis after a few davs'incubation. The organism is a vigorous spreader. when compared with other clostridia. For culture. the material is inoculated in the water of condensation at the bottom of the slope. On incubation in the anaerobic jar at 37°C, a thin film spreads up the slope in a feathery manner, where the organism predominates. Subculture from this feathery edge is then made in the water of condensation of a second tube and after two or three subcultures pure cultures are obtained. *Agar stab.* The growth occurs as a whitee streak and lateral branches develop from the central stern. These brandies are shorter towards the surface and the growth is better seen at the depth of the medium giving the characteristic fir tree appearance. *Cooked-meat medium.* The medium becomes turbid. Meat is not digested but slightly blackened.

Growth requirements

Cl. tetani requires many amino acids and vitamins, when grown on synthetic media. The amino acids are arginine, histidin. tyrosine, valine, leucin, isoleucine, tryptophane and purine, pyrimidine (adenine and uracil) and oleic acid. The vitamins are thiamine, nicotinic acid, riboflavin, pyridoxin, pantothenic acid, biotin, folic acid, etc. Blood or serum improves the growth. The colonies are irregularly round with indefinite edge and granular surface.

Germination of spores

It occurs in an oxygen tension lower than that of normal body tissues. The necrotic tissue, therefore, acts as a favourable nidus for the development of spores and thus the pathogenicity is explained.

Resistance

The vegetative forms of the tetanus bacillus have no greater resistance to heat or chemical agents than the vegetative forms of other microorganisms. Tetanus spores, however, will resist dry heat at 80°C for about one hour and live steam for about five minutes.

Antigenic Structure

Nine of the ten antigen types are recognized by their specific flagellar antigens. Type VI has no flagella. All strains have a common

0 antigen and a second 0 antigen is shared by types II, IV, V, or IX. Fortunately, all strains produce the same antigenic type of toxin which can be neutralized by a single antitoxin.

Bacterial Metabolites

Cl. tetani produces a fibrinolysin and a hemolysin. This hemolysin, discovered and named "tetanolysin" by *Ehrlich.* is destroyed rapidly by oxidation upon exposure to air and can be absorbed by a suspension of red blood cells. The hemolysin is antigenic, giving rise to a specific antihemolysin when injected into animals. Neither of these metabolites, however, is of sufficient potency to render the bacillus pathogenic.

Exotoxin

Virulent strains of *Cl. tetani* produce a powerful neurotoxin which is liberated in the .medium partly by diffusion and partly by autolysis.

The neurotoxin was crystallized by *Pillenter* and his associates in 1946. The crystalline toxin is a simple protein of about the same molecular weight as human serum albumin, and each milligram of nitrogen corresponds to 75,000,000 M.L.D. units.

Murphy and *Alfiller* have extended the work of *Pillemer* and isolated pure toxin by extraction of the living cells. This toxin has an average specific activity of 150×10^6 M.L.D. per mg of N. The polymer formed in the 1 percent protein "toxoiding" reaction is approximately 35 times as large as the monomer. Forhaldehyde causes polymerization of the protein and increases the negative charge.

Human beings are extremely susceptible to the tetanus neurotoxin, and cases of general and sometimes fatal tetanus have occurred in men who were only scratched by a needle which had been used for the injection of the toxin into a horse.

Tetanus toxin is a selective neurotoxin which acts upon the nerve cells of the cerebrospinal axis although it, like the botulinus toxin, also paralyzes the cholonergic motor fibers to the iris of the eye. The nerves in the medulla oblongata are most susceptible to the toxin, which probably explains the generalized convulsions seen in the disease.

There has been considerable controversy for many years about the route by which the toxin reaches the central nervous system after being produced in a peripheral lesion on an extremity. *Meyer* and *Ranson* believed it travelled by way of the motor nerves, while *Abel* and his associates thought it travelled by way of the blood stream. *Bavliis* and G. *Pavling Wright* have presented convincing evidence that it can travel to the central nervous system through the lymph spaces along the nerve trunks, although the possibility of some reaching the medulla oblongata from the blood stream cannot be eliminated. The toxin is believed to act on the synthesis and liberation of acetylcholine. *Zachs* and *Sheff* have found that the tetanus neurotoxin also has a peripheral action on the contraction-relaxation mechanism of muscles.

Antitoxin

Tetanus toxin is an excellent antigen but. unfortunately, is so potent that it is difficult to give a dose that does not produce symptoms. When treated with formalin, the toxin is converted into a toxoid which is nontoxic but still antigenic. For many years commercial antitoxin was made in both horses and cows but now antitoxin is made by immunizing human volunteers. This human antitoxin is more potent than that made in animals and is not destroyed by the immune mechanism of the patient.

It is claimed that the human tetanus immune globulin is at least 100 times more effective, unit for unit, than heterologous sera.

An international conference in 1966 recommended 250 units for prophylactic protection, but *Johnson* recommended 500 units for patients with severe crushing injuries.

Action of toxin

Inoculation of an animal with tetanus toxin is followed by period of incubation from 8 to 24 hours before the toxic spasms start. The site of injection, species of animal, amount of the toxin injected have definite influence on the length of the incubation period. (1) When the toxin is inoculated subcutaneously, spasm begins first in the muscle nearest to the point of inoculation and it spreads gradually until all muscles are involved. (2) Intravenous inoculation produces gereral tetanus of all the muscles. (3) Feeding of the toxin does not produce the disease as the toxin is destroyed by the acid gastric juice and proteolytic enzymes of the gastrointestinal tract.

Tetanus toxin is a selective neurotoxin acting like the botulinum toxin. It acts upon the nerve cells of the cerebrospinal axis and paralyses the cholinergic nerve fibres of the iris muscles, but the nerves of the medulla oblongata are most susceptable to this toxin.

The toxin is believed to act on the synthesis and liberation of acetycholine.

Absorption of toxin

Tizzoni and *Cattain* found that tetanus toxin is transported experimentally, centripetally from any depot in the deeper tissue. This is confirmed now that from the local depot the toxin ascends along the major regional nerve trunk to the central nervous system. *Meyer* and *Ransom* believed that it travelled by the route of motor nerves *but Abel et* al.thought that it travelled by way of blood stream.

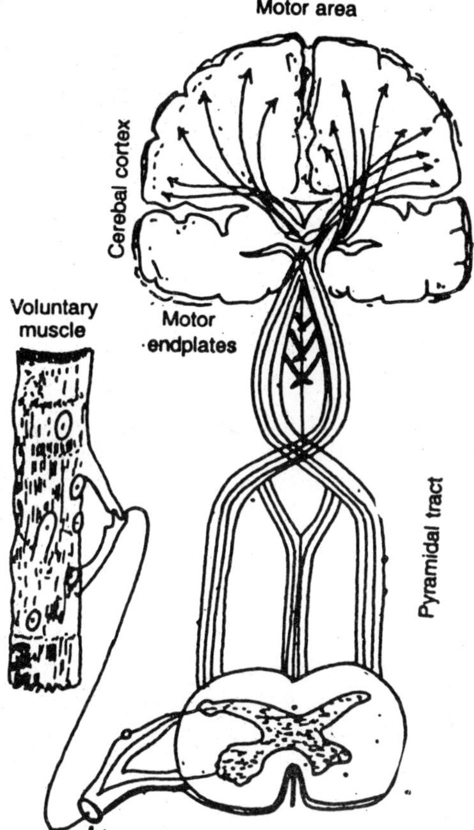

Fig. 18.2. Shows the pathways of tetanus toxin from the peripheral motor nerve via the anterior horn cells and the pyramidal tract to the motor cortex.

Ascent of *toxin* along the peripheral nerve trunk occurs, and the toxin can be recovered from the regional nerve trunk. The route may be through the lymphatics in the epineurium (lymphraume of nerve trunk) or like conduits in a direct continuity through connective tissue interspaces. *Payling Wright* confirmed the passage of toxin through the nerve root and sclerosing agents (like ethanolamine oleate injection in the nerve trunk) could stop the ascent. This has also been proved in parabiotic rats by the study of local tetanus.

It is not possible for the protein of toxin to pass through or diffuse through axoplasm and circulation for diffusion is necessary. So the possibility is that the toxin moves through the tubular clefts between the nerve fibres, the propagating force being high pressure, which is equivalent to arterial.pressure during muscular movements and contraction.

Transmission to the medulla along the cerebrospinal axis: (a) Injection of toxin followed by section of the cord only shows local tetanus upto that segment but injection of toxin above the segment shows generalised tetanus. (b) The tetanus toxin produces tetanus in cat, when injected intravenously, but a dose as small as 1/2000 of the lethal dose will kill the animal, when it is introduced by the intramedullary route. This indicates that the toxin passes through the neural route to the medulla, where very small doses may show fatal action, as the toxin is specific for medulla.

Preparation of antitoxin

The antitoxin is prepared in horses by injecting fonnol toxoid prepared by addition of 0.4 percent formalin to the toxin. It is then incubated at 37°C till the toxin is detoxified. Formalin destroys the toxicity of such a toxin without affecting its antigenic property. 20ml of this toxoid should prove nontoxic to guineapigs by subcutaneous injection. After a series of injections of formol toxoid, crude toxin may be injected. The horse is bled when the titre of circulating antibody is high. Some workers add tapioca or 0.5 percent calcium chloride as adjuvent to increase the antigenic power of the toxin.

Standard Units

There are, however, difficulties about determination of a standard of antitoxin. One American unit is ten times the dose of the antitoxic serum necessary to protect a guineapig, 350 gm for 96 hours against a standard dose of 100 M.L. D. of toxin. The international unit is half of the American unit and based on a standard antitoxin contained in 0.1547 mg of that standard antitoxin. The standardisation is best carried out by the subcutaneous injection of toxin-antitoxin mixtures into mice. The determination of L_o dose is much more convenient than L_+ dose as a basis of standardisation but the latter is followed by many,as it is easier to determine the L_+ dose by the death of the animal. The potency of the purified toxin for prophylactic use can also be measured by flocculation method analogous to Ramon's titration of diphtheria antitoxin.

Pathogenicity

Tetanus toxin is lethal to mice, guineapigs and rabbits when the toxin or the broth culture is injected; a dose of 0.00001 ml is lethal to a mouse weighing 10 gin. The animal dies in a day or two with typical signs of tetanus. The tatanic spasm starts at the site of injection and it is called *local tetanus.* The toxin then reaches the central nervous system through the nerve trunk. being probably absorbed through the end plates and spread up the spaces between the nerve fibres (*Wright et al*.. 1950). In man. the tetanus toxin causes tetanus. Both tetanus and botulinum toxins may act through the interference of vital enzyme systems but the differences between the two has not been explained. Normal choline metabolism of nerve cells is disturbed, resulting in the impairment or availability of acetyl choline.

Clinical Types of Infection in Man

The comparative infrequency of tetanus infection is in marked contrast with the wide distribution of the bacilli in nature. The nature of the wound and the simultaneous presence of other microorganisms seem to be important factors in determining whether or not the tetanus bacilli will proliferate. Deep lacerated wounds in which there has been considerable tissue destruction, and in which chips of glass, wood splinters, or grains of dirt have become embedded, are particularly favorable for the development of these organisms. The injuries of compound fractures and of gunshot wounds easily supply these conditions. In addition to its occurrence following trauma, tetanus has been observed after childbirth, and isolated cases have been reported in which it has followed diphtheria and ulcerative lesions of the throat, performation of the intestines, and even the application of plaster of Paris casts which contained' tetanus spores.

Neonatal tetanus results from infection of the umbilical cord shortly after birth. In many under developed countries this is a major cause of infant mortality.

In a series of 352 cases of tetanus reported in 1968 and 1969 the median incubation period for fatal and nonfatal tetanus cases with known wounds was 6.2 and 7.6 days respectively. Convulsions in patients under 20 indicates poor prognosis. The first symptoms usually consist of headache and general depression, followed rather rapidly by difficulty in swallowing and in opening the mouth, due to spasms or trismus of the masseters. There is slight stiffness of the neck, which makes it difficult for the patient to bring the chin forward on the chest. There develop spasms of the muscles of the cheeks gradually resulting in a drawing up of the tissues about the mouth to give a curious and characteristic expression, the socalled *risus sardonicus.* The spasms extend gradually to the trunk and back, with the development of opisthotonos after several days. Increased difficulty in swallowing may ensue and may be accompanied by involuntary evacuation of urine and feces. The localization of the symptoms follows to some extent the location of the injury.

Treatment

The result of treatment remain poor. In the series of 250 cases published in 1970, 59.2 percent died even though they received antibiotics and antitoxin. In the 15 who received no antitoxin the mortality was 73.3 percent.

The responsibility of the physician to do everything possible to save the patient is very great. The wound should be cleaned and dead tissue cut away. Penicillin should be given in doses of 1,200,000 units daily. Tetracycline or chloramphenicol canbe used for patients who are sensitive to penicillin. The antibiotic therapy should be supplemented by tetanus immune globulin (human) in doses of 500 to 1,000 units daily up to approximately 6,000 to 10,000 units as the total dose.

Early tracheostomy should be performed when the airway is threatened. Muscle relaxants can be used to control spasms. In mild cases phenobarbital, aminobarbital (amytal), or diazepam can be used. If these fail curare can be used to promote total muscular relaxation but should be administered by experts in the Inhalation Department.

Hyperbaric Oxygen Therapy

Pascale and his associates reported the cure of eight of nine patients with hyperbaric oxygen. The single failure was complicated by acute bacterial endocarditis with damage to the brain and kidneys. One patient was given penicillin and sedative but no antitoxin.The symptoms progressed until she was given the hyperbaric oxygen after which she made a rapid recovery. With the new human antitoxin globulin there will be no excuse for not administering at least 3,000 units of antitoxin even for patients who are to receive hyperbaric oxygen.

Active Immunization

The relatively poor results of even the best active treatment is counterbalanced by the remarkably good results of active immunization. The disease could be practically eliminated if all individuals were actively immunized. Not one of the 328 cases of tetanus studied in 1968 and 1969 had received the standard 3 immunizing doses.

Those under 35 years of age show a steadily declining curve while those -35 and over, who were not immunized as children or in the Armed Forces, have decreased very little since 1950.

Effective immunization can be obtained by subcutaneous doses of toxoid and by aerosol immunization.

With minor injuries in an individual who has been previously immunized one booster dose of toxoid will produce adequate antitoxin in one or two days. If there is doubt about the immunization or if the wound is very severe, both toxoid booster and 250 to 500 units of tetanus immune globulin (human) should be given but in a different injection site.

Only five deaths from tetanus occurred in the Armed Forces during World War II between 1942 and 1945. Two of the five received no proven immunization, and one did not get a booster injection at the time of injury. In contrast, there were 2,574 deaths among civilians in the United States during the same years.

TETANUS

Pathology

Tetanus is a condition of toxaemia and the manifestations of the disease are due to the absorption of soluble toxin from the site of infection, usually a local wound, where the tetanus bacillus multiplies. Implantation of tetanus spores into the wound is followed by tetanus, only when the anaerobic condition is maintained. This occurs in a necrotic tissue, where spores can germinate and the organisms can multiply due to the low oxygen potential of such a tissue. According to *Fildes*, low oxygen potential is the determining factor for the germination of tetanus spores. In a healthy tissue, the oxygen potential is sufficient to inhibit their growth but in tissues, specially infected with other aerobic organisms, the oxygen potential falls below its inhibitory level, and the spores germinate and the organism grows in such a tissue. Necrosis, devitalisation of the tissue by injury to the blood vessel and thrombosis and calcium ions derived from soil or haemorrhage act further as contributory factors by reduction of oxygen potential of the tissue.

Incubation Period

It varies from 3 days to 3 weeks, but usually it is 7 days. The period may increase in immunised persons. The incubation period is important, since the severity of the disease and gravity of the case varies inversely, as the incubation period increases or decrease: the milder the attack, the longer is the incubation period.

Portal of Entry

Usually, there is a history of penetrating wound specially caused by an old rusty nail. In other cases, there is a history of wound caused by burns, lacerated wound or wounds by splinters or a street injury contaminated with dust, excreta of horses. In all these cases, the oxygen potential of the tissue is lowered. The wound may be trivial. neglected or completely forgotten. It may even follow a subcutaneous injection of an irritant drug like quinine or emetine. A parturient mother during labour or puerperium may be infected. Newborn babies may be infected through the umbilical cord.

Symptoms

Local spasm may be insignificant. This is followed by trismus or lock jaw which may be the first symptoms noticed due to the tonic contraction,of the masseter. Spasm of the muscles of the face, jaw and neck produces a condition of *rhisus sardonicus*. During the spasm of the muscle, the patient experiences the dread of an impending danger. From the involvement of the jaw muscles, the spasm gradually extends on other skeletal muscles and during the acute spasmodic attack, the patient rests on the head and heels, a condition of *opisthotonus*. Spasms are clonic as well as tonic and the relaxation is incomplete during the interspasmodic interval. Psoas and abdominal muscles often rupture. There is high rise of temperature and the pulse rate is greatly increased. Death occurs due to asphyxia, physical exhaustion or heart failure.

Clinical types of tetanus

(1) *Acute tetanus*. In this, the incubation period is less than 10 days and the symptoms are acute, progressive and the prognosis is grave. (2) *Chronic tetanus*. The incubation period is about one month in these cases and symptoms are less severe. The incubation period may be longer, when the patient receives a prophylactic injection of antitoxin. (3) *Delayed tetanus*. The organism in these cases, remains latent in a wound for years and tetanus is produced when the wound is reopened. (4) *Idiopathic tetanus*. In this, the wound heals and the host does not develop tetanus until the general or local resistance is lowered by some other infection or local trauma. (5) *Local tetanus*. It occurs around the initial wound in subjects, who have received antitoxins. (6) *Head tetanus*. It follows wounds in the distribution of

the facial nerve, as the toxin reaches the central nervous system through the perineural lymphatics. The nerve, when swollen, is caught in the stylomastoid formamen causing paresis of the muscles of expression. (7) *Tetanus neonatorur.* It is due to the infection in the newborn through the wound left after the separation of the umbilical cord. This type is always fatal.

Mortality in tetanus

It is about 80 per cent in untreated cases, when it develops within 10 days following an injury. The serum treatment has little effect on it, when the incubation period is 5 days. But the mortality is substantially reduced. when the incubation period is longer.

PREVENTION AND CONTROL

Prompt and adequate wound toilet and proper surgical debridement of wounds are of paramount importance in the prevention of tetanus as there is an increased risk that tetanus spores may germinate in a wound if there is delay in cleansing or if sepsis develops. Clean superficial wounds that receive prompt attention may not require specific protection against tetanus and it is unreasonable to insist that every small prick or abrasion requires protection with antibiotic or antitoxin. Moreover, some surgeons consider that patients receiving through and prompt surgical treatment of their wounds, plus antibiotic therapy until healing is advanced, do not require tetanus antitoxin in addition, especially if there is a low incidence of tetanus in the area. It is wise to recommend specific prophylaxis in the case of deep wounds, puncture or stab wounds, ragged lacerations, wounds associated with bruising and devitalized tissue, wounds already septic. and animal bite wounds. The need for passive immunization with tetanus antitoxin is avoided if the patient is known to be properly immunized.

Active Immunization

Most authorities consider that all persons should be actively immunized against tetanus in infancy and their immunity maintained by booster doses of toxoid at intervals of five to ten years. This is of particular value in the case of allergic patients for whom serum prophylaxis in the event of wounding carries an increased risk of complications.

Tetanus toxoid is a preparation of refined toxin that has been rendered non-toxic by treatment with formaldehyde ('formol toxoid'). It is a good antigen and the soluble toxoid is made more effective in modern preparations by adsorption on to an aluminium hydroxide carrier ('adsorbed toxoid'). Tetanus toxoid is one of the components of the diphtheriapertussis-tetanus triple vaccine given in childhood, and adsorbed toxoid by itself is used specifically for active immunization against tetanus.

A course of three 0.5 ml doses of tetanus toxoid (preferably the adsorbed toxoid preparation) with intervals of 6 to 12 weeks between the first two, and 6 to 12 months between the-second and third injections, is of proven value in the prevention of tetanus. A reinforcing (booster) dose of 0.5 ml toxoid may thereafter be given at intervals of five to ten years to maintain immunity; but if toxoid is given too frequently there is a risk of sensitization.

A careful record should be kept of all prophylactic injections given. and information should include the batch numbers of the preparations used and the nature of any reactions observed. It is especially important that a record card should be given to the patient or his guardian.

The risk of developing tetanus is primarily related to the local incidence of tetanus and to the immune status of the individual. Whilst some degree of latent immunity is conferred even after only one injection of toxoid, for practical purposes it is wise to differentiate clearly between those likely to .Jave a definite immunity and those who may not be immune. A patient may be regarded as *immune* for six months after the first two injections, or for 5 to 1 O years after three injections (or a booster injection) of a planned course of adsorbed tetanus toxoid. Tetanus antitoxin should not be given to immune patients, but their active immunity maybe enhanced when necessary by giving o.5 ml of tetanus toxoid intramuscularly at the time of injury.

A patient is considered *non immune* if he has never had an injection of tetanus toxoid or if he has had only one such injection. If more than six months have elapsed after a course of two injections, or more than 5 to 10 years after a full primary course of three injections (or a booster injection) of tetanus toxoid, he may be regarded as non-immune, recent evidence suggests that these time limits may be extended. He is non-immune if more than 1 to 2 weeks have elapsed since a previous injection of tetanus antitoxin. He should be considered non-immune if there is any doubt about his immunization history.

Passive Immunization with Antitoxin

Tetanus antitoxin, often called antitetanus serum or ATS, can be obtained by immunizing horses with toxoid. This serum is of value in the prophylaxis of tetanus, if given immediately after wounding. Its use as a curative agent after the development of tetanus is less effective than the corresponding antitoxin treatment of diphtheria.

The usual prophylactic dose of antitoxin is 1500 International Units given by intramuscular or subcutaneous injection as soon as possible after injury. The dose is not reduced for a child. The injection may be repeated at weekly intervals as long as the risk of tetanus persists. Larger initial doses, e.g. 3 000 to 10 000 units, may be given when the wound is severe. Antitoxin is never given intravenously as *a prophylactic* measure.

The administration of equine antitoxin may be associated with untoward reactions and the incidence of unpleasant side effects may be as high as 8 tolO per cent of those that receive this heterologous serum. These include relatively trivial local reactions with erythema and urticaria: serum sickness which may be of the accelerated or delayed types. neuritic sequelae with varying degrees of loss of function; and anaphylactic shock that may occur immediately after the injection or may be delayed for 1 to 2 hours : but fatal anaphylaxis is rare (perhaps 1 death in about 100000 recipients of equine antitoxin).

Some surgeons working in areas in which tetanus is a rare disease have virtually abandoned the use of equine antitoxin. Nevertheless, it should be categorically stated that there is good evidence to justify the administration of tetanus antitoxin to a wounded patient when the circumstances of the wound and the patient's non-immune state warrant it-especially if the wound is sustained in a high-incidence area. The risk of tetanus is greatly increased whea there is delay in dealing with the wound and if sepsis develops. All of these predisposing factors are regularly encountered in many developing countries and it is disturbing that equine antitoxin is being prematurely discarded before there are supplies of human antitoxin to take its place; thus, patients at severe risk are in danger of being denied proper prophylaxis. The recommendations given in Table must be considered carefully in this Context. Even in Britain, human antitoxin is not generally available and it will be necessary to use equine antitoxin for some time to come. If antitoxin is given promptly as a prophylactic, and if proper surgical attention is given, protection is usually but not invariably afforded. In some non-immune patients, antitoxin may be contra-indicated or it may not be considered a sufficient protection. In such cases, the prophylactic use of an antibiotic is reasonable.

Antitoxins have been produced in the cow and the sheep in attempts to produce preparations associated with fewer side effects. These bovine and ovine antitetanus sera are available, but their protective efficacy is only assumed at present.

The use of Human anti-tetanus Globulin (ATG)

The obvious way to avoid the main problems associated with heterologous sera is to develop adequate supplies of homologous antitoxin from human sources. In Britain, supplies of refined human antitetanus globulin are at present released for special prophylactic use or for treatment. This homologous antitoxin is not rapidly removed and a single dose of 250 units suffices for prophylaxis. In treatment, however, there is evidence to support the use of relatively large doses.

Combined Active-Passive Immunization

It is desirable that patients receiving passive protection with antitoxin after injury should also be actively immunized against tetanus with toxoid, because, apart from involving the risk of anaphylaxis, a second dose of antitoxin tends to be more rapidly eliminated than the initial dose and the passive protection afforded on the second occasion is reduced. Purified tetanus toxoid adsorbed or aluminium hydroxide is a powerful antigen released over a period of days and the use of this preparation of toxoid overcomes previous objections to the concurrent administration of tetanus antitoxin for immediate passive protection and tetanus toxoid for active immunization! Thus, an injured non-immune patient may receive from separate syringes, 1500 units of equine tetanus antitoxin or 250 units of homologous ATG intramuscularly in one arm and 0.5 ml of the ***adsorbed*** toxoid preparation in the other. Active immunization is therefore started at an opportune moment and the patient is advised to have a second injection of 0.5 ml of adsorbed toxoid 6 tol2 weeks later.

Antibiotic Protection

Although the prophylactic administration of antibiotics to all cases of open wounds is not recommended, there is justification for the prophylactic administration of an antibiotic such as penicillin to a patient with a previous history of asue severe immediate reaction to horse serum, in which case equine antitoxin is withheld. In the case of a deep contaminated wound or an open wound associated with much devitalized tissue, antibiotic protection should be given in addition to antitoxin because pyogenic infection is likely to occur in such wounds and this favours the development of tetanus. Penicillin may be given at the time of injury and dosage maintained (either by repeated administration or by the use of a long acting preparation such as benzathine, penicillin) until healing is established. As in gas gangrene, this additional safeguard cannot take the place of prompt and adequate surgical wound toilet and it can be criticized on the grounds that strains of *Cl. tetani* vary in their sensitivity to penicillin, that access of antibiotic to the infected area may be impaired, and that penicillinase-producing organisms may also be present. Nevertheless, the prompt administration of antibiotics can prevent the development of tetanus in animals challenged with spores of *C*1. *tetani.* There is good evidence that the combination of a prolonged course of antibiotic plus active immunization with adsorbed tc,xoid at the time of injuiry may prevent tetanus spores germinating until active immunity has developed.

Table slightly amended from that proposed originally by *Rubbo*, illustrates a realistic approach to the integration of antibiotic prophylaxis with the other measures discussed above.

Treatment

In the *treatment* of established tetanus, antitoxin is of proven value. Reliance is frequently placed on the intravenous injection of a large initial dc,se of antitoxin (30 000 to 200 000 units) followed by intramuscular injections; results of current investigations suggest that an initial dose of 50 000 units, given wholly or partly intravenously, gives as good results as those obtained when 200 000 units of antitoxin are injected as the initial dose. When intravenous antitoxin is prescribed, it should be preceded by a subcutaneous test dose, followed by an intramuscular test dose, at half hour intervals. The antitoxin should be diluted, warmed to room temperature and injected very slowly into the recumbent patient. All of the precautions listed below should be observed. Intrathecal administration of antitoxin may cause dangerous reactions.

Encouraging results have been obtained with human anti tetanus serum in the treatment of tetanus, but better results may be at least partly attributable to increasing skill in the general management of tetanus cases.

Precautions to be Observed when Giving Antitoxin

In view of the risk of anaphylactic reactions following injections of antitoxin, routine precautions should be taken before antitoxin is administered. Information should be obtained from the patient regarding previous serum injections and any history of asthma, infantile eczema, urticaria or other allergic condition elicited. In the absence of any of these contraindications the full dose of antitoxin may be injected forthwith, but a sterile syringe and needle with adrenalin (1 ml of 1 in 1000 solution) should be at hand. The patient should, be kept warm before and after treatment and he should be under observation for at least 30 minutes after the injection.

If the patient has had a previous injection of serum, but gives no history of allergy, a subcutaneous trial dose of 0.2 ml antitoxin should be given, and a full dose of antitoxin may be given if no general reactions have occurred within 30 minutes. If the patient gives a history of allergy, the initial trial dose should be 0.2 ml of a 1 in 10 dilution of antitoxin subcutaneously. If no general symptoms develop within 30 minutes, this may be followed by 0.2 nil of undiluted antitoxin subcutaneously. The full dose may be given if there are no general reactions after a further 30 minutes.

Chemotherapy

A course of systemic penicillin or tetracycline therapy should be given in cases of established tetanus. There may be some justification for the local instillation of antibiotic into the wounded area after adequate debridement. Antibiotics may also be required to control complications such as pneumonia.

Dangers of Repeated Booster Doses and Toxoid

Edsall and his associates have warned the medical profession about the dangers of repeated and unnecessary booster doses of toxoid. The public has grown to expect a booster dose of toxoid for each little cut or break in the skin : annually for summer camps, annually in some industrial groups, and routinely at least every four years.

Some individuals develop the immediate type sensitivity, associated with IgE globulins.This type can be demonstrated by the passive cutaneous test. Others develop the delayed type sensitivity which develops more slowly but persists longer. Some patients may have both types of hypersensitivity. The clinical manifestation can be anaphylactic, asthmatic, Arthus phenomenon, peripheral neuritis, generalized urticaria, or severe prolonged induration at the site of inoculation. Treatment for the immediate type reaction is epinepluine and antihistaminic and for the delayed type corticoid hormones. For mixed reactions both types of drugs are needed. *Edsall* and his coworkers titrated the antitoxin levels in the serum of 22 patients who had shown severe reactions to toxoid injections and found that 21 of the 22 had unusually high levels of anti toxin and obviously did not need the booster dose which made them sick.

Prevention of Toxoid Reactions

We support the suggestion of *Edsall* that routine boosters be given every 10 years and emergency boosters be given no closer than 1 year apart. Individuals with a history of a previous reaction to toxoid should have a skin test viith 0.1 ml, or 0.2 L_f of fluid, not alumprecipitated toxoid. A positive skin test of 5 mm or more either at 30 minutes or 24 hours would suggest excessive allergy and a large dose should not be given subcutaneously. Even if there is no skin reaction, the small booster dose of 0.2 L_f should be given.

INDEX

C

M

N

T